T0151959

*Bethsaida*

THE BETHSAIDA EXCAVATIONS PROJECT
REPORTS & CONTEXTUAL STUDIES
GENERAL EDITORS
RAMI ARAV AND RICHARD A. FREUND

THE CONSORTIUM OF THE BETHSAIDA EXCAVATIONS PROJECT (CBEP)
is a consortium of faculty, staff, and students from
Albertson College, USA
Dana College, USA
Doane College, USA
Drew College, USA
Grace University, USA
Hastings College, USA
Jerusalem Center for Biblical Studies, USA and Israel
Michigan State University, USA
Rocky Mountain College, USA
Truman State University, USA
University of Hartford, USA
University of Lodz, Poland
University of Munich, Germany
University of Nebraska at Omaha, USA
Wartburg College, USA
Western Missouri State College, USA

BOARD OF DIRECTORS
Director of Excavations • Rami Arav
Chief Geologist • John F. Shroder
Project Director • Richard A. Freund
Jimmy Albright, Mark Appold, Walter C. Bouzard, Gordon Brubacher,
Denny Clark, John T. Greene, Delvin Hutton, Prof.-Dr. Heinz-Wolfgang Kuhn,
Elizabeth McNamer, John Mark Nielsen, Robert O'Connell, James Olsen,
Charles Page, Nicolae Roddy, Carl Savage, Ilona Skupinska-Lovset,
Mark Smith, Frederick Strickert,
Stanley Udd, James W. Watts

ASSOCIATED STAFF AND RESEARCHERS
Monika Bernett, Michael Bishop, Baruch Brandl, Mina Cohn, Patrick Geyer,
Moshe Inbar, Othmar Keel, Arieh Kindler, Gloria London, Andrea Rottloff,
Ktziah Spanier, Robert Shuster
Artist and Draftsperson • DreAnna Hadash
Conservationist • Orna Cohen
Photographer • Ophir Palmon
Restorer • Charleen Green
Zooarchaeologist • Toni Fisher (Tessaro)
Assistant to the Director of Excavations • Sandra Fortner
Project Coordinator • Wendi S. Chiarbos

# BETHSAIDA

## A CITY BY THE NORTH SHORE
## OF THE SEA OF GALILEE

EDITED BY
RAMI ARAV AND
RICHARD A. FREUND

VOLUME TWO
BETHSAIDA EXCAVATIONS PROJECT
REPORTS & CONTEXTUAL STUDIES

TRUMAN STATE UNIVERSITY PRESS

Copyright ©1999
Truman State University Press
Kirksville, Missouri, 63501 USA
*tsup@truman.edu*

**Library of Congress Cataloging-in-Publication Data**
Bethsaida Excavations Project Reports and Contextual Studies.
    p.    cm.
    Includes bibliographical references and indexes.
    Contents: v. 2. Bethsaida : a city by the north shore of the Sea
of Galilee / edited by Rami Arav and Richard A.Freund
    ISBN 0-943549-49-3 (casebound) ISBN 0-943549-48-5 (paper-
back)
    1. Bethsaida (Extinct city). 2. Excavations (Archaeology)—
Israel—Bethsaida (Extinct city). 3. Bible—Antiquities. 4. Rabbini-
cal literature—History and criticism. I. Arav, Rami. II. Freund, Richard A. III. Bethsaida Excavations Project Reports and Contextual
Studies.
    DS110.

                                                                    CIP
[CD-ROM with ten site maps, in both PDF and TIFF formats, attached to
inside back cover.]

Text is ITC Stone 10/13. Cover by Tyler Schmitt, Truman State University.
Printed in U.S.A. by Sheridan Books, Chelsea, Michigan.

*Dedicated to the Memory of*
*Dr. John J. Rousseau*
*Scholar, Colleague, Friend*
*Director, Bethsaida Excavations Project*
*at the Graduate Theological Union*
*1991-1996*

# Contents

PART ONE

ARCHAEOLOGY AND GEOLOGY OF BETHSAIDA

# Figures, Plates, and Tables

## PLATES

TABLES

# Abbreviations

| | |
|---|---|
| *BA* | *Biblical Archaeologist* |
| *BAR* | *Biblical Archaeology Review* |
| BCE | Years before Common Era. Equivalent to BC dates of modern Western convention. Add 2,000 years for BP or CE date equivalency. |
| BP | [Years] Before the Present |
| BT | Babylonian Talmud |
| CE | Common Era. Equivalent to AD dates of modern Western convention |
| EI | Eretz-Israel |
| *IEJ* | *Israel Exploration Journal* |
| MT | Masoretic Text |
| NT | New Testament |
| OT | Hebrew Bible (Old Testament) |
| PT | Palestinian Talmud |

# Acknowledgments

THE EXCAVATIONS OF BETHSAIDA in the period between the completion of the first volume and the completion of the second volume have been extensive. The excavations continued in 1996 between February 12 and July 12, and in 1997 between January 5 and July 25. The researchers, staff, and directors of Bethsaida met frequently at the site and at regional, national, and international conferences to discuss the results of these two years and especially at two research conferences, one entitled "From Athens to Jerusalem" held at the University of Nebraska at Omaha, April 18–20, 1996, and another held at the completion of the 1997 excavations, when we met for a day-long symposium on Bethsaida held at a conference of the International Society of Biblical Literature in Lausanne, Switzerland, on July 29, 1997. This latter symposium will form the basis for the third volume of Bethsaida Reports and Studies. Professor Kuhn's introduction to the literature section of the present volume was presented at the former conference.

This volume is the result of a day-long symposium on Bethsaida held at a conference of the International Society of Biblical Literature in Budapest, Hungary, on July 24, 1995, with Bargil Pixner, OSB, as the respondent. In the symposium, reports or papers were presented by Rami Arav, Baruch Brandl, Mary Craig, Sandra Fortner, H. W. Kuhn, John Greene, Richard Freund, Mark Appold, Elizabeth McNamer, and Fred Strickert. Also, invited chapters included a coauthored paper entitled "Iron Age Pottery from Bethsaida" by Gloria London from the University of Washington and Robert Shuster from the University of Nebraska at Omaha; "The Two Julias" by Mark Smith from Albertson College; three separate contributions by Arie Kindler (emeritus) from the Eretz Israel Museum in Tel Aviv, Israel; "Two Maacahs" by Ketziah Spanier from New York University; and a joint geological paper coauthored by John F. Shroder, Jr., Michael Bishop, and Kevin J. Cornwell from the University of Nebraska at Omaha and Moshe Inbar from Haifa University. The cartography was provided (as in volume 1) by Marvin Barton, staff cartographer in the Department of Geography and Geology at UNO. The main artists for this volume were DreAnna

Hadash of Omaha and James Olsen of Dana College. Orna Cohen provided the conservation, and Charleen Green was the restorer for the Project and provided technical support. In 1996, the Project initiated two multiyear studies concerning the flora, fauna, and glass finds at the site. Patrick Geyer of Arizona State University, under the supervision of Dr. James Schoenwetter of the Department of Anthropology at Arizona State University, began a study of pollen samples from the site while systematic zooarchaeology at the site was initiated by Toni Tessaro at the University of Tennessee (as part of her graduate studies there) and overseen by Dr. Walter Klippel of the Department of Anthropology. Andrea Rottloff of the University of Munich has been working on the Hellenistic and Roman glass samples and will have a chapter in the next volume in addition to chapters by Tessaro and Geyer in forthcoming volumes. In this regard we acknowledge the help of Penina Shore of the Antiquities Authority of Israel in the preparations for the loan of animal bones and glass finds from the site. The final preparations for this volume were aided by a number of UNO students. Irina Tsed of UNO provided some of the drawings, and official photography was provided by Dr. Arav, Ophir Palmon, and Jeff Bundy of Omaha. Typing and secretarial support for the preparation of the text were provided by Debbie Besser of Bellevue University, Omaha, and secretaries Teri Rydl and Kendra Johnson of the Department of Philosophy and Religion at UNO as well as Vickie Stone from International Studies and Programs.

The Project's activities in the public arena during this same period have been prodigious as well. An exhibition of antiquities entitled "Cities of David: From Bethsaida to Jerusalem" was seen in a number of locations around the United States; approximately ten thousand people passed through the exhibition of antiquities from Bethsaida and from a site just north of Jerusalem (Tell en-Nasbeh). The exhibition formed a part of Jerusalem 3000 activities held nationwide and was a part of the meetings of the Jesus Seminar held at Santa Rosa College in 1996 and the aforementioned research conference "From Athens to Jerusalem" held at the University of Nebraska at Omaha in 1996. The exhibit visited Truman State University in November 1995, Arizona State University in January 1996, the Badé Archaeological Museum on the campus of the Graduate Theological Union/Pacific School of Religion in early February 1996, Santa Rosa College in late February 1996, and San Diego State University in March 1996 before arriving in Omaha for two long-term exhibitions, one held at the University of Nebraska at Omaha in April 1996 and the other at the Jewish Community Center of Omaha from May through August 1996 before being shipped back to Israel. As in 1994, the exhibition cases were specially built by a local craftsman and friend of the Project, John Ainsworth, and designed by Robert Bodnar of the Robert Bodnar Company. The exhibition's safe arrival in and departure from Omaha were facilitated through the good offices of Midwest Express Airlines and Delta Airlines. The 1996 exhibition was made possible thanks to major funding from the Marguerite A. Scribante Foundation. Margie Scribante first visited Bethsaida in 1995 and has been an important part of the Project's ongoing educational and academic efforts ever since. In years to come many will benefit from her investment in the Bethsaida Excavations Project activities in biblical archaeology. The 1996 exhibition provided the basis for a permanent display for biblical archaeology at the University of Nebraska at Omaha. A renovated office and display space for the Project in Arts and Sciences Hall at the University of Nebraska at Omaha was dedicated on May 20, 1997, by Israel's deputy prime minister and minister of tourism, Mr. Moshe Katsav. Other funding for these activities came from member institutions, individuals throughout the United States, the Nebraska Humanities Council, the Henry Monsky Lodge of B'nai B'rith of Omaha, the dean of the College of Arts and Sciences, the Department of Philosophy and Religion, the dean of International Studies and Programs and the Committee on Research at UNO.

Dean Thomas Gouttierre of International Studies and Programs has been the driving force behind the Project's development at the University of Nebraska and he has taken a leading role in the yearly funding and direction of the Project, thus contributing to the success of the Project. He and his associate, Merry Ellen Turner, in International Studies and Programs have made Bethsaida one of the crown jewels of the University's system and a major part of UNO's international connections. Dean Gouttierre, together with Dean of Arts and Sciences John Flocken, and then-Chancellor Del Weber (now emeritus) of UNO, ensured that Bethsaida had a central part in the humanities programs of the University, and the new chancellor of the University of Nebraska at Omaha, Dr. Nancy Belck, has given us every reason to believe that this support will continue for many years to come.

Our thanks to Director Amir Drori of the Antiquities Authority of Israel for allowing the University to have the loan of the antiquities in 1994 and again in 1996 and the Badé Archaeological Museum and its director, Kevin Kaiser, for his work in preparing the traveling exhibit from Tell En-Nasbeh to supplement the Bethsaida antiquities in the 1996 exhibition. Also, the Project would like to thank Hava Katz of the Antiquities Authority of Israel,who prepared the antiquities in Israel and Baruch Brandl of the Antiquities Authority for his assistance in facilitating the selection and preparation of the items for loan. Our thanks to Professor Mark Appold at Truman State University, Professor Joel Gereboff at Arizona State University, Professor Lawrence Baron at San Diego State University, the late Professor John Rousseau at the Graduate Theological Union as well as Kevin Kaiser at the Badé Archaeological Museum and Professor Sandy Lowe at Santa Rosa Junior College, who made on-site arrangements and publicity for the exhibit and ensured its great success.

A fifty-six-minute documentary about the site prepared by the University of Nebraska at Omaha Television entitled "The Lost City of Bethsaida" was completed in March 1997 and premiered at UNO and then later on the Nebraska Educational Television stations statewide. The Alumni Association of UNO provided much of the funding for the premiere of the movie and we thank Alumni Center director Jim Leslie, and coordinator Lori Bechtold, who helped prepare the event. Producer, director, and writer Dave Rotterman, the director of photography Cec Barton, production coordinator at UNO Television, and Brian Shaeffer all went to Israel in the summer of 1995 and filmed the main part of the documentary. Although the Bethsaida Excavations Project provided major funding for the production, the enormous resources necessary to produce a full-length documentary were made possible by UNO Television and its general manager, Debbie Aliano, and Executive Producer Gary Repair. The rest of the funding for the documentary came from a generous grant from the Gilbert M. and Martha H. Hitchcock Foundation and especially its secretary, Mr. Thomas Burke. The funding for the film combined Israeli and American resources. Coordinating these efforts was the University of Nebraska Foundation. Thanks go to those who worked on Bethsaida's behalf for the Foundation including John Niemann, John Erickson, Deb Kohler, and Jeff Dempsey. The Project acknowledges the continuing support of the Israel Tourist Corporation and its past and present directors, but the driving force behind the successful completion of the film and the archaeological park was Mr. Aviad Sar Shalom of the Tourist Corporation, who deserves special praise. The Nebraska Humanities Council, the University of Nebraska at Omaha, Hastings College, Dana College, Doane College, and Truman State University all took part in the production of the Bethsaida documentary. The documentary is presently being distributed nationwide and represents an important achievement for the Bethsaida Excavations Project. In the course of filming the documentary in Israel and the final production and premiere of the movie, support was provided by the people of the village of Tuba-Zangariya, Kibbutz Gadot, Kibbutz Ginosar, and especially Katy Bar-Noff, the administrator of the Kibbutz Ginosar Bed and Breakfast where we stayed during 1995, 1996, and 1997. Thanks are due Nitza Kaplan and her staff at the Bet Yigal Allon Museum at Kibbutz Ginosar for the laboratory, storage space, offices, and display space which have allowed the Project to develop. Funding for some of the activities mentioned above was provided in part by the Golan Regional Council, especially Uri Meir and Itzhaq Wiseman, the Truman State University Press, and particularly its director and editor-in-chief Paula Presley. The Egged Bus Company of Israel, Amsalam Tours of Tiberias, Europcar, Eurodollar, and Sa-Gal Car Rental of Israel, and Murray's Travel in Saint Louis, Missouri, helped with the travel arrangements in Israel and the United States, and we appreciate their help. Finally, the Bethsaida Excavations Project has been immeasurably aided by the addition of a full-time coordinator, Ms. Wendi Chiarbos, of UNO. Wendi, a 1996 graduate of the Department of Philosophy and Religion at UNO, made sure that all the activities mentioned in these acknowledgments were accomplished with success. We thank her for her efforts.

The Bethsaida Excavations Project now includes a large board of directors and staff of researchers, including Dr. Rami Arav, director of excavations, University of Nebraska at Omaha (UNO); Dr. John F. Shroder, chief geologist, UNO; Dr. Michael Bishop, chief geographer, UNO; Dr. Heinz-Wolfgang Kuhn, The University of Munich, Germany; Dr. John T. Greene, Michigan State University; Dr. Richard A. Freund, UNO project director, corresponding secretary of the consortium; Dr. Frederick Strickert, Wartburg College; Dr. Mark Appold, Truman State University; Dr. Elizabeth McNamer, Rocky Mountain College; Dr. John Currid, Reformed Theological Seminary; Dr. Charles

Page, Jerusalem Center for Biblical Studies; Dr. James W. Watts, Hastings College; Dr. Delvin Hutton, Dr. John Mark Nielsen, and Dr. James Olsen, Dana College; Dr. Gordon Brubacher, Doane College; Dr. Denny Clark, Albertson College; associated staff and researchers include affiliated research staff of Dr. Moshe Inbar, Haifa University; Dr. Walter C. Bouzard, Wartburg College; Dr. Monika Bernett, University of Munich; Dr. Gloria London, University of Washington; Dr. Mark Smith, Albertson College; Dr. Dale Stover, University of Nebraska at Omaha; Patrick Geyer, Arizona State University; Baruch Brandl, Antiquities Authority of Israel; Kevin Freese, Oxford University; Mina Cohn, Archaeological Encounters Canada. For petrology/petrography, Dr. Robert Shuster; UNO artist DreAnna Hadash; UNO Conservation, Orna Cohen; Jerusalem Restoration, Charleen Green; UNO Zooarchaeology, Toni Tessaro of the University of Tennessee; glass studies, Andrea Rottloff of the University of Munich; assistant to the director of excavations, Sandra Fortner of the University of Munich

We thank the following people for their participation in the preparation of the site: Yonah Kolman, who worked on the graphics, signage and brochures for the site; Dr. Omri Boneh of the Jewish National Fund; Aliza Rapaport, architect for the new park; Dr. Tzvika Gal, the Antiquities Authority's regional archaeologist; and Yosi Broida and Ilan Kedar of the Antiquities Authority of Israel for their conservation work at the site. In addition to the summer scientific photographs for the regular documenting of the site, other photographers were involved in some of the necessary photographs. We thank in particular, Dubi Tal and Moti Haramati at Albatross Studios in Tel Aviv, Ilan Sztulman in Jerusalem for his expert photography of many of the coins, and A. Shemesh, photographer for some of the artifacts.

As this second volume is being sent to press, the final preparations are being made at Bethsaida for the opening of the site to the public in 1998. This has been a major undertaking headed by Uzi Egoz of the Jewish Agency for this area of the country and involving many committees and the joint efforts of architects, archaeologists, contractors, accountants, and administrators from the Jewish National Fund, the Antiquities Authority of Israel, the Jordan Park, the Israel Tourist Corporation, and the Golan Regional Council among others. Thanks to the generous gifts from the Vatican and the Archdiocese of Omaha, two shaded meditation spots have been created for visitors to enjoy

the commanding views of the Jordan River valley and the Sea of Galilee which must have captivated Bethsaida's occupants for thousands
of years. Our thanks go to Msgr. Dr. Richard Mathes, chargé of the
Holy See in Jerusalem, and the Most Reverend Elden Francis Curtiss,
archbishop of Omaha, for their ongoing support and for facilitating
these gifts. It is hoped that many visitors will soon have the opportu-
nity to visit this site whose history is only beginning to be told.

# Part I

# Archaeology and Geology of Bethsaida

*Rami Arav*

# Bethsaida Excavations: Preliminary Report, 1994-1996

THE 1994 TO 1996 SEASONS MARKED A CHANGE in the history of the excavations. The length of the seasons spent on the field was extended and the number of finds exceeded all the previous seasons. The result is that much more light has been shed on the history and the material culture of the site. The seasons extended between May 1 and December 31, 1994, March and July 1995, and February and July 1996, during which individuals of the Bethsaida Excavations Consortium and hundreds of students participated. During the last four months, a group of hired workers from Tiberias, Safed, Merar, and Buq'ata assisted in the dig.

Staff members for the three seasons were: Dr. Rami Arav, director of the excavations, and Dr. Richard Freund, director of the project and corresponding secretary at the University of Nebraska at Omaha. Area supervisors included: Dr. Mark Appold (Truman State University), Dr. Monika Bernett (University of Munich), Dr. Denny Clark (Albertson College), Sandra Fortner (University of Munich), David Goren (of Israel), Andrea Gramann (University of Munich), Dr. John T. Greene (Michigan State University), Dr. Delvin Hutton (Dana College), Itai Orgad (of Israel), Dr. John Rousseau (University of California at Berkeley), Dr. Mark Smith (Albertson College), Dr. Frederick Strickert (Wartburg College), and Toni Tessaro (University of Tennessee at Knoxville). In addition to this team there were: Dr. Heinz-Wolfgang Kuhn

(University of Munich), Dr. Elizabeth McNamer and a group of students (Rocky Mountain College). Land survey was conducted by engineer Alexander Weisberg; restoration by Beth Seldin-Dothan, Abraham Spivak, Rick Baesler, and Charleen Green; recording by Denise Baesler and Denis Leon; numismatics by Dr. Arie Kindler; drawing by Bruno Castelhano, Rick Baesler, DreAnna Hadash; computer operation by Uri Arav; and metals restoration by Orna Cohen.

## METHODOLOGY

Almost every expedition develops its own recording method. However, all modern excavations use similar data elements, such as basket numbers, locus numbers, and levels. Of course, these records are now also kept in computer databases. The methods we use at Bethsaida have been developed from techniques used by various Israeli institutions and universities. The idea is to record as much information as possible, as accurately as possible. In 1992, we introduced a computerized recording method to facilitate quick reporting and easy access to stored information. This computer program was written on database software. The system leads the operator through a sequence of interconnected windows to the desired menu and program. The first menu is the Subsystem Menu, which offers five options:

1. Entering Excavation Details
2. Base Tables
3. Reports
4. Printing Base Tables
5. Disk Handling

Selecting the first alternative, Entering Excavation Details, opens the window through which most of the data are entered. This window presents four options (fig. 1).

1.1. Entering General Details. This is, in fact, the field log of the dig. In order to make the program user friendly, it is similar in form to the daily dairy used at the site.

1.2. Photo Table. This is where verbal descriptions of all the photographs are stored.

1.3. Finds Inventory. All the data on the individual finds are stored here.

1.4. Walls. All information about walls is recorded here.

Selecting Base Tables in the Subsystem Menu will open a
window that offers five choices:

2.1. Catalogue of Finds Tables. This is a collection of all types of
finds discovered at Bethsaida. The finds are assorted by
materials, periods, and types. Pottery vessels are arranged
according to time period, and within the period they are
arranged from the large open forms to the closed forms.
Each type has a code number. Each time a new type is discovered it is assigned a code number and added to the catalogue. The "reading" of the finds from the table into the
computer file is done by using the code numbers. This
method saves plenty of time, particularly when long and
repeated descriptions of types occur, such as "Hellenistic
globular cooking pot with lid device." The Bethsaida catalogue can store 99,999 different types of finds. This number
is, of course, arbitrary and may be extended if all catalogue
numbers become occupied.
2.2. Sites Table. The user can work with more than one site in
this program.
2.3. Materials Table. This is a coded table of various materials that
compose a find.
2.4. License Table. This stores all the license numbers according
to years. They are useful when reports that indicate the year
of the dig are required.
2.5. Wall Material Table. This enables one to define quickly the
materials used to construct the described walls.

Selecting Reports, on the Subsystem Menu will open a window in
which nine different reports can be generated. They are as follows (see
fig. 4):

3.1. Entering General Details Report (fig. 1), which presents the
field log as it is arranged during the daily activities.
3.2. Locus Report (fig. 2), which presents the data about loci. It
selects information from the Field Diary that pertains to
any locus requested.
3.3. Stratum Report, which selects all information for a requested
stratum. *Go to p. 9*

| | | | | | Entering General Details | | | |
|---|---|---|---|---|---|---|---|---|
| | | | | | FIELD DIARY | | | |
| | | | Site: | 1 Bethsaida | Area: A | Date: 23/06/96 | | |
| Basket No. | Locus & Photos | Square | Level | Description | | Final Locus | Stratum | Finds (F5) |
| 2785 | 187 | J 51 | 168.65 | CONTINUE TO REMOVE DIRT, EXPOSE LARGE STONES | | 0 | | |
| 2786 | 188 | J 51 | 166.88 | OPENING NEW LOCUS S W CORNER OF J 51 E HALF OF HIGH SPOT BESIDE BENCH MARK | | 0 | | |
| 2787 | 175 | F 54 | 168.27 | CONTINUE TO REMOVE DIRT, EXPOSE LARGE STONES | | 0 | | |
| 8529 | 851 | I 50 | 167.50 | CLEANING LOCUS IN SOUTH PART OF THE SQUARE | | 0 | | |

Fig. 1. "Entering General Details" screen from Subsystem Menu

| | | | Locus Report | | |
|---|---|---|---|---|---|
| | | Site: | 1 Bethsaida | Area: A | |
| | Date: 23/06/95 | Locus: 851 | Stratum | | |
| Basket No. | Square | Level | Description | Final Locus | Finds |
| 8529 | I 50 | 167.50 | Cleaning locus in south part of the square | 0 | |

| Catalog No. | Find Description | State of preservation | No. of Finds | Status |
|---|---|---|---|---|
| 0.01 | Mixed pottery | p | 780 | - |
| 11.01 | EB II Hole mouth jar | p | 1 | + |
| 41.00 | IRON AGE II, bowls | p | 1 | + |
| 41.00 | IRON AGE II, bowls | p | 1 | + |
| 44.60 | Iron Age II, Jar - Red slip | p | 1 | + |

Fig 2. Locus Report with "Finds Option" Submenu

| Level Report<br>Site:    Bethsaida    Area: B   Stratum:<br>Locus: 228   Date 19/06/96   Level: 167.00 | | | | | |
|---|---|---|---|---|---|
| Basket No. | Cat. No | Find Description | No. of Finds | Status | State of Preservation |
| 2173 | 1599,99 | Bones | 69 | + | P |
| 2173 | 40.00 | Iron Age II, general | 88 | R | P |
| 2173 | 910.00 | Brick | 80 | - | P |
| 2173 | 40.02 | Iron Age II, clay whorl | 1 | + | I |
| 2173 | 41.00 | Iron Age II, bowls | 2 | R | P |
| 2173 | 45.00 | Iron Age II, jugs | 1 | R | P |

Fig. 3. Level Report

| Bethsaida<br>FINDS REPORT<br>Catalogue No.: 59.50     Athenian black pottery | | | | | | | | | |
|---|---|---|---|---|---|---|---|---|---|
| Area | Stratum | Square | Locus | Level | Basket No. | Date | No. of Finds | Status | State of Preservation |
| A | J | 53 | 0 | 0.00 | 2508 | 01/03/96 | 1 | + | P |
| A | J | 54 | 150 | 166.9 | 2556 | 30/04/96 | 1 | + | P |
| A | J | 53 | 150 | 167.31 | 2530 | 27/03/96 | 1 | + | P |
| A | H | 52 | 153 | 0.00 | 2553 | 29/04/96 | 1 | + | P |
| A | I | 52 | 153 | 0.02 | 2547 | 29/04/96 | 1 | + | P |
| A | I | 52 | 158 | 167.03 | 2594 | 02/05/96 | 1 | R | P |
| A | I | 52 | 158 | 167.30 | 2589 | 02/05/96 | 1 | R | P |
| A | I | | | | | | | | |
| A | G | | | | | | | | |
| A | G | | | | | | | | |

AT Bethsaida   , BETWEEN:
AREA A TO AREA A,
STRATUM   TO STRATUM 7,
LOCUS 0    TO locus 999,
LEVEL 0.00 TO LEVEL 170.00,
AND BETWEEN THE DATES 01/01/96 AND 18/11/96

| THERE ARE | 6 | Athenian black pottery | Status | (R) |
|---|---|---|---|---|
| THERE ARE | 8 | Athenian black pottery | Status | (+) |
| THERE ARE | 0 | Athenian black pottery | Status | (-) |
| THERE ARE | 0 | Athenian black pottery | No Status | |
| TOTAL NO.: | 14 of Athenian black pottery | | | |

Fig. 4. Finds Report

| WALL REPORT FOR SITE BETHSAIDA | |
|---|---|
| WALL NO.: 191 STRAIGHT WALL RADIUS:  0 | |
| Start X Coordination: H485 Start Y Coordination: 43475 Wall width: 80.00 | End X Coordination J 482 End Y Coordination: 42020 |
| Wall upper level: 166.23 | Wall bottom level: 167.90 |
| Wall material: basalt stone | |
| Description: Wall composed of small to large stones. Wall intersects W192 at J310, and W190 at H470 | |

Fig. 5. Subsystem Menu, Wall Report

| CATALOGUE OF FINDS TABLE PRINT | |
|---|---|
| Catalogue No. | Find Description |
| 75.00 | Hellenistic globular cooking pots, L.71 |
| 75.01 | Hellenistic cooking pot ware |
| 75.02 | Hellenistic cooking pot, local ware |
| 75.03 | Hellenistic Roman globular small cooking pot |
| 75.05 | Hellenistic cooking pot, everted rim |
| 75.10 | Hellenistic globular cooking pot, without lid device, L.71.1 |

Fig. 6. Catalogue of Finds Table Print

| Main Details | | | | | | | |
|---|---|---|---|---|---|---|---|
| Site | Date | Area No. | Basket No. | Locus | Level | Square | Stratum |
| Bethsaida | 03/06/96 | B | 2104 | 225 | 166.11 | I | 35 |
| Bethsaida | 03/06/96 | B | 2105 | 225 | 166.00 | I | 35 |
| Bethsaida | 03/06/96 | B | 2106 | 226 | 166.87 | H | 34 |
| Bethsaida | 03/06/96 | B | 2107 | 226 | 165.99 | H | 34 |
| Bethsaida | 04/06/96 | B | 2108 | 225 | 166.04 | I | 35 |

Fig. 7. Sample Report

| Finds Inventory of Bethsaida<br>License: G-46/1990 | | |
|---|---|---|
| Inventory No.: 350 | Material: Ivory | |
| Catalogue No.: 570.00 | Type Description: Ivory object | |
| Area: B<br>Square: G36 | Locus: 364    Date of discovery: 04/07/90<br>Basket No.: 4134    Level: 167.44 | |
| DIMENSIONS;<br>Height; 7.6    WIDTH: 2.3    Diameter: 2.4<br>Description: Ivory handle, dense but hollowed out in the center for the handle. Incisions in fishbone pattern along the handle. Two horizontal lines on top.<br>Period: Iron Age II | | |
| Parallels: | | |
| Roll No.: 9314 | Photo No.: 21 | Drawing No.: 93.000 |

Fig. 8. Finds Inventory

3.4. Level Report (fig. 3), which displays information that pertains to a requested excavated level. This report serves to isolate information for any level. The operator has to insert the range level numbers.

3.5. Finds Report (fig. 4), which generates a report of a single type of discovery and will indicate all dates, areas, loci, and baskets in which the requested find was found. It also indicates whether the find was discarded, saved, or reconstructed as well as the number of the occurrences of the discovery and a total of all finds.

3.6. Photo Report, which indicates lists of photographs pertaining to loci.

3.7. Wall Report (fig. 5), which contains information about walls.

3.8. General Details Report, which describes particular baskets.

3.9. Catalogue of Finds Table (fig. 6), which contains all the types of finds recorded in this catalogue.

Entering General Details (fig. 1) is the primary file for generating information about the project. The main vehicle of data is the basket. As with the manual diary, the General Details Report is confined to locus, square, and elevation. The Table of Description contains all the excavation activities for the day and the circumstances under which the finds of the basket were made. By and large, it does not contain descriptions of the finds. The latter is done in a separate table into which the types of finds, which are recognized and defined, are read from the Catalogue of Finds Table (fig.6) in a numbered code system. When a type is recognized and read into the table, its state of preservation is indicated; e.g., whether it was found in fragments, complete but broken, or intact. The number of occurrences of the find is indicated as well as its status—whether it was discarded, saved, or taken to restoration.

Sample Report (fig. 7) concludes the main details. It includes fields for site, date, area number, basket number, locus level, square, and stratum.

Finds Inventory (fig. 8). Unlike the Catalogue of Finds Table, which describes type of pottery, the Finds Inventory entries describe each find individually with dimensions, and the Inventory lists parallels (if any exist). It also bears the photo number and drawing number of the particular find.

The walls at Bethsaida, which all were given numbers, are recorded in this system in verbal form. At a certain period during the dig there was an attempt to number the walls systematically, with north-south walls bearing even numbers and east–west walls bearing uneven numbers. In addition to the wall numbers, there is also an indication in the reports of where coordinates begin and end, whether they are straight or curved, loci with which they are associated, and what photographs were taken of the walls.

## THE DAILY SCHEDULE

Bethsaida Excavations is fundamentally an educational program offered by the Bethsaida Consortium, which teaches about archaeology, and the Bethsaida site is where students study and share in practical fieldwork at the site. Each session in this program lasts three weeks. The students dig during the morning hours, participate in laboratory work during the afternoons, and attend lectures in the evenings. Each weekend is devoted to field trips to see and learn about other sites. The amount of learning and knowledge the students acquire in the dig surpasses the amount of study in a regular frontal class. Undergraduate and graduate students, in addition to fieldwork, write papers concerning a topic of the excavation or issues on the relationship between the Bible and archaeology.

The expedition was housed at the guest rooms of Kibbutz Gadot (1994) and Kibbutz Ginosar (1995, 1996), and we are grateful for their help and warm hospitality. The laboratories of the excavations— which include pottery restoration laboratories, storage rooms, and offices for associate field experts (in fields such as bones, pollen, geology, and geomorphology), a small finds display room, and a general business office—were provided by Kibbutz Gadot (1994) and Beit Alon Museum (1995, 1996). We are indebted to them and their efforts, which helped the expedition in many ways. In particular, the Beit Alon Museum and its director, Nitza Kaplan, deserve special praise for their forethought and creativity in serving the expedition, which in turn significantly adds to humankind's understanding of ancient Galilee, a primary mission of the museum. The daily schedule of the expedition was as follows:

4:30  Wake-up call.
5:15  Bus leaves for the site.
9:00  Breakfast at the site.
13:00 Return by bus to the kibbutz and lunch.
16:30 Afternoon lab work and/or pottery reading.
19:00 Supper.
20:00 Evening lecture.

## RESULTS OF THE EXCAVATIONS
### SETTLEMENT PATTERN AND CITY PLANNING (FIGS. 9, 10)

The 1994–1996 campaigns at Bethsaida were the longest that work has been carried out at the site. As a result, the pattern of settlement through the ages has become much clearer and more obvious. Almost from the beginning, we thought that Bethsaida consisted of two main cities, the lower city and the upper city. The two cities were built on an extension of a lava flow to the Sea of Galilee, and during the early period of the first millennium BCE it was surrounded by the sea on both the southern and the western shores. The shallow and normally still water (which is so desirable around the shore of Sea of Galilee) together with its abundance of fish, its location at the estuary of the Jordan river, and its excellent view of the entire lake, are advantages that made this location a most preferable place to encamp and found a city, and these factors were presumably the main reasons for its success. The upper city was situated on the eastern ridge of the extension hill, somewhat farther away from the water but with a commanding

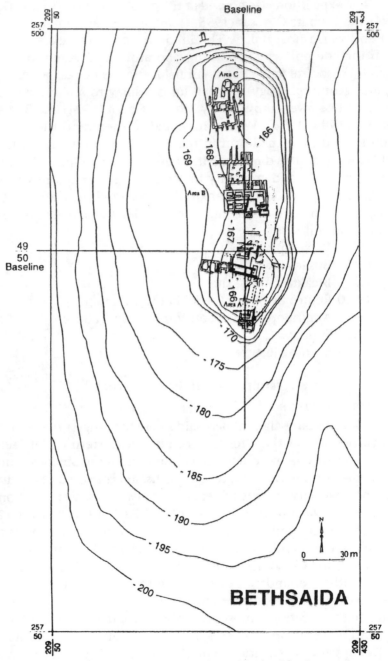

Fig.9. General ground plan of Bethsaida site

Fig. 10. Aerial shot looking south, showing Bethsaida plain in the foreground and the Sea of Galilee in the background. The excavation concentrated on the northeast side of the mound.

view of the entire settlement and the lake. Thus the city wall, remains of which we have unearthed and which dates from the tenth century BCE, is shared by the lower and the upper city on the east side. The city was found to be heavily fortified; details on these fortifications are described in the following pages. The gate to the city was found at the eastern section of the city, just below the upper city, and it is approached by a long walk in the shadow of the eastern city walls. Those entering the city through a four-chamber gate would be in the upper city; to enter the palace compound a turn to the right at the end of the gatehouse would lead to the palace gate. There is perhaps more than one gate. A water gate should be located closer to the lake in the lower city. No remains of this proposed gate have been discovered thus far, but the remains of the city wall are easily discernible in some sections. They survive in some places at a thickness of about 1.2 m.

The Hellenistic settlement was completely different. It does not seem to have been a town, but rather a large village, composed of very large courtyard houses arranged next to one another and connected by alleys or spacious openings. Since the Iron Age city was built so durably, with heavy massive walls, many of the walls and structures projected out of the debris of the houses and were put into secondary and tertiary use in the Hellenistic and Roman periods. This habit of reusing walls most probably saved a great deal of energy and effort for the later Hellenistic and Early Roman construction workers, but it did not work so beneficially for the archaeologists who came to explore the ruins. The stratigraphical problem of identifying the dates of construction and destruction of every segment of the walls in this mound is one of the most difficult of its kind, and it is the hope of the author that this analysis is as close as possible to the reality of one period.

STRATIGRAPHY

In volume 1 of this series, seven levels were observed. We still maintain this number; however, the attribution of structures to the different levels has not yet been fully established and may change as the result of future excavations. Further research will focus especially on the Iron Age levels and will observe the possibility of defining more sets of layers within this long period. The levels thus far are:

LEVEL 1. The top level consists of remains from the Middle Ages to the modern period (fourteenth to twentieth centuries). This level includes only a few fragmentary buildings and installations that were constructed sporadically on the mound. It also contains a group of more than one hundred Bedouin tombs that date from the sixteenth century to the twentieth century. The latest phase of use on the mound belonged to the modern Syrian military position, which crisscrossed the mound with trenches, bunkers, houses, and armor installations. This phase was the most destructive in the history of the site incorporated in our Level 1 remains.

LEVEL 2. The second level (which dates from the fourth century BCE to the second century CE) consists of four layers of constructions and reuse of buildings during the Hellenistic–Early Roman period.

During the excavation campaign of 1996, a level of occupation that dates from the second century CE was revealed; for convenience, the descriptions of these remains are incorporated within this level.

LEVEL 3. The third level consists of the remains of structures of the Persian period (540–332 BCE). This is a fairly long period, but very few structures were built at the site during this period.

LEVEL 4. The fourth level dates from Iron Age IIC, III. This level contains the remains of the city after the Assyrian conquest (732 BCE) to the end of the Babylonian period (540 BCE). In a few instances there is gradual shift from Level 4 to Level 3; therefore, we leave open the question of the end of this level and await further excavations to elucidate this point.

LEVEL 5. The fifth level dates from Iron Age IIB (925–732 BCE). This level and Level 6 are where most of the building activities took place. Further excavations would clarify the particular date of the structures in these levels.

LEVEL 6. The sixth level dates from Iron Are IIA (1000–925 BCE). It is likely that the city wall and the Bit Hilani palace were constructed during this period.

LEVEL 7. The seventh level dates from the Early Bronze Age (3050–2700 BCE). Only shards of pottery and a very few architectural remains can be ascribed to this period.

The natural way to present the finds at the site would have been to describe (in order) the approach to the city, then the city walls, then the fortifications, and finally the structures within the city. However, in keeping with archaeological tradition, the descriptions will proceed chronologically (from the earliest level to the latest) and alphabetically (from Area A through Area C).

## AREA A (MAPS 1 THROUGH 6)

STRATIGRAPHY AND ARCHITECTURAL REMAINS

This area includes the remains of the Iron Age II city gate structure as well as the city walls and its fortifications. The Hellenistic–Early Roman remains of this area include walls and floors of unidentified structures and the remains of a building we have interpreted as the temple of Roman imperial cult, most particularly of Julia-Livia.

The stratigraphy of Area A is not yet fully established. The section in Map 1 shows the situation at the end of 1994 season. Section

A-A crosses squares 58 and shows, on the right, the pavement on the outside of the city wall, which is ascribed to Levels 6 through 4. Immediately after and associated with it is the city wall, which was cut through by a Hellenistic-Roman chamber that is ascribed to Level 2. The city wall inside the town is 77 cm deeper than at the outside. It reaches a depth of 170.77 m. A towerlike projection, which may be interpreted as a segment of the upper city fortifications, is formed by walls W300, W307, W314. These walls are presumably revetment walls that support the construction of the upper city.

## LEVEL I

The latest physical occupation at the site in Area A belongs to the modern Syrian military destruction, which prevailed at Bethsaida during the 1960s. Trenches crisscrossed the area and caused great damage, particularly to the upper levels. The main entrance to the military trenches was made in squares M54–56. At square K54, just above the Iron Age gateway to the city, the trench split into two sections. One led to a fortified position at H49 and the other led to a series of trenches at the line of square 57 and to an underground bunker of 5 by 7 m at E55. The disturbances not only mixed the authentic context of the levels at the area of the trenches, but by dumping the contents on the shoulders, they also created a mixture of finds on the shoulders. Further references to the disturbances will be given throughout the descriptions of the various levels.

A different kind of disturbance is found in the upper layers, and was made by numerous Bedouin tombs dug into the earlier levels. The tombs never exceeded 1.5 m below the surface, but in some cases they lay across remains of ancient walls, some of which were reused as one wall of the grave. This may be seen in W10 in square J50. Two tombs were built on top of W7 in square L52, two tombs were built over W27 in square K56, and one tomb with multiple burials was built on top of W300 in square J58. Sometimes dismantled public buildings were used for the tombstones (fig. 11). Most of the tombs date from the sixteenth century to the late nineteenth century. This date is established on evidence of coins that were found in the tombs. Further analysis of the Bedouin remains will be published in future volumes.

Above the layer of the tombs, the remains of a late medieval or early Ottoman period structure were found. One wall, W310, is seen in the plan in square J58. Another wall in an east–west direction was

Figs. 11a and 11b. Stones from dismantled public building used for nine-teenth-century Bedouin tombs, found in Area A

found at the southern end of W310 and was 6 m in length; a third wall lay in a north-south direction, parallel to W310. The stones for these walls, including a single limestone construction block, were taken from older buildings. Among the finds are several clay pipes that may belong to the house contents or may have been brought in at a later date.

## LEVEL 2

This level consists of more than one layer of structures, including all the Hellenistic and Roman construction activities. Many of these activities put to use remains of the previous level that stood out. The phenomenon of reusing old—but stable—walls was widespread throughout the different levels of occupation and is found at many sites. In areas where the hard and durable basalt stones served as the main material of construction, this method was even more intensified. While it made for easier construction, it creates tremendous difficulties for the archaeologists who encounter it. The distinction between the various construction phases and layers is the main focus of any archaeological undertaking; therefore, further analyses may modify the interpretations and conclusions made thus far.

Although the Iron Age city gate was destroyed and burnt (presumably in 732 BCE) and became a huge heap of dirt and debris, the remains of the thick, strong walls were obvious in the later periods, and some were reorganized to form the Hellenistic and Roman levels. Such is the case of W10 and W7.

The upper layer of Level 2 was above any remains of the Iron Age structures. This layer consists of a large area that was paved with fieldstones and some poor walls that were built within or on top of the pavement. The purpose of the pavement is unknown thus far, although it was discerned in a wide area. The significance of this layer is that squares H–I 53–52 obviously superimpose W64 and implies that the structure associated with this wall was out of use during the life of this layer. The finds of this layer include a small number of coins and pottery that date to the second half of the second and third centuries CE.

A ROMAN TEMPLE(?) (MAPS 2 AND 3). The layer under the pavement of H52 poses a real challenge for the excavators. The main building in this layer is superimposed over the Iron Age city gate; its builders made use of sections of the walls that were seen above the ground.

This building, which is proposed to be a temple (fig. 12), is an oblong structure measuring 6 by 20 m, with the narrow walls facing roughly east-west. It is situated in squares G–K 51–53 and consists of walls W64, W65, W62, W69, and the wall west of W65.

Most of the remains of this building were already seen a few years ago. W62, W69, and most of W64 were encountered as early as 1988. Only scarce remains of W62 were discovered, due to a distur-

Figs. 12. Proposed Roman temple, seen from east to west. Notice in the fore-ground the foundation of the column base.

bance caused by a Syrian military trench that went through it from northwest to southeast in J52. The average width of these walls is 1.2 m. It is noteworthy that this is larger than the average width of a private building from this level, which is 0.7 m. Some large sections of the walls seem to be nicely constructed with large slabs and field-stones. A blocked entrance in H51 may indicate that the wall was used prior to its final function. W62 in I52 presents an interesting picture of destruction. The southern face of the wall is partially missing, as a result of looting, and partially inclining inward, as if destroyed by an

*Rami Arav*

earthquake (fig. 13 shows the inclined wall). The southern wall of the building, W64, was found in a poor state of preservation, although the excavated segments demonstrate nice masonry. Perhaps one of the oddest features of the building is that the *antae* that create the porch are not equally extended. For unknown reasons, the southern wall, W64, stretches out more to the east than W62. This southern *antis* was severely destroyed by the Syrian trench and we believe that the remnants behind the Syrian trench represent this extension. Almost at the center of the porch, foundational remnants of a column 48 cm in diameter were unearthed. This would suggest a room for two adjacent

Fig. 13. W62 in I52. Southern face of wall inclining inward

columns in the style known in the first century CE,[1] which would fit a distyle temple. A large flat stone next to it would suggest that the floor of the building was not lower than -167.07 m.

The western wall of the porch to the building is W65, which was rebuilt over the remains of the Iron Age W7 and follows its external lines. W7 is 2.5 m wide and the superimposed wall is reduced to only 1.1 m. This wall was heavily destroyed by the Syrian trench and only a few stone remnants of the wall remained. The Syrian trench pushed aside from its in situ position a dressed threshold—the single dressed stone that was found at the site close to the in situ position. The stone measures 0.8 by 0.35 m (fig. 14). It is indeed a small threshold for a main entrance and it may have served as one of the side doors to the building.

Fig. 14. Threshold of the proposed Roman temple

Limited portions of the wall that may form the back of the *pronaos* were found. A Syrian military position that was built on top of it has ruined it almost entirely. There were not any remains left of the doorway. The elevation of -167.73 m for the bottom of the lowest course conforms with the elevation of -167.07 m for foundations of the floor.

The main room of the building is a large rectangular space that measures 9.1 by 3.85 m. This room was found totally empty. The wall at the back, W69, connects the two long walls of the building. Below W63, which is what was left of the upper layer, there are remains of an entrance threshold to a back side porch at the west. The porch was flanked by two *antae*.[1] Part of the southern *antis* was removed by a later pit at the point where it met a previously reported round structure.[2]

The general ground plan, the stone decorations, and the small finds in the immediate vicinity of this building indicate that it may have been a temple. Most of the important components of a temple were employed in this building. They include the east-west orientation of a rectangular building, the porch situated in *antae* in both east and west ends, remains of a column foundation, a room that may be interpreted as a *pronaos,* a room that may be interpreted as a *cella,* and a porch that can be viewed as the *adyton.* The stone decorations found in the vicinity of the building bolster this assumption. Thus far, four decorated stones have been discovered at Bethsaida. Some were found in a secondary use in Bedouin tombs and information on three of them has been published.[3] Near the western porch several pits containing vessels were discovered, which formed, presumably, the cache of the temple.[4] In another pit, 10 m southwest of the building, an incense shovel was unearthed (fig. 15). The shovel is clearly indicative of a nearby sanctuary, dedicated most probably to the Roman imperial cult. In this vicinity a clay female figurine, which may be interpreted as the image of Julia-Livia, was discovered.[5] In addition, a few other female figurines were revealed; one of them is wearing a veil over a tiara (fig. 16). Temples of the first century CE are not very common in this region—or more precisely, none of them have been found in this area. However, at a further distance and in particular in the Hauran and in northern Syria a few were found and reported. Most are built of fine dressed stones and resemble very vaguely the building at Bethsaida.[6]

Nevertheless, a few elements speak against this interpretation. While the building is situated on an ideal place for a temple (the highest spot of the mound, over a huge pile of debris of the extraordinarily large Iron Age city gate, and overlooking the entire city below, and

Fig. 15. Discovery of incense shovel in a pit southwest of the temple

Fig. 16. Figurine wearing a veil over a tiara

over one of the better lookout points of the Sea of Galilee), it is obvious that, unlike many other Hellenistic-Roman temples, this building is not constructed on a podium.[7] It is possible that the Bethsaida temple's construction depended upon constraints caused by the massive Iron Age gate debris. It is impossible to know whether the building originally had a paved floor, because no traces of pavement of the interior floor were found. It is likely, however, that the floor was thoroughly looted, together with the rest of the dressed and decorated stones that may have adorned the interior and the exterior of the building. If this is the temple built by Philip the Tetrarch, the son of Herod the Great, for the cult of Livia-Julia, the wife of Augustus and the mother of the reigning emperor Tiberius,[8] then it was indeed a very modest temple in comparison with the structures that Philip's father had built at Samaria and Caesarea Maritima.[9]

In connection with the conjectured temple, or perhaps a layer below, we have discerned some rough fieldstone pavement that covered a large area in squares J53–54. The walls associated with it do not make any coherent ground plan thus far. Perhaps further excavations will clarify these points. The walls are inconsistent in their construction. Some are built of one line of heavy boulders and others by smaller fieldstones in two faces.

A few other remains of an unknown structure were found in squares K53–54. These include a well-constructed wall in an east–west direction that is 1.1 m wide and, connected to it, a north–south wall 0.7 m wide. An important clue for a relative dating of this wall is found in the foundation trench of the east–west wall. The trench has removed about 1.4 m of the Iron Age pier of the city gate, but has not touched the end of what we refer to as the southern *antis*. In addition, the first course of the wall is 0.3 m deeper than W64. This is an obvious indication that the wall was constructed after the Iron Age and prior to the construction of W64; i.e., during the Late Hellenistic period.

SOUTHERN SECTION OF AREA A, LEVEL 2. Very few remains were discovered in the area south of the supposed temple. The building activities in this area during Level 2 activity were confined to small alterations and rebuilding from the more ancient Iron Age structures. These were found in squares I–K, 59–60. A single-room house was built into the Iron Age city wall in square K59. The single, solid wall was built on top of the city wall in square K60 and perhaps also served as a city wall. No further remains of this wall were encountered in other parts of the mound. The tops of other Iron Age walls were reused and served as the foundation for one-face walls of unidentified structures. All in all, the entire layout of this level in this area is remarkably humble and poor.

## LEVELS 3 AND 4

No remains have been attributed to these levels thus far. Future research will attempt to discover whether there were any structural activities in this area during this period.

## LEVEL 5

This level is very problematic, although the various structures are obvious and easily defined. The level consists of the Iron Age city gate and the associated remains of the city walls as well as the pavements outside the gate. The main problem is the correlation and the relative association of all the elements. Further investigation will concentrate on these issues and imply adequate reconstruction.

CITY GATEHOUSE (MAP 4). Segments of the city gate were excavated during the previous seasons; unfortunately, they were not identified as such when they were first encountered (see Arav [1995], 7-15). The main reason for this was the method we initially employed of leaving the balks unexcavated until we obtained a thorough visible perception of the building. During the 1996 season we removed the balks, and only then did the structures become clear to us.

The gate is situated in squares J–N, 51–57, which set it at the eastern side of the city. It is apparently also the entrance to the upper city. It is set far off from the northernmost vulnerable point and in a place where the unarmed right flank of an enemy would have to advance near the (presumably) guarded city walls. This location came somewhat as a surprise to us since we did not expect to find a city gate at the highest point of the mound. As a matter of fact, it became the highest point of the mound as a result of the fierce conflagration caused by the Assyrian assault, evidently in 732 BCE. This destruction left an enormous heap of debris. Other structures did not suffer such severe destruction and thus perhaps survived to the next period.

Although we have not excavated the gate in its entirety, the main features and scope are visible. The approach to the gate was made at the eastern city wall. The city wall in this place is situated on an artificial rampart, 6 to 7 m in width, where the slope in the east descends sharply into a deep ravine. We have not yet investigated the rampart but it obviously dates from the construction of the gate. The ravine effectively protected the city wall from the east and prevented the pouring of a dike for the use of battering rams. It is presumed that the approach to the city gatehouse was protected by watchtowers and an external gate, in the same fashion as at Dan,[10] Megiddo,[11] and Lachish.[12] These external structures may be located on the area where the rampart is substantially wider, in squares O47–48.

The city gatehouse represents a right-angle axial approach to the city. Those who entered had to make a right turn from the rampart in order to enter the city. A right-angle approach is found in city gates from almost all periods. This simple technique made it difficult for those who wished to assault the city with battering rams, cavalry attacks, or with foot soldiers. The city gatehouse is built of large, roughly dressed basalt boulders and is meticulously constructed. As exposed thus far, it measures 17.35 by approximately 35 m. The gate consists of four deep chambers and a 4-m-wide passageway in between (figs. 17, 18). The towers that flank the passage have not been fully

Fig. 17. Pavement of passageway. Notice the plaster on the pier between chambers 3 and 4.

Fig. 18. Remnants of pavement inside the gate. Stele is seen on the right, leaning on the southwestern pier.

excavated yet, but their dimensions are pretty well established based upon a section from squares M–O 51, which measure 5.75 m wide by 13.5 m long. The length is projected from the passage between the chambers. No part of the southern tower has been excavated thus far, but it is assumed that it is identical to the northern one. It is also assumed that, as in Megiddo and Carcemish, there would be recessions that would lead into the passage.[13] Remnants of pavements in squares O51 and M58 suggest that the entire area outside the gate was paved similarly to the pavement at Dan.[14] A short *glacis* made of crushed limestone and dirt descends from the city wall to a length of 5.5 m. A similar *glacis* was observed in the excavations of the northern city wall in Area C. It is noteworthy that both *glacis* are not only built in the same system, but also slope at an identical angle of 32 percent. The core of the tower was made of various sizes of fieldstones, as a small section in square M52 indicates.

As mentioned above, four chambers flank the passage. They were only partially excavated. Chamber 4, the northeast chamber, measures 10.25 m long by 3.5 m wide. The size of the chamber was figured from small probes in its corners and along the wall. A pier, 2.35 m wide (W7), divides chamber 4 from chamber 3. The pier is built of very massive stones that were carefully put together. The side of the pier that faces the gateway was nicely plastered in red with layers of whitewash on top.

Chamber 1 measures 10.7 by 3.4 m. Three squares (I 54, 55, 56), were excavated, which contain portions of the chamber, the pier (W319), and the face of the pier to the passage. Remains of a wall at the northern end of the chamber may indicate a later attempt to block the chamber. A well-constructed and worn threshold, which measures 15 cm in height, was found at the entrance of the chamber.

Chamber 2, the southeastern chamber, is perhaps similar in size to chamber 4. Only one square was unearthed: K56, which contained sections of the chamber and the pier between chambers 1 and 2 (W21) and the end of the pier facing the passage. The chamber contained a layer of 0.75 m of ashes. As with the other piers, this one is built of solid and massive fieldstone with very coarse dressings.

Chamber 3, northwest of the gate, measures 10.1 by 3.4 m and is the most excavated chamber. Sections of its walls (W10, W500, and W7) were exposed already in previous years. These walls are very thick and are all 2.35 m wide.

Chamber 4 (see fig. 19), the northeast chamber, measures 10.25 m long and 3.5 m wide. The size of the chamber was figured from small probes in its corners and along the wall. A pier that measures 2.35 m wide (W7) divides chamber 4 from chamber 3. The pier is built of very massive stones that were carefully put together. The side of the pier that faces the gateway was nicely plastered in red with layers of whitewash over it.

The main passage was meticulously paved with relatively small stones. This pavement was found smooth and worn from long usage. The piers that faced the passageway were all plastered in clay with a thick whitewash. The pavement of the passageway is most probably connected to patches of pavement in areas outside the city wall (W160, W315) and together they undoubtedly formed a continuous pavement. This pavement tends to rise slightly to the south in the extramural section, and more steeply where one would enter the city gate. The elevation of the pavement at the northern exterior pavement (O52) is 170.41 m, and the southern exterior pavement (M58) is at 170.87 m. The interior passageway (J54) is 168.83 m high.

Above the passage we discovered a thick layer of bricks that came from the ceiling. The bricks measure 35 by 60 by 15 cm. Some of them bear reed imprints and may be evidence of a flat ceiling sup-

Fig. 19. Probe showing northeast corner of chamber 4

ported by a reed-and-beams bedding. Brickwork most probably constituted the upper courses of the walls from an average level of 1.5 m
above the floor.

The gate was destroyed by a fierce conflagration. The bricks
came off the walls and ceiling and then melted into yellowish-black
glazed clinkers that amalgamated pottery, plaster, and bricks. The
thermal conditions to produce such clinkers must have been exceed-
ingly high. No fuel materials were discerned and it is presumed that
the wooden doors together with oil and other organic materials were
ablaze for a relatively long time. On top of the burnt bricks and debris
a number of large spots of gray ashes were revealed, which indicate a
fire hearth that covered the destroyed gate.

The northwest corner of the city gate served also as an entrance
to the palace complex (perhaps "the king's gate," as in Esth. 4:2). The
entrance, 1.7 m wide, was made between W10 and W25. The northern end of W10 was of thick construction and built in three recessions. This section was built with extremely huge boulders that
weighed a few tons each. One of the boulders measures 1.6 by 1.2 by
0.6 m. It served perhaps as a huge platform for a tower that overlooked the entrance of the palace complex. Inside the plaza, at the

east side (the right-hand side of the entrance) was a row of several stones in upright position, probably indicating stelae or *matzevot* for offering purposes.[15]

## Southern Section, Levels 4-6 (Maps 5 and 6)

The southern section of the city gate poses difficulties in relation to the city gate. Future investigations will focus on the connecting parts in order to clarify it. The order of the levels and their content are clear and obvious, but the connection of it to the city gate needs to be established.

### Level 6

W315 represents the city wall, which was found in a seriously destroyed condition. The outside face of the wall is conjectural and based upon a 6-m average of the city wall. The remains of the pavement outside the wall support this reconstruction. Large sections of the wall were removed by a modern Syrian military trench. The inner face of the wall has been found, although sections were reused during the Hellenistic and Early Roman periods. It seems, however, that the city wall is connected to W300, under the superimposed W311, which is situated in an east–west direction. This wall turns to the south in W307 and turns west in W314. It is assumed that these walls form large revetments to support the upper city in which the city gate and the palace complex are situated. If this is the case, then the upper city was set apart from the lower city by a sequence of bastions or towers that served also as a huge revetment wall to form the upper plateau of the upper city. Clues for this theory may be found in the shape of the hill. Originally the natural hill consisted of large boulders in various shapes. In order to overcome obstacles, the builders confined the upper city site with a thick and solid revetment wall, poured filling on top of the ground, and created a flat plateau on which the pubic structures were built.[16]

### Level 5

Level 5 marks a great change in the appearance of this area. A fierce destruction caused the collapse of the superimposed structures of the revetment walls, which came down, covered the towers and the floor, and sealed off this level. The only remains of the previous level was the old city wall, which because of its thickness was presumably still towering over the debris. A new wall W311, built with very large boulders, was attached to the city wall, making the latter even thicker. This wall, together with other corresponding walls (W304, W306, W313, W300, W310), forms a building with spacious rooms that served perhaps for public purposes. The entrance to this edifice was between W310 and W313. This entrance led to an elongated room that measures 7.5 by 3 m. There are three other openings to this room: One is at the north in W310, which led to an unknown destination in the vicinity of the city gate. The second was opposite the first one, at the southern wall W306, and led to an elongated room, which measures 7.5 by 2.4 m and is similar to the first room. An opening at the eastern end of W306 connected the two rooms again. This interesting room is obviously part of a larger building, the purpose of which is still unknown.

The building was destroyed in a ferocious blaze. Thousands of pottery shards, particularly of large jars, were discovered on the floor together with ashes and remains of the fire (fig. 20). It is interesting that only a few jars could be restored. The date suggested for this destruction is the third quarter of the eighth century BCE, and perhaps more precisely, the campaign of the Assyrian king Tiglath Pileser III in 732 BCE.[17]

## SELECTIVE FINDS FROM AREA A

During the 1994–1996 excavation season we discovered and recorded in Area A more than 300,000 shards of pottery (of which 101,560 shards were found during the 1996 excavation season). A third of all the shards was taken to our restoration laboratories. To this amount one has to add a large number of small finds made of stone, metal, or bone in order to calculate the total number of small discoveries at the site. It is practically impossible to give a full account of all the finds in printed media. Every report would be very selective, very interpretive, and perhaps somewhat biased. The best way to produce a full account of the finds with an attempt to reduce to the essential minimum the imposition of the excavator's opinion is by a computerized report on a CD-ROM. This is perhaps the only means for access to all the material that has been excavated. It should be noted, however, that in a CD-ROM report, the personal interpretations of the excavator cannot be totally eliminated. A CD-ROM report will be presented in the future. The purpose of this report is to sketch briefly selective finds

Fig. 20. Thousands of pottery shards, particularly of large jars, discovered
among ashes and remains of a fire in a Level 5 room

and to present them with traditional formality from the excavator's
point of view.

FIGURINE. A fragment of a female figurine (fig. 21) was discovered at Area A in locus 151, square 53 (basket 2538), which is the area
of the proposed temple. The figurine was cast in a mold. The fragment
measures 5 by 3.5 cm, and it is estimated that the entire item could
have been approximately 12 cm long. It shows a female dressed with
a chiton over a long draped cloth. The proximity of the discovery to
the temple implies that the find was associated with the temple.

INCENSE SHOVEL. On May 7, 1996, a bronze incense shovel (fig.
22)  was found in locus 152 (sq. G54) at the level of 167.47 m. The
shovel was assigned basket number 2660.

*Archaeological Context:* Locus 152, where the shovel was found,
is a refuse pit located at the western section of the square. The pit was
excavated during the second half of the first century CE into an east–
west wall (W506) of an unknown building. It contained pottery shards
accumulated over a relatively long period of time. There were Late
Hellenistic cooking pots of the type identified by us as "tall neck
straight,"[18] first-century casseroles with an everted rim, cooking pots

Fig. 21. Collection of figurines found in vicinity of temple. *Clockwise from top:* veiled figure with tiara; unidentified figure; female figure with chiton; and right-hand side of female figure found in Area C.

of the type identified by us as triple ridge.[19] This type is also known as 4B and 4C Kefar Hanania,[20] Capernaum type A5,[21] Khirbet Shema types 1.1 and 1.2.[22] The common dating for the type is mid-first to mid-second centuries CE. In addition, there was a so-called Herodian bow-spouted oil lamp that dates to the first century CE, and first- and second-century-CE bowls of the type known as Galilean Bowl.

On the chart below (table 1), the numbers represent the different types of pottery rim fragments. It is obvious that the rim fragments are an accidental discovery from the pit; any additional fragments that may be added to the pit information would change the picture only slightly. At present, there is no better method for analyzing and dating the data of the pit than to present its contents, discern the latest materials in it, and to record the main bulk of the discovery. The catalogue and quantities are listed here.

The earliest finds are the Hellenistic second- and first-century-BCE table fineware (also known as Eastern Terra Sigillata, or ETS). The most prevalent rim fragments at the pit were the Galilean bowls which were produced during the first and early second centuries CE, which

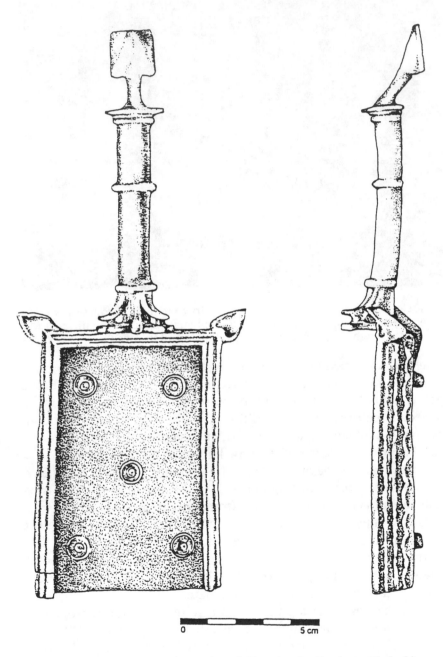

Fig. 22a. Bronze incense shovel (drawing by DreAnna Hadash)

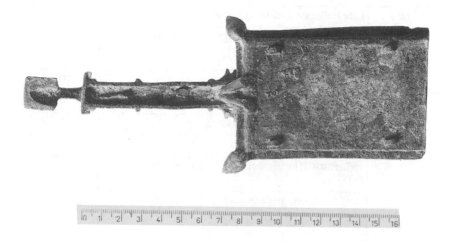

Fig 22b. Bronze shovel found at Bethsaida

*Rami Arav*

## Table 1. Rim Fragments from Area A

| Cat. Nos. | Rim Fragment Types | Amounts |
|---|---|---|
| 40–60 | Iron Age material | 2 |
| 62.2 | Hemispherical small deep bowl, first century CE | 1 |
| 75.3 | Late Hellenistic cooking pot with a tall neck | 7 |
| 75.2 | Late Hellenistic cooking pot with lid device | 3 |
| 75.4 | Early Roman cooking pot with short neck | 5 |
| 75.5 | Early Roman cooking pot with triple ridge | 10 |
| 76.4 | Early Roman Casserole with an everted rim | 7 |
| 96.2 | Bow-spouted Herodian oil lamp | 1 |
| 96 | Hellenistic oil lamp | 1 |
| 98 | Hellenistic Fineware, a/k/a Eastern Terra Sigillata (ETS) | 9 |
| 110.1 | Galilean Bowl, first and early centuries CE | 14 |
| 78.08 | Roman jar with everted rim | 1 |
| 102.05 | Roman-period cooking pot lid. | 2 |

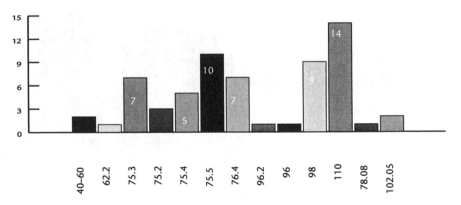

Table 2: Graphic representation of rim fragment types found in Locus I 52

are also the latest finds in the pit. First-century-CE cooking pots comprise the next largest group and it buttresses the dating of late first century CE for the main bulk of the deposit. Along with these rim fragments was found the incense shovel.

*Description of Incense Shovel:* X-ray photographs of the shovel show clearly that it was cast in one piece of bronze (fig. 23). That is a significant observation since it excludes the possibility that the shovel was made of various molds and brazed together in a manner that Yigal Yadin suggests as one possibility for the shovels he discovered in the "Cave of Letters."[23] (He did not favor such an interpretation however.) It would also exclude the possibility that some parts could have been employed in combination with other shovels or other objects. The similarity of the shovels therefore, is based on their style and not on their method of construction. The shovel consists of four parts: handle, pan, ear brackets, and feet. The measurements, given in cm, of the shovel (fig. 23) are:

length: 20.5
width: 6.7
height of the pan: 1.5
height of the handle: 3.1
length of handle: 11.2
length of pan: 9.1
length of column with the capital: 8.1.

*The handle* is shaped in the form of a column halved down its length. It rests on a base that bears a Corinthian capital. At two-thirds length of the column there is a ring decoration. Inside the column there are marks of the casting procedure, which can be also seen in the X-ray photo. A short leg (2.7 cm) with a square base extends from the handle and supports the shovel to balance it from tipping back. The Corinthian capital has five schematic freestanding leaves in two lines. The handle is attached to the pan by an abacus at the top of the capital and two short bars below the pan (fig. 24).

*The pan* is rectangular in shape (5 by 8.6 cm). It has two ear-bracket decorations at the corners that resemble horns of an altar. The pan has projecting sides that support rims. The rims of the pan are formed in a triple ridge design very similar in style to the design and size of the rims of the globular cooking pots that date from the end of the first century CE to the early second century CE.[24] The similarity of

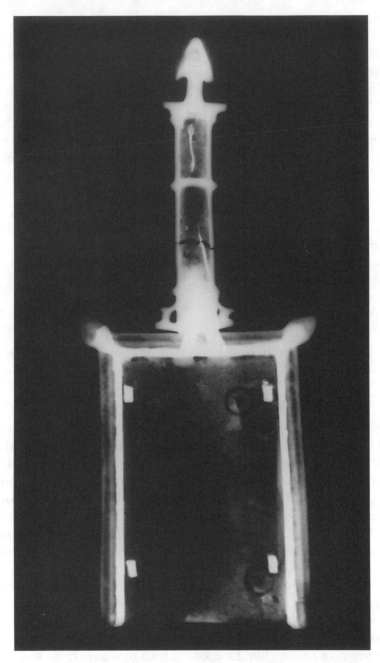

Fig.23. X-ray photograph of bronze incense shovel.

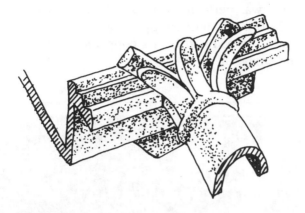

Fig. 24. Detail of capital attachment to the pan. Notice the cross section of the handle and pan. Drawing by Jim Olsen.

design indicates not only the actual date but also the origin of these shovels. If this observation is correct, then perhaps all the shovels with this design were manufactured in the Near East.[25] Five concentric circles decorate the bottom of the pan. The purpose of these circles is unknown, but it should be noted that they appear on the pan found in the Judean caves[26] and on others.

The *rims* of the shovel are slightly longer than the pan (this feature was found also on the shovels discovered by Yadin in the Cave of Letters[27]). Along the sides of the pan is a decorative wave design.

There are four short *legs* that support the pan at the bottom. They were made to correspond in level, the leg emerging from the handle to balance the shovel.

METALLURGICAL OBSERVATIONS
The shovel was examined by Mrs. Hana Ziv at the metallurgical laboratories of Raphael Institute in Israel on November 20, 1996.[28] Two spots were selected for the analysis, at the rear side of the handle and at one of the legs of the pan. The samples were polished and analyzed for chemical elements with a scanning electronic microscope (SEM). The results did not show conformity of materials and therefore the magnification of elements was carried out. The analyses were made on a small enlargement in order to obtain maximal surface analysis.

Three analyses were performed on the leg, four were performed on the handle, and one was performed on an 800x enlargement of a lead grain (photo 2497). Element mapping was produced and demonstrates clear grains of lead within the copper surface (see fig. 25, photographs of the analysis).

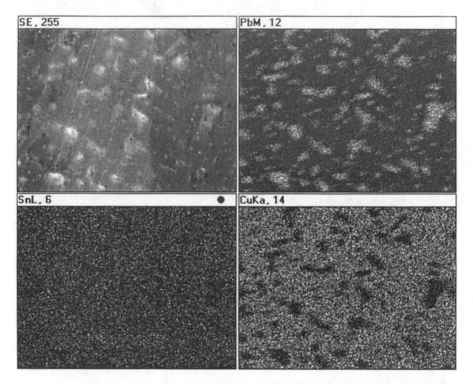

Fig. 25. Element mapping shows clear grains of lead within the copper surface
of the incense shovel

The analysis shows clearly that there is no uniformity of elements throughout the shovel, which indicates that the raw material from which the shovel was fabricated was not homogenized. This low-quality bronze was produced at a low melting temperature or by a poor stirring of the different elements. The main element in the shovel is copper, which comprises between 77.18 percent and 82.46 percent of the material. In the point analysis of the lead grain there was only 16.16 percent of copper. Tin was found in a relatively low percentage, 6.39 percent to 7.28 percent. Lead is an element that normally is not mixed with bronze; it was found in relatively large percentages, between 9.42 percent and 15.69 percent. The point analysis of the lead grain shows a large concentration, 81.69 percent, of lead. Since a good solid bronze would be comprised of 40 percent tin and 60 percent copper it is therefore obvious that the raw material of the shovel was of low-quality bronze. Even higher percentages of copper were found in the Cave of Letters shovels, and Yadin noted a similar occurrence of lead elsewhere.[29] Since tin is absent in the eastern basin of the Mediterranean and had to be imported either from Spain or from the Iranian plateau, it is suggested that the lead found in the shovel was not an accidental introduction but derives rather from lack of tin. It means, therefore, that the raw material was indigenous and perhaps the entire product is indigenous as well. It is noteworthy, however, that it was customary in antiquity to transport unused bronze vessels for the purpose of melting them down again and casting new vessels. This practice causes difficulties in identifying the place of manufacture for the vessels. It would be more helpful if more element-tracing analyses were carried out on a large quantity of bronzes from the eastern basin of the Mediterranean.

DISCUSSION

Forty-five shovels are known today from the ancient world. Most of these shovels were bought from dealers and their provenance is doubtful. However, most of the shovels seem to appear in the Eastern Roman Empire rather than in the west. The shovel of Bethsaida bears similarities to the shovels discovered by Yadin in the Cave of Letters. Shovel number 5-57.23 from the Cave of Letters is the closest parallel to the Bethsaida shovel. Both shovels have five concentric circles and a similar display, similar ear brackets, and similar handle. The Bethsaida Corinthian capital is similar to the shovel number 6. A further analysis dealing with the entire collection of shovels will be carried out and reported in a future article.

The discovery of the shovel in the vicinity of what is proposed to be a temple leads to the conclusion that the shovel played a role in rituals of the Roman imperial cult. It is noteworthy that this is not the only discovery that may be attributed to this cult at Bethsaida. In volume 1 we reported on the discovery of a female figurine wearing a veil. Her hairstyle, together with the veil, indicates that it was a rendering of Julia, the wife of Augustus and mother of Emperor Tiberius.[30] The discovery of the shovel and its role in the Roman imperial cult sheds light on the discovery of more shovels by Yadin. In 1961, he discovered a hoard of vessels in the Judean desert in a place known today as the Cave of Letters.[31] He speculated that the hoard, which contained five shovels together with an elaborately designed *patera* and sixteen other vessels, was taken as booty from a Roman military camp situated almost above the cave. But since soldiers rarely own such vessels, it is reasonable to suggest that the Cave of Letters collection may have been derived from a much more important location than a desert field camp. One suggestion is that the hoard was taken from a Roman imperial cult center, and perhaps most plausibly, from the temple of Jupiter that Hadrian had built, where offerings were made for his health, namely the Temple Mount at Jerusalem.

Interestingly, Josephus recounts a strikingly similar situation that occurred sixty years prior to this, in which the temple vessels at Jerusalem were taken by rebels. Among the vessels were some that were donated by Emperor Augustus and his wife and by other "foreigners." During the last days of the first Jewish revolt, John of Gishala melted down

> many of the temple offerings and many of the vessels required for public worship, bowls, and salvers [Gk. *pinakas*[32]] and tables, nor did he abstain from the vessels for pure wine sent by Augustus and his consort. For Roman sovereigns ever honored and added embellishment to the temple, whereas this Jew pulled down even the donations of foreigners, remarking to his companions that they should not scruple to employ divine things on the Divinity's behalf, and that those who fought for the temple should be supported by it.[33]

John of Gishala and the rebels, who were in need of financial resources, obviously wished also to cleanse the temple of impure vessels. Did not the Bar Kokhba rebels wish to do practically the same thing by removing the vessels from the temple of Capitoline gods in Jerusalem? Definitely, more research is required.

TABLE 3: SEQUANT RESULTS
Spectrum label: Bronze 13 X200
System resolution = 108 eV
Quantitative method: ZAF (2 iterations)
Analyzed all elements and normalized results

| Element | Spect. Type | Element % | Atomic % | Element % | Atomic % | Element % | Atomic % | Element % | Atomic % |
|---|---|---|---|---|---|---|---|---|---|
| Si K | ED | -0.04 | -0.09 | 0.08 | 0.2 | -0.02 | -0.05 | 0.06 | 0.16 |
| Cu K | ED | 81.28 | 91.87 | 78.44 | 90.35 | 83.32 | 92.51 | 77.18 | 89.40 |
| Sn K | ED | 6.67 | 4.03 | 7.09 | 4.37 | 7.28 | 4.33 | 6.79 | 4.21 |
| Pb L | ED | 12.09 | 4.19 | 14.40 | 5.09 | 9.42 | 3.21 | 15.69 | 5.57 |
| S L | ED | | | | | | | 0.29 | 0.66 |

| Element | Spect. Type | Inten. Corrn. | Std. Corrn. | Element. | Sigma | Atomic |
|---|---|---|---|---|---|---|
| Si K | ED | 1.102 | 1.00 | 0.01 | 0.09 | 0.04 |
| Fe K | ED | 1.129 | 1.00 | -0.15 | 0.18 | -0.40 |
| CE K | ED | 1.690 | 1.00 | 16.16 | 0.44 | 37.97 |
| Mo L | ED | 0.940 | 1.00 | 2.10 | 0.65 | 3.26 |
| Sn L | ED | 0.697 | 1.00 | 0.20 | 0.32 | 0.25 |
| Pb M | ED | 0.988 | 1.00 | 81.69 | 0.76 | 58.87 |
| Total | | | | 100.00 | | 100.00 |

| Element | Spect. Type | Element % | Atomic % | Element % | Atomic % | Element % | Atomic % |
|---|---|---|---|---|---|---|---|
| Si K | ED | -0.02 | -0.051 | 0.06 | 0.05 | -0.06 | -0.16 |
| Cu K | ED | 81.32 | 91.92 | 82.46 | 92.17 | 82.26 | 92.07 |
| Sn K | ED | 6.39 | 3.87 | 6.59 | 3.94 | 6.47 | 3.87 |
| Pb L | ED | 12.30 | 4.26 | 10.89 | 3.73 | 11.17 | 3.83 |
| S L | ED | | | | | 0.17 | 0.38 |

COLUMN PART. An interesting discovery was made under the proposed temple in square I52. There a basalt column part (fig. 26) was discovered thrown in a pit. The pit contained Hellenistic and Early Roman pottery shards. The column base (or capital), however, is non-classical in appearance and it is apparent that it derives originally from an unknown Iron Age structure. A similar column base found in secondary use was recorded previously in the dig and reported in volume 1.[34] The column measures 48 cm in diameter; the largest diameter is

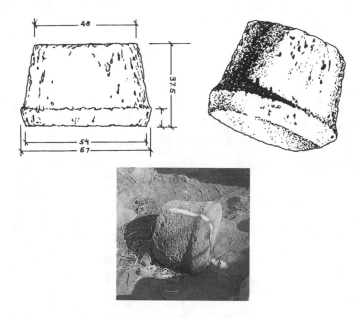

Fig. 26. Basalt capital. Drawings by Jim Olsen.

57 cm, and it is 37.5 cm in length. The column part is slightly conical, with a ticketing towards the largest diameter and then it turns in an opposite conical direction. A similar column part was recorded in the Bit Hilani at Zincirli.[35] Neither the purpose nor the original function of the column is clear yet.

## AREA B (MAPS 7 AND 8)

Area B is assigned to the north of grid line number 46, which is north of Area A. It comprises the Iron Age palace complex and the superimposed Hellenistic and Early Roman buildings. Some of the Iron Age and Hellenistic–Early Roman finds have been reported in volume 1.[36] This report will complete the description of the structures and elucidate their functions.

Since all walls were made of strong basalt stones and were in constant use for centuries, they were observed in more than one level. In the description of the levels in this area, we divert from the more traditional method of describing the levels from top to bottom; for convenience, the description will follow the levels from the lowest known to the latest.

LEVEL 6, THE BIT HILANI PALACE (FIG. 27, MAP 8)

Fig. 27. Bit Hilani palace seen in aerial photograph. The Bit Hilani is the thick-walled structure on the right side of the photograph.

The plaza that leads from the gatehouse to the palace was described in the past report.[37] The latest excavations made it clear that the wide entrance at the south side of the plaza (in square J51) leads, in fact, from the gate area to the palace plaza. The few stones standing in upright position in the plaza that were also reported and identified as stelae or *matzevot*,[38] are now better understood in the light of the discovery of a similar practice in Tel Dan.[39]

The immediate connection between the plaza and the palace (in square lines 45, 46) was thoroughly destroyed by a large Syrian trench. However, the difference (0.23 m) in elevations between the floor of the plaza (167.19 m) and the floor of the palace (167.42 m) leads us to estimate that the original lower level of the plaza[40] corresponds with the construction of the palace.

The palace faces to the south and is identified with the Bit Hilani type (see Arav [1995], 24). It is a rectangular, closed building that measures 15 by 27.7 m and is a meticulous construction of very massive, strong boulders, some of which are roughly dressed. The average width of the walls is 1.4 m and the average weight of the stones reaches several hundred kilograms. The maximal state of preservation of the walls was recorded near the entrance of room 7 and it reaches to 1.5 m. It is presumed that higher than this point the walls were made of baked bricks, many of which were discovered at the dig. The bricks had an average size of 60 by 30 by 13 cm, which means that they were laid in two or four rows alongside the width of the wall.

The palace consists of an entrance to a vestibule, a main hall, and eight rooms around it. There is no central courtyard nor any indications of another entrance to the edifice. These two features and others discussed below are essential elements of a palace of Bit Hilani type.[41] The entrance to the building is at the eastern half of the long southern wall (W318). Only one pillar base was discovered (W83), which measures 2.5 by 1.5 m. An Early Roman wall superimposes the area where the gap between the wall and the second pillar would normally be found, making it difficult to assess whether there was another pillar. Thus far two entrances to the vestibule have been discovered, a narrow one of 1.6 m, and a larger one.

The vestibule behind the entrance is a fairly large, broad room, which measures 14 by 2.7 m and leads directly to the main hall. The elevation of the vestibule may not be the elevation of the earliest level of the building: it was found to be at 167.41 m, which is about 0.6 m above the average level of the floors of all the rooms at the building. The vestibule contains the following loci: 211, 227, 228, 229, 400, 403, 431, 438, 439, 442, 581, 585, 606, 631, 694. The multiple-loci method used in the dig was an attempt to differentiate between every single change in the excavated terrain in order to receive, as much as possible, clear and clean loci from upper or lower layer deposits. It must be admitted that with this effort there was always mixed pottery from different periods involved in the finds due perhaps to the long duration of the building occupation and the excavations of the modern Syrian military, particularly in squares L42–43 and H42–43.

The main hall is situated on an east–west axis. Those who entered it had to turn left in order to reach its inner portion and perhaps its more important area. If we are to assume that there was a throne in this hall it would have been here. The main hall measures 19.7 by 4.5 m and is flanked by eight rooms, any of which the person who received guests could appear from or retreat to. There are no indications to the way this room was lit; if light did not penetrate from a light well in the ceiling, then the room probably was quite dark. The western end of W191 was removed and excavated to determine the elevation and construction of the floor. The floor, found at elevations of 168 m, was built with crushed and compacted limestone. This layer of limestone was about 50 cm in several places and was constructed on a layer of compact dirt and in a few places on bedrock. The main hall consists of the following loci: 411, 416, 419, 421, 422, 423, 427, 428, 430, 431, 432, 433, 437, 580, 583, 584, 586, 605, 607, 608, 616, 617, 621, 623, 628, 635, 638. Among the most important finds is the Egyptian figurine of the dwarf god Pataekos.[42] The figurine was found in locus 638, at the eastern end of the hall. Another important discovery was an Iron Age IIB jar handle bearing three Hebrew letters MKY [מכי], which reads perhaps *Mikhyahu,* which is another form of Michael (see discussion on p. 91 below). The rooms around the main hall are indicated by numbers. As a rule, all rooms have their entrances near the corners.

Room 1 is one of the better preserved rooms. It measures 5 by 2.7 m, and like the rest of the building, it was built with amazingly heavy boulders. The room is connected directly to the main hall. The meager remains of a floor was made of crushed, packed limestone. It was discovered at an elevation of 167.9 m and this is perhaps the level of the earliest floor. The following loci were attributed to this room: 421, 423, 425, 571, 579, 693, 697. The finds from this room were thoroughly mixed. An intact Hellenistic ray-beam motif oil lamp was found in a lower level together with other Iron Age II and Hellenistic pottery shards.

Room 2 measures 4.3 by 2.7 m. Its southern wall, W318, was altered in antiquity. The building suffered severe destruction, particularly the southwestern corner, by a Syrian military trench. It is an interior room that opens to room 3 only. A few baked red clay bricks were found next to W391, which may indicate a bench next to the wall. The floor of this room was found at 167.9 m. The following loci were attributed to this room: 587, 590, 591, 614, 648.

Room 3 suffered a destiny similar to that of room 2. It measures 4.3 by 2.9 m. There were two openings to this room, one at the east to the back of the main hall and another at the south to room 2. As a rule, all openings were made at the end of the walls and not in the middle (which would seem to have made more sense for the opening between rooms 2 and 3). The northern wall of this room, W87, serves also as the symmetry axis of the entire palace. It is important to note that this axis is parallel to the facade of the palace and is perpendicular to the entry axis. The floor of the room was found at 168.02 m. The following loci form this room: 421, 423, 424, 570, 587.

Rooms 4 and 5 correspond to rooms 3 and 4, but vary in their size. They are situated at the northeastern corner of the building. Room 4 measures 4.3 by 2.3 m. The room was connected to the main hall by an opening at the southeast corner of the room. The floor level was found at 168.02 m. The following loci form this room: 411, 416, 420. Room 5 is situated at the corner of the building. The very corner of the building was destroyed almost to the first course. The room measures 4.3 by 2.7 m and was entered from room 4 by an entrance at the west section of W84. The floor of the building was found at 168.06 m. As with the other rooms, it contained a mixture of finds dating also from the Hellenistic period together with two Hellenistic coins, one from Tyre that was found at an elevation of 167.64 m, and the other a Seleucid coin found at an elevation of 167.81 m. Two Iron Age II kohl sticks were discovered also in this room. Room 5 contained the following loci: 401, 405, 408, 411, 414.

Room 6 is situated along the northern wall of the building. It measures 5 by 2.7 m. It equals and is parallel to room 1 in the axis of symmetry of the building. The floor of this building is at 168.04 m. The entrance faces the main hall and is the only one that was left closed at our dig; we have removed obstructions from all the other entrances. The room contains loci 411 and 417. It is important to note that among the finds was the ninth century bulla (reported in vol. 1[43]), discovered in a locus slightly north of the building's northern wall (W67). It is presumed that the bulla came from a second floor of the building.

Room 7 was the best preserved room in terms of finds. It is similar in size to rooms 1 and 6, and measures 5 by 2.7 m. As with room 6, entrance to the room was made at the western end of the southern wall W84. The entrance to the room was blocked, but the obstruction was removed during the dig. Room 7 was the first room that was unearthed and yielded more than twenty complete vessels and a large number of basalt tools, such as shallow, flat, and deep bowls. The pottery content of the room was published in volume 1 under finds of locus 365. Neither of the other rooms of the palace contains intact pottery vessels. The floor excavated thus far is at 167.47 m.

| Room | Length (m) | Width (m) | Floor Level (m) | Entrance Width (m) | Special Find |
|------|-----------|-----------|-----------------|--------------------|--------------|
| Vestibule | 14.0 | 2.7 | 167.41 m | 4.00(?) | |
| Main hall | 19.7 | 4.5 | 168.00 | | Pataekos; MKY handle |
| Room 1 | 5.0 | 2.7 | 167.9 | 1.35 | |
| Room 2 | 4.3 | 2.7 | 167.9 | 0.75 | |
| Room 3 | 4.3 | 2.9 | 168.02 | 1.00 | |
| Room 4 | 4.3 | 2.3 | 168.02 | 1.00 | |
| Room 5 | 4.3 | 2.7 | 168.06 | 0.75 | |
| Room 6 | 5.0 | 2.7 | 168.04 | 1.35 | bulla in north of room |
| Room 7 | 5.0 | 2.7 | 167.47 (?) | 1.35 | intact vessels |
| Room 8 | 6.5 | 2.7 | 167.65 | 3.5 | |

Table 4: Rooms of Bit Hilani Palace

Room 8 is situated at the northeast corner of the building. It is the largest among the rooms that surround the main hall, measuring 6.5 by 2.7 m. Unlike the other rooms in the building, this room has a large entrance that measures 3.5 m and is at the western end of W310. The floor of the room was established right on top of bedrock. The elevation of this room is 167.67 m, which is 0.3 m above the rest of the building. At the eastern end of the room there is an opening to a large cave that penetrates below the east wall of the building at W305; this cave has not yet been explored. The room contains the following loci: 620, 626, 634, 639, 641, 658, 662, 665, 666, 667.

*Rami Arav*

POTTERY FINDS FROM THE BIT HILANI

As mentioned above, only one room in the Bit Hilani was found to contain intact vessels (see plates I and II). The pottery finds from the rest of the building were quite disappointing. Not only was there no intact pottery, but it was also impossible to reconstruct a single pot. A great number of shards was found, particularly in the main hall, but attempts to reconstruct did not yield a single vessel. Thousands of vessel rims were found; only three hundred rim fragments will be presented in this report. This presentation will cover the rooms of the palace only. A more specific report on selected pottery shards from loci associated with the construction of the building is presented elsewhere in this volume.[44]

VESTIBULE. This room contained a large number of late material and one shard of a red slip and burnished, step-footed bowl (fig. 28), similar to the bowls found in room 1 (pls V.1, 55, 11–23) and dates from Iron Age IIB, and an Iron Age I cooking pot ( pl. I.1). A few Late Hellenistic and Early Roman cooking pots were also discovered in this room (pl. I.16, 17).

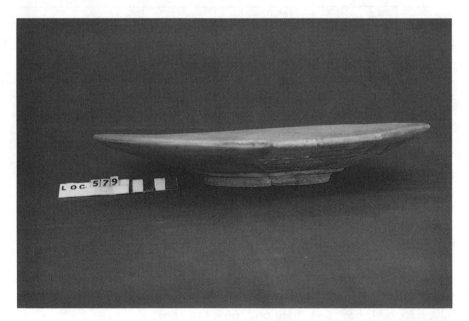

Fig. 28. Red slip and burnished step-footed bowl, known as "Samarian Ware"

Main Hall. The few drawings presented in plate II do not represent the bulk of the material that was discovered in this room for the main hall contained the largest amount of pottery shards in the entire building. Our efforts to restore these shards did not yield a single restored pot. However, we have discovered an intact spouted juglet (pl. II.1). This juglet may be dated from Iron Age IIB. The bowls represented in the plate date from this period too.

Room 1: A fairly large number of cooking pots were discovered in the room. They are distinguished by an emphasized ridge below the rim and date from Iron Age I or early Iron Age IIA (pl. IV.1–11). Other vessels that date to Iron Age IIB are the shallow light red slip-and-burnished bowls of step-footed type (pl. V.1, 4, 11, 12, 13). Vessels that date from Iron Age IIB and IIC comprise the large bulk of the room, as seen by the craters (pl. V.16–19). Large quantities of jar fragments were also discovered in the room (pl. III.2–10). Hellenistic shards (pl. XIII.8–11) indicate the long occupancy of this room. Noteworthy among these discoveries is a bowl with palmette decorations as well as a single Early Bronze Age II shard of a platter (pl. V.14).

Room 2. This room presents a small variety of Iron Age IIA cooking pots (pl. VI.10–20), large craters (pl. VII.1–5), Iron Age IIB jars (pl. VII.6–13), and an Iron Age IIb strainer (pl. VII.16). A large variety of Hellenistic pottery testify a long use of this room from the fourth-century-BCE craters (pl. VI.1–2) to Early Roman casseroles (pl. VI.8–9), and a Galilean bowl (PL. VI.2).

Room 4. This room presented one shard of an Iron Age IIA cooking pot (pl. IX.7). The main bulk of the finds were Iron Age IIB large, deep bowls (pls. VIII.1–16, IX.2), which may imply the purpose of the room. This room contains a few Hellenistic bowls (pl. IX.5–6) and one shard of Roman Galilean bowl (pl. IX.3).

Room 5. This room contained Iron Age IIA cooking pots (pl. XII.8–10). Iron Age II cooking pots (XII.15, 16), and a large number of Iron Age II jars (pls. XIII.26; XIV.1–7), which may indicate that this was a jar storage room. The Hellenistic occupation of this room left cooking pots (XII.2–5, 18) and juglets (XIV.9, 10).

Room 6. This room features an Iron Age II cooking pot (pl. XV.4–10), a few Iron Age II jars (pl. XIV.16, 17), and a few bowls (pl. XIV.20–23) and some craters (pl. XV.13–17). Only a few shards of later material were found here (pl. XIV.14, 17, 18).

ROOM 8. This Room contained Iron Age IIA cooking pots (pl. XVI.1–6), an Iron Age IIB cooking pot (pl. XVI.8), bowls (pl. XVII.4–10), jars (pl. XVII.12–17), a few basalt stone objects such as a bowl (pl. XVII.11), a grinding stone (pl. XVI.11), two clay pierced whorls (pl. XVI.12, 13), and a stone weight used perhaps for fishing (pl. XVI.10).

DISCUSSION

North Syrian Bit Hilani similar to those discovered in Tel Halaf, Zingirli IV–G, Tel Tayinat IV, Sakzeguzü, and Tel Hassan, share the following characteristics:

1. They were built near the city walls in the vicinity of the city gate.

2. They are broad, large edifices, which means that their facade is in their long wall.

3. They lack an interior courtyard or patio.

4. They consist of an elaborate facade with one or more pillars or columns, a vestibule, a main hall, and adjacent rooms.

5. The axis of the vestibule and the main hall is parallel to the facade of the building.

The chart on the next page summarizes the dimensions and finds in these palaces for comparison with Bethsaida.[45]

Collection of pottery vessels from the Bit Hilani at Bethsaida

| Site | Extension of Building | Extension of Main Hall | Special Attributes |
|------|----------------------|------------------------|--------------------|
| Bethsaida | 27.7 x 15. 0 m | 19.7 x 4.5 m | one pillar (?), set close to city wall, piazza, opposite public building (Hilani?) |
| Tell Halaf | 52.0 x 30.0 m | 37.0 x 8.2 m | three pillars, secured by a gate inside the fortified city, raised piazza, opposite public building |
| Zincirli J | 31.0 x 43.0 m | 25.5 x 8.5 m | one column, piazza, related to a second Hilani (K) |
| Zincirli K | 28.0 x 20.0 m | 23.0 x 8.0 m | three columns, stairwell, piazza, related to a second Hilani (J) |
| Zincirli I | 52.0 x 34.0 m | 22.0 x 8.0 m | no traces of pillars/columns |
| Zincirli II | 40.0 x 32.0 m | 25.0 x 9.5 m | no traces of pillars/columns, stairwell |
| Zincirli III | 32.5 x 29.0 m | 20.0 x 8.5 m | two columns, stairwell, built into the city wall, piazza, related to a second Hilani (IV) |
| Zincirli G (west) | 24.0 x 24.0 m | 17.5 x 6.0 m | one column, set close to city wall, courtyard, related to second Hilani (G-east) Zincirli G |
| Zincirli G (east) | 21.0 x 12.5 m | 11.5 x 4.5 m | one column, set close to city wall, courtyard, related to second Hilani (G-west) |
| Tell Tayinat I | 58.5 x 29.0 m | 25.0 x 7.0 m | three columns, stairwell, piazza, related to opposite Hilani (I) |
| Tell Tayinat IV | 41.0 x 39.0 m | 34.0 x 8.5 m | two columns, stairwell, piazza, related to opposite Hilani (I) |
| Sakzegyzü | 25.0 x 25.0 m | 14.0 x 6.0 m | one pillar, stairwell, integrated into city wall, piazza |
| Tell Hassan | 31.5 x 21.0 m | 18.5 x 6.0 m | no traces of pillars/columns (awaits further excavation |

Table 5: Comparison of Bethsaida with Selected Sites

PLATE I. VESTIBULE, AREA B: POTTERY FINDS

| Plate No. | Locus | Classification and Clay Color | Clay Composition and Decoration | Firing |
|---|---|---|---|---|
| I.1 | 403 | IA II cooking pot. Surface: reddish-brown | — | High |
| I.2 | 403 | IA IIB crater. Surface: red | — | Med. |
| I.3 | 403 | IA IIB crater. Surface: reddish-brown | — | Med. |
| I.4 | 400 | IA IIB deep bowl. Surface: reddish-brown | — | Med. |
| I.5 | 400 | IA IIB bowl. Surface: reddish-brown | — | Med. |
| I.6 | 403 | IA IIB bowl. Surface: reddish-brown | — | Med. |
| I.7 | 403 | IA IIB jug. Surface: medium brown | — | Med.-Low |
| I.8 | 400 | IA IIB crater. Surface: reddish-brown | — | Med. |
| I.9 | 400 | IA IIB sloped bowl. Surface: reddish-brown | — | High |
| I.10 | 403 | IA IIB jar. Surface: brown | — | Med. |
| I.11 | 403 | IA IIB jar. Surface: medium brown | — | Med. |
| I.12 | 400 | IA IIB jar. Surface: medium brown | — | Med. |
| I.13 | 403 | IA IIB crater. Surface: reddish-brown | — | Med. |
| I.14 | 403 | IA IIB cooking pot. Surface: reddish-brown | — | High |
| I.15 | 400 | IA IIB deep bowl. Surface: reddish-brown | — | Med. |
| I.16 | 403 | Roman cooking pot. Surface: reddish-gray | — | High |
| I.17 | 400 | Roman cooking pot with triple-groove rim. Surface: red-gray | — | High |
| I.18 | 400 | Roman juglet. Surface: reddish-brown | — | Med.-High |

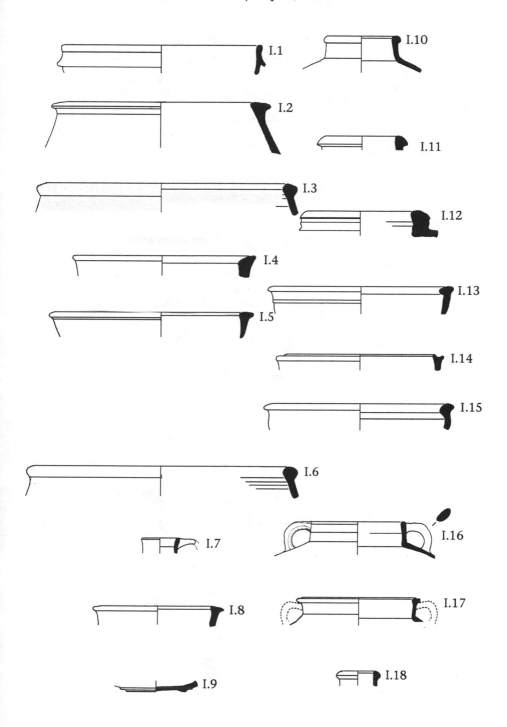

PLATE II. MAIN HALL, AREA B: POTTERY FINDS

| Plate No. | Locus | Classification and Clay Color | Clay Composition and Decoration | Firing |
|---|---|---|---|---|
| II.1 | 427 | IA II spouted juglet. Surface: brownish-red | — | Med.-High |
| II.2 | 428 | IA II bowl. Surface: reddish-brown | — | Med. |
| II.3 | 428 | IA II bowl. Surface: reddish-brown | — | Med. |
| II.4 | 428 | IA II crater. Surface: reddish-brown | — | Med. |
| II.5 | 427 | IA II jar. Surface: brown | — | Med.-High |

PLATE III. (1 : 5)

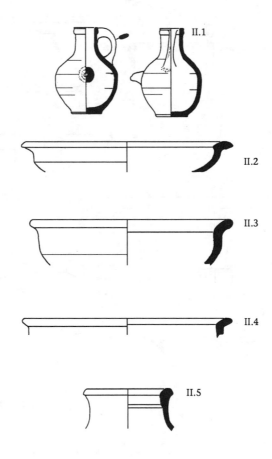

PLATE III. ROOM 1, AREA B: JUGS, JARS, STRAINERS

| Plate No. | Locus | Classification and Clay Color | Clay Composition and Decoration | Firing |
|---|---|---|---|---|
| III.1 | 579 | IA IIB trifold jug. Core & surface: pink | Grits: medium-dark, reddish brown, large, gray. Grog: medium-large | Med. |
| III.2 | 579 | Hellenistic jar or jug. Core & surface: very pale brown | Grits: large, white; medium brown. Org. grit: large. Grog: large | Low |
| III.3 | 579 | Hellenistic jar. Core & surface: light yellowish brown | Grits: large, dark; brown/white. Org. grits: medium Grog: medium | Med. |
| III.4 | 579 | Hellenistic jar. Core: very pale brown. Surface: pink | Grits & Org. grits: small | Med.-high |
| III.5 | 571 | Hellenistic jar. Core & surface: very pale brown | Grits: small | Med. |
| III.6 | 693 | Hellenistic jar. Core: brown. Outer band & surface: light brown | Grits: medium | — |
| III.7 | 579 | Hellenistic jar. Core & surface: pink | Grog: range brown/cream. | Low |
| III.8 | 579 | Hellenistic jar. Core: very pale yellow. Surface: reddish yellow | Org. grits: small | Low |
| III.9 | 579 | Hellenistic or IA IIB jar. Core: pink. Surface: very pale brown | Grits: large, dark & light brown/white. Org. grits & grog: large | Med. |
| III.10 | 571 | IA IIB jar. Core & surface: reddish yellow | Grits: medium-dark | Med. |
| III.11 | 579 | IA IIB strainer. Core & surface: pink | Grits: Large, white/pink/brown. Org. grits & Grog: large | Low |
| III.12 | 693 | Hellenistic jar. Surface: pink | Grits: small/none Org. grits: small | — |
| III.13 | 579 | Roman jar/jug; horiz. rim; 3 ridges. Core & surface: yellowish red | Grits: small | High |

PLATE III. (1 : 5)

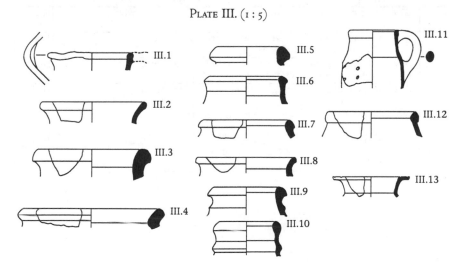

PLATE IV. ROOM 1, AREA B: COOKING POTS

| Plate No. | Locus | Classification and Clay Color | Clay Composition and Decoration | Firing |
|---|---|---|---|---|
| IV.1 | 579 | IA IIB cooking pot. Core: brown. Outer bands: red. Surface: red | Org. grits: medium, white. Grog: medium, pearly. Clay composition appears to be crushed shell | Med. |
| IV.2 | 579 | IA IIB cooking pot. Core: dark gray. Outer bands: reddish brown. Surface: reddish brown | Grits: small to medium | High |
| IV.3 | 571 | IA IIB cooking pot. Core: dark gray. Surface: dark reddish gray | Grits: small, white. Org. grits: medium | High |
| IV.4 | 697 | IA II cooking pot. Core: very dark gray. Surface: reddish brown | Grits: small, white. Org. grits: medium | High |
| IV.5 | 579 | IA II cooking pot. Core & surface: reddish yellow | Grits: large. Org. grits: large. Grog: large. | Med. |
| IV.6 | 579 | IA IIC cooking pot. Core: dark gray. Outer bands: brown. Surface: pale brown | Grits: small. Org. grits: small. | Med. |
| IV.7 | 579 | IA IIC cooking pot. Core: light reddish brown. Outer bands: reddish yellow. Surface: light reddish brown | Grits: medium gray. Org. grits: large (1mm) | Med. |
| IV.8 | 579 | IA IIC cooking pot. Surface: reddish yellow | Grits: medium-dark brown. | Med. |
| IV.9 | 579 | IA IIC cooking pot. Core: very dark gray. Outer bands: Surface: dark brown | Grits: medium-large. Org. grits: large | Med. |
| IV.10 | 579 | IA IIC cooking pot. Core: light gray. Outer bands: light reddish brown. Surface: light reddish brown | Grits: large-medium brown. Org. grits: large. Grog: large | Med. |
| IV.11 | 693 | IA IIC cooking pot. Core: dark gray. Surface: dark gray | Grits: large | High |
| IV.12 | 579 | IA IIB cooking pot. Core & surface: reddish yellow | Grits, org. grits, grog: large | — |
| IV.13 | 571 | IA IIA cooking pot. Core: white. Surface: very pale brown | Org. grits: small. Grog: small, gray | Med. |
| IV.14 | 579 | Persian period cooking pot. Core & surface: red | Grits: small, white | High |
| IV.15 | 579 | Hellenistic globular cooking pot, tall neck. Core & surface: yellowish red | Grits: none | High |
| IV.16 | 579 | Hellenistic globular cooking pot. Core: weak red. Outer bands: red. Surface: red | Grits: small | High |
| IV.17 | 571 | IA II cooking pot. Core: gray. Surface: yellowish red | Grits: small | High |
| IV.18 | 693 | Early Roman cooking pot, 3 ridges on rim. Core & surface: red | Grits: none | High |
| IV.19 | 579 | Hellenistic cooking pot, globular. Core: dark gray. Outer bands & surface: dark reddish brown | Grog: small, light gray | High |

PLATE IV. (1 :5), ROOM 1, AREA B: COOKING POTS

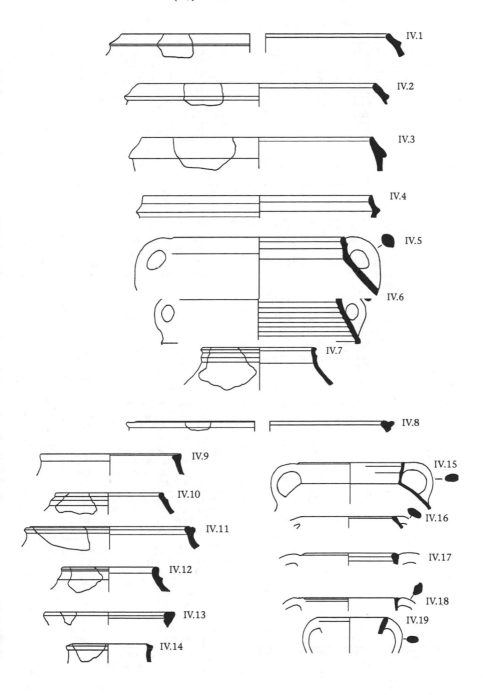

PLATE V. ROOM 1, AREA B: BOWLS, PLATTER, CRATERS

| Plate No. | Locus | Classification and Clay Color | Clay Composition and Decoration | Firing |
|---|---|---|---|---|
| V.1 | 425 | IA IIA deep bowl. Core & surface: very pale brown | Grits: small. Decoration: reddish yellow slip and burnished | High |
| V.2 | 693 | IA IIB bowl. Core: gray. Outer bands: very pale brown. Surface: light reddish brown | Grits: large. Org. grits: large | Med. |
| V.3 | 693 | IA IIB l bowl, large. Core: light gray. Surface: pink mottled; white/reddish brown | Grits, Org. grits, and Grog: large | — |
| V.4 | 579 | IA IIA bowl. Core & surface: reddish yellow | Grits: medium, gray. Org. grits: medium. Decoration: reddish yellow slip and burnished | High |
| V.5 | 693 | Hellenistic bowl, incurved rim. Core & surface: pink | Grits: small/none | Low |
| V.6 | 693 | Hellenistic bowl, incurved rim. Core & surface: reddish yellow | Decoration: very, very thin, dark red slip inside, which is rubbing off | Low |
| V.7 | 579 | Hellenistic bowl, incurved rim. Core & surface: reddish yellow | Grog: small. Decoration: thin, dark reddish brown, semi-glossy slip inside | Med. |
| V.8 | 693 | Hellenistic bowl, incurved rim. Core & surface: pink | No grits or grog. Decoration: (inside) thin, well-preserved, glossy slip; (outside) faint, poorly preserved black stripes(?) | Med. |
| V.9 | 573 | Hellenistic bowl, incurved rim. Core: light reddish brown. Surface: peeled black slip over light reddish brown | Decoration: (inside & outside) thin, peeling, black slip | Med. |
| V.10 | 579 | Hellenistic bowl, incurved rim. Core & surface: pink | No grits or grog. Decoration: (inside) thin, well-preserved reddish brown slip; (outside) weak red slip | Med. |
| V.11 | 579 | IA II bowl. Core & surface: reddish yellow | Grits: medium gray. Grog: medium. Decoration: reddish yellow slip, burnished outside and inside | High |
| V.12 | 579 | IA II bowl. Core & surface: reddish yellow | Grits: medium gray. Grog: medium. Decoration: reddish yellow slip, burnished outside and inside | High |
| V.13 | 579 | IA II bowl. Core & surface: reddish yellow | Grits: medium gray. Grog: medium. Decoration: reddish yellow slip, burnished outside and inside | High |
| V.14 | 579 | Early Bronze platter. Surface: reddish yellow | Grits: medium | Low |
| V.15 | 579 | Roman crater. Core & surface: light red | Grits: small-medium Grog: medium. Decoration: (inside) very thin, red slip; stamped palmette or leaf design; (outside) slip to emphasize leaf design | Med. |
| V.16 | 579 | IA IIB crater. Core: gray. Outer bands: light yellowish brown. Surface: brown | Grits, Org. Grits, Grog: small-medium | High |
| V.17 | 697 | IA II B crater. Core: yellow. Surface very pale brown | Org. grits: medium Other: indication of large handle | Med. |
| V.18 | 579 | IA IIB crater. Core and outer bands: reddish brown. Surface: medium-dark | | Med.-High. |
| V.19 | 693 | IA IIB crater. Core & surface: light gray | Grits, Org. Grits, Grog: large | Med. |

PLATE V. (1:5) ROOM 1, AREA B: BOWLS, PLATTER, CRATERS

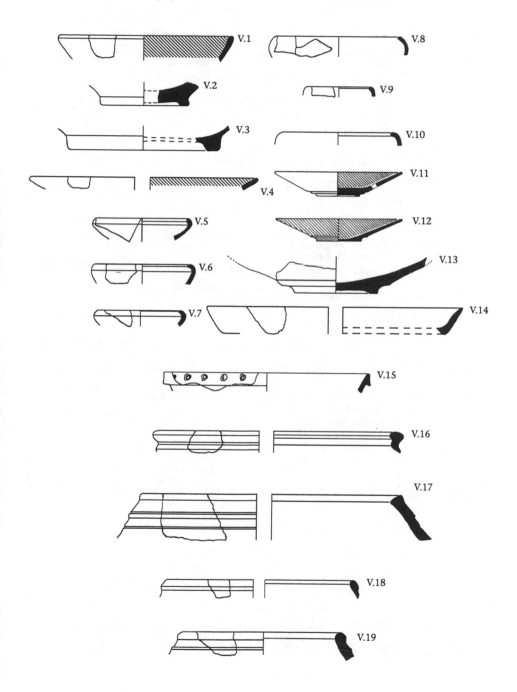

PLATE VI. ROOM 2, AREA B: BOTTLE, BOWLS, CASSEROLES, AND COOKING POTS

| Plate No. | Locus | Classification and Clay Color | Clay Composition and Decoration | Firing |
|---|---|---|---|---|
| VI.1 | 588 | Hellenistic bottle. Core & surface: pale yellow | Grits small. Org. grits: medium | High |
| VI.2 | 588 | Early Roman Galilean bowl. Core: weak red. Surface: weak red | Grits: small | High |
| VI.3 | 588 | Late Hellenistic incurved bowl. Core: very pale brown; very fine clay body. Surface: slip covered | No grits or grog. Decoration: (inside) nonglossy, red slip; (outside) mottled red-dark reddish brown, thin, nonglossy, well-preserved | Med. |
| VI.4 | 588 | Late Hellenistic incurved bowl. Core: gray. Surface: gray | Grits: small. Org. grits: small. Grog: small. | Med. |
| VI.5 | 587 | Hellenistic incurved bowl. Core & surface: pink | Org. grits: small. Grog: medium. Inside slip: worn, thin, red. Outside slip: nearly worn away on rim; red/dark red | Med. |
| VI.6 | 588 | Hellenistic bowl. Core: light red. Outer bands: brown. Surface light brown | Grits: medium, light & dark brown | Med |
| VI.7 | 588 | IA II bowl. Core: light red. Outer bands: brown. Surface: light brown | Grits medium, light-dark brown | Med. |
| VI.8i | 588 | Hellenistic casserole with horiz. rim. Surface red | Grits: small | High |
| VI.9 | 588 | Early Roman casserole, everted rim. Core and surface: red | Grits: small (hard to determine) | High |
| VI.10 | 588 | Early Roman cooking pot. Core: red. Surface: reddish brown | Grits: small (hard to determine) | High |
| VI.11 | 588 | Early Roman cooking pot, 3 ridges on rim. Core & surface: red | Grits: small, dark gray; no org. grits or grog | High |
| VI.12 | 588 | Hellenistic globular cooking pot. Core & surface: red | Org. grits: small | High |
| VI. 13 | 588 | Hellenistic globular cooking pot. Surface: dark reddish gray | Grits: small, dark gray | High |
| VI.14 | 590 | IA IIA cooking pot | Grits, org. grits, grog: none. Slip (inside) thin, red; (outside) nearly absent, poorly preserved black | — |
| VI.15 | 588 | IA IIA cooking pot. Core: dark reddish gray. Outer bands: yellowish red. Surface: reddish yellow | Grits: medium, white. Grog: medium | — |
| VI.16 | 588 | IA IIA cooking pot. Core & surface: light reddish brown | Grits: medium, white & gray | Med |
| VI.17 | 588 | IA IIA cooking pot. Core: gray. Surface: light reddish brown | Grits: small. Org. grits: small-medium, white | Med. |
| VI.18 | 588 | Cooking pot. Core: very dark gray. Surface: reddish brown | Grits: medium Org. grits: many, medium | High |
| VI.19 | 587 | IA IIB cooking pot. Core: reddish brown. Outer bands & surface: red | Grits: small | High |
| VI.20 | 588 | Hellenistic globular cooking pot. Core: gray. Outer bands & surface: reddish yellow | Grits: small, dark gray. Org. grits: large | Med. |

PLATE VI. (1 : 5) ROOM 2, AREA B: BOTTLE, BOWLS, CASSEROLES, AND COOKING POTS

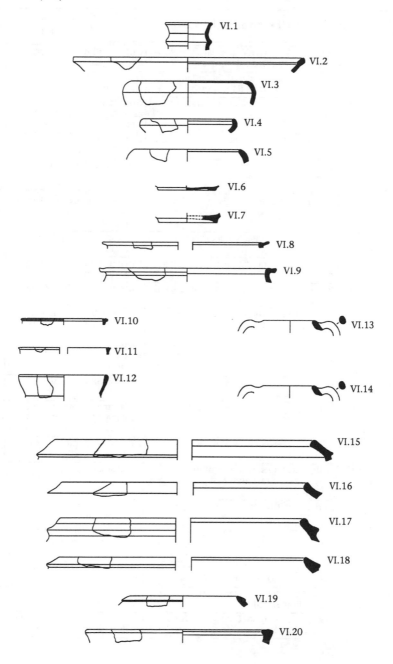

PLATE VII. ROOM 2, AREA B: CRATERS, JARS, AND OTHER ITEMS

| Plate No. | Locus | Classification and Clay Color | Clay Composition and Decoration | Firing |
|---|---|---|---|---|
| VII.1 | 587 | IA crater. Core: gray. Outer bands: yellowish red. Surface: reddish brown | Grits: small-medium. Org. grits: few, large | High |
| VII.2 | 587 | IA crater. Core: dark gray. Outer bands: light brown. Surface: light brown. | Grits: medium-large, dark gray. Grog: med | High |
| VII.3 | 588 | IA II crater. Core: dark gray. Surface: reddish brown | Grits: large, dark brown & pink. Org. grits: large. Grog: large | High |
| VII.4 | 587 | IA II crater. Core & surface: very pale brown | Grits: medium Org. grits: large. Grog: large | |
| VII.5 | 587 | IA II crater. Core: gray. Outer bands: light brown. Surface: brown | Grits: small. Org. grits: medium Grog: medium-large | Med. |
| VII.6 | 588 | Hellenistic jar. Core & surface: very pale brown (surface slipped) | No grits or grog. Slip (inside): thin, peeling, red, semiglossy; (outside) worn, thin, black-dark gray | Med. |
| VII.7 | 587 | IA II jar. Core: white. Surface: very pale brown. | Grits: small. Org. grits: medium | Med. |
| VII.8 | 588 | IA II jar. Core: gray. Surface: light brown | Grits: medium, white. Org. grits: medium | Med. |
| VII.9 | 588 | IA II jar. Core: very dark gray. Outer bands & Surface: reddish brown | Grits: medium Grog: large | High |
| VII.10 | 587 | IA II jar. Core: very pale brown. Surface: covered with red slip | Grits: small, gray and white. Decoration: (inside): glossy, thin, well-preserved, red slip; (outside): well-preserved, glossy, think red slip. Med. burnish | High |
| VII.11 | 588 | IA II jar. Core: dark gray. Outer bands & surface: light brown | Grits: small-medium | |
| VII.12 | 588 | IA II jar. Core: gray. Outer bands & surface: yellowish red | Grits: small, white; medium, dark gray; large, very hard. Faint thumbprint inside curve | High |
| VII.13 | 588 | IA II jar. Core: reddish yellow. Surface: very pale brown | No grits, org. grits, or grog | Med. |
| VII.14 | 587 | Hellenistic juglet, wheel trimmed foot. Core: pink. Outer bands & surface: very pale brown | Grits: small | Med. |
| VII.15 | 588 | IA II goblet. Core & surface: light brown | Grits: medium, dark gray. Org. grits: medium | Med. |
| VII.16 | 590 | IA II strainer. Core & surface: reddish yellow | Grits: small, gray; medium, dark brown. Org. grits & grog: small | Med. |
| VII.17 | 588 | Hellenistic mortaria. Core: pink. Outer bands & surface: yellowish red | Grits: small, light brown tiny, white | High |
| VII.18 | 587 | Hellenistic mortaria. Core: dark gray. Surface: yellowish red | Grits: small-medium, dark gray | Med. |
| VII.19 | 587 | Hellenistic mortaria. Core: gray. Outer bands: pink. Surface: reddish brown | Grits, org. grits & grog: large | High |

PLATE VII. (1 : 5) ROOM 2, AREA B: CRATERS, JARS, AND OTHER ITEMS

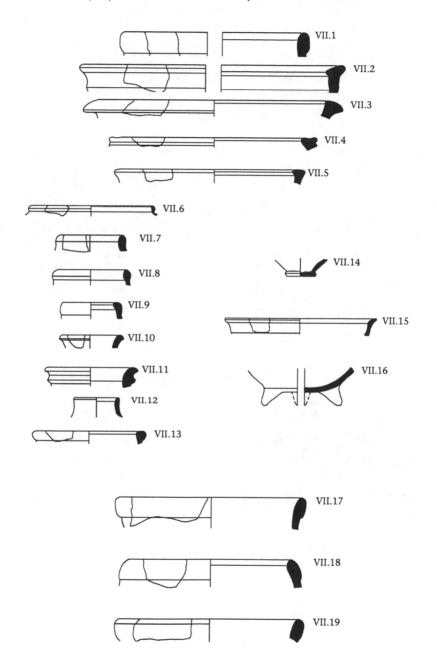

PLATE VIII. ROOM 4, AREA B: BOWLS

| Plate No. | Locus | Classification and Clay Color | Clay Composition and Decoration | Firing |
|---|---|---|---|---|
| VIII.1 | 420 | IA II large deep bowl. Core and surface: yellowish brown | Grits: small white & medium black. Org. grits: large | Med |
| VIII.2 | 416 | IA II large deep bowl. Core: dark gray. Outer bands reddish brown. Surface: reddish brown | Girts: small medium, dark gray. Org. grits: small | High |
| VIII.3 | 420 | IA II large deep bowl. Core: dark gray. Surface: light brown | Grits: small light brown, medium gray. Grog: small light brown, large | High |
| VIII.4 | 416 | IA II large deep bowl. Core: dark gray. Outer bands: brown. Surface: brown | Grits: medium gray. Org. grits: large. Grog: medium | Low |
| VIII.5 | 416 | IA II large deep bowl. Core: dark gray. Outer bands and surface: light brown | Grits: medium gray. Org. grits: large. Grog: small | Low |
| VIII.6 | 416 | IA II large deep bowl. Core: gray. Outer bands and surface: reddish yellow | Grits: medium gray & white. Org. grits. medium | High |
| VIII.7 | 420 | IA II large deep bowl. Core: brown. Outer bands: light brown. Surface: brown | Grits: medium white/gray. Org. grits and grog: medium | Med. |
| VIII.8 | 420 | IA II large deep bowl. Core: dark gray. Outer bands and surface light brown | Grits: medium white & large black. Org. grits. medium Grog. small | Med. |
| VIII.9 | 420 | IA II large deep bowl. Core: gray. Surface: light brown | Grits: small dark gray. Org. grits: small | Med. |
| VIII.10 | 420 | IA II large deep bowl. Core: gray. Surface: light brown | Grits: medium gray. Org. grits and grog: small | High |
| VIII.11 | 420 | IA II bowl. Core and surface: dark brown | Grits: medium black. Org. grits and grog: medium. Decoration: burnished, low | Med. |
| VIII.12 | 416 | IA II bowl. Core: gray. Outer bands and surface: light brown | Grits: medium–dark gray. Org. grits and grog: medium | Med. |
| VIII.13 | 416 | IA II bowl. Core: dark gray. Outer bands and surface: yellowish red | Grits: medium–dark brown and white. Org. grits: medium–large. Grog: med | High |
| VIII.14 | 416 | IA II bowl. Core, outer bands, and surface: light brown | Org. grits and grog: small | Med. |
| VIII.15 | 420 | IA II bowl. Core: light yellowish brown. Surface: reddish yellow | Grits: small pink/white; medium–dark gray. Org. grits: small | Low |
| VIII.16 | 420 | IA II bowl. Core: very pale brown. Surface: reddish yellow | Org. grits: small. Decoration: burnished–high | Low |

PLATE VIII. (1 :5) ROOM 4, AREA B: BOWLS)

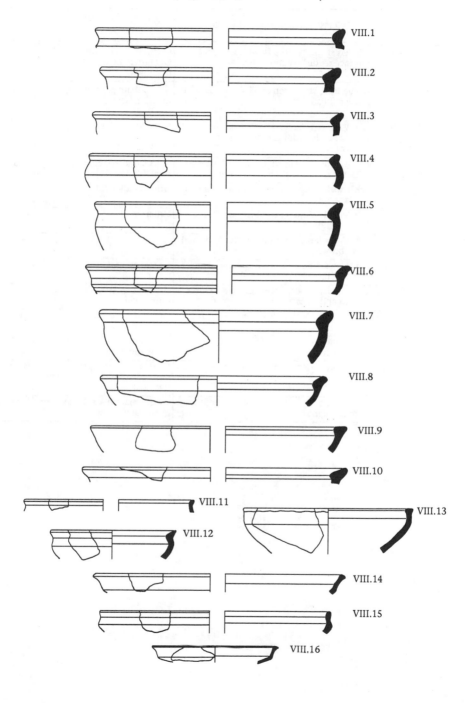

PLATE IX. ROOM 4, AREA B: BOWLS AND COOKING POTS AND CRATERS

| Plate No. | Locus | Classification and Clay Color | Clay Composition and Decoration | Firing |
|---|---|---|---|---|
| IX.1 | 420 | Hellenistic large deep bowl. Core: pink. Surface reddish yellow | Grits: medium white & red. Org. grits: medium Surface: medium | Med. |
| IX.2 | 420 | Hellenistic large deep bowl. Core: gray. Surface: reddish yellow | Grits: small; gray/brown; medium white. Org. grits: small | Med. |
| IX.3 | 416 | Early Roman Galilean bowl. Core: light red. Outer bands: reddish brown. Surface: reddish brown | Grits: small; dark gray | High |
| IX.4 | 416 | Hellenistic deep bowl. Core: pinkish gray. Outer bands & surface: reddish brown | Grits: large, red & black. Grog: small | High |
| IX.5 | 416 | Hellenistic globular cooking pot. Core and surface: red | Grits: small, white | High |
| IX.6 | 407 | Hellenistic globular cooking pot. Core and outer bands: red | Grits: small | — |
| IX.7 | 407 | IA IIA cooking pot. Core, outer bands: reddish brown | — | — |
| IX.8 | 420 | IA II cooking pot. Core and outer bands: reddish brown | Org. grits: medium | Med. |
| IX.9 | 416 | IA II cooking pot. Core: light gray. Outer bands and surface: very pale brown | Grits: small, dark gray. Org. grits: large | High |
| IX.10 | 420 | IA II crater. Core: brown. Surface: brown | Grits: medium white/black. Grog: medium | Med. |
| IX.11 | 420 | IA II crater. Core: gray. Outer bands and surface: light brown | Grits: medium, white/black. Grog: medium | Med. |
| IX.12 | 420 | IA II crater. Core: gray. Surface: brown | Grits: small, dark gray/white. Org. grits: small. Grog: large, light red | High |
| IX.13 | 416 | IA II crater. Core: brown. Outer bands and surface: light brown | Grits: medium–dark gray. Org. grits: medium | Med. |

Plate IX. (1 : 5), Room 4, Area B: Bowls and Cooking Pots and Crater

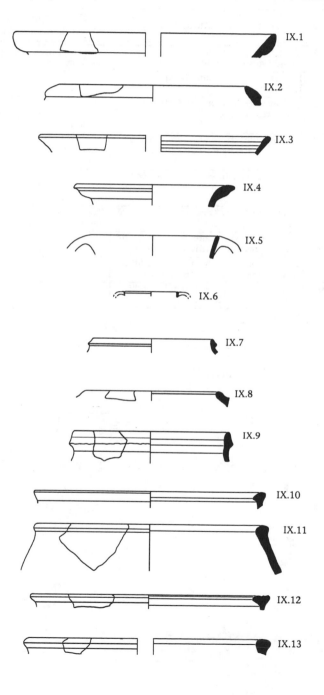

PLATE X. ROOM 4, AREA B: JARS

| Plate No. | Locus | Classification and Clay Color | Clay Composition and Decoration | Firing |
|---|---|---|---|---|
| X.1 | 420 | IA II jar. Core: gray. Outer bands: brown. Surface: very pale brown | Grits: large, white. Org. grits: small. Grog: small | High |
| X.2 | 407 | IA II jar. Core: gray. Outer bands: light brown | — | — |
| X.3 | 416 | IA II jar. Core: light brown. Outer bands and surface: reddish yellow | Grits: medium, dark gray/white. Org. grits: large. Grog: medium | Med |
| X.4 | 420 | IA II jar. Core: gray. Outer bands: reddish yellow. Surface: light reddish brown | Grits: small, gray; medium white. Orig. grits: small. Grog: none | Med. |
| X.5 | 416 | IA II jar. Core: light brownish gray. Outer bands: very pale brown. Surface: very pale brown | Grits: medium–light & dark brown. Org. grits: medium Grog: medium | High |
| X.6 | 416 | IA II jar. Core: gray. Outer bands & surface: brown | Grog: small, white & dark gray. Grog: small to medium | High |
| X.7 | 407 | IA II jar. Core: gray. Outer bands: reddish yellow. Surface: light reddish brown | — | — |
| X.8 | 407 | IA II jar. Core: gray. Outer bands: reddish yellow. Surface: light reddish brown | — | — |
| X.9 | 407 | IA II jar. Core: gray. Outer bands: reddish yellow. Surface: light reddish brown | — | — |
| X.10 | 407 | Early Bronze Age jar | — | — |
| X.11 | 416 | IA II jar. Core, outer bands, and surface: red | Grits: small. Decoration: burnished-high | High |

PLATE X. (1 : 5)

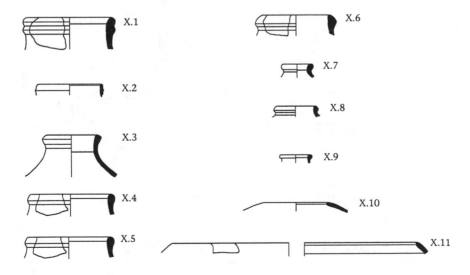

X.1 X.2 X.3 X.4 X.5 X.6 X.7 X.8 X.9 X.10 X.11

## Plate XI, Room 5, Area B: Bowls

| Plate No. | Locus | Classification and Clay Color | Clay Composition and Decoration | Firing |
|---|---|---|---|---|
| XI.1 | 411 | Hellenistic everted rim bowl. Core: gray. Surface: yellowish red | Grits: small, gray. Decoration: very pale brown, glossy to dull slip on outside, of varying thickness. Poorly preserved | High |
| XI.2 | 414 | Hellenistic inverted rim bowl. Core: reddish yellow. Surface: reddish yellow, slip-covered | Grog: small, white. Decoration: thin, red, glossy, peeling slip | Med. |
| XI.3 | 404 | IA II bowl | — | — |
| XI.4 | 408 | IA II bowl. Core: reddish gray. Surface: light reddish brown | Grits: small, gray. Org. Grits and grog: small | Med. |
| XI.5 | 411 | Medieval bowl. Core: yellowish red. Surface: pale yellow | Grits: small. Decoration: green glaze inside | High |
| XI.6 | 414 | IA II bowl. Core: light red, slip covered and medium burnished | Grits: small, pink/gray. Grog: small. Decoration: inside, medium semiglossy slip, nearly peeled away; outside, red medium thick, semiglossy slightly peeling slip | — |
| XI.7 | 414 | IA IIB large deep bowl. Core: gray. Surface: light brown | Grits: small, white/gray | Med. |
| XI.8 | 401 | IA II bowl. Core and surface: light brown | — | — |
| XI.9 | 401 | IA II bowl. Core and surface: light brown | — | — |
| XI.10 | 411 | IA IIB large bowl. Core: dark gray. Surface: dark brown | Grits: medium, gray/white. Org. grits: small. Grog: medium | High |
| XI.11 | 414 | IA II large deep bowl. Core & surface: red | Grits: small, white/gray | High |
| XI.12 | 401 | Early Roman Galilean bowl. Core & surface: reddish | Grits: reddish | — |

Plate XI. (1 : 5)

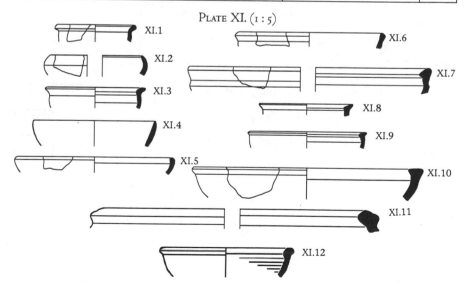

*Rami Arav*

PLATE XII. ROOM 5, AREA B: COOKING POTS

| Plate No. | Locus | Classification and Clay Color | Clay Composition and Decoration | Firing |
|---|---|---|---|---|
| XII.1 | 414 | IA II cooking pot. Core: gray. Surface: red | Grits: small, white/gray | — |
| XII.2 | 414 | Hellenistic globular cooking pot, tall neck. Core: dark gray. Surface: reddish brown | Grits: small, white/gray. Decoration: Clay added near top of handle | High |
| XII.3 | 408 | Hellenistic globular cooking pot. Core: dark red. Surface: red | Grits: small, dark gray/white | High |
| XII.4 | 411 | Hellenistic globular cooking pot. Core: gray. Surface: reddish brown | Grits: small, gray. Org. Grits: small | High |
| XII.5 | 411 | Hellenistic globular cooking pot. Core and surface: red | Grits: small, gray. Decoration: thin red matte slip inside | — |
| XII.6 | 408 | IA II cooking pot. Core and surface: light reddish brown | Org. grits: medium Grog: large | High |
| XII.7 | 411 | IA II cooking pot. Core: brown. Surface: yellowish red | Grits: small, white. Org. grits: medium | Med. |
| XII.8 | 411 | IA IIA cooking pot. Core: dark brown. Outer bands and surface: light red | Grits: small, white/brown/gray. Org. grits: medium | Med. |
| XII.9 | 414 | IA IIA cooking pot. Core and surface: light brown | Grits: medium, gray. Org. grits: small | High |
| XII.10 | 414 | IA IIA cooking pot. Core and surface: very dark grayish brown; core mottled | Grits: large, dark gray. Org. grits: medium Grog: large | High |
| XII.11 | 414 | IA II cooking pot. Core: very dark gray. Surface: reddish brown | Grits: small, white. Org. grits: small | High |
| XII.12 | 411 | IA II cooking pot. Core and surface: brown | Grits: small, black/brown/white. Grog: small | Med. |
| XII.13 | 411 | IA II cooking pot. Core: gray. Surface: red | Grits: small, gray. Grog: medium | High |
| XII.14 | 401 | IA II cooking pot | — | — |
| XII.15 | 411 | IA IIC cooking pot. Core: dark reddish gray. Surface: yellowish red (may have had colored slip) | Grits: small, white/medium gray | Med. |
| XII.16 | 411 | IA II C cooking pot. Core: weak red. Surface: reddish brown | Grits: small, white/dark gray | High |
| XII.17 | 411 | IA IIB cooking pot. Core: dark gray. Surface: reddish brown. | Grits: small, gray | High |
| XII.18 | 411 | Hellenistic cooking pot with everted rim. Core: gray. Surface: red | Grits: small, white. Orig. grits: small, gray | High |
| XII.19 | 405 | Early Hellenistic crater. Core: gray. Surface: light red | Grits: small, white. Grog: medium | High |
| XII.20 | 401 | Hellenistic crater. Core and surface: yellowish | — | — |

PLATE XII. (1 : 5) ROOM 5, AREA B: COOKING POTS, CASSEROLE, CRATERS

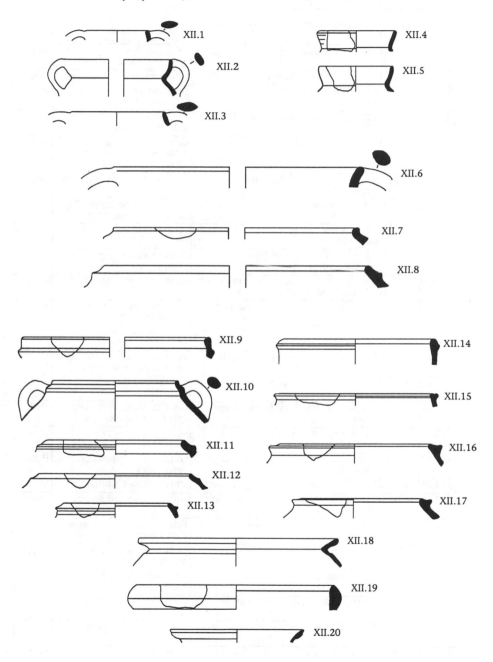

PLATE XIII. ROOM 5, AREA B: JARS

| Plate No. | Locus | Classification and Clay Color | Clay Composition and Decoration | Firing |
|---|---|---|---|---|
| XIII.1 | 411 | IA II jar. Core: dark gray. Surface yellowish red | Grits: medium, brown/white/gray. Grog: large | High |
| XIII.2 | 408 | IA II jar. Core: gray. Surface: light brown | Grits: small-medium white | Med. |
| XIII.3 | 408 | IA II jar. Core: dark gray. Surface: light brown | Grits: medium, white/gray. Org. grits: medium | Med. |
| XIII.4 | 408 | IA II jar. Core: gray. Surface: light brow. | Grits: small, white/gray. Org. grits: small. Grog: small | Med. |
| XIII.5 | 414 | IA II jar. Core dark gray. Outer bands and surface: light brown | Grits: small, dark gray and medium, white. Org. grits: small. Decoration: neck ridge | High |
| XIII.6 | 405 | IA II jar. Core: gray. Outer bands and surface: light brown | Grits: small, white. Org. grits and grog: small | High |
| XIII.7 | 408 | IA II jar. Core: dark gray. Outer bands and surface: reddish yellow | Grits: small, white/gray. Org. grits: small. Grog: small | High |
| XIII.8 | 401 | IA II jar. Core: dark gray. Outer bands and surface: brown | — | — |
| XIII.9 | 408 | IA II jar. Core: gray. Outer bands and surface: light brown | Grits: small, white/gray. Grog: small | Med. |
| XIII.10 | 408 | IA II jar. Core: very dark gray. Outer bands and surface: light brown | Grits: medium, brown/white | Med. |
| XIII.11 | 414 | IA II jar. Core: gray. Surface: reddish yellow | Grits: medium, dark gray/white. Grog: small | High |
| XIII.12 | 414 | IA II jar. Core: very dark gray. Surface: reddish yellow | Grits: medium, white/light brown. Org. grits: small | High |
| XIII.13 | 408 | IA II jar. Core: dark brown. Surface: light brown | Grits: small, white/gray. Decoration: ridge under rim | Med. |
| XIII.14 | 401 | IA II jar. Core: dark gray. Surface: light brown | — | — |
| XIII.15 | 414 | IA II jar. Core: dark gray. Surface: light brown | Grits: medium, white. Org. grits and grog: medium | Med. |
| XIII.16 | 414 | IA II jar. Core: dark gray. Surface: light brown | — | — |
| XIII.17 | 414 | IA II jar. Core: gray. Outer bands and surface: pink | Grits: small, white/black. Grog: small | High |
| XIII.18 | 408 | IA II jar. Core: gray. Surface: light brown | Grits: medium, white/gray | Med. |
| XIII.19 | 408 | IA II jar. Core: black gray. Surface: reddish yellow | Grits: medium, white/gray | Med. |
| XIII.20 | 408 | IA II jar. Core and surface: pink | Grits: pink. Org. grits: small, pink/white/gray. Grog: med. | Med. |
| XIII.21 | 414 | IA II jar. Core: gray. Surface: pink | Grits: small, gray/light brown, and large, white | High |
| XIII.22 | 408 | IA II jar. Core and surface: light brown | Grits: small, gray; medium, white | Med. |
| XIII.23 | 405 | IA II jar. Core: very dark gray. Surface: light brown | Grits: small, white. Org. grits: small. Grog: small | High |
| XIII.24 | 411 | IA II jar. Core and surface: very pale brown | Grits: small, gray; medium, white | High |
| XIII.25 | 408 | IA II jar. Core: gray. Outer bands and surface: pink | Grits: small, gray; medium, white | High |
| XIII.26 | 414 | IA II jar. Core: very dark gray. Surface: pink | Grits: small, gray; med., white. Org. grits: med. Grog: small | Med. |

PLATE XIII. (1 : 5). ROOM 5, AREA B: JARS

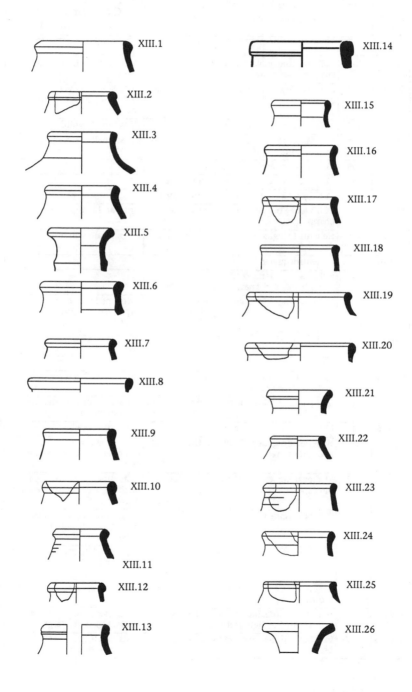

XIII.1

XIII.2

XIII.3

XIII.4

XIII.5

XIII.6

XIII.7

XIII.8

XIII.9

XIII.10

XIII.11

XIII.12

XIII.13

XIII.14

XIII.15

XIII.16

XIII.17

XIII.18

XIII.19

XIII.20

XIII.21

XIII.22

XIII.23

XIII.24

XIII.25

XIII.26

PLATE XIV. ROOMS 5 AND 6, AREA B: JARS, JUGS, BOTTLE, STRAINER, TABLEWARE, BOWLS

| Plate No. | Locus | Classification and Clay Color | Clay Composition and Decoration | Firing |
|---|---|---|---|---|
| ROOM 5 | | | | |
| XIV.1 | 405 | IA II jar. Core: gray. Outer bands and surface: reddish yellow | Grits: small, white. Grog: small | Med. |
| XIV.2 | 414 | IA II jar. Core: dark gray. Surface very pale brown | Grits: small, gray; medium, white. Org. grits: medium Grog: medium | High |
| XIV.3 | 414 | IA II jar. Core and surface: reddish yellow | Grits: small, white/reddish | Low |
| XIV.4 | 408 | IA II jar. Core: light gray. Outer bands and surface: pink | Grits: small, white/gray | High |
| XIV.5 | 404 | IA II jar. Core and surface: light brown | — | — |
| XIV.6 | 404 | IA II jar. Core and surface: light brown | — | — |
| XIV.7 | 404 | IA IIC jar. Core and surface: light brown | — | — |
| XIV.8 | 405 | IA IIB jug. Core and surface: very pale brown | Grits: and org grits: small | Med. |
| XIV.9 | 405 | Hellenistic juglet. Core and surface: light red | Grits: small, white | Med. |
| XIV.10 | 404 | Hellenistic juglet | — | — |
| XIV.11 | 411 | Hellenistic juglet. Core: very pale brown Outer bands: light red. Surface: light brown | — | High |
| XIV.12 | 408 | IA IIB strainer. Core: very dark gray. Outer bands and surface: reddish yellow | Grits: medium, light brown. Org. grits: medium Grog: small | Med. |
| XIV.13 | 405 | Hellenistic fine tableware. Core and surface: reddish yellow | No grits or grog | Med. |
| ROOM 6 | | | | |
| XIV.14 | 417 | Hellenistic bottle. Core: very pale brown. Surface: light gray | Grits: small, light gray | Med. |
| XIV.15 | 417 | IA II jar. Core: pink. Surface: reddish yellow | Grits: medium, white. Org. grits: medium | Med. |
| XIV.16 | 417 | IA II jar. Core and surface: pale brown | Org. grits: small | Med. |
| XIV. 17 | 417 | Hellenistic jug. Core: light red. Outer bands and surface: red | Grits: small, white/light brown. Decoration: pinkish gray | Med. |
| XIV.18 | 417 | Medieval jug. Core: light gray. Surface: pinkish gray | Grits: small, black/red. Grog: medium. Decoration: reddish brown slip inside and outside | High |
| XIV.19 | 417 | Fine tableware. Core: white | No grits or org. grits. Decoration: dark gray slip inside and outside | Med. |
| XIV.20 | 417 | IA II bowl. Core: gray. Surface: light brown | Grits: small to medium, dark gray/white. Org. grits: medium | Med. |
| XIV.21 | 417 | IA II bowl. Core: reddish yellow. Surface: brown | Grits: small, gray. Grog: small | Med. |
| XIV.22 | 417 | IA II bowl. Core: brown. Outer bands: brown. Surface: light red | Grits: medium, gray/large, white. Org. grits: large | Med. |
| XIV. 23 | 417 | IA II bowl. Core: dark gray. Surface: reddish brown | Grits. small, gray/ Med., white. Org. grits. medium | Med. |

PLATE XIV. (1 : 5)
ROOM 5, AREA B: JARS, JUGS, BOTTLE, STRAINER, TABLEWARE, BOWLS

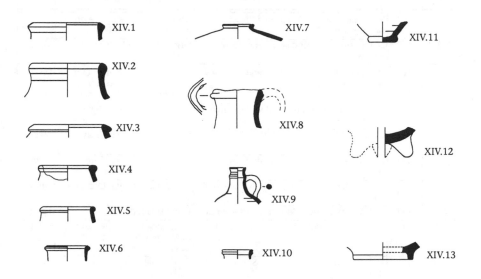

ROOM 6, AREA B: BOTTLE, JARS, JUGS, TABLEWARE, BOWLS

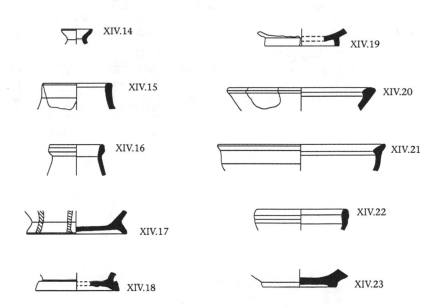

PLATE XV. ROOM 6, AREA B: BOWLS, COOKING POTS, CRATER

| Plate No. | Locus | Classification and Clay Color | Clay Composition and Decoration | Firing |
|---|---|---|---|---|
| XV.1 | 417 | Medieval bowl. Core: reddish brown. Surface: very pale brown. | Decoration: green glaze on inside; some on outside | Med. |
| XV.2 | 417 | IA IIB bowl. Core and surface: reddish yellow | Org. grits: small. Grog: medium | Med. |
| XV.3 | 417 | IA II large deep bowl. Core: reddish yellow. Surface: brown | Grits: small, dark gray. Org. grits: medium. Decoration: light horizontal lines incised | Med. |
| XV.4 | 417 | IA II cooking pot. Core and surface: light brown. | Grits: small, gray. Grog: small | High |
| XV.5 | 417 | IA IIA cooking pot. Core: dark gray. Surface: yellowish red | Grits: medium, dark gray | Med. |
| XV.6 | 417 | IA IIA cooking pot. Core: gray. Surface: brown | Grits: small and medium, black. Org. grits: small | High |
| XV.7 | 417 | IA II cooking pot. Core: gray. Surface: pinkish gray | Grits: small, white. Org. grits: small | High |
| XV.8 | 417 | IA IIA cooking pot. Core and surface: red | Grits: small, dark gray | High |
| XV.9 | 417 | IA IIA cooking pot. Core: dark gray. Surface: light red | Grits: small, dark gray and medium, white. Org. grits: small | High |
| XV.10 | 417 | IA IIB coking pot. Core: gray. Surface: light brown | Grits: small, gray/brown/red. Grog: small | Med. |
| XV.11 | 417 | IA cooking pot. Core and surface: pink | No grits or grog | Low |
| XV.12 | 417 | IA II cooking pot. Core: gray. Surface: very pale brown and mottled gray | Grits: medium, gray/white | — |
| XV.13 | 417 | IA II cooking pot. Core: dark gray. Outer bands and surface: light reddish brown | Grits: small, dark gray, and medium Grog: small | High |
| XV.14 | 417 | IA II cooking pot. Core and surface: light reddish brown | Grits: small, gray/white | — |
| XV.15 | 417 | IA II cooking pot | — | — |
| XV.16 | 417 | Hellenistic globular cooking pot. Core: gray. Surface: red | Grits: small, gray. Org. grits: small. Grog: small | High |
| XV. 17 | 417 | IA II crater. Core and surface: light brown | Grits: small, white/black/brown. Org. grits: small | Med. |

Plate XV. (1:5) Room 6, Area B: Bowls, Cooking Pots, Crater

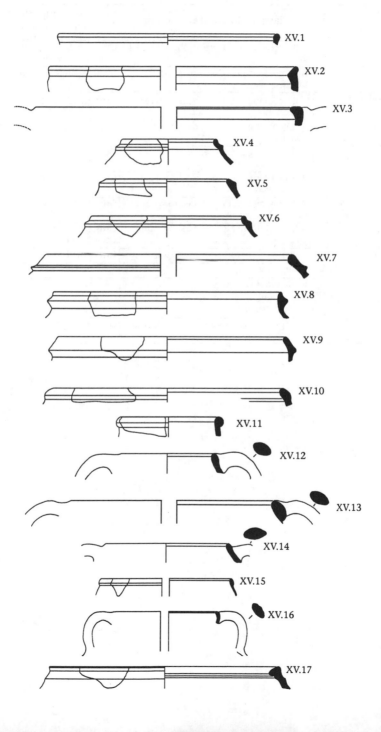

*Rami Arav*

PLATE XVI. ROOM 8, AREA B: COOKING POTS, CASSEROLE, MISCELLANEOUS

| Plate No. | Locus | Classification and Clay Color | Clay Composition and Decoration | Firing |
|---|---|---|---|---|
| XVI.1 | 634 | IA IIA cooking pot. Core and surface: dark gray | Grits: small, gray/brown/red/ white and medium, gray | — |
| XVI.2 | 626 | IA IIA cooking pot. Core and surface: brown | Grits: medium to large, gray | Med. |
| XVI.3 | 626 | IA IIA cooking pot. Core: yellowish red. Surface: mottled, dark, reddish brown | Grits: small, light brown/gray | High |
| XVI.4 | 634 | IA IIA cooking pot. Core: dark brown. Surface: light reddish brown | Grits: small, gray. Grog: small | — |
| XVI.5 | 658 | IA IIA cooking pot. Core, outer bands, and surface: reddish brown | Org. grits: small | Med. |
| XVI.6 | 626 | IA IIA cooking pot. Core: very dark gray. Surface: reddish brown | Grits: medium and large, gray | High |
| XVI.7 | 634 | IA II cooking pot. Core: pale brown. Surface: reddish yellow | Grits: small, gray | — |
| XVI.8 | 641 | IA IIB cooking pot. Core: dark red. Surface: red | Grits: small, gray/brown. Grog: small | — |
| XVI.9 | 626 | Hellenistic casserole. Core and surface: red. | Grits: small, gray | High |
| XVI.10 | 634 | Basalt stone weight | — | — |
| XVI.11 | 634 | Basalt grinding stone | — | — |
| XVI.12 | 634 | Clay spindle weight. Core: dark gray. Surface: reddish yellow | Grits: small, gray. Org. Grits: small. Grog: small | Low |
| XVI.13 | 634 | Clay spindle weight. Core: light red; white. Surface: light red; white | Grits: medium, gray | Med. |

PLATE XVI (1:5), ROOM 8, AREA B, COOKING POTS, CASSEROLE, MISCELLANEOUS

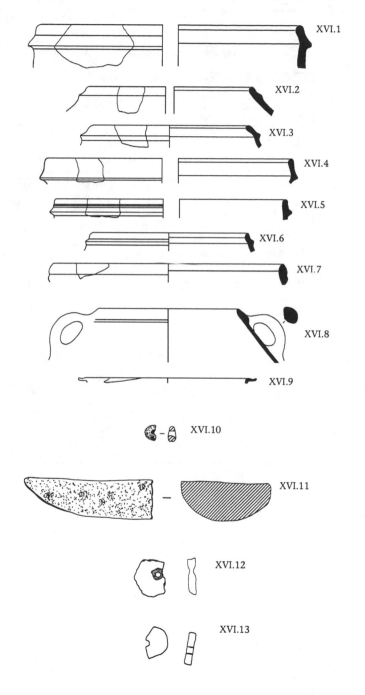

PLATE XVII. ROOM 8, AREA B: BOWLS AND JARS

| Plate No. | Locus | Classification and Clay Color | Clay Composition and Decoration | Firing |
|---|---|---|---|---|
| XVII.1 | 639 | IA II large bowl. Core and surface: dark gray | Grits: small, gray/brown/white/red, and medium, gray | — |
| XVII.2 | 634 | IA II large, deep bowl. Core: gray. Surface: pink | Grits: small, dark gray | Med. |
| XVII.3 | 634 | Hellenistic bowl with inverted rim. Core: gray. Surface: reddish yellow | Grits: small, gray | High |
| XVII.4 | 639 | IA IIB deep bowl. Core: gray. Surface: reddish yellow | Grits: small, light and dark gray/white | High |
| XVII.5 | 626 | IA IIB large, deep bowl. Core: dark reddish brown. Surface: reddish brown | Grits: small, white. Org. grits: small. Grog: small | High |
| XVII.6 | 620 | IA IIB bowl. Core: white. Surface: mottled light reddish brown | Grits: small, red. Grog: small, light brown | Med. |
| XVII.7 | 641 | IA IIB large, deep bowl. Core: gray. Surface: pink | Grits: large, white/gray/red. Grog: large | High |
| XVII.8 | 620 | IA IIB bowl. Core and surface: red | — | High |
| XVII.9 | 620 | IA IIB bowl. Core: dark gray. Surface: light brown | Grits: small, white/gray. Grog: small. Decoration: low burnish | Med. |
| XVII.10 | 620 | IA II bowl. Core and surface: very pale brown | Grits: small, brown/white | High |
| XVII.11 | 634 | Basalt bowl | — | — |
| XVII.12 | 620 | IA IIB jar. Surface: white | Grits: small, red/gray/white. Grog: small | Med. |
| XVII.13 | 634 | IA IIB jar. Core and surface: light brown | Grits: small, gray. Grog: small | Med. |
| XVII.14 | 620 | IA II jar. Core: light gray. Outer rim and surface: reddish yellow | Grits: small, gray. Org. grits: small | Med. |
| XVII.15 | 634 | IA IIB jar. Core: gray. Surface: reddish yellow | Grits: small, light and dark gray/white | High |
| XVII.16 | 639 | IA IIB jar, Core and surface: brown | Grits: medium, gray. Grog: medium | Med. |
| XVII.17 | 626 | IA IIB jar. Core and surface: light brown | Grits: small, white and large, dark gray. Grog: large | High |

PLATE XVII. (1:5), ROOM 8, AREA B: BOWLS AND JARS

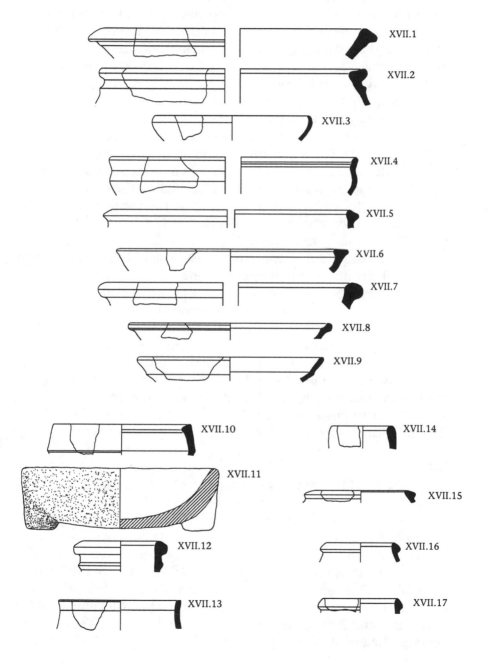

## LEVEL 5 AND LEVEL 4

Because of uninterrupted and continuous use of the building it is not easy to distinguish and assign the later alterations of the building to the different levels of the site. However, some important changes occurred and caused a drastic change in the appearance of the building and perhaps also to its usage. It has been noticed by scholars that a Bit Hilani type of building was built by strict architectural standards that made it impossible to introduce changes in the ground plan without converting the building into a thoroughly different architectural entity.[45] The order of the later changes cannot be traced and we find it difficult to date. The alterations are presented here in random order.

1. A wide and massive wall, W195, was built in front of the building, blocking a section of its eastern half of the facade.
2. A smaller structure was annexed at the western half of the facade. It consists of walls W304, W301.
3. The entrances to rooms 1,6,7, were blocked.
4. A wall the width of one stone, W191, was built across the main hall, dividing the hall into two long rooms.
5. Two brick benches were added along the wall, the newly added wall, and the wall of room one (square J43).

Because of all these changes it seems that the building lost its Bit Hilani appearance and was altered to suit new demands. Apparently the new occupants were not interested in the old palace fashion and it ceased to be a Bit Hilani. Was the function of the building as a palace changed? It is the opinion of the excavators that the building served different purposes in levels 5 and 4. It is, however, difficult to draw political or sociological conclusions from this change.

## CITY WALL (MAP 8)

East of the Bit Hilani runs the city wall (W303). It was found in a deteriorated situation. In its center was a Syrian military trench that led to a bunker, which we eventually removed (in square M–N46). Similar to other portions of the city wall, this section was built with large, massive boulders on the outside and inside faces, and the core was filled with smaller fieldstones and rubble (fig. 29). The average thickness of the wall is 6.2 m, and occasionally it was widened to both the outer and interior faces in the form of bastions. This thickening added between 1 and 2 m to the width of the wall, making these places between 7.2 and 8 m thick. This treatment of a city wall was rarely

Fig. 29. City wall section (W 303) showing core filled with small fieldstones and rubble, three stones of the outer face of the wall and remains of a floor

used in Iron Age cities of the land of Israel and is only recorded in Tel Dan.[47] Changes in the course of the walls were made at these bastions, as may be observed in M42. Similar changes are seen at the northern section of the wall.

LEVELS 3 AND 2

A few walls continued to be used on these levels, one of which is W304, which together with W81 forms, in fact, one wall. A lower floor that is associated with this wall is at 167.63 m and dates from Iron Age IIC as does an upper floor paved with small pebbles at an elevation of

Fig. 30. W304 with two successive floors. The lower one is Iron Age IIC and the upper one is a Roman floor. The upper wall is leaning inward, most probably as a result of an earthquake.

166.72 m that carried pottery shards dating from the Early Roman period (fig. 30). This upper wall is connected to both W82 and W192. The function of these walls is unknown because of modern Syrian military disturbances. W198 is a remnant of a wall; it is impossible to follow its pattern or to date it more precisely.

THE ROMAN HOUSE (MAP 7). At the eastern section of the area, the remains of an Early Roman house are slightly better preserved. A Syrian bunker destroyed the northern end of W193 and made it impossible to reconstruct the rest of the house. The room that belongs to this wall was approached by an entrance at W306. Near this entrance there was an oven, which may indicate an open courtyard. Two rooms were built east of W197 and along the more ancient Iron Age city wall. The walls were constructed of relatively small fieldstones that could have been handled by one or two persons. Smaller stones were inlaid between the larger ones. Dirt plaster mixed with pottery shards covered the wall from the outside. This fact helped date the walls to the Early Roman period (figs. 31, 32).The entrance to the southern rooms was made through W197. An opening in W300 led to an interior room. The eastern wall of this house was the old Iron Age city wall, which means that the Iron Age city wall was high enough to be reused almost a millennium later. It is noteworthy that the inhab-

Fig. 31. Wall 197 of the Roman house, small oven on the Iron Age pavement. Notice the gap between foundation of the Roman house and the Iron Age floor

Fig. 32. Shard of Early Roman fineware found in situ at the foundation of the Early Roman house

Fig. 33. The Roman house next to the city wall. Notice the two entrances, left,
to an adjacent room and at the west, presumably to a courtyard

itants of this house presumably did not like the recession in the city
wall and filled it with smaller stones in order to create one straight line
(see figs. 33, 34). The rooms of the Roman House were partially paved
with coarse paving (fig. 35). At the corner of W197 and W199 there
was a flour-threshing device that was built to fit the corner. A very similar device was discovered at Gamla and dates to the first century CE.[48]

THE FISHERMAN HOUSE. This building was reported already in *Bethsaida*
1:22–23, 26-28. During further digging, finer stages of it preservation
and use were discerned, and a detailed discussion will be presented in
the next volume.

SMALL FINDS FROM AREA B

JAR HANDLE WITH INSCRIPTION. In the course of removing a balk
between squares K42 and K43, a handle bearing an inscription was
unearthed (fig. 36).The particulars of the discovery are that it was discovered in Area B, stratum 2, locus 584, level 167.05 m, basket 6469,
date 12.5.95.

Fig. 34. The Roman house adjacent to the Iron Age city wall. The north-south wall is the city wall. The large stone at the foreground is the city wall's offset. The east-west walls are Roman

The upper section of the balk contained the northern portion of W193. The lower section contained W395, which is the eastern continuation of W191. At the bottom of the balk, at the elevation of 167.31 m, there is the floor of the main hall of the Bit Hilani. W193 is a Roman-period wall that runs in a north-south direction; its northern end was destroyed by the Syrian military installation. The stratification of the balk is not a simple one. The establishment of the trench in W193 perhaps caused some Roman shards to descend to the level of the Iron Age pottery. The construction of the Syrian military installation undoubtedly caused greater confusion in the original stratifica-

*Rami Arav*

Fig. 35. The Roman house in Area B

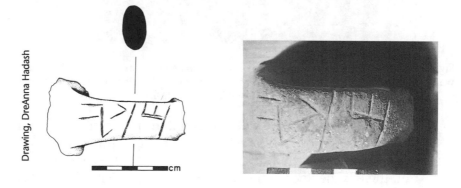

Drawing, DreAnna Hadash

Fig. 36. Jar handle with מכי (MKY) inscription

tion, which means that the handle was not discovered in situ. However, the main bulk of the finds, consisting of more than 500 shards of pottery, date from Iron Age II, but no more than a dozen are Early Roman shards.

The inscription was on a handle of a jar that could not be restored; it was incised with a sharp object after the firing procedure was completed. The letters are large (22 by 16 mm) and easy to define. The script is in three Hebrew Phoenician characters: מכי (MKY). This is most probably the short spelling (without vowels) of the proper name Micaiah. The proper name Mikha/Micah derives from this name. This proper name exists, in fact, in two theophoric versions, Mikhyahu and Michael. The meaning of the name is "Who is like God?"

Micaiah is a frequent name in the Hebrew Bible. It denotes at least seven different persons. The most interesting in relation to our inscription, but not necessarily relevant to it, is Micaiah the mother of Abijah, king of Judah (2 Chr. 13:2). Interestingly, the mother of Abijah is identified in a parallel passage in 1 Kings 15:2 with "Maachah the daughter of Abishalom." Furthermore, in 2 Chr. 11:20 (a list of King Rehoboam's wives and offspring) she is referred to as "Maachah, the daughter of Absalom." There is no need to speculate that Abishalom and Abshalom are two different persons, as a few scholars suggest,[49] not because the name Abshalom is rare in the Bible, but because they both have daughters with similar names who were married to the same king, and it seems that Abshalom named his daughter after his mother. As stated above, our inscription may have nothing in common with the persons mentioned above, but it is interesting to find that this name occurs in the relevant territory of the Geshurites precisely in the area from which Maachah and Abshalom are believed to have come.

EGYPTIAN PATAEKOS FIGURINE (FIG. 37). On August 30, 1994, a small Egyptian figurine depicting the Egyptian god Pataekos was discovered during leveling a 10-cm sediment of red burnt soil in locus 638.[50] The soil elevation was between 167.96 and 168.04 m. This level is approximately the floor level of the palace. Above the level of the red soil was another layer of red brick debris of 30 to 40 cm. Below the figurine level there was a brown-red soil down to the bedrock (168.04–168.37 m). Locus 638 forms the eastern end of the main hall of the Bit Hilani.

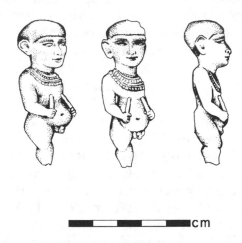

Fig. 37. Egyptian Pataekos faience figurine

The figurine is made of faience. Most of the blue glazing is faded or peeled away except for a few deposits under the right arm and under the neck, which indicate its original turquoise color. The figurine was severely damaged in antiquity for an unknown reason. Most of the rear half together with the left side of the back of the head, the left ear, left arm and shoulder, and left leg are missing. The figurine was also cut off below the right foot, and the square base on which these figurines are frequently posted is missing too. This is very regrettable because occasionally the figures stand on crocodiles, and the bottom of the bases often bears inscriptions or magic symbols. The current state of preservation measures 6.1 cm. Together with the conjectured base, the height of the figurine might have been between 7 and 8 cm. Although the state of preservation does not permit speculation on the function of the figurine, its fairly large size makes it unlikely that the figurine served as an amulet.

The figurine depicts a standing dwarf male. The head is spherical and has pronounced ears, rendered in a realistic style to minute details. A fine groove on the forehead indicates a close-fitting cap. The upper eyelid is elevated and stresses an elongated line. The head is overproportioned in relation to the body, and has no distinct neck. The figurine is wearing no clothes but is not entirely naked. A collar of three rows of square beads covers the entire chest. The bulbous abdomen is marked with a deep naval. The preserved right arm is held alongside the body. Right and left hands rest on the abdomen, at the height of the navel. Each hand is clenched around an object which appears to be a knife or a dagger. Both hands clearly show marked individual fingers. Male genitals indicate the sex of the figurine. The figure is not standing upright. The only leg preserved has a thick thigh and calf and is bowed outward and slightly bent.

This figurine represents clearly the Egyptian Pataekos, who is identified as a dwarf god. The name derives from Herodotus' describing a certain aspect of the image of the Egyptian god Ptah, which he refers to for his Greek readers as Hephaistos.[51] He calls this image Pataekos and reminds his reader that it is very similar to the images the Phoenicians carry at the prow of their ships. For those who had never seen a Phoenician ship, he adds shortly that it bears the likeness of a dwarf. Pataekos would mean in this sense "the little Ptah." The Pataekos is in fact very common in archaeological contexts. In Israel alone, 184 Pataekos figurines have been discovered thus far. In fact, this is the most common Egyptian find after the Eye of Horus. However, in spite of its being very common, the Egyptian name of this god and worship practices related to it are still unknown.

HANDLE WITH ANCHOR INCISION. During the 1994 excavations a handle of a Hellenistic jar incised with an anchor was found (fig. 38), in locus 674, which is located at square L39, among Hellenistic–Early Roman pottery shards. The handle, 6 cm long by 3 cm wide, is typical of a large variety of Hellenistic jars of yellow-greenish ware. The incision was made when the jar was still "skin wet," just before it was put into the kiln. The inscribed anchor is 5 by 2.4 cm, and perhaps depicts a metal anchor. It has a long narrow bar, with a crossing bar at the upper side and two curved bars at the bottom. This type of anchor was discovered at the Sea of Galilee and is associated with first-century-CE fabrication.[52] It is interesting to note that the most common anchor in the Sea of Galilee during the Hellenistic and Roman periods was a basalt stone pierced with a hole (see Fortner's chapter, p. 282).

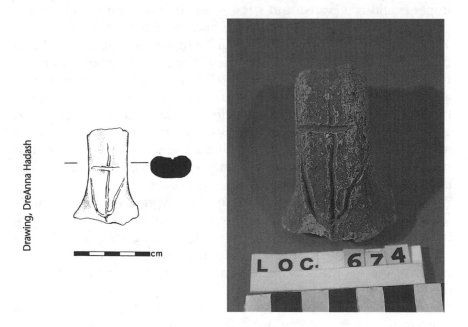

Fig. 38. Handle with anchor incision

FIGURINE OF GODDESS. This figurine (fig. 39) was found in Area B in locus 453, square K44, at the entrance to the palace. The figurine is made of clay that was compressed into a mold. It depicts a woman with the Egyptian Hator hairstyle. She has very pronounced large eyes that are emphasized with double lines; her nose and lips are worn away. She is wearing two large double earrings and a tied necklace. Some remains of hair locks can be seen on the left side of her face. The style of the figurine together with pottery from the locus help to date it to Iron Age II.

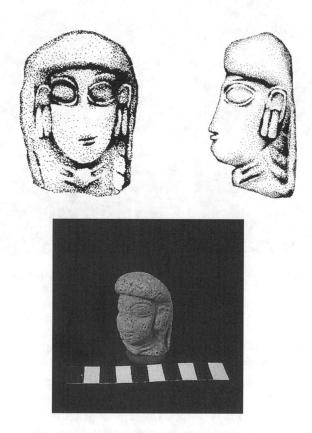

Fig. 39. Figurine of goddess, found in Area B.
Drawing by DreAnna Hadash

## Area C (Maps 9–10)

Area C (fig. 40) was excavated extensively during the 1994–1995 seasons. The finds from this area include the northern city walls, a large courtyard house ("house of the vintner") adjacent to remains of another courtyard house, a subterranean structure ("wine cellar"), remnants of what might be a street, remnants of a house across the street, and remains of extensive habitation (but with little substantial architectural remains) from the medieval period.

Fig. 40. Aerial shot showing Area C, courtyard house, kitchen, and other rooms in the north

### Level I

A few remains were discerned at Area C that belong to this level; the purpose of the remains is not clear. In square G26 was a crude structure that included a single room built with irregular walls of different sizes and construction. W234 runs from south to north; it measures 2.5 m at the south and is reduced to 1.8 m at its north; it then loops to the east and south and narrows down to 0.8 m when it meets W234 again. No floor was observed that belongs to this wall. The pottery and coins collected from this area indicate that the structure existed during the fourteenth to fifteenth centuries. South of this wall the area was severely disturbed by some kind of medieval activity. Our initial assumption is that the area served as limestone kilns. This was based upon the recognition of five round large pits that contained basalt stones covered with white patches. However, geological investigations of the white patches revealed that the white patches are travertine sediments of water and not lime created by kilns.

Fig. 41. House of the Vintner in Area C, looking from the courtyard to the kitchen

LEVEL 2 (RESIDENTIAL QUARTER)

This level was found in a poor state of preservation. Level 1 structural activities had removed large sections and introduced a mixture of shards and finds from the lower and upper layers.

HOUSE OF THE VINTNER. This house is situated in squares E–I 29–32 (fig. 41). It is 16.2 by 18 m in size and it is a courtyard-type house.[53] Although the house seems to be a complete unit, it made use of old Iron Age walls. Thus, the oldest wall in this house is W209, which by and large served as the northern wall of an Iron Age house. That explains also the slight irregularity of this room in comparison with the other walls. L900, the kitchen, was perhaps the first room to be built in this house. The entrance to the house was made in the southern wall, and sometime later it was narrowed. This entrance led to a spacious courtyard (12 by 12.80 m at L911). Traces of pavement found at the southwest corner of the courtyard and a hard, crushed, bitten limestone floor was found below debris at the southeast corner of the house, suggesting that the courtyard was partly roofed at the east along W201. A large medieval cavity was excavated in the center of the courtyard, which destroyed the paved floor and disconnected it from its entire surrounding. Among the special finds from the courtyard was an iron strigilis that was found at the northern half of the courtyard.

An opening in the eastern wall of the courtyard, W201, leads to L900, which is interpreted as the kitchen of the house. Some paved remnants at the southeast corner of the kitchen indicate that the entire floor might have been paved. Pavement at the northern half of the room suggests a lower layer of pavement. Near the entrance was an oven, and along the southern wall, W209, was a large collection of kitchenware. Two basalt threshing boards together with a basalt stone flour mill were found near the pavement (fig. 42). In addition, three bronze pruning hooks and a gold earring were also among the finds of this house (see vol. 1, p. 33, fig. 21, and p. 34, fig. 23). Other notable finds were three bent iron nails found near the opening (which perhaps belonged to the door hinges) and an iron key (fig. 43) similar to known Hellenistic Roman keys.[54]

The northern wall of the courtyard led through an opening to the northern section of the house. Near the entrance, still in the courtyard, the door lintel was discovered. The room north of this (defined by W205, W206, W213, W211) is a nice, spacious room that served perhaps as the *triclinium,* or dining room, of the house. W211 is a double wall with a bench at the west side. The opening at this wall leads to an irregular room, of which W214 serves as the western wall of the room. The reason for this irregularity was, perhaps, the desire not to block the street that ran at the west side of the house. The room east of the *triclinium* is difficult to interpret; its walls were found in a poor condition and there was no obvious entrance to it.

East of the kitchen (locus 900), a subterranean structure was discovered (locus 948). It measured 4.5 by 2.85 m. Two walls, partly built under the ground, support a roof made of long basalt beams (figs. 44

Fig. 42. Demonstration of operation of basalt threshing board and flour mill, found in Area C

and 45). The construction technique and its overall measurements resemble very closely the Byzantine *Miqve* (ritual baths) at Chorazim,[55] but there are no indications of other necessary *Miqve* architecture at Bethsaida. More importantly, in the Bethsaida subterranean structure, four large jars, together with a casserole found in this locus, may indicate a wine storage facility. Our present hypothesis is that it was a wine cellar, but this cannot be proven. The jars and the casserole (fig. 45) date from the end of the second to the early first century BCE. Because of the so-called wine cellar and the pruning hooks, the entire building is now designated as House of the Vintner.

Fig. 43. Iron key and spearhead found in House of the Vintner

Fig. 44. Basalt beams from roof of a subterranean structure

Fig. 45. A cellar, found with jars, adjacent to the kitchen in the Late
Hellenistic courtyard house, Area C

At the northeastern corner of this house, the remains of another house were discovered (squares H–I, 26-29, fig. 40). Although there were only a few remains of the house, it was most probably a courtyard house. W236, W233, and W237 constitute its outer wall; W240, W239, and W242 form presumably the courtyard. The entrance to the house was perhaps at the south. Remnants of pavement were discovered at the western end of W239 and may indicate pavement throughout the entire house. The northwestern corner of the house was destroyed by the medieval structure of Level 1. The definition of the eastern end of the building is unclear as well.

Remnants of pavement that may be interpreted as street pavement were discovered in the east and northeast parts of the House of the Vintner. The pavement is attached to W224 and W219, which presumably form a corner of a building at the east side of the street.

### LEVEL 3

There are no structures that are ascribed to this level with great certainty. Finds, however, show that there is a strong presence of the Persian period in this area. Perhaps the northeast house could be dated to this level although stratigraphically this building is not different from the House of the Vintner.

### LEVEL 4, CITY WALLS W259 (FIG. 46, MAP 10)

No particular remains were discovered in the residential quarter from this level although many of the walls in the upper levels were in fact first built and used during level 4. The most important remains from this level are the remains of the city walls, which were discovered 17 m north of the residential quarter and present state-of-the-art Iron Age II military fortifications.

A 56 m length of these walls was unearthed and together with the fortification installations form a considerably heavy fortification system. The northern approach to the city is the most natural approach. The western and the southern sides of the city faced the Sea of Galilee during the Iron Age; during the Hellenistic and Roman periods, they faced the lagoons, while the eastern side faces a ravine that slopes steeply towards the south. The northern side, where the mound seems to stretch out from the low basalt extension, provided the only accessible—and most vulnerable—point of the city. Perhaps this is why the city was so formidably fortified at the north. It is plausible

Fig. 46. City wall (W259) with segment of tower on *left* of photo.

that a moat preceded the entire system; this however has not yet been investigated. A section that we excavated at the north (squares D19, 20, 21) suggests the following system of fortification.

A solid revetment wall built of large boulders (some measure 0.9 by 0.7 by 0.5 m) at the outer face, together with smaller stones, form the core of this revetment wall. This wall was constructed on the bedrock, which was originally cleared of all dirt and soil; then a glacis was poured in. The glacis was made of crushed limestone mixed with red soil that was taken from the riverbed. The glacis was short (it has a span of 2 m) but was quite steep. It reaches the top of the revetment wall, which is more than 2 m high. That would make a slope of 32 percent, which was observed also in a section near the city gate.

The revetment wall followed the course of the city wall at a distance of 3.5 m. This would leave a free rampart near the city walls. The latter were built of enormous boulders in carefully constructed masonry construction. In order to eliminate vulnerable corners the city wall turns north-northeast at squares G-H-I 21, 22, 23 and then turns east west at F20, 21. The turning point was reinforced with a massive protrusion of 11.4 m, which forms a shape similar to offsets or bastions. Two further offsets were excavated. One was at a distance of 9.5 m from the large offset. Its length is 2.6 m and it projects 0.6 m from the city wall. The second is at a distance of 8 m from the last one and projects to 1.5 m from the city wall. The core of the wall was densely filled with smaller rocks and fieldstones. Small segments of the inner wall were excavated and surveyed. They show clear evidence that the wall at the north was constructed similarly to the eastern city wall, which means that the inner wall was a mirror image of the outer wall. Thus, the widths of the city walls vary from 6.2 to 7 m. This technique has no peer in the fortification of Iron Age cities in Israel outside of the city of Dan, and it is perhaps a further northern innovation.[56] The purpose of these offsets is not yet clear. Although, on one hand, it seems reasonable that any thickening of the wall would result in better reinforcement, it would, on the other hand, be too small to support a tower. Our reconstruction shows two alternatives, which could be either a rather small tower or a buttress.

## Small Finds from Area C

Bearded Man Figurine. Just outside of the House of the Vintner, near the entrance at the south and the western end of wall W209, a small figurine of a bearded head was discovered (fig. 47). The figurine is made of clay, and was not made in a mold. It was perhaps a freestanding piece of a large statuette or sculptured group.The head of the figurine is removed from its neck and from the top of what seems to be a tall headgear. A section of the nose is missing too. The fragment that is preserved measures 74 mm high, 60 mm wide, and 45 mm in profile. It depicts a pronounced beard and pronounced elongated eyes. He wears a very slim smile and has slightly projected cheeks. His hairstyle is rendered as a wig; incisions mark the hair locks. The figure is wearing what should have been a long and pointed headgear, which comes down to its neck at the back and is fitted on his headdress. The artistic style, particularly the pointed beard, the slim smile, and the hairstyle

Fig. 47. Figurine of bearded man found in Area C.
Drawing by DreAnna Hadash

appear to be Near Eastern artwork with a conspicuous Greek archaic influence. A similar figurine was discovered at Tel Amrit (ancient Arvad) in the north Phoenician coast (today Syria), and is dated from the fourth to the fifth centuries BCE.[57] We propose this dating for our figurine as well.

CRUCIFORM MARKING ON A SHARD (FIG. 48). The House of the Vintner produced a few interesting finds. Near the entrance of the main room at the north of the courtyard, which is identified as the *triclinium* of the house (locus 924), there were a few fragments of a jar. No rim fragments or base parts were discovered and no complete restoration could have been achieved. The fragments were observed by Yoval Goren of the Antiquities Authority and were found to be a typical production of western Galilee.[58] Pottery and numismatic evidence of the locus point to the first century BCE for latest deposition of the jar.[59]

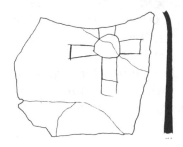

Fig. 48. Cruciform marking on shard found in Area C. See also cover of vol. 1.

The cruciform marking was incised on the outside face of the jar by a sharp, hard, pointed tool after the firing process. The lines of the incision correspond to the lines of the jar, which indicate that the jar was intact when the incision was made, and it was not meant to be an ostrakon. However, it also means that the incision was not necessarily done in western Galilee. The style of the incision leaves no doubt that it was deliberately meant to appear as it is, and it was not a result of a quick or casual production.

The restored fragment was assembled from four pieces, and it measures 20.7 by 19 cm. The upper part of the cruciform is missing and it is only a conjecture that it is similar to the other arms. The incision presents a four-arm cruciform with a circle at its center. The cruciform measures 10.7 cm from right to left and 10.6 cm (of what is preserved) from top to bottom. Some of the incisions were made over again and appear in double lines. All arms are oblong in shape and almost equal to each other. The right arm measures 3.1 by 2.8 cm; double incisions are seen on the lower line of the arm. The lower line measures 3 by 2.2 cm. An additional extension prolonged the cruciform to 6 cm. Double strikes are noticed on the left line. The left arm is 3.6 by 1.8 cm and double incisions are noticed on the four lines of the oblong. The upper arm was only partly preserved; it is 2.5 cm wide and only 1 cm was preserved of the long lines. It would be similar to the right and left arms if 2 cm were added to it. Obvious attempts are discerned in shaping the center into a circle. The incision begins in the lower left side and was made, most probably, in a counterclockwise direction. It seems that the incised design began with the circle and the arms were added.

## SUMMARY

The Iron Age city was no doubt very heavily fortified. Its 6- to 8-m-thick city walls are almost without precedents. The city gate was installed in the east, above a deep ravine, making it difficult to storm and conquer the city. The northern section of the city wall is formidably constructed. Undoubtedly, these strong defense systems were made in order to withstand the most powerful assault machinery used from the tenth century BCE and onward, namely, battering rams.[60] The revetment walls together with the short and steep glacis would make it extremely difficult to install a battering ram. In addition, by placing the walls at a distance, behind a free rampart, they were removed outside the range of battering rams and reduced the risk of the city wall's being breached. If we may judge from the evidence that the Bethsaida city walls provide, these walls were never conquered from the northern side. The only evidence of military conquest was observed at the city gate and its southern area. Presumably the city walls fulfilled their function perfectly.

The city walls were reused also during the Hellenistic and Roman periods and perhaps even later. In fact, the only Byzantine remains to be found at Bethsaida were near the city walls, where a few shards of pottery and a cooking pot were found.

The fortifications together with the palace complex that included the plaza and the Bit Hilani palace strengthen our previous assumption, that Bethsaida was a city of major importance during Iron Age II. We suggest in volume 1 that the site could have been the capital of the kingdom of Geshur. The name of the capital of this kingdom is not recorded in the Bible,[62] and it has long been speculated that it resided in the town of Karnaim, further to the east, simply because Karnaim became the Assyrian capital of the province after its conquest at the end of the eighth century BCE.[63] The finds of Bethsaida together with the discoveries made in other Iron Age II sites in the vicinity[63] present a settlement pattern in which a major dominant town governs a vast area at the eastern territories of the Sea of Galilee, in which small satellite towns such as Tel Hadar or Ein Gev serve, respectively, as storage sites or rural and commercial centers.

The religion of the Geshurites is better understood today because of the Bethsaida excavations. The figurines of a male wearing *Atef* headgear, the female with the Hator hairdressing, and the Egyptian figurine of Pataekos indicate that the Geshurites had a syncretistic religion that was, evidently, not much different from that of their neighbors. Egyptian influence was strongly manifested through the appearance of figurines and other images made in Egypt and brought to the region. This exchange as well as past Egyptian dominance and the closeness of the site to the international trade routes resulted in the local Geshurite deities carrying strong Egyptian influence. It is assumed, therefore, that the eclectic Egyptian elements present on the figurines reflect the essence of an eclectic Geshurite religion. There was, however, a change during Iron Age IIC, when a stronger Aramean influence penetrated, as is attested by the discovery of the figurine in Area C.

The residential quarter in Area C presents an environment of a humble community of country people who lived in poor dwellings and were occupied in fishing, viticulture, livestock raising, and other farming occupations. Their houses were occupied for a relatively long period of time. A few of the houses were built during the fourth century BC and were continuously inhabited for a few centuries. The excavated area reflects perhaps the oldest residential nucleus of the Hellenistic town. A few homes were apparently abandoned when their inhabitants moved to newer homes slightly south, down the slope of the mound. Although humble and poor, the inhabitants were not remote from the main thoroughfare of communication and were aware of the happenings in the centers of civilization. They purchased from time to time good-quality pottery and perhaps also other objects. The buildings did not carry any Greek classical elements; there were no columns or Greek capitals, not even after the Roman temple was constructed in their neighborhood. Was it because of the higher expenses of maintaining these homes, or because the Greek architecture did not appeal to them? This question has not been answered yet, and it is perhaps the concern of a larger environmental and socioeconomic reconstruction.

If we interpret the building at Area A properly as a Roman temple dedicated to the Roman imperial cult and more precisely to the cult of Julia, then it presents definitely a picture of an imposition of the cult from above, with little to do with the population of the town. Although built on the highest spot of the town, it was not constructed in the midst of a busy quarter, but perhaps intentionally rather far from the busy downtown. It is a modest temple, far removed from the more luxurious examples that Philip's father, Herod the Great, had constructed. In its appearance, however, it resembles more the style of the northern Syrian temples at Palmyra than those in Samaria and Caesarea Maritima. In short, similar to the earlier Iron Age architectural influence on Bethsaida, the northern styles may have continued to influence throughout the Roman period.

## CHAPTER NOTES

1. For definition and discussion see: Robertson (1969), 39:383, and Fletcher (1987), fig. 130A.
2. For the round structure see Arav (1995a), 16, fig. 2.
3. Kuhn and Arav (1991), 77–106. Other fragments will be published in a separate article that deals with the identification of the building. The largest piece is that of a lintel (see Kuhn and Arav [1991], 106, pl. 2:5), probably seen and reported more than a century ago on the top of the mound (see Frei [1886], 118).
4. some of the vessels were published and indicate first century CE for the pits. See Arav (1995a), 19, pls. VI:1–3, VII:1–4, VIII:2.
5. See: Arav (1995a), 21, fig. 13.
6. Distyle temples are quite frequent in the Levant; some have adytons. See Ward-Perkins (1994), 340, 356, 500. A distyle temple with adyton was discovered at Qanawat; see butler (1907–1922), 351, fig. 124; 365–402.
7. Further excavations will reveal whether the revetment wall east of the city gate was not, in fact, the eastern retaining wall of a podium that was made out of the ruined Iron Age city gate. Small temples without distinctive podia were discovered in the region. See for example the temples at Caesarea Paneas (Banias); Ma'oz (1993a), 140ff.; (1993b), 534ff.; and Dar (1993), 616–17.
8. The renaming of Bethsaida to Julias was undoubtedly a result of the imposition of the Roman Imperial Cult on his tetrarchy. See Arav (1994), 246. The idea that Julia is identified with Julia/Livia, the wife of Augustus and the mother of Tiberius, was presented by A. Kindler in a symposium at Haifa University, April 1987. See Kindler's chapter in this volume. This has been reinvestigated and published by Kuhn and Arav (1991), 85–91, and by Strickert (1995), 165ff.
9. Herod the Great had built the temple at Samaria already in 27 BCE. This was among the first Roman Imperial Cult temples erected in the Roman Empire. The temple in Caesarea was built about 20 BCE.
10. The city gate at Dan shows a close resemblance to the gate at Bethsaida, especially the external pavement; it differs, however, in its direct approach. See Biran (1992), 4–6; (1994a), 4–6.
11. The city gate at Megiddo shows close parallel to the gate at Bethsaida, although it is not so large.
12. For research of city gates see Herzog (1976) and Herzog (1992), 848–852; Mazar (1990), 467–70.
13. The southern gate of the inner city at Carcemish is perhaps a good parallel to Bethsaida. Both share pavement in the passageway only and four large chambers. See Wooley (1921), pl. 12; Naumann (1955), p. 272, figs. 335, 337. See also Mazar (1990), 457–70.
14. Biran (1994b), 8–15.
15. Arav (1995a), 14, fig. 6.
16. Is this technique identical to the "Milo" that King Solomon had built in Jerusalem to support the Temple Mount (1 Kings 9:15)? See Shiloh (1993), 703–704; Mazar (1990), 379–80.
17. The campaign of Tiglath Pileser III was very destructive for many cities in northern Israel (Ahlstrom [1993], 607–753). Levels of destruction were observed in Dan (Biran [1994b], 15), Hazor (Yadin [1993], 603). For recent study on Tiglath Pileser III documents, see Tadmor (1994).
18. Tessaro (1995), 141. This type was dated by Negev to 4 BCE and 63 CE; see Negev (1986), 94.

19. Tessaro (1995), 133.
20. Adan-Bayewitz (1993), 127,192.
21. Lofreda (1979), 32.
22. Meyers, et al. (1976), 193.
23. Yadin (1963), 48.
24. Tessaro (1995), 133.
25. Some of the shovels with the triple ridge design were reportedly coming from Hauran area and also in Pompeii and Herculaneum; see Yadin (1963a), 54–58, pls. 15, 16, 28.
26. Yadin (1963a), fig. 14, shovel no. 5–57.23.
27. Yadin (1963a), fig. 14, shovel no. 5–57.23.
28. We gratefully acknowledge the Raphael Institute and its laboratory director, Dr. David Gorney, and laboratory operator, Mrs. Hana Ziv, for their kind and helpful support.
29. Yadin (1963), p. 48, n. 21.
30. Arav (1995a0, 21.
31. Yadin (1963), n. 22.
32. This is most probably the *Pinkha,* in Hebrew (פנכה), that means small bowls.
33. Josephus, *Wars,* book 5:562–64, translated by Thackeray.
34. Arav (1995a), 1:11.
35. The column bases in Zincirli are slightly smaller. One is 25 cm high and 38 cm in diameter, and the other is 25 cm high and 45 cm in diameter. See Koldewey (1898), fig. 90; republished by Naumann (1995), p. 130, fig. 123 (third and fifth figures from the top).
36. Arav (1995a), 22-27.
37. Arav (1995a), 22-27.
38. Arav (1995a), 12.
39. See Biran, (1994b), 1–17.
40. Three layers of pavement were distinguished. See Arav (1995a), 24-27.
41. The *Pataekos* is published in a separate article; see Arav and Bernett (1997).
42. These features are suggested by H. Frankfort as the main features of a bit Hilani style palace. See Frankfort (1996), 282–90.
43. Brandl (1995), 141–64.
44. See London and Shuster in this book.
45. A detailed discussion on the Bit Hilani in Bethsaida and those in Northern Syria will be published by Arav and Bernett. This table was prepared by Monika Bernett.
46. See also Fritz (1983) and Mazar (1990), 378–79.
47. Biran (1992), 4–6.
48. See S. Gutman (1993), 459ff.
49. Schearing ((1992), 429–30.
50. See Arav and Bernett (1997).
51. Herodotus, book 3, p. 37
52. An anchor similar to this but without the crossing bar was found not far from the boat discovery at Magdala. See Wachsmann (1990), 107–10.
53. The kitchen and the courtyard of the house were discovered in 1992–93 and are reported briefly in Arav (1995a),29–34; selected finds are on 51–52.
54. A similar key made of bronze was found by Y. Yadin in the cave of the letters in the Judean desert; see Yadin (1963), 67.
55. Z. Yeivin (1993), 302–303.

56. In many other places (e.g., Megiddo, Gezer), whenever there was an offset at the outer line of the city wall, there was an inset at the inner line of the wall, which retains the width of the city wall equally. The Bethsaida technique is different and was also observed in Tel Dan; see Biran (1992), 14:4–6.
57. This figurine is made of stone from Tel Amrit and is in the national Museum in Damascus; see Klengel (1980), fig. 79.
58. The observation and analysis were carried out at the offices of Antiquity Authorities in Jerusalem and were communicated orally to BEP. We thank Dr. Y. Goren for his preliminary report.
59. A Hellenistic coin dating to Antiochus III, 223–187 BCE was discovered in the vicinity of the jar. See Arie Kindler's coin report in this volume. A full report on the finds of the locus is being prepared by Sandra Fortner and will be published in this series.
60. See Yadin (1963), 61
61. We have suggested that this place be identified with the biblical Zer in Joshua 19:35; see Arav (1995b), 193–201.
62. For their own reasons, the Assyrians did not always retain the old capitals after they conquered other kingdoms, but sometimes established new capitals for local governors. Examples are Megiddo and Ramoth Gilead. See Aharoni and Avi-Yonah (1993), fig. 151.
63. See Kochavi (1996), 184–201.

## LITERATURE CITED

Adan-Bayewitz, David. 1993. *Common Pottery in Roman Galilee: A Study in Local Trade.* Ramat Gan, Israel: Bar Ilan University Press.

Aharoni, Yohanan, and Avi-Yonah, Michael. 1993. *Macmillan Bible Atlas.* New York: Macmillan.

Ahlstrom, Gosta W. 1993. *The History of Ancient Palestine.* Minneapolis: Fortress Press.

Arav, Rami. 1994. Julia the Mother of God: First Century CE Roman Imperial Cult in Palestine, in *AAR/SBL Abstracts Annual Meeting 1994.* Atlanta: Scholars Press.

———. 1995a. Bethsaida Excavations, Preliminary Report, 1987–1993, in Arav and Freund (1995) (q.v.), 3–63.

———. 1995b. Bethsaida and the Fortified Cities of Naphtali, in Arav and Freund (1995) (q.v.), 193–201.

Arav, Rami, and Richard A. Freund. 1995. *Bethsaida: A City by the North Shore of the Sea of Galilee.* Vol. 1. Kirksville, Mo.: Thomas Jefferson University Press.

———, and Monika Bernett. 1997. An Egyptian Figurine of Pataekos at Bethsaida, IEJ 47:3–4, 198–213.

Biran, Avraham. 1992. *Tel Dan.* Excavations and Surveys in Israel. Vol. 14. Jerusalem: Israel Department of Antiquities.

———. 1994a. *Dan, 25 shenot hafirot be-Tel Dan.* English: *Biblical Dan.* English version, Joseph Shadur. Jerusalem: Israel Exploration Society; Hebrew Union College; Jewish Institute of Religion.

———. 1994b. Tel Dan: Biblical Texts and Archaeological Data, in M. D. Coogan, J. C. Exum, L. E. Stager, *Scripture and Other Artifacts: Essays on the Bible and Archaeology in Honor of Philip J. King.* Louisville: Westminster John Knox Press, 1–17.

Brandl, Baruch. 1995. An Israelite Bulla in Phoenician Style from Bethsaida (et-Tell), in Arav and Freund (1995) (s.v.), 141–156.

Butler, H. C. 1907–1922. *Ancient Architecture of Syria.* Publication of the Princeton University Archaeological Expedition to Syria in 1904–1905 and 1909, Vol. IIA–B. Leiden.

Dar, Simon. 1993. Hermon, Mount, in Stern (1993) (q. v.), 2:616–17.

Fletcher, Banister. 1987. *A History of Architecture.* 19th edition, ed. John Musgrove. London: Butterworth.

Frankfort, Henri. 1996. *The Art and Architecture of the Ancient Orient.* New Haven: Yale University Press.

Freedman, David Noel, ed. 1992. *Anchor Bible Dictionary.* New York: Doubleday.

Fritz, Volkmar. 1983. Die syrischen Bauformen des Hilani und die Frage seiner Verbreitung. *Damaszener Mitteilungen* 1:43–58.

Gutman, Shmaryahu. 1993. Gamala, in Stern (1993) (q.v.), 2:459–63.

Herodotus. 1982. *The History.* Translated by William Sheperd. Cambridge: Cambridge University Press.

Josephus, Flavius. [*Works,* English & Greek, 1958–]. Loeb Classical Library. 9 vols. Trans. H. St. J. Thackeray. Cambridge, Mass.: Harvard University Press; London: W. Heinemann, 1958–1965.

Kindler, Arie. 1989. "The Coins of the Tetrarch Philippus and Bethsaida," *Cathedra for the History of Eretz-Israel and its Yishuv* no. 53 (September). Jerusalem (Hebrew).

Klengel, Horst. 1980. *Geschichte und Kultur Altsyriens.* Wien: Schroll.

Kochavi, Moshe. 1996. The Land of Geshur: History of a Region in the Biblical Period, in *Eretz Israel* 25: 184–201 (Hebrew).

Koldewey, Robert. 1898. *Ausgrabungen in Sendschirli.* Vol. 2. Berlin.

Kuhn, Heinz-Wolfgang, and Rami Arav. 1991. The Bethsaida Excavations, Historical and Archaeological Approaches, in: *The Future of Early Christianity: Essays in Honor of Helmut Koester.* Ed. B. A. Pearson. Minneapolis: Fortress Press.

Loffreda, Stanislao. 1974. *La Ceramica Cafarnao.* Vol. 2. Jerusalem.

Mazar, Amihai. 1990. *Archaeology of the Land of the Bible, 10,000-586 BCE.* New York: Doubleday.

Myers, Eric M., C. L. Kraabel, and J. F. Strange. 1976. *Ancient Synagogue Excavations at Khirbet Shema', Upper Galilee, Israel, 1970–1972.* Durham, NC: ASOR, 42:193–96.

Naumann, Rudolf. 1955. *Architektur Kleinasiens von ihren Anfangen bis zum Ende der spathethitischen Zeit.* Tubingen: Verlag Ernst Wasmuth.

Negev, Avraham. 1986. *The Late Hellenistic and Early Roman Pottery of Nabataean Oboda: Final Report.* Quedem Series 22, no. 14. Jerusalem: Hebrew University Institute of Archaeology.

Robertson, D. S. 1969. *Green and Roman Architecture.* Cambridge: Cambridge University Press.

Schearing, L. 1992. Maachah, in Freedman (1992) (q.v.), 4:429–30.

Shiloh, Yigal. 1992. Jerusalem, in Stern (1993) (q.v.), 2:701-12.

Strickert, Fred. 1995. "The Coins of Philip, " in Arav and Freund (1995), 165–89.

Tadmor, Hayim. 1994. *The Inscriptions of Tiglath Pileser III, King of Assyria.* Jerusalem: Israel Academy of Sciences and Humanities.

Tessaro, Toni. 1995. Hellenistic and Roman Ceramic Cooking Ware from Bethsaida, in Arav and Freund (1995), q.v., 127–34.

Wachsmann, Shelley. 1990. *The Excavations of an Ancient Boat in the Sea of Galilee (Lake Kinneret).* Atiqot: English series, no. 9. Jerusalem: Israel Antiquities Authority.

Yadin, Yigael. 1963. *Judean Desert Studies: The Finds from the Bar Kokhba Period in the Cave of Letters.* Judean Desert Studies Series. Jerusalem: Israel Exploration Society.

———. 1963b. *The Art of Warfare in Biblical Lands in the Light of Archaeological Study.* 2 vols. Trans. M. Perlman. Jerusalem: International Publishing.

———. 1993. Hazor, in Stern (1993) (q.v.), 2:594–603.

Yeivin, Zeev. 1993. Chorazin, in Stern (1993) (q.v.), 1:301–304.

*John F. Shroder, Jr., Michael P. Bishop,*
*Kevin J. Cornwell, Moshe Inbar*

# Catastrophic Geomorphic Processes and Bethsaida Archaeology, Israel

T HE LOCATION OF THE ANCIENT CITY OF BETHSAIDA has been disputed for nearly sixteen hundred years. Some traditions concerning the site survived in medieval and local Bedouin lore, but by and large the people who searched for the place through the centuries were unable to definitively declare its location. In the late nineteenth and early twentieth centuries, however, et-Tell, a mound of debris several kilometers northeast of the edge of the Sea of Galilee, was recognized as the most probable location, although other small ruins nearby were cited by some as possible contenders. Beginning in 1987, it remained for the University of Haifa and our Bethsaida Excavation Project to assess the immediate region, probe the ruins, begin major excavations, and determine the geomorphic evolution of the region.

Shroder and Inbar (1995) provided the geologic and geographic background to the Bethsaida site. They were able to show, through their tripartite shoreline-change model, that the Beteiha Plain coastline at Bethsaida had shifted from an estuarine or lagoonal environment to dry land. This occurred through some combination of uplift of the land along the great Dead Sea–Jordan rift or transform fault system ("shore-up" hypothesis), change of water level in the unstable Sea of Galilee ("water-down" hypothesis), and building out of the shoreline in the Jordan delta past Bethsaida ("shore-out" hypothesis).

115

The latter two hypotheses of unstable water levels and delta growth also showed the high improbability that the el-Araj site on the lake and delta edge could date back to the time of Bethsaida, confirmed also by the archaeological probes. Unexplained, however, were the details of the original formation of open water at Bethsaida, and the eventual elimination of the estuarine environment. It is the purpose of this paper to show how the stratigraphy and landforms of the Beteiha Plain relate to catastrophic and noncatastrophic geomorphic processes associated with parts of the Jordan River and Sea of Galilee in late Pleistocene and Holocene times.

## Dead Sea – Jordan Rift Fault System

The geological setting and background of the Dead Sea–Jordan (Levant) transform fault system is fundamental to understanding the very great effects upon human history in the region that this profound crustal discontinuity represents. Recognition that this area is alone in the world in having the longest written record of earthquakes provides us a unique data set to interpret associated geomorphologic and archaeologic phenomena (Garfunkel et al. 1981; Russell 1980, 1985; Ben-Menahem 1991).

The geometry of the faults surrounding the Sea of Galilee indicates that it formed under extension of the Earth's crust, perhaps as a pull-apart basin along an offset in the greater Levant transform fault system. In detail, a plethora of major and minor faults make up the rift system in the direct vicinity of Bethsaida, but with the overall east region moving generally north, and the west region moving generally south (left-lateral movement). Within this context there is a good deal of up and down and rotational motion as well (Heimann and Baer 1995; see fig. 1).

Directly to the north of the Sea of Galilee, the Korazim and Yehudiyya plateaus, on the west and east respectively, reflect overall uplift along both sides of the fault system in this area. The fault system here is comprised predominantly by the main Jordan fault in the Jordan River gorge and the Almagor fault a few kilometers to the west on the edge of the Korazim plateau. Both faults are left-lateral strike-slip faults (Heimann 1990, 1995); however, they differ in that almost no differential vertical uplift is known for the Jordan fault, whereas the Almagor fault has up to 150 meters of vertical offset (Heimann and

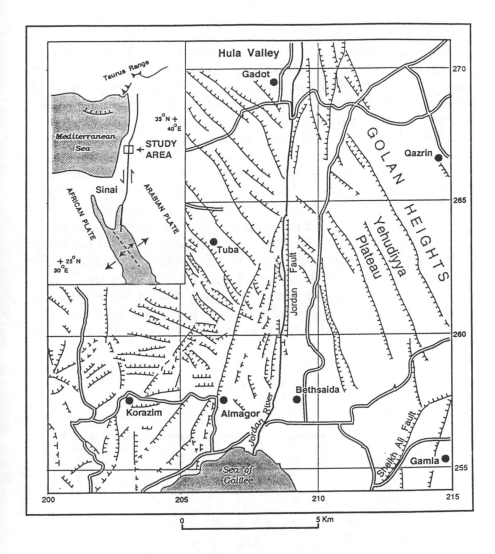

Figure 1. Map of faults in Jordan gorge and on Korazim and Yehudiyya Plateaus between Hula Valley and Sea of Galilee (after Heimann, 1995).

Baer 1995), assuming that tectonism and not mass movement was the primary displacing agent. Morphological observations, archaeological evidence, and recent seismic activity indicate late Holocene or historical to ongoing activity on the Almagor and Jordan faults (Heimann 1990, 1995).

ATERET FORTRESS OFFSET

The Crusader castle of Ateret was established in 1178 CE about 1 km south of the present Benot Ya'aqov bridge and 10 km north of Bethsaida (fig. 2; table 1). Its walls and associated water ducts have been variously affected by the Jordan fault since their construction (Agnon 1995). Direct lateral offset as much as 2.1 meters as well as bending suggest both single seismic episode displacement as well as possible slow creep. Either condition is reflective of long-term rates of local deformation by which we may better assess possible upwarping conditions at nearby Bethsaida. Most of the observed fault displacement at Ateret was thought by Agnon (1995) to be best explained by a single large earthquake. The large seismic event recorded throughout the Levant, which occurred in 1202, was suggested as a good candidate, although other significant earthquakes in 1546, 1759, and 1837 were also recognized as possible times of ground rupture in rapid lateral movement. From the point of view of the Bethsaida Project, however, the significance of an offset of 2.1 meters in the past 818 years, since construction of the fort, is that this enables us to better appreciate pos-

Table 1: Geomorphologic subdivisions of the upper Jordan River valley between the Hula Depression and the Sea of Galilee (fig. 2).

| |
|---|
| Hula Paleo-Embayment Geomorphic Control |
|    Gadot and Benot Ya'aqov Formation carbonate and clastic-controlled topography |
| Jordan and Almagor Rift Fault Control |
|    Upper canyon incision |
|    Large slope failures (Tuba I & II) |
|    Catastrophic flood landforms (boulder fans and terraces) |
|    Unstable ground between Jordan and Almagor faults; shutter ridges |
|    Small slope failures (post-1968 flood) |
| Lake Lisan and Sea of Galilee Paleo-Embayment Geomorphic Control |
|    Upper (Lisan) embayment boulder braided fan pattern |
|    Middle (Lisan) embayment sand-braided delta fan pattern |
|    Western Beteiha Plain (Sea of Galilee embayment) meander delta fan pattern |
|    Modern Jordan delta |

sible uplift and downwarp rates at the edge of the Sea of Galilee near Bethsaida.

The top of a black, organically rich clay layer noted at Bethsaida by Shroder and Inbar (1995) is indicative of quiet water estuarine conditions there. This black, organically rich clay is at the extreme outer edge of the 2-to-3-km-wide Beteiha Plain, itself clearly emergent from the Sea of Galilee through differential uplift and outward delta building. Radiocarbon dates of 2455 to 2035 years BP (table 2) for the top of the black, organically rich clay and its present-day position about 5 meters above the existing level of the Sea of Galilee would require an uplift rate of ~2.22 mm yr$^{-1}$ to move the black, organically rich clay up out of the water at the level of the present Sea of Galilee to its present position. Shroder and Inbar (1995) instead had hypothesized a possible uplift rate of about 1 mm per year at Bethsaida, based on known rates of long-term downwarping of the Galilee basin. It was thought that the uplift of the Beteiha Plain could have been at an approximately similar rate, albeit in the opposite sense of motion. Although the lateral offset rate at the Crusader fort is certainly not directly equatable to an uplift rate at Bethsaida, still it can be seen that high rates are possible in this area, whether produced in a single abrupt seismic event or in long-term creep laterally or vertically upward or downward. We hypothesize that some uplift at the Bethsaida site probably decreased water depths over time and raised the black, organically rich clay above the present level of the lake. Some other high-energy factor, however, clearly produced the boulder gravels that both underlie and overlie the estuarine muds. In this context, catastrophic floods were seen to be the only possible surficial process capable of producing such deposits.

## CATASTROPHIC FLOODS

The most significant result from fieldwork conducted during the summers of 1994 and 1995, was the discovery of the importance of the Tuba I and Tuba II slope failures (fig. 2; table 3 ) that had first been noted by Harash and Bar (1988). Our field investigations and laser theodolite measurements indicated that these large landslides had originally dammed the Jordan River. This would have impounded a significant volume of water behind each landslide dam. Slope failures creating natural dams are very common in environments exhibiting steep slopes where external factors such as seismic and/or precipita-

Figure 2. Geo-
morphological
map of Jordan
gorge showing
fault geomorphic
controls, chief
landforms, paleo-
embayments
extending south
from the Hula
Valley and north
from the Sea of
Galilee, and loca-
tions of boulder
fields, radio-
carbon dates, and
chief archaeologi-
cal sites. Table 2
lists the geomor-
phological subdi-
visions displayed
on this map.

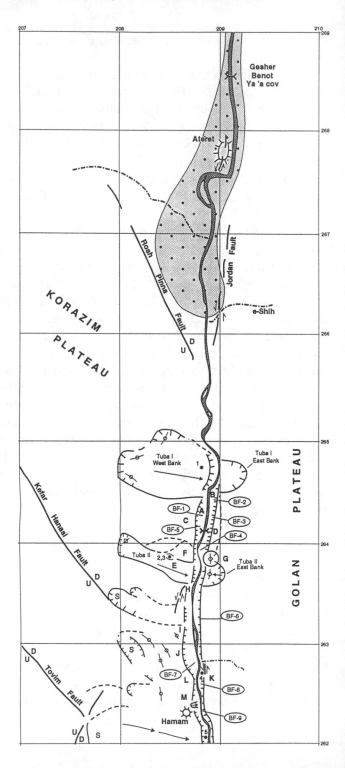

BF-1
Boulder Field
Measurements

- - -
Trace of Landform

Escarpment

Less Eroded Slump Block

More Eroded Slump Block

D
U
Fault with Downthrow
and Upthrow

Wadi (dry valley)

Fault with Lateral Motion

S
Slump or
Down-dropped block

A-P
Terrace

Slope Failure
Movement Direction

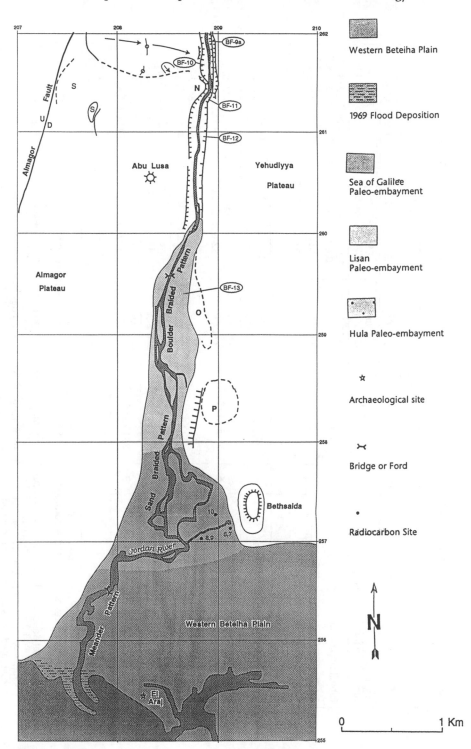

Table 2: Radiocarbon dates for material from Jordan River gorge and Beteiha Plain. Site numbers located on fig. 2

| Location Material | Site No. | 14C Date (yr BP)[a] | Calibrated calendrical mean date[b] (yr BP) (yr BCE/CE)[c] | 1 sigma[d] calibrated yr BP calibrated yr BCE/CE | 2 sigma[e] calibrated yr BP calibrated yr BCE/CE |
|---|---|---|---|---|---|
| **Jordan River Gorge** | | | | | |
| Tuba I slope failure soil pit @ 1.7m | 1 | 7965 ±340 | 8369 BP 6420 BCE | 8854–8013 BP 6904–6063 BCE | 9276–7683 BP 7326–5733 BCE |
| Tuba II slope failure slip plane clay | 2 | 11,070 ±145 | 12,601 BP 10,652 BCE | 12,753–12,434 BP 10,803–10,484 BCE | 12,899–12,233 BP 10,949–10,283 BCE |
| Tuba II slope failure bedded slope gravel beneath slip plane | 3 | 2295 ± 485 | 1882 BP 68 CE | 2475–1326 BP 525 BCE–624 CE | 3076– 884 BP 1126–1066 BCE |
| Terrace K paleosol above flood boulders | 4 | >20,500 | | | |
| Hamam slope failure slip plane clay | 5 | 9040 ±630 | 9652 BP 7703 BCE | 10,360–8963 BP 8410–7013 BCE | 11,325–8172 BP 9375–6222 BCE |
| **Beteiha Plain** | | | | | |
| Bethsaida spring bone @ 0.5m in lacustrine clay beneath flood gravels[f] | 6 | 2035 ±170 | 1575 BP 375 CE | 1798–1386 BP 152 BCE–564 CE | 1979–1250 BP 29 BCE–700 CE |
| Bethsaida spring organic lacustrine clay @ 0.5m beneath flood gravels[f] | 7 | 2455 ±90 | 2087 BP 138 BCE | 2190–1966 BP 240–16 BCE | 2315–1864 BP 365 BCE–86 CE |
| SLP 32 lacustrine clay @ 1.94m | 8 | 3450 ±50 | 3327 BP 1378 BCE | 3365–3257 BP 1415–1307 BCE | 3424–3200 BP 1474–1250 BCE |
| SLP 32 bivalve shells @ 4.22m | 9 | 8310 ±65 | 8866 BP 6917 BCE | 8949–8686 BP 6999–6736 BCE | 8989–8564 BP 7039–6614 BCE |
| SLP 12 bivalve shells @ 3m | 10 | 15,040±170 | 17,526 BP 15,577 BCE | 17,732–17,320 BP 15,783–15,370 BCE | 17,936–17,108 BP 15,986–15,158 BCE |

a. Back-calculate dates from before the present (BP) starting at 1950 CE.
b. Radiocarbon dates are calibrated according to Stuiver &Pearson (1986), Pearson & Stuiver (1986), and Stuiver & Reimer (1993); method A was used.
c. Calendrical designator BC (before Christ) = BCE (before common era); AD (anno Domini/year of our Lord)) = CE (common era).
d. 1 sigma = 68.3% chance that real date will fall within this range of one standard deviation from the mean.
e. 2 sigma = 95.4% chance that real date will fall within this range of two standard deviations from the mean.
f. Uncalibrated dates reported in Shroder and Inbar, 1995.

Table 3: Morphologic characteristics of Tuba I and Tuba II slope failure complexes

| MORPHOLOGIC CHARACTERIS-TIC | TUBA I | | TUBA II | |
|---|---|---|---|---|
| | West Bank | East Bank | West Bank | East Bank |
| Altitude of crown | 200 m a.m.s.l | 140 m | 195 m a.m.s.l. | 50 m |
| Altitude of toe | 0 m a.m.s.l. (sea level) | 0 m a.m.s.l. (sea level) | -60 m b.m.s.l. | -60 b.m.s.l. |
| Length | 875 m | 225 m | 775 m | 175 m |
| Width | 475 m | 250 m | 150–200 m | 200 m |
| Area | 288,000 m$^2$ | 53,000 m$^2$ | 58,000 m$^2$ | 13,000 m$^2$ |
| Thickness | ~50 m | ~25 m | ~30 m | ~25 m |
| Volume | 14.5 x 10$^6$m$^3$ | 1.3 x 10$^6$m$^3$ | 1.7 x 10$^6$m$^3$ | 3.25 x 10$^5$m$^3$ |

tion events can initiate slope failure (Code and Sirhindi 1986; Costa and Schuster 1988). Water flowing over the top of each dam would quickly erode and transport large quantities of sediment, initiating dam failure and catastrophic flooding. Consequently, a major objective of our fieldwork was to identify geologic evidence of catastrophic flooding within the Jordan gorge to assess its effects on the Beteiha Plain.

## Methodology

Discovery of the unusual slope failures, flood boulders, and associated landforms in the gorge of the Jordan River, and the stratigraphy in the Beteiha Plain (Shroder and Inbar 1995) necessitated a multifaceted approach to better understand the complex morphology and chronology of the area. We used geomorphological mapping, subsurface stratigraphic reconstruction, granulometry, paleontology, radiometric age dating, geographic information system technology, and hydrologic computer modeling of catastrophic floods using the BREACH and HEC–2 computer simulation programs to analyze the problems. The integration of these approaches enabled us to understand and reconstruct original environmental conditions.

### Geomorphological Mapping

Aerial photographs and large-scale (1:10,000) topographic maps were used to map geomorphology. The topographic maps were produced in

1966, three years prior to the devastating flood of 1969 in which 214 m$^3$ s$^{-1}$ of water in the Jordan River altered the topography of the gorge by eroding many new scarps along the river's edge (Inbar 1974, 1977, 1982, 1987; Inbar and Even-Nir 1989; Inbar and Schick 1979). We remapped topographic changes and used laser theodolite measurements to produce more accurate and detailed landform maps and cross sections (fig. 2). In our geomorphological mapping we concentrated upon structural, mass movement, and fluvial boulders and landforms in order to better understand the subsurface stratigraphy we encountered.

Fieldwork in 1994 and 1995 consisted of examination of the geologic evidence for flooding, and the collection of data required for hydrologic computer simulations. Consequently, fieldwork consisted of mapping the patterns of erosion and identifying depositional features. Data acquisition involved ground photography and the use of global positioning system (GPS) technology to ensure accurate location information. Specifically, we were interested in identifying high-water marks in the gorge which represent minimum estimates of the maximum flood stages associated with the larger Tuba I slope failure event. These locations represent control points which were used to verify the results of computer simulations. In addition, we recorded general information regarding the characteristics of the gorge such as cross section configuration, landscape complexity, water-flow constriction locations, elevated boulder deposits, and boulder field locations in the bottom of the gorge (fig. 2).

Mapping of boulder deposits also involved measuring the long axis (a-axis), intermediate axis (b-axis), and thickness (c-axis) of individual boulders. Fifty of the largest boulders for each boulder field were sampled. The data were used to generate hydraulic estimates of mean velocity, shear stress, and stream power. A flow competence equation (Komar 1989) provided a relatively simple evaluation of a flood's mean-flow shear stress from the diameter of transported boulders:

$$\tau = 0.045 \ (ps\text{-}p) \ g \ D_{50}^{0.65} D_{bi}^{0.35} \qquad (1)$$

where: $\tau$ = mean-flow shear stress having units of Newtons (N m$^{-2}$)

ps = relative density of the boulder clast

p = density of water

g = gravity

$D_{50}$ = median diameter of clasts in the sediment bed

$D_{bi}$ = intermediate axial diameter of the clast

Komar (1989) discussed some of the limitations associated with applying equation 1 to flow competence assessments. The equation is generally realistic with $D_{bi}/D_{50}$ ratios less than or equal to 22.0. Conversely, the equation is not valid using large $D_{bi}/D_{50}$ ratios. The largest boulders measured in the Jordan gorge were over 200 cm in diameter. Therefore, a $D_{50}$ value of at least 9 cm is required. We used estimates of $D_{50}$ ranging from 9 to 70 cm. Previous work indicated that mean bedload particle sizes for the Jordan and Meshoshim Rivers range from 10 to 70 cm (Inbar and Shick 1979). A conservative estimate of water density at 1 gm cm$^3$ was used. Highly sediment-laden waters can have higher densities (e.g. Lord and Kehew 1987). Standard flood modeling methodology, however, is to use conservative estimates, although smaller density estimates result in production of less conservative shear stress estimates.

Mean-flow velocities were generated using Costa's (1983) threshold velocity equation:

$$\upsilon = 0.18 \ D^{0.49} \qquad (2)$$

where: $\upsilon$ - refers to the threshold mean-flow velocity in m s$^{-1}$

D = intermediate particle diameter

Stream power refers to the power or time rate of energy expenditure per unit area of the stream bed and can be expressed as:

$$\omega = \tau\upsilon \qquad (3)$$

where: $\omega$ – refers to stream power in watts (W m$^{-2}$)

$\tau$ – shear stress

$\upsilon$ – velocity

These hydraulic parameters are important to examine in an attempt to characterize the local and spatial hydraulic conditions associated with transportation and deposition of boulders. The ability of rivers to erode and transport sediment is related to shear stress (Baker and Costa 1987), while the concept of stream power is intimately tied to sediment transport capability (Baker and Costa 1987). Therefore, the hydraulic parameters generated from geologic evidence were compared to hydraulic parameters generated from computer simulations in order to provide insight into the transportation and deposition of boulders in the gorge, although we were aware that multiple floods in the Jordan confound the task of differentiating which floods moved which boulders.

### STRATIGRAPHIC RECONSTRUCTION, GRANULOMETRY, AND PALEONTOLOGY

Following excavation of two backhoe trenches near the Bethsaida spring in 1993 and discovery of the black, organically rich clay there (Shroder and Inbar 1995), we decided the following year to put in twenty-four more backhoe trenches between the lakeshore and Bethsaida, and two deep boreholes near Bethsaida to sample the sediments and reconstruct the stratigraphy through vertical stratigraphic columns into standard fence diagrams.

### RADIOMETRIC AGE DATING

Radiocarbon dates on wood, bone, shells, soil humic matter, paleosols, and buried lacustrine organic matter were performed by conventional and accelerator mass spectrometer (AMS) techniques by Beta Analytic, Inc., of Miami, Florida; Geochron Laboratories of Krueger Enterprises, Inc., in Cambridge, Massachusetts; and The Weizmann Institute of Rehovot, Israel (table 2).

### GIS ANALYSIS

Geographic information system (GIS) technology was used to analyze the topographic characteristics associated with the damming of the Jordan River and subsequent water impoundments. A GIS database was developed using ARC/INFO software. All global positioning system (GPS) data and associated attribute information were imported. Point coverages were displayed depicting sample locations, control points, boulder fields, and terraces. We digitized a 1:10,000 topographic contour map along the entire length of the Jordan gorge, from the southern edge of the Hula Valley to the Sea of Galilee. This resulted in an arc coverage which was used to generate a triangular irregular network (TIN) model of the topography that we used for GIS analysis.

Water volume and surface area estimates for the Tuba I and II impoundments were generated by systematically increasing the water surface elevation in relation to the topography behind each of the landslide dams. An estimate of the time required for the water surface to reach the upper dam surface was calculated using modern-day average daily discharge estimates from the Jordan River and GIS volume estimates. Surface area and impoundment geometry information was required as input into computer simulations, to estimate the peak discharge and timing of dam failure.

## HYDROLOGIC COMPUTER MODELING

Our analysis involved computer modeling of hydrologic conditions in an attempt to simulate a first-order approximation of flood magnitudes. Two hydrologic models were used to characterize different aspects of the flood events. In this way, peak discharge estimates generated from both models could be compared. Specifically, the National Weather Service (NWS) BREACH model was used to initially estimate peak discharge based upon GIS analysis and water impoundment information. The model produced a flood hydrograph which was used to estimate the timing of dam failure. Once the dams were broken and the floods simulated, the Hydrologic Engineering Center HEC-2 hydrologic model developed by the U.S. Army Corps of Engineers was used to conduct water surface profile analysis. These simulations provided information regarding local hydraulic conditions and peak flood discharge.

## NWS BREACH MODEL

In an effort to determine the approximate peak discharges associated with the Tuba I and Tuba II slope failure dams, the BREACH dam break model was used. The computer program enables mathematical reconstruction of an earthen dam and simulates dam failure by the development of a trapezoidal breach. Simulations result in a peak discharge hydrograph. Simulations are based on the geometrical and physical properties of the dam itself, principles of hydraulics, soil mechanics,

Table 4: BREACH model input parameters for the Tuba I and Tuba II dam break

| Input Parameter | Units | TUBA I Value or Range | TUBA II value or Range | Justification |
|---|---|---|---|---|
| Initial elevation of water surface in reservoir | m | 49.69 | 34.83 | field measurements (overtopping failure) |
| Elevation of top of dam | m | 49.69 | 34.83 | field measurements |
| Inflow to reservoir | $m^3$ | 17.33 | 17.33 | modern flow |
| Time associated with reservoir inflow | hours | 103 | 57 | calculated |
| Surface area of reservoir | $m^2$ | $3\times10^5$ | $2.14\times10^5$ | GIS calculations |
| Elevation associated with surface area | m | 49.69 | 34.83 | field measurements |
| Top widths of tailwater sections | m | 0–360 | 0–159 | field measurements |
| Manning number | unitless | 0.035 | 0.035 | field estimation |
| Dam slopes | unitless | 1.0–2.5 | 1.0–2.5 | field estimation |
| $D_{50}$ of dam material | mm | 95–200 | 95–200 | Inbar (1989) |
| Porosity of dam material | unitless | 0.3–0.4 | 0.3–0.4 | literature estimate |
| Unit weight | $kg\ m^{-3}$ | 7.48–10.59 | 7.48–10.59 | literature estimate |
| Internal friction angle | unitless | 10–16 | 10–16 | Donovan (1996) |
| Cohesive strength | $kg\ m^{-2}$ | 0–4893 | 0–4893 | Haras and Bar (1988) |
| $D_{90}/D_{30}$ ratio | unitless | 4 | 4 | Inbar (1989) |
| Width of dam crest | m | 10.6 | 10.6 | field measurement |
| Length of dam crest | m | 219 | 212 | field measurement |
| Downstream channel slope | $m\ km^{-1}$ | 40.2 | 40.2 | field measurement |

sediment transport, and reservoir properties (table 4). The model is minimally sensitive to most of the numerical parameters but is most sensitive to the internal friction angle of the dam's materials, its cohesive strength, and the slope ratio of the upstream and downstream faces of the dam.

DAM FAILURE. The manner in which dam failure occurred for either Tuba I or Tuba II slope failure dams, whether as reservoir filling, overtopping and headward erosion, piping failure through the dam, or as an increase of internal pore pressure gradients to the point of complete hydrodynamic failure is unknown. Little modern evidence is available to indicate whether any or all of these conditions may have precipitated failure since most of the dams have been washed away. For our simulations we have chosen to assume that complete reservoir filling and overtopping precipitated the initial development of each breach. Subsequent erosion along the front of each dam face and into the sides of each breach eventually produced catastrophic failure. Reasonable estimates for sensitive input parameters were based on the following factors.

*Cohesive Strength:* Harash and Bar (1988) described the area in general as consisting of "irregular sequences of blocky, in places weathered, vesicular basalt flows with interlayered fat clay (fossil soil) and soft tuffs that also fill joints and voids within the rock." They characterized the existing cohesive properties of the materials in Tuba I and Tuba II as ranging from ~1950–3900 kg m$^{-2}$. It is quite likely that upon failure and deposition, the cohesive strength of slope failure material would have been lower as a result of the disruption to the sediment and soil internal matrices as well as positive pore pressures in saturated and undrained zones in the slope failure mass. Cohesive strength estimates between 0–4900 kg m$^{-2}$ were used in simulation runs.

*Internal Friction Angle:* Several springs are present at different elevations on the Tuba I and Tuba II slope failures, which indicates the occurrence of several groundwater horizons perched on locally clayey interbeds (Harash and Bar 1988). Whether or not these conditions occurred in the prelandslide condition is unknown, but the condition is probable. If the slope failures resulted from seismic activity, it is likely that saturated and near-saturated prelandslide materials, after shaking and settling, were under positive pore pressure gradients. Considering the relatively quick reservoir fill time and subsequent dam failure, little draining of these reorganized sediments would have been possible, with the result that the internal friction angle of the sediment, or the maximum angle at which frictional stress is maintained in the sediment matrix, would likely have been low (oral comm., R. Donovan 1996). The internal friction angle was varied between 10 and 16 degrees during the simulations.

$D_{50}$ *Grain Size:* Previous work on the smaller Jordan gorge landslides (Inbar 1989) provides a basis for estimating $D_{50}$ values, as it is difficult to accurately sample these large slope failures. Reasonable $D_{50}$

values, could range from ~95 mm to a maximum of 200 mm. Simulations were run using a $D_{50}$ estimate of 150 mm.

*Upstream and Downstream Dam Face Slopes:* The slopes of the upstream and downstream dam faces in the valley bottom have been largely removed by erosion. Modified slope fragments today measure close to 1-to-1 in places. Depending upon material types, natural slopes tend to form 2-to-1 or lower slope angles. We varied our simulations from 1-to -1 to 2.5-to-1.

## HEC-2 MODEL WATER SURFACE PROFILE ANALYSIS

The computer program HEC-2 was developed to calculate water surface profiles. It is designed to simulate water flow in natural and human-made channels. It has been used extensively by the engineering community (Chow 1959; Feldman 1981) and for geomorphological and paleohydrologic investigations (Ely and Baker 1985; Webb 1985; Jarrett and Malde 1987; Florsheim and Keller 1989; O'Connor 1993).

The model simulates changes in water surface elevation from cross section to cross section, based upon cross-section geometry and hydraulic parameter estimates. The program uses a numerical method called the "standard-step" or "step-backwater" computation (Hoggan 1989). The step-backwater method of modeling is based upon the principles of conservation of mass and the conservation of energy associated with one-dimensional flow (O'Connor 1993). Hoggan (1989) indicated that the model produces satisfactory results in many applications even though the model is based upon several simplifying assumptions.

Water flow through the Jordan channel was assumed to be steady. The distinction between steady and unsteady flow relates to constant or varying water depth, velocity, and discharge over time for a particular cross section. A steady-flow model can be used for catastrophic flood modeling because flood waves rise and fall gradually (Hoggan 1989) and reasonable first-order approximations can be obtained (O'Connor 1993). Similarly, gradually varied flow is also assumed. Varied flow represents changes in the water depth and velocity over longer distances along a stream. Rapidly varied flow occurs if depth and velocity dramatically change over a relatively short distance. Flow conditions are largely controlled by structural characteristics such as bedrock resistance and changes in the bottom slope and cross-section geometry. The model also assumes that river channels have small slopes (< 0.1). Inbar (1987) indicated that for the entire gorge reach, the average channel slope is 0.02, while slope values are 0.04 for 100 m reach lengths.

In order to compute water surface elevations, the program requires detailed information regarding flow geometry and hydraulic estimates. Specifically, data inputs include: cross-section geometry, reach lengths, loss coefficients, flow regime, starting water elevation, and discharge.

Cross sections represent channel boundary geometry for the analysis of flow, while reach lengths are the measured distances from cross section to cross section. Step-backwater calculations are particularly sensitive to channel geometry (O'Connor 1993) and cross sections must be adequately spaced and placed in order to account for expansions, constrictions, and changes in slope so that energy losses resulting from geometry are characterized. The basalt-bedrock-confined channel of the Jordan gorge represents an ideal environment for this analysis, as channel geometry is relatively stable, thereby reducing energy loss due to changing boundary conditions. Two reaches were identified as suitable for analysis, based upon model assumptions and the presence of geologic evidence for major flooding. Reach 1 represents a relatively short segment of the gorge immediately downstream from the Tuba I failure and extending to the Tuba II failure (fig. 2). Reach 2 represents a longer segment of the gorge ranging from Tuba II to a major constriction point at point N (see fig. 2) approximately 5 km downstream. All cross sections were digitized from a 1:10,000 scale topographic map. Interpolated cross sections were also utilized. Cross sections were evenly spaced within both reaches due to relatively homogeneous geometry, although expansions and constrictions were adequately represented. Reach lengths ranged from 20 to 100 meters.

Several types of energy loss coefficients are used by the program to calculate head losses and thereby to determine water surface elevation. The Manning's coefficient of roughness (n) is used to characterize the roughness of the channel that influences energy loss, velocity, and the magnitude of hydraulic parameters such as shear stress and stream power. Consequently, Manning's n composite estimate (0.048) was consistently assigned to cross sections based upon the estimation procedures of Chow (1959). Contraction and expansion of flow due to geometry changes also influence energy loss. Expanding and contracting flow from cross section to cross section along each reach was relatively small. Therefore, contraction and expansion coefficients of 0.0 and 0.0001 respectively were used.

The program also requires the selection of a water-flow regime. Flow regimes are subcritical, supercritical, or critical. All reaches were initially modeled assuming subcritical flow conditions. This assumption was tested by examining profile calculations. Computed water surface elevations are not permitted to cross critical depth. Consequently, initial flow regime assumptions are invalid if the program defaults to critical depth without balancing energy equations.

Initial water surface elevations were estimated using a range of elevations. Critical depth was used as one end of the range and normal depth as an intermediate value. Other estimates were based upon the local geological evidence. Discharge estimates were based upon results from BREACH simulations. Reasonable discharge estimates should result in the calculation of water surface elevations that approximate elevations interpreted from geologic evidence.

Output from computer simulations consisted of key hydrologic variables including water surface elevation, top width, velocity, energy slope, and conveyance ratio. Each variable was closely examined for each cross section to ensure that changes from cross section to cross section were reasonable. Significant changes in the magnitude of these variables from section to section may be the result of erroneous input and invalid modeling of energy losses (Hoggan 1989). In addition, the hydraulic parameters shear stress and stream power were compared to the same parameters calculated from boulder measurements. In this way, sediment transport conditions would provide insight into the ability of the flood to influence the downstream portion of the gorge.

Before the HEC-2 model was used to simulate the Tuba I and Tuba II flood events, it was calibrated based upon the observed and measured 1969 flood event. Inbar (1987) described the hydraulic conditions associated with the event and indicated that peak discharge was 214 m$^3$ s$^{-1}$ with maximum velocities of 6–7 m s$^{-1}$. Our simulation model was calibrated using the peak discharge of the 1969 flood to produce reasonable estimates of hydraulic conditions associated with the flood. It was then used to produce estimates of the hydraulic conditions and peak discharge of the larger Tuba I flood event.

GEOMORPHOLOGY OF THE JORDAN RIVER GORGE

The upper Jordan River passes from its sources in northern Israel and Lebanon, through the Hula Valley depression, before entering the upper Jordan gorge. Both sides of the Jordan River gorge are a volcanic plateau tilted down towards the Sea of Galilee. The river has cut down through the basalt lava layers and exposed the separate flows. Because of offset along the Levant transform fault system, no parallelism occurs between the different flows across the two sides of the gorge and correlation is not possible. The narrow basaltic canyon of the Jordan is about 10 km long and 800 meters wide, with a depth from the upland edge to the channel of about 200 to 250 meters. The left (east) bank of the Jordan gorge here is the lower Golan Heights, source of several volcanic centers which produced some of the Plio-Pleistocene basalt of the area. The right (west) bank is the Korazim plateau (Heimann 1995), which also covered with similar but slightly older basalt. The Jordan River exits from the gorge into a large embayment near Bethsaida and part of the western Beteiha Plain for about 4 km before spilling into the Sea of Galilee.

Inbar and Even-Nir (1989) noted that the longitudinal channel slope of the upper Jordan Gorge from the Hula Valley to the Sea of Galilee is 2 percent, from the +60 meters above mean sea level to -210 meters below mean sea level at mean lake level. Two basic morphologic units in the gorge were distinguished: the valley escarpments and the Jordan floodplain. The valley slopes are commonly greater than 15 degrees and are composed of multiple lava flows between 3 and 5 meters thick and intercalated with scoria and weathered basalts, all of which are overlain by colluvium, slope wash, and weathered mantles. A number of large and small slope failures occur in the gorge (Harash and Bar 1988; Inbar and Even-Nir 1989) and are the focus of much of our attention in this report. In addition a variety of polygenetic terraces produced by faulting, river erosion, deposition, and catastrophic floods occur along the lower valley walls and are discussed in detail below. The floodplain segments include the active channel about 10 to 15 meters wide and lower boulder terraces that were deposited and fluvially modified both in prehistoric and historic times.

Geomorphologically the upper Jordan gorge can be subdivided into a number of subsidiary geomorphic units that facilitate understanding (fig. 2, table 1). These subunits are controlled by basic underlying bedrock geology, different geomorphic events, and varying geo-historical development.

## Hula Paleo-Embayment Geomorphic Control

From north to south for ~4 km (Israeli map grid crossings 270–266), the upper Jordan gorge has been predominantly influenced by sedimentation controlled by the paleo-Hula depression. The rise and fall of ancestral Hula lake waters produced fluvial clastics and lacustrine carbonates of the Gadot Formation, the Benot Ya'aqov Formation, and other formations preserved there, which rift faulting subsequently fractured into fault blocks and inclined at various attitudes (Horowitz 1978; Goren-Inbar and Belitsky 1989; Goren-Inbar et al. 1992). The northern part of the gorge containing these soft sedimentary units is thus more shallow, open, and more gently sloping than farther south. Geomorphologically of course, this is the primary topographic reason that the ancient bridge (Geshur) Benot Ya'aqov was established in this location in antiquity as the major Jordan crossing point on the way to Damascus.

## Jordan and Almagor Rift Fault Geomorphic Control

From about grid crossing 266 to 265 the gorge is progressively more narrow and deeply incised, with a prominent fault-controlled shutter ridge closing the mouth of the Wadi e-Shih valley coming in from the east. From about grid crossing 265.1 to 263.6 are the massive Tuba I and Tuba II slope failures, which are discussed in detail below. Because these slope failures engendered temporary impoundment of the Jordan River and catastrophic breakout floods in antiquity, well-scoured bedrock, boulder fans, and boulder terraces occur along the gorge all the way from the slope failures to the canyon outlet at grid crossing 260.

This fault-controlled part of the upper Jordan gorge also has a number of other associated landforms that result from the convergence of the Almagor fault with the main Jordan fault at about the sites of the Tuba I and II slope failures. This 9-km-long and 2-km-wide triangular wedge of ground on the west wall of the Jordan gorge occurs between the two left-lateral transform faults. It is effectively being torn apart and rotated by the west side slipping north and the east side south. The ground between is replete with undrained graben-like depressions, horstlike ridges subparallel with the gorge, shutter ridges, mass-movement features, springs, and other indications of long-term tectonic and slope instability. In fact the ubiquitous down-dropped blocks or sag ponds, undrained depressions behind slump blocks, and other hummocky and undrained topography are characteristic of both mass movement and fault-related geomorphic genesis, which makes landform differentiation of the two genetic types impossible in many locations. For example, directly south of the Tuba II slope failure, four major down-dropped blocks occur within 3 km. All have arcuate headscarps and wrinkle ridges or slump blocks oriented across slope, with zones of slope failure in which movement has been from west to east and downslope into the Jordan gorge. It is clear that the Almagor fault has ruptured the bedrock and set up the right (west) bank of the Jordan for massive slope failure (fig. 3). In fact a good case can be made that much of the postulated vertical motion on the Almagor fault (Heimann 1995) may actually have a significant mass movement component to it. In any case such mass movement has occurred many times, some of it certainly in response to seismicity but other examples probably because of high magnitude precipitation events. In addition, on both sides of the lower walls of the gorge next to the floodplain, numerous subsidiary slope failures (rock falls, debris falls) occurred in response to undercutting by the catastrophic flood of 1969 in which peak flows of 214 m$^3$ s$^{-1}$ nearly doubled to quadrupled normal peak flows.

## LAKE LISAN AND SEA OF GALILEE PALEO-EMBAYMENT GEOMORPHIC CONTROL

From the Jordan gorge outlet at grid crossing 260, to 4.5 km south to the Sea of Galilee at 255.5, the fluvial geomorphology is largely controlled by prior higher levels of Lake Lisan in the late Pleistocene time period and by the minor vertical fluctuations of the paleo-Sea of Galilee for the past 10,000 years of Holocene time (fig. 2). Thus in the grid square 260 to 259, where the gradient changes abruptly coming out of the Jordan gorge, clays from ancient Lake Lisan 5 meters below the surface at the broken bridge crossing (itself at about -165 meters altitude) show that the Jordan River of Lisan time would have had to drop all of its coarse load above that point, and probably somewhat back into the gorge as well. Later as the level of Pleistocene Lake Lisan declined, this coarser load would have extended out over the Lisan lake clays. In aggregate this produced a narrow fan-shaped deposit

Figure 3. Rounded flood boulders overlain by paleosol, slip-plane clays, and uppermost slope failure gravels of the Hamam area, occurring between terraces M and N (figure 2). The person has his hand on site 5 material that dates to about 9040±630 [14]C yr B.P. (table 2). Unknown is whether or not this slope failure blocked the Jordan River for a time, but it certainly added to gravel and boulder sedimentation downstream on the Jordan River floodplain and the Beteiha Plain.

about 300 meters wide at the head of the Lisan paleo-embayment that Inbar (1989) mapped as a "boulder braided pattern." Rock-cut terrace O (fig. 2) on the east side of this area may be either an early wave-formed feature from Lake Lisan or a later strath produced by lateral planation of the Jordan River flowing off a formerly higher fan surface here.

From grid crossing 259 for 2 km downstream to the Bethsaida tel where the valley widens to as much as 1.1 km east to west, the gradient of the Jordan continues to decrease. Sediment has been deposited there in a "sand braided pattern" (Inbar 1989). The Jordan floodplain in the Galilee paleo-embayment at Bethsaida covers Lisan clays several meters down that we have dated at ~15,000 $^{14}$C yr. BP, overlain by Galilee clays at about 0.5 meters depth that we dated at ~2000 to ~2500 $^{14}$C yr BP (Shroder and Inbar 1985 and table 2). The lower, older clays are clearly a result of deposition in the higher waters of Lake Lisan. As previously mentioned however, the younger clays occur ~5 meters above the present level of the Sea of Galilee, which means that they must have been uplifted since deposition because the Sea of Galilee cannot have been that much higher 2,000 years ago or it would have drowned such ports as Tiberias, which we know did not happen. To further explain the anomalous high position of these young clays without resorting to an uplift hypothesis, Shroder and Inbar (1995) also hypothesized a possible fluvial gradient starting with lagoonal clays in a protected fluvial backwater and thence down a riverine slope of the Jordan and into the Sea of Galilee.

From the Sea of Galilee embayment at Bethsaida and across the northwestern edge of the Beteiha Plain to the lakeshore, the Jordan River channel morphology changes into more of the "meander pattern" of Inbar (1989). In this case the channel deepens to several meters, widens to several tens of meters, and assumes more of a single winding channel than the upstream braid pattern. This change is probably a reflection of the close base level of the Sea of Galilee as well as of the more restricted erosion afforded by the sticky, cohesive, and water-retentive montmorillonitic lake clays characteristic of the Beteiha Plain. An uppermost thin (<0.5 m) layer of gravel and small boulders extends across the lake clays from near Bethsaida to the lakeshore and is the result of past catastrophic floods that have swept across the lake plain from the Jordan and the Meshoshim Rivers, including the flood of 1969 (Inbar 1974; Shroder and Inbar 1995).

## Slope Failure Geomorphology

The catastrophic floods generated by the damming of the Jordan River, impoundment of significant water bodies upstream, eventual overtopping of slope failure dams, and water breakouts significantly altered the stratigraphy and geomorphology of the Jordan gorge and Beteiha Plain at least twice. Exposition of these failures and the flood events each generated enable better determination of the processes and chronology by which the lagoonal areas at Bethsaida were first produced and then later destroyed. The Tuba I and Tuba II slope-failure complexes each consist of a west bank main failure into the bottom of the Jordan gorge, a flood breakout escarpment on both sides of the gorge bottom, and a flood-produced, east bank failure back into the gorge. Their shared morphologic characteristics attest to a similitude of process but not of chronology as the soils on Tuba I are much thicker and more extensively developed than those on Tuba II.

Tuba I Slope Failure

At 14.5 x $10^6$ m$^3$, this massive slope-failure complex on the west bank is the largest of the Jordan gorge landslides (table 3). The rocky main scarp is ~50 meters high and includes a subsidiary scarp of similar height to the north. Thick, partially vegetated bouldery lobes of talus occur below each. Both west-bank escarpments have at their bases large back-tilted slump blocks 150 to 200 meters long with rounded summits. The north scarp has only one large block and the south main scarp has two near the top and at least four more downslope. The toe of the failure is large, lobate, and nearly horizontal on its top high above the Jordan River (fig. 4).

The material of this slope failure is largely basalt boulders, although considerable fine-grained scoria, weathered basalt fragments, and clays make up the matrix as well. A complex slope failure (Varnes 1978) is a combination of types of material and types of movement. In this case, the movement is basically that of a slump block and rock slide, although a case could be made that rock comminution in transport, coupled with pre- and postslide weathering, actually make this failure a slump and debris slide. In any case the mass occurs at about the convergence of the Almagor and Jordan faults, and was probably precipitated abruptly into the valley by a seismic event. At present the timing of this event is unknown, although the presence of thick soils on the slope failure attests to a considerable antiquity. Well-developed soils over a meter in thickness occur throughout the slide, with an organic A horizon of 60 to 65 cm and a rubified B horizon of 40 to 55 cm. Recurrent failures at the steep toe above the Jordan River

Figure 4.  View north to the toe of the Tuba I slope failure. Water was impounded behind this barrier on the opposite side almost to the skyline and behind where the dark shrub occurs in the center of the photo. The piles of boulders between the road and the slope-failure toe are large-clast remnants of terrace A (figure 2) deposited after the initial breakout flood and left behind following a recent gravel-pit operation there. The smaller boulder fields (BF-4 & BF-5; figure 2)) in the left foreground were partly remobilized in the 1969 flood.

have caused soil superposition in some places as one soil slid on top of another. Our original working hypothesis for the timing of the Tuba I slope failure was ~25,000 years old, based mainly upon thick soils but also upon the presence of Bronze Age pottery, stone structures, and older lithic materials on top of the slide. The bottom of one of the thick soils on the top of the toe provided a minimum date of 7965±340 [14]C yr BP (table 2), or about three times younger than we think the Tuba I failure really is. Greater timing certainty will have to await cosmogenic radionuclide dating of the olivine-rich basalt boulders on the failure surface or [14]C dating of organic material from slip planes beneath the slope failure, should such become available through natural or artificial excavation in the future.

The toe of the mass is ~50 to ~75 meters thick and clearly blocked the Jordan River when it was emplaced. The resulting impoundment backed water several kilometers up the Jordan River to a point just south of the Crusader castle of Ateret. Although the duration of such landslide impoundments is almost never very long (Costa and Schuster 1988), the water would have backflooded and saturated all banks, rock joints, scoria zones, and weathered basalts with which it came in contact. Eventually as water overtopped the slide mass, or perhaps broke through in piping failure as well, the breakout flood breached the toe and undercut both the west and east banks. As is common in such situations, the catastrophic dewatering of the east bank, coupled with its undercutting, then would have led directly to its failure as well. The resulting boulder and debris-laden flood wave would have poured down the Jordan gorge (figs. 5 and 6) and

Figure 5. View north from Hamam up the main breakout flood zone of the Jordan gorge to the Tuba I and Tuba II slope failures. Terrace L (fig. 2) in the foreground was swept across by floodwaters that rounded and imbricated boulders on terrace M nearby. Terrace K on the extreme right edge has flood boulders up to 20 m above the valley bottom.

Figure 6.  Terrace K with sloping bedded fluvial gravels that pass up and over the bedrock spur and Jordan rift fault beneath the tree. The arrow to the left of the tree is the site of the paleosol directly above the flood gravels that dates to >20,500 $^{14}$C yr B.P. (site 4; table 2).

debouched into the Lake Lisan embayment north of the Bethsaida peninsula. Unknown at present is how far this flood of boulders and coarse sediment progressed into the lake, although it is likely that a prior relatively curvilinear, embayed coastline would have been considerably altered with islands and bars of new gravel in it. We hypothesize that this new complex coastline configuration would have contained many new bays and backwaters that attracted early settlement nearby. The emerging town of Bethsaida would have then grown up on its peninsular site because of its strategic location, spring water, thoroughfare access, and rich livelihood opportunities in the new lagoons and surrounding arable lands (Shroder and Inbar 1995).

## Tuba II Slope Failure

In total volume the Tuba II slope failure on the west bank is about eight and a half times smaller than the Tuba I failure (table 3). Tuba II is also a complex slump and rock slide–debris slide, with a sharp angled, ~50-meter-long slump block at its head, zones of fresh boulder lobes in its midsection, and a lobate toe composed of boulders and considerable fine-grained weathered basalt material (fig. 7). On the left

Figure 7. Tuba II slope failure in 1994 prior to 9-m gully incision at the site of the arrow (terrace section E; fig. 2). Terrace section F (fig. 2) occurs beneath the box on the right-hand side and is bedded colluvial sediment emplaced prior to the Tuba II slide by slope processes. Terrace section F was partly overridden and concealed by the Tuba II slope failure.

(north) side of the toe a torrential rain in early spring of 1995 eroded a 9-meter-deep cut through the slope failure and into the bedrock beneath (section E). This fortuitous exposure and that of the flood-cut Terrace F another 100 meters directly downslope in the inner gorge of the Jordan enable establishment of a relative chronology of events here (fig. 8, table 5).

The interpretation of the stratigraphy of section E is that weathered corestones developed from the basalt bedrock of the area (unit 1, table 5). Chemical weathering produced clay minerals from the

Figure 8. Terrace section E on the left or north flank of the Tuba II slope failure. Units are described in table 5. Slip plane of the slope failure is indicated by dark line with an arrow for sense of motion. Rock outcrop below slip plane to right of tape measure line is spheroidally weathered corestones of basalt (unit 1, table 5). Below slip plane to the left of the tape is bedded slope gravels with organic matter dating at 2295±485 $^{14}$C yr B.P. (site 3; table 2). Overlying slip plane clays anachronistically date at 11,070±145 $^{14}$C yr B.P. (site 2; table 2), presumably because of contamination by older material smeared out along the slip surface and exaggerated by the sensitive $^{14}$C AMS technology.

Table 5: Stratigraphic description of: Terrace section E and terrace section F. From bottom to top in order of superposition, the stratigraphy and events deduced are presented here

| STRATIG-RAPHY | EVENTS | |
| | TERRACE SECTION E (south wall of exposure on left/north lateral toe of Tuba II slope failure, west bank) | TERRACE SECTION F (weakly stratified terrace gravels 100 m directly downslope of Terrace section E) |
|---|---|---|
| Top | Surface of Tuba II slope failure | Terrace tread surface |
| Unit 5 | Weakly developed to nonexistent soil | Weakly developed to nonexistent soil |
| Unit 4 | Tuba II slope failure boulders and debris, 4–5 m thick. Plentiful internal shear zones. Rubified zones where prior weathered basalts were smeared out through the deposit. | Clast-supported boulder gravel, 5 m thick. |
| Unit 3 | Slip plane clays of basal Tuba II slope failure, 25 cm thick. Lenticular. Dry color 7.5YR 32, dark brown; 10YR 44, dark yellowish brown; 2.5Y 20, black. Site 2 (table 2), anachronistic date 11,070 ±145 [14]Cyr BP. | Clast-supported pebble and cobble gravel, 4 m thick. |
| Unit 2 | Bedded slope gravels; angular pebble and gravel deposit; ~1 m thick; crudely stratified. Probably sorted through gravitative and kinematic filtering. Correlative with coarser angular rubble of Terrace section F exposed directly downslope. Clay lenses in upper part. Dry color 10YR 44; dark yellowish brown. Deposit interpreted as talus deposited at top of denuded slope following initial breakout flood from Tuba I slope failure and flood event. Site 3 (table 2) 2295±485 [14]C yr BP. | Matrix-supported boulder gravel, 5 m thick. |
| Discon-formity | Produced by same event that denuded surrounding slopes, probably breakout flood from Tuba I slope failure. | — |
| Unit 1 | Weathered corestones above less-weathered basalt bedrock. Weathering has continued since lava emplacement to break down the mafic minerals and feldspars. Corestones have been progressively rounded from formerly more angular joint blocks of the original basalt. | Clast-supported cobble gravel, 6 m thick. |
| Bottom | Basalt bedrock. | Jordan River floodplain |

basalts, among which were considerable montmorillonite types, well known for high shrink and swell capacities which contribute to slope instability. At some point a severe environmental change, possibly the seismic event of the Tuba I slope failure or the breakout flood immediately thereafter, caused denudation of the lower slopes of the gorge and produced fresh rock cliffs and a new surface upon which rock talus could accumulate. The lowest part of the valley received plentiful talus rock which rolled, slid, and fell into the gorge as a normal, piecemeal accumulation of such materials as they come loose from slopes above and are gravitatively transferred to slopes below. This gravitative transfer exerts a certain kinematic or momentum-based sorting such that large particles tend to travel farther than small ones. Such gravitative sorting produced talus slopes with course materials at the bottom and fines at the top. In this case the course slope materials are exposed in section F (table 5) at the bottom of the valley and the uppermost fines occur as the bedded slope gravels of unit 2 in section E. Because there are at least four sets of slope gravels exposed in section F, we presume that a considerable length of time passed to allow emplacement of the several different units. This depositional sequence ended in uppermost bedded gravels at site 3 with organic matter dating at 2,295± 485 $^{14}$C yr BP (table 2). The next major event to occur for which we have clear evidence is the catastrophic failure of the upper slopes and the sliding down of the Tuba II slope failure over the prior materials of sections E and F. This produced a smearing out of formerly surface soil clays and incorporated them as the slip-plane clays of unit 3 in section E (table 5). The anachronistic date at site 2 here is much older than that of site 3 and is regarded as unreliable in that a slight contamination would have been disproportionately exaggerated by the $^{14}$C AMS technology that was used. Above this the rock and debris of the Tuba II slope failure were emplaced, commonly with multiple shear-plane lenses of weathered and rubified basalt materials.

The mass of the Tuba II slope failure–west bank moved directly into the bottom of the gorge of the Jordan River and must have dammed the river to cause an upstream inundation. The toe of this slope failure is only ~30 meters thick, which means that a smaller body of water was impounded behind it than that of the Tuba I event. In addition, the Tuba II slope failure also was sufficient to disrupt the opposite, east bank and cause it to fail as well, again probably through catastrophic dewatering following the breakout flood that must have occurred. In spite of its smaller size, the mass of water, rocks, and mud resulting from this second breakout flood would still have been sufficient to pour across the Lisan embayment, the Bethsaida lagoon, and the Jordan River inlet and the nearby western Beteiha Plain. This may be the source of the half meter to a meter of gravel, which contains stratigraphically jumbled potsherds of widely varying antiquity up to Roman glass, that was deposited onto the lagoonal black clays at Bethsaida and el-Araj.

The radiocarbon date of the bedded slope gravels directly beneath the Tuba II slope failure means effectively that the landslide and breakout flood occurred after, or younger than the calibrated date of about 68 CE (table 2). This is entirely consistent with a failure and flood date resulting from the major earthquake in 363 CE (Russell 1980), which apparently destroyed the former quiet-water conditions at Bethsaida. Thus although one radiocarbon date cannot categorically prove the precise timing we originally suspected from the archaeological data, the carbon 14 date does support our hypothesis.

## FLOOD GEOMORPHOLOGY

A great many fluvial erosion features and depositional terraces occur along both sides of the Jordan gorge. Some are minor benches of old lava flows where the resistance of the underlying rock allowed development of a small strath of no particular recognized geomorphic significance. Other terraces, such as the large one at -135 meters altitude ($T_3$, Shroder and Inbar 1995; terrace P, this paper) 1 km directly northwest of Bethsaida, is ~50 meters above the floodplain and may represent an old beach of an early stage of Lake Lisan, a fault block, or other nonfluvial landform. Many of the terraces, however, are related to catastrophic flooding of the Jordan, as attested to by the large boulders on the terraces, the imbricated boulders on some, and other evidence of catastrophic flooding described below. As is typical of valleys with repetitive catastrophic floods of unknown magnitude and timing, however, attribution of each specific landform to a particular flood is commonly difficult or impossible (Cornwell 1994). In this case we know that at least three major floods have occurred in the Jordan gorge; one in late Pleistocene, one in late Holocene, and one in historically recent time (1969). Probably others have occurred as well, but the palimpsest record of flooding has overprinted flood stratigraphy and landforms to the point of chaotic complexity or obliteration. In general we attribute the highest and largest flood landforms in the gorge to the clearly oldest and biggest flood associated with the Tuba I event. Stratigraphy from this event is largely buried beneath younger sediments on the Beteiha Plain. On the other hand, except possibly for the stratigraphy of flood gravels containing Roman glass and older potsherds overlying the lagoonal clays at Bethsaida, the flood associated with the Tuba II event is as yet almost entirely unknown from the landform data. Further careful soil and paleosol stratigraphy, coupled with plentiful radiocarbon dates, might better elucidate the Tuba II flood.

LANDFORMS OF THE JORDAN RIVER FLOODS

Until such time as other rigorous measures suggest otherwise, we assume that the landforms and stratigraphy described here were almost entirely generated by the breakout flood associated with the Tuba I event in Late Pleistocene time. We are reasonably certain of this attribution because we are mainly concerned only with the larger and higher landforms that would have been produced by the larger event. They are described below in sequence down the gorge, and from one side to the other, beginning directly downstream from the Tuba I landforms.

Beginning at the Tuba I slope failure on both sides of the river, there occurs a boulder and gravel fan (terraces A and B; fig. 2) whose apex lies several meters inset into the slope failure where it is cut through by the Jordan River. The distal portion of this fan was not observed, presumably because it was obscured or removed by the 1969 or other flood. On the west side of the river this fan (terrace A) has provided a ready source of gravel in historical construction projects, leaving behind there >40 remnant boulders ~2 meters in diameter (fig. 4). On the east side where the bulldozers could not excavate so readily, remnants of the original fan surface survive (terrace B) and show it to have been ~6 meters above the present river water level. The lower 4 meters of the fan are largely clast-supported boulders up to 2 meters in diameter, with an overlying 2 meters of fluvially stratified sands, coarse gravels, and smaller boulders. We interpret this fan to have been deposited in the waning stages of the original breakout flood event.

Also on the west bank above the breakout flood fan where the switchback road crosses the river in a ford, from about grid crossing 264.45 to 263.95, scoured basalt bedrock in the hillslope occurs for about half a kilometer downstream that we interpret as directly attributable to the breakout flood (terrace C; fig. 2). It appears that as the flood burst out it was directed somewhat to the southwest to remove sediment from the bedrock on that side. The bedrock here is mostly exposed corestones. Directly opposite on the east bank, on the other hand, a prominent depositional terrace (D) of boulders runs for ~0.6 kilometer that we interpret as having been emplaced in the initial outburst flood. This terrace is ~110 meters wide at the base, ~45 meters wide at the tread top, and stands 26 meters above the Jordan River floodplain. Soil-carbonate-encased boulders in its tread top range from 1 to ~3 meters in long axis. We hypothesize that the 26-meter height above the floodplain of this terrace and its boulders attests to the size and stream power of the initial breakout flood only 300 meters downstream from its initiation.

Directly downstream from the scoured bedrock (terrace C; fig. 4) of the west bank occurs terrace F (fig. 4), mentioned above in connection with the Tuba II stratigraphy. Across the river from terrace F, terrace G occurs, which is a slump block considerably older than the Tuba II landform. Terrace F seems to have begun accumulating as talus after the breakout flood of the Tuba I event, and perhaps the terrace G slump block was similarly emplaced into the gorge in response to undercutting by the same flood.

The Tuba II slope failure on both sides of the river is considerably smaller than Tuba I mass but it too has a breakout fan whose apex begins slightly inside the Tuba II slope failure mass alongside the right bank of the river. This terrace H is up to 5 meters above the Jordan, has a basal 3 meters of clast-supported subrounded to angular basal boulders overlain by well-stratified, thin-bedded cobble to pebble gravels and pebble to granule-sized sand lenses. The fan extends several tens of meters along the west bank to where it dies out near a prominent exposure of columnar basalt and rift-fault gouge that stands up to 50 meters above the river. The lava-flow surface of the columnar basalt dips 70 degrees and roughly parallel with the slope; presumably having been inclined from its nearly horizontal lava-flow emplacement position by movement on the fault (Harash and Bar 1988). South ~200 meters along the strike of the fault occurs a prominent shutter ridge that shows appropriate left-lateral displacement to the north of ~50 meters of a small wadi that comes down the west bank. Directly upslope 0.5 to 0.75 km occurs two curvilinear escarpments that wrap around down-dropped blocks that are either slump failure or fault sags; perhaps a combination of both. Thus except for the Tuba II breakout fan, this section of the gorge shows only rift fault and related geomorphology. Across the river on the east bank only scoured bedrock occurs for over 0.8 km from about grid crossing 263.6 to 262.8.

On the west bank from about 263.2 to 263.1 terrace I occurs. The terrace top is overlain with ~5 meters of angular colluvium, but the interior and steep (39°) face of the landform up to 28 meters above the river has flood-smoothed and rounded boulders ~1 meter in diameter in a light colored (2.5Y 5/2) grayish-brown sandy matrix. The interior of the terrace is a bedrock knob that projects outward a few tens of meters into the valley, which may have impeded the flood flow and caused the flood boulders to be emplaced so high upon this side. We thus interpret this boulder deposit as emplaced by the Tuba I breakout flood with the height of its flood boulders determined by the overall channel constriction at this point. At about 263 on the west bank where the valley widens out, terrace I passes into terrace J, which has declined to ~14 to ~15 meters above the river but still contains boulders 1 to 2 meters in diameter.

At about 262.7 on the east bank the unusual terrace K occurs up to 20 meters above the river (fig. 6). This terrace has rift-faulted bedrock at each end, with 5 to 10 meters of flood gravels, an organic-rich paleosol about 50 cm thick, and ~10 meters of overlying colluvium exposed in a reentrant between the rock outcrops. The lowermost flood gravels extend horizontally across the face of the outcrop downstream for several tens of meters before climbing up at ~20° to pass over the bedrock obstruction on the downstream side. We interpret this as a flood-emplaced primary bedding rather than as a fault-affected dip because no visible offsets occur in the underlying flood gravel or in the overlying paleosol or colluvium. This terrace K extends from this stratigraphic exposure for several hundred meters downstream and about 20 meters above the valley bottom. The paleosol that had developed on the upward sloping flood gravels dates at >20,500 $^{14}$C yr BP (table 2), which is entirely consistent with emplacement by the Tuba I breakout flood.

On the opposite, west side of the valley occurs a low (5-10 m) boulder terrace L that accumulated on the upstream side of the Hamam bedrock block and first major valley constriction (fig. 5). The terrace rises downstream to a position 25 to 30 meters above the river where imbricated boulders occur on its edge in terrace M. This site faces directly upstream into the course of any oncoming catastrophic flood and is the first major obstruction and valley constriction below Tuba I. Thus the high, imbricated boulders here probably reflect that relationship to the flood. The Hamam slope failure (fig. 3) deflected south around the bedrock knob of Hamam and slid into the Jordan gorge between terraces M and N. From this point onward downstream the gorge is progressively more constricted between bedrock (east bank) and colluvial (west bank) walls. At 261.45 the valley contracts to its narrowest at <75 meters where a veneer of rounded boulders is plastered over bedrock on the west bank to a height of 26 meters above the valley floor in terrace N (fig. 9). Above the top of the rounded boulders occurs an additional 5-meter thickness of angular colluvial boulders. For the next 1.3 km downstream the gorge has no significant deposits or terraces of note that enable geomorphologic reconstruction until it opens out into the Lisan embayment.

Figure 9. Photograph of the narrowest constriction at terrace N (fig. 2) in the Jordan gorge.

# FLOOD MODELING RESULTS

## GIS ANALYSIS AND WATER IMPOUNDMENTS

Results of GIS analysis indicated that a water impoundment of significant volume was associated with the Tuba I and II slope failure events. Based upon a modern-day average daily discharge rate of $1.7 \times 10^6$ m$^3$ (Inbar 1987), the amount of time was calculated it would take for the water to reach the top of each landslide dam. This average daily discharge rate represents an estimate of the discharge rate of the Jordan River during the rainy season. Inbar and Even-Nir (1989) indicate that although landslides are caused by seismic events, most of the slides in the gorge are caused by rainfall events. Although we cannot rule out the possibility that the slope failures were initiated by a seismic event and occurred during the low-flow summer season, our time estimates are conservative. These estimates are based upon the assumption that modern-day rates approximate the actual discharge at the time of the events.

The top of the toe of the Tuba I landslide was estimated to be at 50 meters above sea level. Consequently, it would take about four days for the water to reach this level. The water elevation rapidly increased as water volume slowly increased, a result of the very narrow and V-shaped configuration of the gorge. At approximately 20 meters elevation, where the valley widens, the slope of the curve changes, indicating that the water volume increased rapidly while the water elevation increased slowly. We estimated the total volume of the impoundment to have been ~$6.4 \times 10^6$ m$^3$. This would have flooded the upper reach of the gorge, with the impoundment extending approximately 2.7 km toward the Hula basin (fig. 2).

The top of the toe of the Tuba II landslide was estimated to be at sea level. Therefore, it would have taken about 2 days for the water to reach this level. As with the Tuba I impoundment, the configuration of the gorge dictated the change in slope of the elevation–volume line. The major difference between the Tuba I and II water impoundments was that of size. The smaller Tuba II slope failure produced a smaller impoundment. We estimated the total volume of the impoundment to have been ~$3.6 \times 10^6$ m$^3$. This would have flooded the immediate upstream reach of the gorge, with the impoundment extending approximately 1.3 km to the north.

BREACH Simulations

Results of statistical analysis of BREACH simulations (table 6) indicated that the model is sensitive to the dam-face slope ratio which affected failure time significantly.

Table 6: Simulation results of the Tuba I and Tuba II dam failures

| Dam face slope ratio | Number of runs | Mean maximum discharge $(m^3 s^{-1})$ | Standard deviation $(m^3 s^{-1})$ | Mean time of failure after overtopping (hr) | Standard deviation (hr) |
|---|---|---|---|---|---|
| TUBA I | | | | | |
| 1:1 | 12 | 57943 | 6244 | 2.5 | 0.09 |
| 2.5:1 | 12 | 36466 | 1910 | 23.3 | 0.000001 |
| TUBA II | | | | | |
| 1:1 | 12 | 28327 | 2127 | 1.6 | 0.07 |
| 2.5:1 | 12 | 15691 | 427 | 15.9 | 0.000001 |

For the Tuba I event and a ratio of 1:1, the mean peak discharge was $5.8 \times 10^4$ $m^3$ $s^{-1}$ ± 12 x $10^3$ $m^3$ $s^{-1}$. Using a lower slope angle resulted in a mean peak discharge of $3.6 \times 10^4$ $m^3$ $s^{-1}$ ± 4 x $10^3$ $m^3$ $s^{-1}$. Failure times ranged on average from 2.5 to 23 hours (fig. 10). These results indicated that peak discharge could have ranged from 3.0–7.0 x $10^4$ $m^3$ $s^{-1}$.

Tuba II results are similar, although peak discharge estimates are smaller. For a 1:1 ratio, the mean discharge was $2.8 \times 10^3$ $m^3$ $s^{-1}$ ± 4 x $10^3$ $m^3$ $s^{-1}$. For a 2.5:1 ratio, the mean peak discharge was $1.5 \times 10^3$ $m^3$ $s^{-1}$ ± 800 $m^3$ $s^{-1}$. Failure time ranged on average from 1.6 to 16 hours (fig. 11). Consequently, the peak discharge associated with the Tuba II event could have ranged from 1.5–3.0 x $10^3$ $m^3$ $s^{-1}$.

HEC-2 Simulations

*Calibration:* HEC-2 simulations for two reaches along the Jordan gorge were used to estimate the peak discharge of the flood event. Prior to running simulations using geologic evidence, the model for each reach was calibrated based upon the work of Inbar (1987).

Inbar (1987) reported that a catastrophic flood on the Jordan River occurred 19-23 January 1969. He indicated that the event was caused by a rare climatic event and that the flood was $10^8$ $m^3$ in vol-

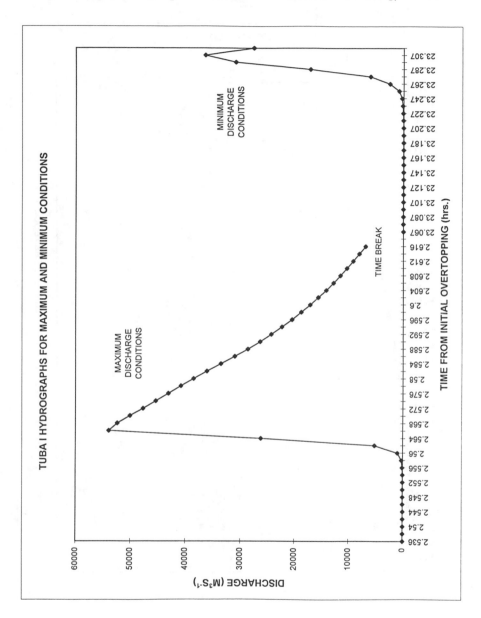

Figure 10. Hydrographs of Tuba I flood for independent maximum and minimum conditions, marked by time break for clarity

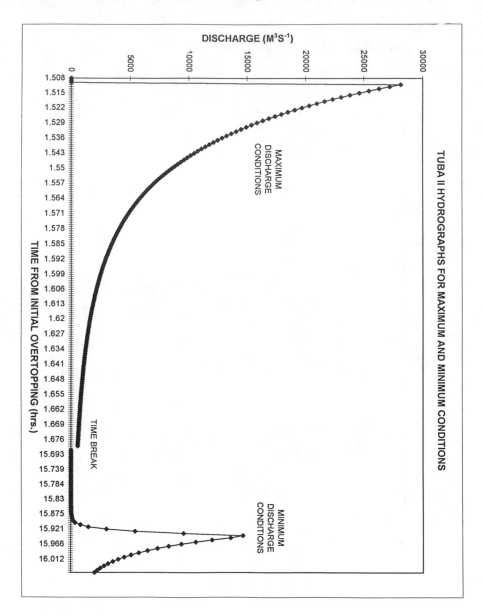

Figure 11. Hydrographs of Tuba II flood for independent maximum and minimum conditions, marked by time break for clarity

ume, with a peak discharge and velocity of 214 m$^3$ s$^{-1}$ and 6–7 m s$^{-1}$ respectively. The valley floor was reworked, although large boulders from the upper portion of the gorge were not transported great distances (Inbar 1987). The event dramatically changed the channel and floodplain due to relatively high stream power (Inbar 1987).

Initial runs of the model assuming subcritical flow were not successful. The program defaulted to critical depth, indicating that the energy equations could not be balanced using this flow regime. Baker and Costa (1987) indicated that supercritical flow is more common in bedrock channels and can be sustained for longer periods of time. Consequently, the supercritical flow regime was used. Calibration of the model to the 1969 event resulted in the production of reasonable hydraulic parameter estimates. Water velocity estimates for cross sections ranged from 5.5 to 7.0 m s$^{-1}$. These estimates are very similar to the results reported by Inbar (1987). The spatial variation of velocity along each reach was examined, and velocity variations were associated with channel gradient and channel geometry variations. Higher velocities would be associated with larger gradients and narrow channels (Magilligan 1992). For most cross sections, however, the water velocity ranged from 6.0 to 7.0 m s$^{-1}$.

It is important to model the energy conditions appropriately, as the derivation of the shear-stress and stream power are directly dependent upon the local energy slope (O'Connor 1993). Energy conditions were also modeled reasonably. Energy head losses for cross sections were < = 0.1 m, with energy slopes ranging from approximately 0.02 to 0.03. This resulted in the production of boundary shear-stress estimates ranging from 250 to 500 N m$^{-2}$ and stream power estimates from 1300 to 3500 W m$^{-2}$. Many cross sections exhibited shear-stress and stream power estimates near 400 N m$^{-2}$ and 2400 W m$^{-2}$ respectively. The largest stream power estimates were associated with channel geometry changes where greater rock resistance and increased water depth account for higher stream power.

Williams (1983), reported that a stream power of 1000 W m$^{-2}$ will move boulders with intermediate diameters of 1.5 meters, whereas shear stresses of 500 N m$^{-2}$ will move boulders with intermediate diameters of 3 meters. Our simulation results produced energy conditions along each reach that are capable of modifying the channel and floodplain. In addition, they are capable of transporting boulders the distances reported by Inbar (1987) without transporting the largest boulders down the entire gorge and onto the Beteiha plain. Consequently, simulation results related to sediment transport of the 1969 flood are considered to be reasonable.

*Reach I (Tuba I to Tuba II):* At a control location on the east bank near the Tuba I slope failure, we measured the height of the boulder berm in terrace B to be 26 meters above the channel (fig. 12). This equates to a minimum water surface elevation slightly above mean sea level (1 m). Reach I was modeled so that simulated water surface

Figure 12. Flood boulders deposited on terrace B close to breakout point of Tuba I flood (fig. 2)

elevations would match elevations interpreted from the geologic evidence. To accomplish this, peak discharge estimates were systematically increased, starting at $3.0 \times 10^4$ m$^3$ s$^{-1}$. The discharge parameter is known to have the largest influence on water surface elevation (Hoggan 1989). The starting point represented a low estimate of peak discharge based upon BREACH simulation results.

Initial results indicated that the flow was supercritical and that water surface elevations were 5–6 m less than spot elevations for cross sections down the reach. Peak discharge was systematically increased and simulation results that produced the best fit to the geological evidence were associated with a peak discharge of $4.0 \times 10^4$ $m^3$ $s^{-1}$ (fig. 13). The results are very close to the 1 m elevation estimated for this control location.

Water elevation changes are the result of changes in channel geometry. Water surface elevation generally increases as the valley becomes narrow. This is most noticeable in the lower half of the reach where constriction locations are associated with higher elevations (fig. 14). Geometry changes are also responsible for the range in cross section water depths (21 to 27 m). Energy slopes ranged from 0.02 to 0.03. Energy head losses for cross sections were generally < =0.1 meter.

The simulation resulted in the production of velocity estimates that ranged from 18 to 20 m $s^{-1}$. Highest velocities were associated with narrow segments of the gorge, whereas most cross sections exhibited velocities from 18 to 19 m $s^{-1}$. Boundary shear-stress estimates ranged from $2.5–3.1 \times 10^3$ N $m^{-2}$, whereas stream power estimates ranged from $4.6–6.3 \times 10^4$ W $m^{-2}$.

*Reach II (Tuba II to Major Constriction Terrace N):* Simulations were also run for the upper portion of reach II to determine if the peak discharge could account for flood boulders deposited approximately 25 to 30 meters above the Hamam constriction point. This height equates to a water surface elevation of at least -60 meters below sea level.

Simulation results indicated that water depths ranged from 21 to 32 m. The increased water depth is reflective of the narrow segment of the upper portion of reach II compared to reach I. In addition, this segment exhibits two moderate constriction locations. These constrictions would force the water surface elevation to increase (fig. 15). A peak discharge of $3.7 \times 10^4$ $m^3$ $s^{-1}$ at terrace M near Hamam (fig. 16) would result in a water elevation of -60 meters, which would then account for the deposition of large boulders at this location.

Appropriate modeling of energy slopes and head losses for cross sections in the upper reach produced ranges of 0.01 to 0.02 and < 0.1 meter respectively. Water velocity estimates were less than those of reach I and ranged from 13 to 18 m $s^{-1}$. Similarly, boundary shear-stress and stream-power estimates were less than estimates from reach

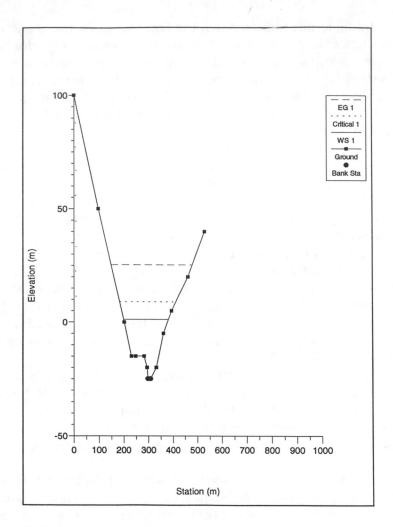

Figure 13. Cross section at terrace B control point near the Tuba I slope failure (vertical exaggeration 9:1). Simulated flood water surface elevation is based upon a peak discharge of $4.0 \times 10^4$ m$^3$ s$^{-1}$ and was found to correspond closely to a high water mark at ~1 m altitude above mean sea level. EG 1 is the energy gradient; Critical 1 is the critical depth; WS 1 is the simulated floodwater surface; ground indicates the valley bottom profile; Bank Sta indicates the ground control points at the edge of the present-day river channel.

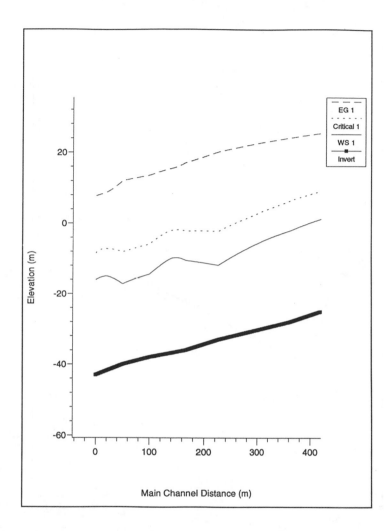

Figure 14. Simulated water surface elevation in longitudinal section along the channel near the Tuba I slope failure breakout point (vertical exaggeration 6.6:1). EG 1 is the energy gradient; Critical 1 is the critical depth; WS 1 is the simulated floodwater surface; Invert (the heavy dark line) is the floodplain bottom.

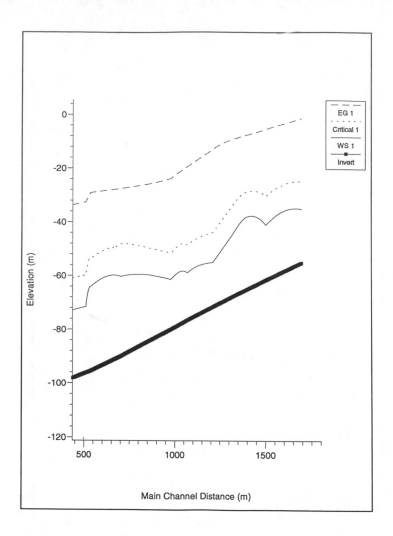

Figure 15. Simulated water surface elevation in longitudinal section along the channel for the upper segment of reach II (vertical exaggeration is 17.1:1). Moderate constrictions along this segment of the reach influence water depth and elevation. EG 1 is the energy gradient; Critical 1 is the critical depth; WS 1 is the simulated floodwater surface; Invert (the heavy dark line) is the flood-plain bottom.

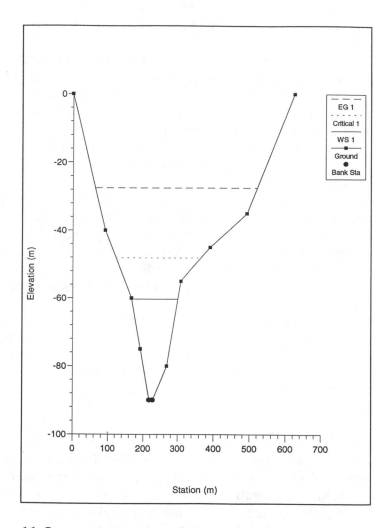

Figure 16. Cross section at a control point near the Hamam constriction (vertical exaggeration 9.5:1). Simulated floodwater surface elevation is based upon a peak discharge of $3.7 \times 10^4$ m$^3$s$^{-1}$ and was found to correspond closely to a high water mark at -60 m altitude below mean sea level. EG 1 is the energy gradient; Critical 1 is the critical depth; WS 1 is the simulated flood-water surface; Ground indicates the valley bottom profile; Bank Sta indicates the ground control points at the edge of the present-day river channel.

1, and ranged from 1.5 to 2.7 x $10^3$ N m$^{-2}$ and 2.1 to 4.7 x $10^4$ W m$^{-2}$ respectively.

The lower portion of reach II was analyzed and modeled in order to explain boulder deposits 26 to 30 meters above the floodplain at the major constriction at terrace N (fig. 9). Energy conditions were such that large boulders were deposited at -84.0 to -88.0 meters.

Initial runs of the model using supercritical flow were not successful. Subcritical flow conditions produced results consistent with the geological evidence. Energy slopes for cross sections ranged from 0.01 to 0.0009.

Water depths ranged from 25 to 46 m above the surface of the floodplain, with the maximum water depth associated with the maximum constriction location (fig. 17). It is interesting to note that water velocities ranged from 6 to 13 m s$^{-1}$. Similarly, shear-stress estimates decreased and ranged from ~200 to 1.5 x $10^3$ N m$^{-2}$. The lower energy conditions would enable the deposition of large boulders at relatively high elevations.

The decrease in energy conditions can be explained by the fact that only a certain amount of water could pass through the constriction and the stream gradient is less steep. In addition, the flow of water was not confined to the narrow gorge. The cross section at terrace N (fig. 17) shows that water flowed over the top portion of the constriction.

DISCUSSION

The results discussed above indicate that the Tuba I flood was exceptionally powerful. High energy conditions depend upon the combination of gradient, water depth, and velocity (Baker and Costa 1987). Examination of the characteristics of the gorge and simulation results indicates that supercritical flow could be maintained along selected segments of the gorge. Energy conditions at peak discharge would have exceeded the threshold or critical tractive force needed to initiate particle motion and transport boulders a significant distance down the gorge. Because of the high stream power associated with peak discharge, deposition would have been associated with the temporal variation in energy conditions at most cross sections. Deposition at constriction locations, however, resulted from low energy conditions. It is difficult, however, to relate simulated energy conditions to hydraulic parameters generated from boulder measurements collected in the

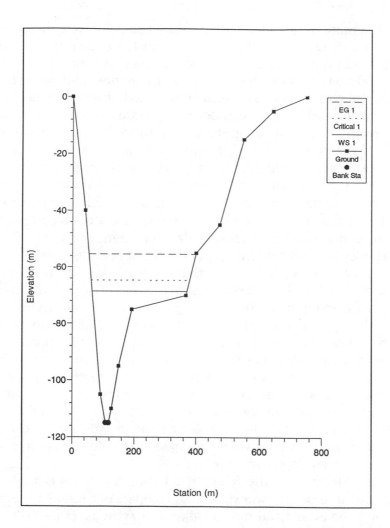

Figure 17. Cross section at the major constriction point at terrace N (fig. 2) in the Jordan gorge (vertical exaggeration 9.3:1). Water flow was not entirely confined to the narrow channel below the terrace, but flowed over the top portion of the constriction. Lower energy conditions there resulted in the deposition of large boulders at relatively high elevations on the terrace tread.

field. Assumptions include: (1) all measured boulders were transported by this flood, (2) the boulders were deposited at or near peak discharge, and (3) maximum boulder sizes represent variation in transport conditions. Clearly, these assumptions are not valid. Some boulders in the gorge must have been transported by subsequent floods and smaller boulders may be associated with various slope failure and flood events. Given the magnitude of simulated energy conditions, many of the boulders were probably deposited during lower discharges after peak discharge. Similarly, because of closely spaced cooling joints in the basalts, large boulders > 2 to 3 meters are quite uncommon in the Jordan gorge. Consequently, hydraulic parameter estimates generated from boulder sizes are postulated to be only the limiting conditions for sustaining clast transport, and are probably not representative of true energy conditions at peak discharge.

It is also important to note that this analysis and the peak discharge estimates are based upon channel geometry as depicted from a 1966 topographic map. The topographic data represent the terrain before the 1969 flood occurred but after both the Tuba I and Tuba II events. It is highly probable that the canyon prior to the Tuba I event exhibited a quite different fault geometry and constriction due to talus deposits, as well as less vertical relief because of greater floodplain storage of sediment. The Tuba II flood occurred in a valley more like that of the present. Minimum estimates of high water marks attributable to the Tuba I flood indicate that our estimate of peak discharge is conservative and would compensate for differences in channel geometry developed over time.

In order to place the Tuba I and Tuba II flood events and their magnitude into better context, we can compare our results to several historic flood events and modern-day river systems (table 7). These data show that high shear-stress and stream power are not necessarily related to high discharge rates. The Amazon and Mississippi River systems exhibit relatively high discharge rates with relatively low shear-stress and power. This is primarily a function of low water flow velocities. During most flood events water flows at higher velocities, which accounts for larger shear-stress and stream-power values. In addition, channel characteristics affect energy conditions. Alluvial channels can accommodate high flow velocities such that channel erosion and transportation of sediment reduce energy conditions and result in lower shear-stress and stream-power values. In resistant bedrock chan-

Table 7: Historic and prehistoric floods and river hydraulic conditions; after Baker and Costa (1987)

| River System | Discharge (m³ s⁻¹) | Stress (Nm⁻²) | Power (Wm⁻²) | Channel |
|---|---|---|---|---|
| Amazon River, SA | 300,000 | 6 | 12 | alluvial |
| Mississippi River, NA | 30,000 | 6 | 12 | alluvial |
| Big Thompson River Flood, CO | 799 | 597 | 3,943 | bedrock |
| Rapid City Flood, SD | 357 | 326 | 1,669 | bedrock |
| Eel River Flood, CA | 21,300 | 156 | 719 | bedrock |
| Teton River Flood, ID | 64,000 | 819 | 10,700 | bedrock |
| Lake Bonneville Flood, NA<br>Red Rock Pass<br>Grande Ronde<br>Pittsburg Landing | 1,000,000 | 2,500<br>1,282<br>1,730<br>2,931 | 75,000<br>31,131<br>52,641<br>120,863 | mixed |
| Jordan River, Israel, Tuba I Flood | 40,000 | 1,571 | 21,800 | bedrock |

nels, such as the Jordan gorge, channel geometry is relatively stable and increases in flow velocities and depth increased shear-stress and stream power.

## Conclusion

Geomorphologic analysis and computer simulation of multiple flood events in the Jordan gorge have enabled reconstruction of the most probable sequence of geomorphic events there for the past 25,000 years. The initial condition began with Lake Lisan extending past the Bethsaida peninsula and into the mouth of the Jordan gorge. Lacustrine muds were deposited in this quiet water embayment. A major seismic event several tens of thousands of years ago may have triggered the Tuba I slope failure, which in any event, slid down into Jordan gorge and impounded a lake (block diagram no. 1; fig. 18). In about a week the Jordan River inundated the canyon behind the unstable dam until it failed, producing a catastrophic breakout flood that left a boulder fan and flood terraces in the upper part of the gorge. In the Lisan embayment the flood waves of boulders, gravel, and mud came to an irregular stop, leaving piles and heaps of sediment spread out in a chaotic fashion wherever the forward velocity of the flood wave was impeded by variations in water depth and prior deltaic sed-

1

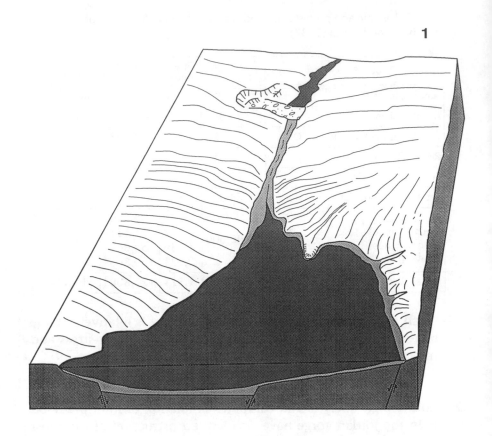

Figure 18. Block diagram no. 1 is ~25,000 years ago with the Lake Lisan precursor to the Sea of Galilee extending past the Bethsaida peninsula and into the lower part of the Jordan gorge. The Tuba I slope failure has just blocked the Jordan River and impounded a body of water behind it.

imentation from the Jordan River. The result was formation of a protected embayment at the Bethsaida peninsula (no. 2; fig. 19). Following continued decline of the level of Lake Lisan, coupled with continued riverine sedimentation and, perhaps, with other slope-failure-generated flooding and sediment increases from the Hamam site, the bay at Bethsaida continued to fill up with sediment. Early settlers on the Bethsaida peninsula would have found protected lake water in an adjacent bay, fertile soils nearby, and an entirely habitable site upon which to begin a new settlement (no. 3; fig. 20). In the ensuing millennia as Bethsaida became a substantial town, the nearby shore-

2

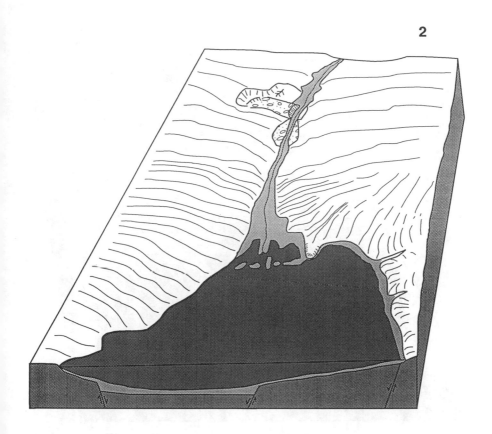

Figure 19. Block diagram no. 2 is immediately following the breakout flood of ~25,000 years ago where the irregular boulder and gravel beds were deposited into the Lake Lisan and Sea of Galilee paleo-embayments. At that time a somewhat protected bay or lagoon was produced directly west of the Bethsaida peninsula.

line continued to change through a combination of tectonic uplift (shore up), Jordan delta sedimentation extension lakeward (shore out), and perhaps also through the continued decline of the level of the Sea of Galilee (water down). Even so, the embayment at Bethsaida was maintained, probably through the combined flow of the Jordan River and the spring at Bethsaida (no. 4; fig. 21). Then perhaps some 1,800 years ago another fatal slope failure caused a new flood of water and gravel to burst from the mouth of the Jordan gorge and over-

3

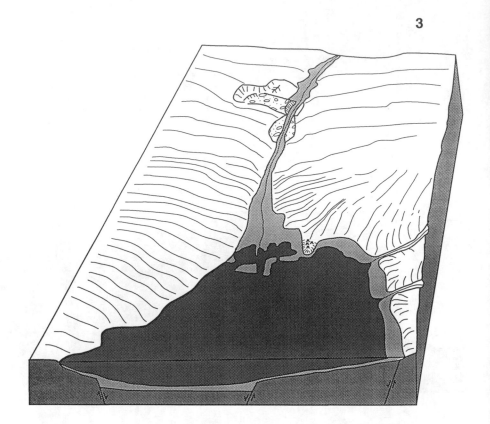

Figure 20. Block diagram no. 3 shows initiation of the first settlements on the Bethsaida peninsula some 15,000–20,000 years after the Tuba I slope failure and breakout flood. Continued deltaic sedimentation by the Jordan and other rivers has built out the coastline, and uplift of the east and north coast has extended the shoreline as well.

whelm the quiet water at the base of the Bethsaida peninsula. In combination with turmoil produced by the recent Roman invasion of the time, this last flood destruction changed the shoreline further (no. 5; fig. 22) and thereafter eliminated Bethsaida as a viable dwelling place.

**4**

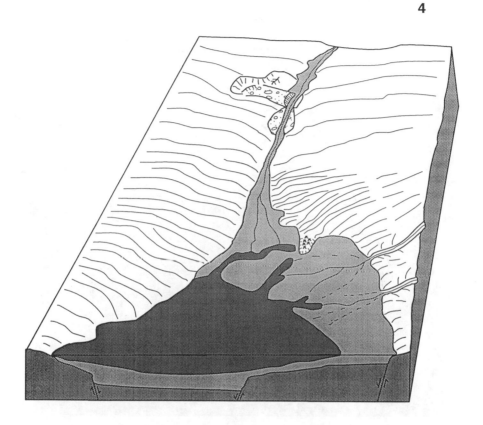

Figure 21. Block diagram no. 4 is Bethsaida at its acme, perhaps 3,000–2,000 years ago, with a considerably extended or prograded shoreline. The original embayment at Bethsaida has been restricted but is still navigable. Another extends in from the south.

**5**

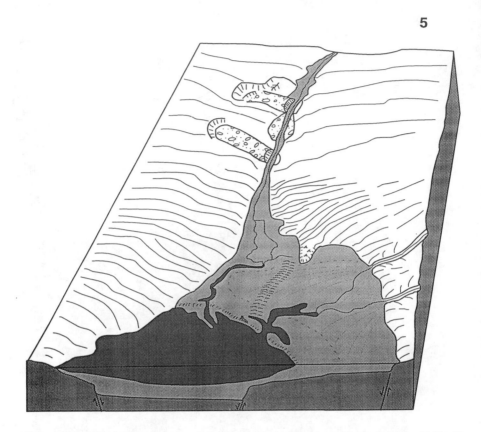

Figure 22. Block diagram no. 5 is the present-day situation after the Tuba II slope failure and breakout flood, which eliminated the original embayments near Bethsaida. El Araj has been established on a beach ridge at the edge of the Sea of Galilee. The Jordan delta has been extended out past the beach ridge as a result of the 1969 flood.

## Literature Cited

Agnon, A. 1995. Stop 16: Ateret Fortress: Active Faulting of a Crusader Fortress' Wall. In: A. Heimann and G. Baer, eds. *Dykes in Israel and Their Tectonic and Magmatic Setting*. Third International Dyke Conference, Excursions Guidebook, Report GSI/17/95; 39–41.

Amiran, D. H. K., E. Arieh, and T. Turcotte. 1994. Earthquakes in Israel and Adjacent Areas: Macroseismic Observations since 100 B.C.E. *Israel Exploration Journal* 44, nos. 3–4: 260–305.

Bagnold, R. A. 1966. An Approach to the Sediment Transport Problem from General Physics. *U.S. Geological Survey Professional Paper* 422–I, 37 pp.

———. 1977. Bed Load Transport by Natural Rivers. *Water Resources Research* 13:303–12.

———. 1980. An Empirical Correlation of Bedload Transport Rates in Flumes and Natural Rivers. *Proceedings of the Royal Society* 372A:453–73.

Baker, V. R., and J.E. Costa. 1987. Flood Power. In: *Catastrophic Flooding*. Ed. L. Mayer and D. Nash. London: Allen Unwin, London, 1–21.

Ben–Menahem, A. 1991. Four Thousand Years of Seismicity along the Dead Sea Rift. *Journal of Geophysical Research* 96, no. B12:20,195–20,216.

Chow, V. T. 1959. *Open–Channel Hydraulics*. New York: McGraw-Hill, 690 pp.

Code, J. A., and S. Sirhindi. 1986. Engineering Implications of Impoundment of the Indus River by an Earthquake–induced Landslide. In *Landslide Dams: Processes, Risk, and Mitigation*. Ed. R. L. Shuster. Geotechnical Special Publication Number 3: 97–110.

Cornwell, K. J. 1994. Evidence of Quaternary Breakout Floods Along the Middle Indus Valley and in the Peshawar Basin of Northern Pakistan. Unpublished Ph.D. dissertation, University of Nebraska–Lincoln, 183 pp.

Costa, J. E. 1983. Paleohydraulic Reconstruction of Flash–flood Peaks from Boulder Deposits in the Colorado Front Range. *Geological Society of America Bulletin* 94:986–1004.

Costa, J. E., and R. L. Shuster. 1988. The Formation and Failure of Natural Dams. *Geological Society of America Bulletin* 100:1054–68.

Ely, L. L., and V. R. Baker. 1985. Reconstructing Paleoflood Hydrology with Slackwater Deposits, Verde River, Arizona. *Physical Geography* 5:103–26.

Feldman, A. D. 1981. HEC Models for Water Resources System Simulation: Theory and Experience. *Advances in Hydroscience* 12:297–423.

Florsheim, J. L., and E. A. Keller. 1989. Hydrologic Geometry of Riffle–pool Sequences: A Modeling Approach. *Geological Society of America Abstracts with Programs* 21:79.

Garfunkel, Z., I. Zak, and R. Freund. 1981. Active Faulting in the Dead Sea Rift. *Tectonophysics* 80:1–26.

Goren–Inbar, N., and S. Belitsky. 1989. Structural Position of the Pleistocene Gesher Benot Ya'aqov site in the Dead Sea rift Zone. *Quaternary Research* 31:371–76.

Goren–Inbar, N., S. Belitsky, K. Verosub, E. Werker, M. Kislev, A. Heimann, I. Carmi, and A. Rosenfeld. 1992. New Discoveries at the Middle Pleistocene Acheulian Site of Gesher Benot Ya'aqov, Israel. *Quaternary Research* 38:117–28.

Harash, A., and Y. Bar. 1988. Faults, Landslides and Seismic Hazards along the Jordan River Gorge, Northern Israel. *Engineering Geology* 25:1–15.

Heimann, A. 1990. The Development of the Dead Sea Rift and Its Margins in Northern Israel during the Pliocene and the Pleistocene. *Geological Survey of Israel*, Report GSI/28/90.

Heimann, A. 1995. The Dead Sea Rift. In Heimann, A. and G. Baer (Editors). 1995, Dykes in Israel and their tectonic and magmatic setting. Third International Dyke Conference, Excursions Guidebook, Report GSI/17/95; p. 39–41.

Heimann, A., and G. Baer, eds. 1995. Dykes in Israel and Their Tectonic and Magmatic Setting. *Third International Dyke Conference, Excursions Guidebook*, Report GSI/17/95, 146 pp.

Hoggan, D. 1989. *Computer–assisted Floodplain Hydrology and Hydraulics*. New York: McGraw-Hill.

Horowitz, A. 1978. The Quaternary Evolution of the Jordan Valley. In *Lake Kinneret*, ed. C. Serruya, 33–44. The Hague: W. Junk Publishers.

Inbar, M. 1974. River Delta on Lake Kinneret Caused by Recent Changes in the Drainage Basin. *Geomorphologische Prozesse und Prozesskombinationen in der Gegenwart unter verschieden Klimabedingungen*. Report of the Commission on Present–day Geomorphological Processes (International Geographical Union). Gottingen: Abhandlungen der Akademie der Wissenschaften in Gottingen. 197–207.

———. 1977, Bedload Movement and Channel Morphology in the Upper Jordan river. Unpublished Ph.D. thesis, The Hebrew University, Jerusalem.

———. 1982, Measurement of the Fluvial Sediment Transport Compared with Lacustrine Sedimentation Rates: The Flow of the Jordan River into Lake Kinneret. *Hydrological Sciences Journal* 4:439–449.

———. 1987, Effects of a High Magnitude Flood in a Mediterranean Climate: A Case Study in the Jordan River Basin. In: *Catastrophic Flooding*, ed. L. Mayer and D. Nash. Boston: Allen and Unwin, Boston. 333–53.

———. 1989, Landslides in the Upper Jordan Gorge. *Pirineous, Journal on Mountain Ecology* 134:23–40.

Inbar, M. and M. Even–Nir. 1989. Landslides in the Upper Jordan Gorge. *Pirineos, Journal on Mountain Ecology* 134:23–40.

Inbar, M., and A. P. Schick. 1979. Bedload Transport Associated with High Stream Power, Jordan River, Israel. *Proceedings: National Academy of Science, USA, Geology*. 76:2525–2517.

Jarret, R. D., and H. E. Malde. 1987. Paleodischarge of the Late Pleistocene Bonneville Flood, Snake River, Idaho, Computed from New Evidence. *Geological Society of America Bulletin* 99:127–34.

Komar, P. D. 1989. Flow–competence Evaluations of the Hydraulic Parameters of Floods: and Assessment of the Technique. In *Floods: Hydrological, Sedimentological and Geomorphological Implications*. Ed. K. Beven and P. Carling. New York: John Wiley and Sons.

Lord, K. L., and A. E. Kehew. 1987. Sedimentology and Paleohydrology of Glacial–lake Outburst Floods in Southeastern Saskatchewan and Northwestern North Dakota. *Geological Society of America Bulletin*. 99:663–673.

O'Connor, J. E. 1993. Hydrology, Hydraulics, and Geomorphology of the Bonneville Flood. *Geological Society of America Special Paper* 274.

Pearson, G. W., and M. Stuiver. 1986. High–orecision Calibration of the Radiocarbon Time Scale, 500–2500 BC. *Radiocarbon*. 28:839–62.

Russell, K. W. 1980. The Earthquake of May 19, A.D. 363. *Bulletin of the American Schools of Oriental Research* 238:47–64.

———. 1985. The Earthquake Chronology of Palestine and Northwest Arabia from the 2nd through the Mid–8th Century A.D. *Bulletin of the American Schools of Oriental Research*. 260:37–59.

Shroder, J. F., Jr., and M. Inbar. 1995. Geologic and Geographic Background to the Bethsaida Excavations. In: *Bethsaida: A City by the North Shore of the Sea of Galilee*. Ed. R. Arav and R. Freund. Kirksville, MO: Thomas Jefferson University Press. 1:65–98.

Stuiver, M., and G. W. Pearson. 1986. High–precision Calibration of the Radiocarbon Time Scale, AD 1950–500 BC. *Radiocarbon*. 28:805–838.

Varnes, D. J. 1978. Slope Movement Types and Processes. In: *Landslides—Analysis and Control*. Ed. R. L. Shuster and R. J. Krizek. Transportation Research Board Special Report 176, National Academy of Sciences, Washington, DC, 11–33.

Webb, R. H. 1985. Late Holocene Flooding on the Escalante River, South-central Utah. Ph.D. thesis, University of Arizona, Tucson.

ACKNOWLEDGMENTS

We are profoundly grateful to the multiethnic, multireligious people of Israel who gave us their time and effort to make this project so interesting and enjoyable. The residents of Kibbutz Gadot and Kibbutz Ginossar provided excellent accommodations and food. Drs. R. Arav and R. Freund gave unstintingly of advice, assistance, and good companionship in the field. We would like to thank students L. Banker, P. Nieland, A. Schmidt, J. West, and A. Whitten for their field assistance. M. Barton contributed excellent graphics.

*Gloria London*
*Robert Shuster*

# Bethsaida Iron Age Ceramics

T HE IRON AGE MATERIAL presented here comes from a small area of the upper city located at the northeastern edge of Bethsaida. Because it is located close to main roads, the site has suffered for millennia at the hands of looters and scavengers which has resulted in dismantling of the architecture and in disturbances of the deposits. From the seventeenth through the twentieth centuries the El-Talawiyeh Bedouin tribe made use of the site, and more recently Syrian military constructions interfered with the archaeological deposits. As a consequence, the Iron Age deposits excavated thus far have experienced considerable postdepositional disturbances.[1]

At Bethsaida, Iron Age pottery is found virtually on the entire mound. The bulk of this report deals with material excavated in Area B, loci 601 and 417 and with certain published reconstructed pots from Area B, locus 365 (see CD map 7).[2] These deposits relate to the basalt and brick palace, the Bit Hilani. Locus 601, wedged between this building and a city wall, represents a possible pre– or early palatial use of the area, phase 1. Locus 365, noteworthy for its reconstructible pots, basalt vessels, and a stamped clay handle, comes from room 7 in the public building when it functioned as a palace, phase 2.[3] Locus 417, room 6 of the Bit Hilani, contained an abundance of shards, but none belong to complete or reconstructible pots. Locus 417 might date to the same period of use as locus 365, i.e., phase 2 of the palace use; however, it was mixed with later material. Locus 437, also very mixed, belongs to phases 2 and 3, a postpalatial phase, possibly following a destruction episode in the last quarter of the eighth century. Locus 437, part of the Main Hall, appears to have little red slipped and/or burnished pottery. Room 5, the westernmost room along the north wall (W67) of the Bit Hilani, had not been excavated at the time of this study. In phase 3, the subdivision of the Bit Hilani into small rooms signals a change in function for the building. Loom weights found in locus 427 imply that by phase 4 the structure was no longer a palace.

The repertoire presented here spans several architectural periods or phases of use. Other than the more complete pots from room 7 (locus 365), most Iron Age shards are small and worn, and for the most part they do not belong to reconstructible pieces. This leads to speculation concerning their depositional history and uncertainty about their date and the date of the building. A sample suite of thirty-one shards selected for petrographic analyses includes the full range of shapes present, both those with decorated and plain surface treatments. Robert Shuster of the University of Nebraska at Omaha carried out the petrographic analysis, which he and Gloria London then analyzed together. The emphasis of the petrographic analysis is on distinguishing among different wares present at the site to learn what types of pottery could have been produced within the region and which forms represent imports. The findings have implications concerning the organization of the ceramics industry in the Iron Age. Other topics treated here include (1) differences in the manufacturing techniques (2) the relationship among pyrotechnology, surface treatment, and nonplastics used to temper the wares, and (3) dating of the evidence.[4]

## Repertoire

At Bethsaida the excavated areas of Iron Age II produced a repertoire noteworthy for its dearth of store jars. This contrasts with the variety of open and closed pots in the small and medium size ranges. Such a repertoire could reflect the use of the Bit Hilani as a building not normally functioning as a place for the long-term storage of basic commodities. There are few differences between the types of pots found in each locus, other than the abundance of cooking pots in room 6 (locus 417). Rather than the result of pure chance, this could reflect the postpalatial use of the building (table 1).

Given the presence of Bit Hilani, one might expect a plethora of luxury artifacts, yet this is not so regarding the ceramics. Perhaps pres-

Table 1. Distribution of vessel types in Iron Age deposits

| LOCUS[a] | VESSEL TYPE | | | | | | | | | TOTAL |
|---|---|---|---|---|---|---|---|---|---|---|
| | Bowl | Chal-ice | Crater | Jug | Juglet | Store Jar | Cooking Pot | Lamp | Strainer | |
| 601 | 14 | 0 | 4 | 9 | 3 | 1 | 6 | 1 | 2 | 40 |
| 417 | 13 | 1 | 6 | 8 | 0 | 5 | 15 | 0 | 2 | 50 |
| 365 | 4 | 0 | 4 | 1 | 4 | 1 | 1 | 2 | 0 | 17 |
| TOTAL | 32 | 0 | 11 | 21 | 4 | 10 | 22 | 3 | 4 | 107 |

a. Locus 601 contains forty diagnostic shards; locus 417 contains fifty. Locus 365 includes reconstructible pots only and is not entirely comparable to the other loci listed here. This table represents the minimum number of pots present based on the number of shards. Bases were not included to prevent counting a pot twice. Vessels listed as strainers might be incense burners as well.

tige items were of metal rather than of clay. Bronze artifacts could easily have been melted down once they were no longer serviceable or were removed from the site by scavengers or others. Thus far, the entire Iron Age remains that have been uncovered have been scavenged and the best artifacts were most likely removed following the use of the building as a palace. Large stationary jars are underrepresented throughout the Iron Age deposit and in the petrographic sample suite, but smaller transportable jars are present in locus 365 of room 7. Sample selection for the petrographic analysis represents the diversity of clay bodies and contributes to the large number of decorated vessels in the sample. The thin section analysis includes a total of eight cooking pots of different rim types to determine whether there is a correlation between rim type and clay body. Most of the Iron Age material is fragmentary in nature and rather worn, often displaying mere traces of the red or brown slips that once covered the surfaces. An Early Bronze Age holemouth jar was sampled and serves as reference point (table 2).

Table 2. Petrographic samples, Bethsaida

| Sample | Registration No. | Locus | Vessel type |
|---|---|---|---|
| P30 | 5811.19 | 601 | Construction material |
| P31 | 5811.1 | 601 | Bowl, red slip and burnish |
| P32 | 5811.14 | 601 | Cooking pot, with compact rim |
| P33 | 5311.5 | 601 | Jug |
| P34 | 5811.2 | 601 | Jug, red slip and burnish |
| P35 | 5811.9 | 601 | Juglet |
| P36 | 5824.2 | 601 | Jug |
| P37 | 5834.1 | 601 | Bowl, red slip and burnish |
| P38 | 5834.1 | 601 | Cooking pot, white inclusions |
| P39 | 5834.1 | 601 | Cooking pot, black inclusions |
| P40 | 5834.7 | 601 | Bowl |
| P41 | 5834.1 | 601 | Jug, painted |
| P42 | 5834.5 | 601 | Jar, slipped; with potter's mark |
| P43 | 5834.3 | 601 | Bowl, large |
| P44 | 5834.9 | 601 | Bowl, hemispherical |
| P45 | 5824.4 | 601 | Bowl, with paint |
| P46 | 5165.1 | 417 | Bowl, large |
| P47 | 5168.8 | 417 | Jar, holemouth, Early Bronze Age |
| P48 | 5168.2 | 417 | Bowl, large |
| P49 | 5168.13 | 417 | Cooking pot |
| P50 | 5168.10 | 417 | Crater |
| P51 | 5176.6 | 417 | Bowl, with exterior grooves |
| P51 | 5176.2 | 417 | Bowl |
| P53 | 5176.3 | 417 | Chalice [?], burnished |
| P54 | 5176.8 | 417 | Strainer/incense burner |
| P55 | 5180.5 | 417 | Bowl, hemispherical |
| P56 | 5163.1 | 417 | Cooking pot, with compact rim |
| P57 | 5163.2 | 417 | Cooking pot |
| P58 | 5163.3 | 417 | Cooking pot |
| P59 | 5854.1 | 601 | Crater |
| P60 | 5811.20 | 601 | Cooking pot |

## Petrographic Analysis

##### Characterization of the petrographic groups 1-5.

Samples selected in the field were numbered P30 through P60 without regard to vessel type, date, or surface treatment and they include a wide variety of shapes and surface treatments. All but one date to the Iron Age. It is not the opinion of the authors that the selection is a representative sample of the ware distribution at the site, but it comments on the diversity of the ceramics industry as a whole and the origin of the wares. In addition to the macroscopic examination of the shards, thin sections were examined under a polarizing petrographic microscope using magnifications of x40 and x100. Features recorded include the type, size, shape, orientation, frequency, and sorting of the rock and mineral inclusions as well as the voids of burned out organic material in the clay matrix. For the thirty-one samples, five general groups are discernible. Both the presence and absence of basalt and the quantity of basalt serve as the primary criteria for assigning each sample to one of the groups. The first three groups are differentiated according to their decreasing percentages of basalt whereas groups 4 and 5, five shards in all, lack basalt entirely (figs. 1, 2; table 3).

##### Basalt Tempered Wares

Group 1: Basalt-Rich Ware, N=11
            Samples P32, 39, 42, 44, 47, 48, 49, 50, 56, 57, 60
Basalt predominates in eleven samples accounting for 70 percent or more of the total inclusions. In five samples, the basalt is 80 percent or more. Angular to subrounded and rounded basalt fragments are present in sizes ranging from 0.5 to 2.5 mm. For P56 and 60, cooking pot samples, 50 percent of the basalt is free olivine. Of the other nonplastics, the most common is grog or crushed pottery representing 5 to 20 percent and measuring 0.1–4.0 mm. Samples 32 and 48 lack grog. Quartz grains account for 5 to 10 percent of the rock and mineral inclusions and range in size from 0.01 to 0.2 mm. Opaques, equant in shape and 0.01 to 1.2 mm in size, are present at 5 to 20 percent. Oval and rectangular voids of burned out organic material are 10 to 30 percent of the total clay body and range in size from 0.02 to 2.0 mm. Calcite is entirely absent in this basalt-rich ware, whereas it has been identified in several of the other groups. The inclusions are well mixed throughout the clay matrix. In size they correspond well to wall thickness: pots with thicker walls have the larger inclusions. The basalt-rich

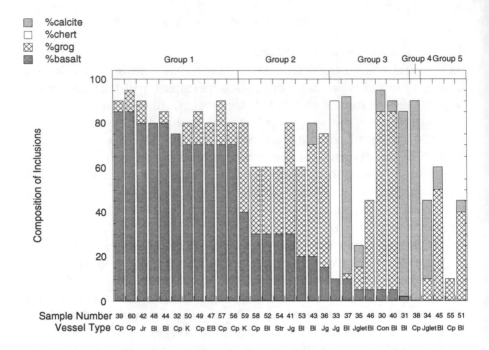

Figure 1. Petrographic samples P30 through P60 arranged according to inclusion type and quantity into groups 1–5.

ware typifies large thick-walled containers. In contrast, thinner-walled vessels in groups 2 and 3 might contain a single large basalt inclusion.

For this basalt-rich ware, the proportion of clay, in contrast to the voids and inclusions, is relatively low, at 50 percent or less of the clay matrix for all but one of the eleven samples (fig. 2). Only P42, a decorated jar, has a higher proportion of clay at 70 percent. It is the only painted vessel of this ware group. Pottery types in this ware group include cooking pots, jars, craters, large bowls, and one small slipped bowl.

Group 2:  Medium Basalt Ware, N=8
          Samples P36, 41, 43, 52, 53, 54, 58, 59.

Basalt, now limited to 15 to 40 percent, is supplanted by grog as the dominant inclusion for the eight samples of this group. Grog and basalt are either equal in quantity or grog is greater, ranging from 30 to 60 percent of the total inclusions. Rounded and angular grog fragments vary in size from 0.4 to 3.0 mm, comparable to the basalt-rich

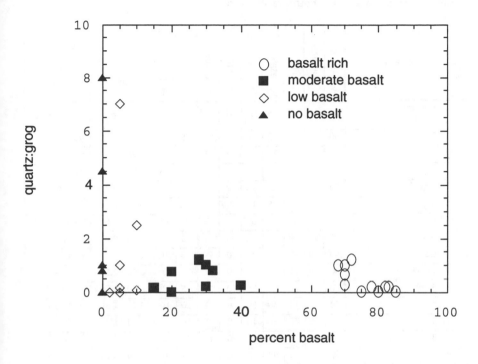

Figure 2. Petrographic samples P30 through P60 plotted according to percentages of basalt and the ratio of quartz : grog. Groups 1–3 are differentiated and groups 4 and 5 are together in the category of "no basalt."

wares, but with one difference. Whereas grog inclusions of all sizes are found in each ware type, for the medium basalt wares, the large grog fragments can be a minority within each shard. For example, although P53 includes one fragment measuring 3.0 mm across, the majority are 0.3 to 1.3 mm. Larger fragments are only occasionally found, which suggests that some sorting had occurred to create a slightly fine, less porous clay body. All inclusions are well mixed throughout the clay matrix. The slightly smaller sizes of the inclusions in this group correspond to the thinner walls and smaller pot forms in contrast to the basalt-rich ware.

Basalt inclusions range in size from 0.5 to 2.0 mm, with a concentration between 0.5 and 1.5 mm. This represents a smaller size distribution than found in the basalt-rich ware. The upper size limit of

Table 3. Characterization of petrographic samples

| Sample | Vessel Type | % clay | % nonplastics | % voids | % basalt | % grog | % chert | % calcite | % opaques | % quartz | Size range (mm), of basalt clasts | Size range (mm) of grog clasts |
|---|---|---|---|---|---|---|---|---|---|---|---|---|
| P30 | Construction Material | 50 | 20 | 30 | 5 | 80 | 0 | 10 | 5 | 0 | 0.25 - 1.20 | up to 3.00 |
| P31 | Bowl | 60 | 30 | 10 | 2 | 0 | 0 | 83 | 5 | 10 | 0.20 - 0.50 | none present |
| P32 | Cooking pot | 50 | 20 | 30 | 75 | 0 | 0 | 0 | 25 | 0 | 0.20 - 1.50 | none present |
| P33 | Jug | 40 | 30 | 30 | 10 | 0 | 80 | 0 | 5 | 5 | 0.10 - 1. 00 | none present |
| P34 | Juglet | 70 | 20 | 10 | 0 | 10 | 0 | 35 | 10 | 45 | none present | up to 3.50 |
| P35 | Juglet | 65 | 20 | 15 | 5 | 10 | 0 | 10 | 5 | 70 | 0.10 - 0.50 | 0.15 - 0.75 |
| P36 | Jug | 40 | 30 | 30 | 15 | 60 | 0 | 0 | 1 | 10 | 0.25 - 1.00 | 0.60 - 2.00 |
| P37 | Bowl | 60 | 30 | 10 | 10 | 2 | 0 | 80 | 3 | 5 | 0.10 - 0.25 | 2.50 |
| P38 | Cooking pot | 40 | 40 | 20 | 0 | 0 | 0 | 90 | 10 | 0 | none present | none present |
| P39 | Cooking pot | 50 | 35 | 15 | 85 | 5 | 0 | 0 | 10 | 0 | 0.50 - 2.50 | 0.20 - 0.50 |
| P40 | Bowl | 70 | 20 | 10 | 5 | 80 | 0 | 5 | 5 | 5 | 0.40 - 1.50 | 0.10 - 1.5 |
| P41 | Jug | 70 | 20 | 10 | 30 | 50 | 0 | 0 | 10 | 10 | 0.25 - 1.50 | 0.25 0 2.50 |
| P42 | Jar | 70 | 20 | 10 | 80 | 10 | 0 | 0 | 10 | 0 | 0.20 - 1.20 | 0.50 - 3.00 |
| P43 | Bowl, large | 50 | 35 | 15 | 20 | 50 | 0 | 10 | 20 | 0 | 0.50 - 2.00 | 0.30 - 1.00 |
| P44 | Bowl | 50 | 35 | 15 | 80 | 5 | 0 | 0 | 15 | 0 | 0.10 - 0.70 | 0.10 - 0.70 |
| P45 | Bowl | 50 | 30 | 20 | 0 | 50 | 0 | 10 | 0 | 40 | none present | 0.10 - 0.70 |
| P46 | Bowl | 60 | 30 | 10 | 5 | 40 | 0 | 0 | 15 | 40 | 0.10 - 0.40 | 0.20 - 1.50 |
| P47 | Jar, holemouth, EBA | 50 | 30 | 20 | 70 | 10 | 0 | 0 | 10 | 10 | 0.20 - 1.50 | 0.40 - 0.75 |
| P48 | Bowl, large | 50 | 30 | 20 | 80 | 0 | 0 | 0 | 15 | 5 | 0.10 - 0.75 | none present |
| P49 | Cooking pot | 50 | 40 | 10 | 70 | 15 | 0 | 0 | 5 | 10 | 0.10 - 0.50 | 0.50 - 2.00 |
| P50 | Crater | 50 | 20 | 30 | 70 | 10 | 0 | 0 | 10 | 10 | 0.10 - 1.00 | 0.10 - 1.00 |
| P51 | Bowl | 60 | 20 | 20 | 0 | 40 | 0 | 5 | 15 | 40 | none present | 0.20 - 1.50 |
| P52 | Bowl | 75 | 10 | 15 | 30 | 30 | 0 | 0 | 10 | 30 | 0.10 - 0.50 | 0.20 - 0.75 |
| P53 | Bowl | 70 | 20 | 10 | 20 | 40 | 0 | 0 | 10 | 30 | 0.05 - 0.70 | 0.30 - 1.30 + one 3.00 |
| P54 | Strainer | 60 | 20 | 20 | 30 | 30 | 0 | 0 | 10 | 30 | 0.10 - 0.50 | 0.30 - 2.00 |
| P55 | Bowl | 50 | 40 | 10 | 0 | 10 | 0 | 0 | 10 | 80 | none present | 0.10 - 0.30 |
| P56 | Cooking pot | 50 | 30 | 20 | 70 | 10 | 0 | 0 | 10 | 10 | 0.05 - 1.00 | 0.50 - 2.0 |
| P57 | Cooking pot | 50 | 20 | 30 | 70 | 20 | 0 | 0 | 5 | 5 | 0.20 - 1.50 | 0.50 - 1.50 |
| P58 | Cooking pot | 70 | 15 | 15 | 30 | 30 | 0 | 0 | 10 | 30 | 0.10 - 0.70 | 0.20 - 0.50 |
| P59 | Crater | 50 | 30 | 20 | 40 | 40 | 0 | 0 | 10 | 10 | 0.10 - 0.80 | 0.20 - 4.00 |
| P60 | Cooking pot | 40 | 40 | 20 | 85 | 10 | 0 | 0 | 5 | 0 | 0.10 - 1.50 | 0.15 - 1.00 |

the basalt, which does not exceed 2.0 mm (versus 2.5 mm for the basalt-rich ware), along with the intentionally added grog, reveals that potters purposefully prepared this clay matrix prior to its use. Potters altered the raw material by removing the largest basalt fragments and then added crushed pottery. As a consequence of adding the grog, the overall percentage of basalt was reduced. The ratio of clay : voids : nonplastics differs from the basalt-rich group in that clay at times accounts for over 50 percent of the matrix (n=5 samples), 50 percent (n=3), and 40 percent (n=1). This represents two differences from the basalt-rich ware: (1) more variation in the amounts of clay to nonplastics than in the more consistent basalt-rich group; and (2) a larger proportion of clay to nonplastics. The result is a denser, less porous, more compact ware. As in the basalt-rich ware, oval and rectangular voids from organic material are 10 to 30 percent of the clay matrix and range in size from 0.05 to 2.5 mm.

Vessel types included in the medium basalt ware are a cooking pot (P58), jugs (P36 and P41, a painted jug), a strainer/incense burner (P54), burnished or slipped bowls (P52 and 53), a large bowl (P43), and a crater (P59). Medium-sized vessels predominate along with smaller pieces, some bearing decoration, in contrast to larger containers made of the basalt-rich ware of group 1.

Group 3:   Low Basalt Ware, N=7
            Samples P30, 31, 33, 35, 37, 40, 46.
In this ware type, basalt is present in quantities not greater than 10 percent and drops down to 1 or 2 percent. Angular to rounded basalt inclusions range in size from 0.25 to 1.5 mm. The predominant nonplastic varies and is the determining factor in the subgroups within the low basalt ware. Four subgroups are defined by the quantity of grog, calcite, quartz, and chert as well as a separate category for construction material. Samples 30, 40, and 46 are rich in grog (80, 80, and 40 percent respectively), whereas other samples have 2 to 10 percent grog, and P31 and 33 lack grog. When present, the size distribution of grog is 0.1 to 3 mm, not unlike the other basalt-tempered wares. However, the size range of the basalt shows a marked difference, measuring 0.25 to 1.5 mm. This is a full millimeter smaller than the largest inclusions in the basalt-rich ware.

Group 3A:  Low Basalt Ware: Calcite-Rich Decorated Pottery
            Samples P31, 37.

Calcite constitutes 80 percent of the inclusions found in the two red slipped and burnished bowls P31 and P37. Basalt is present (10 percent or less). Quartz and opaques appear in even smaller amounts, and one piece of grog (2.5 mm across) was identified in P37. Voids account for a mere 10 percent of the clay body, with 60 percent clay and only 30 percent nonplastics. Inclusions are normally fine in size, ranging from 0.01 to 0.5 mm, and they are well mixed throughout the clay matrix. For P31, the tan/gray firing clay appears to be very fine-grained and few if any inclusions are visible with the naked eye. For the thicker-walled P37, firing pink/brown in color, white and gray inclusions appear as specks to the unaided eye, in contrast to a single large (2.5 mm) grog inclusion. In contrast to the other calcite-rich clay matrix of a cooking pot (see below), the calcite in this group is smaller in size and is mainly round and oval in shape, and not the angular forms with rhombs common as in P38. Furthermore, unlike the cooking pot category, basalt is minimally present in the calcite group of decorated pottery.

Group 3B:  Low Basalt Quartz-Rich Ware
            Sample P35.

Whereas other samples contain quartz, P35 has a predominance of quartz, accounting for 70 percent of all inclusions, in addition to a small amount of rounded calcite (10 percent), subrounded grog (10 percent), angular basalt (5 percent), and angular and equant opaques (5 percent). An occasional piece of basalt and grog are present, whereas the quartz, opaques, and calcite are well mixed throughout the clay matrix. Rounded to oval voids of nonplastics measure 0.05 to 1 mm. A slip measuring 0.01 mm in width is measurable under the microscope. This red slipped small jug with trefoil mouth, P35, is similar to bowl P55 in that quartz, opaques, and grog are comparable in each, but P55 lacks calcite and the trace of basalt found in P35. The clay matrix has an almost homogeneous fine-grained appearance as a result of the relatively high percentage of clay at 65 percent clay, 15 percent voids, and 20 percent nonplastics. In the fine-grained tan firing clay matrix it is difficult to discern inclusions with the naked eye. Quartz-rich P35 is indistinguishable from P31, a calcite-rich fine ware without the aid of thin sections and microscope. Both are red slipped and burnished.

Group 3C: Low Basalt Ware: Chert-Rich Ware
　　　　Sample P33.
An abundant fine-grained inclusion (80 percent of the nonplastics) tentatively identified as chert, in rounded to subangular fragments measuring 0.02 to 2.0 mm in size, distinguishes this ware. Basalt represents 10 percent in angular to rounded fragments measuring 0.1 to 1.0 mm. There is a trace of calcite, small quantities of subrounded quartz (5 percent) between 0.03 and 1.0 mm, and rounded opaques (5 percent) measuring 0.05 to 0.1 mm, all found throughout the clay. Voids are plentiful (30 percent), extending up to 10.0 millimeters long and 2.0 mm wide. It is possible that this handle contains more voids than the vessel body of the jug or cooking pot. Potters often add extra nonplastics to accessory pieces to facilitate their drying at the same rate as the rest of the body. As such the clay matrix of the body might contain a lower percentage of voids than the handle. Macroscopically, the ware is rough, coarse, and has the feel of a cooking pot. The proportion of clay is one of the lowest at 30 percent with another 30 percent voids and 40 percent inclusions.

Group 3D: Low Basalt Ware: Construction Material
　　　　Sample P30.
The fragment of construction material (P30) examined petrologically contains small amounts of basalt (5 percent), hematite (5 percent), and calcite (10 percent). Angular to rounded grog predominates, representing 80 percent of the tempering material. The clay was well mixed with inclusions distributed evenly throughout the clay body. Equant to elongate-shaped voids of burned out organic material account for 30 percent, nonplastics 20 percent, and clay 50 percent. Inclusions range in size from 0.25 to 1.2 meters (basalt), 0.3 to 1.2 mm (calcite), 0.2 mm (hematite), and grog fragments are found up to 3 mm in size. Messy and heterogeneous describe the appearance.

　　　The low basalt ware group 3 includes the construction material (P30), slipped bowls (P31, 37, 40), jugs (P33, 35 slipped), and a medium-sized bowl (P46).

NONBASALT WARES

Groups 4 and 5. N=5
      Samples P34, 38, 45, 51, 55.
Five shards of the thirty-one sampled lack basalt altogether. For the present they are divided into two categories: cooking ware and fine ware. It is conceivable that the decorated pieces in group 5 do not constitute a viable group and with a larger sample could be further subdivided.

Group 4.    Calcite-tempered cooking ware.
      Sample P38
Cooking pot P38 lacks basalt but contains 90 percent calcite, with 5 percent each of round grog (0.5 to 2.0 mm) and round to oval opaques (0.04 to 0.1 mm). Grog appears as an occasional fragment whereas the opaques are well mixed as is the calcite (0.1 to 1.0 mm). Angular rhombs are common. Dr. John F. Shroder of the University of Nebraska, Omaha, identified foraminifera diagnostic of the Cretaceous carbonate rocks in the area of Bethsaida. Oval voids of nonplastics are quite fine and measure 0.1 to 0.25 mm. Voids account for 20 percent of the clay body, nonplastics 40 percent, and clay 40 percent. These proportions vary markedly from those of the other calcite group 3A in which voids are 10 percent, nonplastics 30 percent, and clay 60 percent, resulting in a much denser ware than that of cooking pot P38. There is no mistaking the two with the unaided eye.

Group 5.    Quartz-Decorated Fine Ware, N=4
      Samples P34, 45, 51, 55.
Quartz grains in 40, 40, 45, and 80 percent characterize this group of decorated pottery. Also present in varying quantities are grog (10 to 50 percent), calcite (5 to 35 percent but none in P55), and opaques (10 to 15 percent and none in P45). Basalt is entirely absent. Sample P45 contains two distinct grogs, differentiated by their light and dark colors. The percentage of clay is 50 to 70 percent, with nonplastics 20 to 30 percent and voids 10 to 20 percent depending on the sample. Most of the nonplastics are small in size (0.02 to 0.8 mm) except for the grog (0.1 to 1.5 mm with occasional pieces as large as 3.5 mm). For P55, the clay exhibits a very fine-grained appearance, fired grayish brown throughout. Rare medium-sized clasts appear in sharp contrast to the

rest of the clay matrix consisting of fine quartz (0.05 to 0.5 mm), opaques (0.03 0.1 mm), and grog (0.1 to 0.3 mm) inclusions. The voids are similarly infrequent (10 percent), measuring 0.05 to 0.1 mm. Sample P51 has thick interior and exterior slips, a thick dark gray core with thin brown firing margins. White and gray inclusions are visible to the unaided eye. Although this is a less-fine-grained ware than the others in this group, it appears quite compact. P51 contains 60 percent clay and 20 percent each of nonplastics and voids. There might be differentiation within this group, but the sample size is too small at present to warrant further delineation. Uniting the group is the absence of basalt, presence of quartz, and vessel type. All objects included here belong to a category of fine, small, thin-walled decorated shapes. The painted and/or burnished juglet (P34) and bowls (P45, 51) could well represent pottery made at some distance from the site and imported for their contents or aesthetic qualities, but not necessarily from the same place.

## PETROGRAPHIC ANALYSIS: PREPARATION OF THE RAW MATERIALS

Our sample suite includes a variety of vessel types and variations within each type when possible. The primary goal of the study was not to determine the precise source of the clay used for the pottery, nor the production locations, but to learn about the distribution of local versus nonlocal ceramic artifacts and variation within the tradition as a whole. One question concerns whether the potters added or extracted rocks and minerals, or if the nonplastics were native to the raw material. Often this is difficult, if not impossible, to address depending on the specific type of inclusion present. One looks for evidence in the size, shape, and distribution of the inclusions in the clay body. Ethnoarchaeological studies record extant traditional potters working in all parts of the world such as Crete, Africa, Cyprus, and the Philippines, who do not add tempering materials to clay.[5] They add water alone. Potters prefer to learn how to work with the clay at hand instead of spending time and effort to clean and prepare clay. These potters will, however, remove the largest rocks and pieces of organic material that they come across while working the clay. In addition, small-sized organic material remains in the clay to help it sour, thereby rendering it more workable. Another way to create a suitable clay without adding or extracting anything is to mix together two clays. This allows potters to benefit from the properties inherent in each clay, especially if individually each is unsuitable.[6] There is no evidence to conclude that potters who add tempering material represent the norm.

For the Bethsaida Iron Age material, the inclusions provide a partial answer concerning treatment and preparation of the clay, particularly the presence of grog, which figures prominently in our assemblage. Grog, one of the best inclusions potters can add intentionally, is still used by professional potters today. Grog is made by crushing and grinding old or broken pots and shards into small fragments. Since it is clay that has withstood one firing already, it responds well to further fires. It adheres well to other clay particles to form a compact material. It is porous and can absorb paint or slip applied to a vessel surface in contrast to rocks, which are not absorbent. Its porosity further serves to open the vessel wall, which facilitates drying and firing. Grog can be crushed into a variety of sizes. Ideally, potters prefer inclusions that vary in size sufficiently to allow maximum mixing, meshing, and interlocking of clay with the tempering material. Wares with copious rock inclusions often require a slip application before a painted decoration precisely because the paint will not adhere to the rocks that protrude on the surface. The slip serves both to cover the rocks and readily absorb the paint. All five ware groups include samples with grog (fig. 3). There appears to be little correlation between vessel wall thickness and grog size. Thinner walled pots might have a predominance of small and fine sized grog, but individual larger fragments occasionally are present, for example, in P42 and P49.

Fresh breaks in many of the potsherds reveal the presence of black basalt inclusions. The availability of Neogene-Quaternary basalt in the region suggests that potters did not add basalt to the clay but that it was present in the raw material. Our single Early Bronze Age holemouth jar contains basalt as well (P47). The concern here then is to ask whether potters sometimes extracted basalt from the clay; not whether they added basalt. In some instances there is evidence of intentional preparation and cleaning of the clay by removal of the largest fraction of rocks and minerals, especially the basalt; for example, in petrographic groups 2 and 3. A trend for more and bigger basalt nonplastics in the larger pots is discernible when comparing the twenty-three samples with basalt (fig. 4), but given the small sample

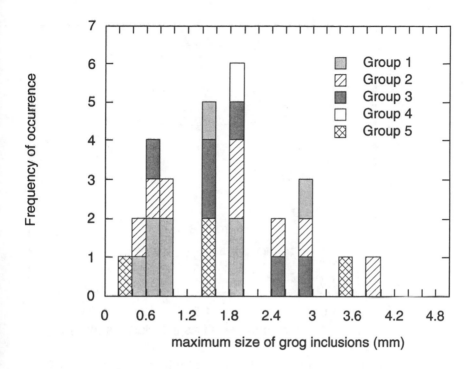

Figure 3. Size distribution of grog inclusions for ware groups 1–5.

size for each ware group, the results are not conclusive. The concentration of small rather than large basalt grains in ware group 3 suggests that potters and their assistants might have taken care to eliminate the large basalt fragments. In other words, there is a tendency for the lower percentages of basalt to correspond with the smaller inclusions.

Other inclusions present in the Bethsaida Iron Age pottery are calcite, quartz, hematite, chert, and opaques. If calcite is the dominant inclusion in cooking pots, potters most likely added it, as ethnographic evidence for this practice documents.[7] In all, three samples (P31, 37, 38) contain large quantities of calcite, but P38 alone is a cooking pot. Voids remaining from organic material that fired away are evidence of yet another inclusion type. They range from 10 to 30 percent of the clay matrix (fig. 5). For the collection as a whole, non-plastics that were intentionally added to the clay include grog and at times calcite and organic materials. For some ware categories, potters intentionally removed the largest basalt fraction. The small size (0.01

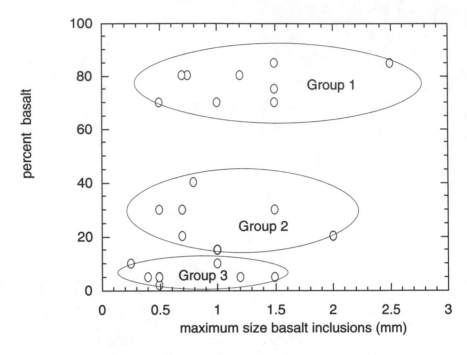

Figure 4. Maximum size of basalt inclusions for basalt ware groups 1–3.

to 0.6 mm) and limited quantities of opaques (3 to 10 percent, with only two samples that contained 20 percent) suggest that the inclusions are native to the clay. For other rocks and minerals, such as the quartz, calcite, chert, it is not clear whether they were native to the clay or potters added them.[8]

## Discussion of the Construction Material

Sample P30, a 26-millimeter-thick piece of fired clay from locus 601, belongs to a vat, chinking material, or a statue. Possibly it does not date to the Iron Age II period and could be more recent. Its nondescript nature precludes typological dating, but it might be a representative of the locally available material since it belongs to a large thick-walled object. One would expect that for thick-walled clay objects, people used nearby clays and not imported materials. For example, bricks examined but not included in this study reveal the presence of basalt and differ markedly from P30. With 30 percent voids of burned-out organic material, this is one of the highest percentages of organic

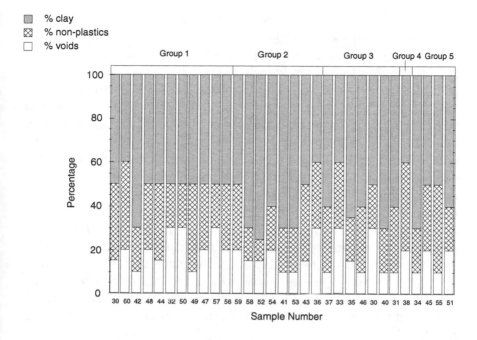

Figure 5. Ratio of clay : nonplastics; voids in each petrographic sample arranged according to ware groups 1–5

material in Bethsaida ceramics. Straw in thick clay objects, such as bricks for example, helps prevent excessive shrinkage and cracking during the drying period.[9] Along with the high percentage of voids, P30 is mineralogically interesting because it contains so little basalt, a mere 5 percent in contrast to the large quantity (80 percent) of grog. It has some calcite (10 percent) and is the only sample with hematite (5 percent). Grog serves as an excellent inclusion if paint or other finish covers the surface since grog readily absorbs an applied treatment. Selection of this sample was designed to establish the local clay deposits even though it is unlikely that the same potters who made pots were those who made large stationary clay objects. This is not to suggest that there is no interaction between brickmakers and potters. To this day construction workers use broken pottery as filler for making bricks. However, the large quantity of grog and minimal amount of basalt reveal little about the composition of the locally available raw materials.[10]

## Manufacturing Techniques

As in most pottery assemblages, more than one manufacturing technique was used to create the Bethsaida Iron Age material.[11] Clays of five ware groups have been identified and there appears to be a correlation between vessel types and clays. A clear association between a specific manufacturing technique and clay type can be ascribed to jugs and cooking pots. To define and describe details of the manufacturing generally requires a large collection of shards as well as reconstructible pots. For the Bethsaida Iron Age deposits, both of these requirements were absent, since the reconstructible pots were reassembled prior to investigation of the manufacturing techniques. Nevertheless, examination of their surfaces allows one to comment on the tradition in general. Wheel-thrown wares are not the norm. Some of the smaller pieces, especially the lamps and perhaps some of the dipper juglets, were thrown from a cone of clay all in one piece and later thinned in the hand. Most shapes were made in the upside-down technique involving a tournette or slow wheel that lacked momentum. Potters continued to coil pots and use molds in combination with turntable rotation.

### Upside-Down Manufacturing Technique

Jugs.   To shape closed vessels, such as jug 4148 (*Bethsaida* 1, pl. XI:3), potters worked on a tournette or mobile work surface instead of a fast-turning wheel. Apparently, the potter punched a hole in a lump or cylinder of clay to open the clay to create a bowl-like shape with a thick lower body. Above the point of carination the body is coil constructed. Following a drying period, the neck was added. Traces of the rough neck join to the body remain. Then the potter added a handle that extended from the neck ridge. Fingerprints or smears on the interior neck remain where the handle was attached first to the neck ridge and then pulled down to the shoulder. Unintentional horizontal grooves on the handle top reveal evidence of the upside-down manufacturing technique. While the clay was wet, but after the handle was added, the vessel was returned to the tournette upside down in a chuck or holder to secure the jug as the potter scraped away the excess clay from the lower body before adding a ring base. The jug body and handle were burnished in several directions corresponding to vessel shape: vertical burnish strokes on the neck below the ridge and multidirectional strokes on the body.

Jug 4196 from locus 365 has a thick rim and a handle that extends from a neck ridge down to the shoulder. It was made of a red firing clay tempered with basalt, grog, and the rectangular voids of organic material. Evidence of manufacture consists of traces of a fibrous material used as external supports at two points of change in angle. On the rounded base are circular smoothing lines that imply a finishing trim was applied as the jug stood upside down on the turntable. Jug 4185 (*Bethsaida* 1, pl. XI:2), with a cone-shaped neck and a handle extending from the neck ridge to the shoulder, displays an irregular, rather asymmetrical body. Uneven pieces tend to stay close to their place of manufacture suggesting a nearby source for this jug. Basalt and grog inclusions confirm this. The neck, whose interior shows ridges, detached separately. Fingerprints are visible on the interior neck where the handle was added. A fillet was added to secure the lower handle attachment. There is a slight omphalso base resulting from the upside-down manufacture. On the base interior, an "s" crack suggests that the potter lacked access or failed to smooth and thin a base so thick that it cracked during the drying. Jug B. Sq. 43/1c 10.4.94, another possible trefoil spout, was also made in the upside-down technique. Jug P36, possibly with a trefoil mouth, displays marks on the neck interior indicative of a clockwise rotation direction for the final rim smoothing. Oblique striations of a smoothing cloth point to the opposite rotation direction.

Three jugs sampled for petrographic analysis (P33, 36, 41) suggest that potters preferred wares 2 and 3 to the basalt-rich ware 1 for jugs. There is one important distinction among the three sampled jugs. Unlike the jugs with a handle from the neck ridge to the shoulder, for P33, the only chert-tempered ware, the handle extends from below the neck ridge to the shoulder. Handle placement is not trivial. Here it differentiates the work of a potter who used a clay different from that used for the other jugs. The implications are that (1) the differences in handle placement represent the work of a different potter or workshop, (2) these differences coincide with specific ware groups, and (3) these differences do not necessarily have chronological significance. Instead they signal the work of different contemporaneous pottery workshops.

Jars. Jar 4173 (*Bethsaida* 1, pl. XIII:1) with two shoulder handles has a rim folded over to the exterior and is extremely heavy for its size. Made of a brown firing clay with a thick gray core, it represents local manufacture based on the presence of basalt and grog along with the rectangular voids of organic material and white inclusions. The uneven egg-shaped base is not especially thick, but the upper body is thick and heavy, possibly because it was coil made. The thin base could have been created after the upper body was complete. To do so involves the upside-down technique. After finishing the upper body and the rim, the piece was placed upside down on the turntable. Another jar, 4153 (*Bethsaida* 1, pl. XIII:2) has a simple slightly thick-ened rim and neck ridge and two handles that extend from the point of carination down to the lower body. It has a pink/tan surface, brown interior wall, and gray core. Inclusions of basalt, grog, white, and rect-angular and circular voids of organic material imply local manufacture.

Bowls. Common to shards of bowls are drag lines on the lower exte-rior body, which suggests that in the initial stage of manufacture the bowl bases were left as thick, heavy lower bodies that required scrap-ing and trimming once each vessel dried slightly. First a cylinder of clay was positioned on the turntable. The potter worked to open it into a rough bowl form to which coils were added to increase the height. After shaping and finishing the rim, the bowl was set aside to dry. Once the rim was sufficiently dry to support the weight of the clay, each bowl was turned upside-down on the turntable and finished by trimming and turning the clay down to the desired thinness.[12] The scraping tool causes drag marks by pulling inclusions across the sur-face. Typically, drag marks are deepest and widest where the inclusion was picked up and as it was pulled across the surface it left a long tail-like indentation in the clay until the inclusion dropped off. Drag marks are evidence of the final thinning and trimming work which, at times, was also responsible for unintentional burnished lower exterior bodies in contrast to the rest of the pot, which remained without the burnish sheen.[13]

Throwing from a Cone or Hump of Clay

Lamp 4185 (*Bethsaida* 1, pl. XIV) of tan clay with traces of soot, has an uneven, irregular spout, and displays rough burnishing on the exterior. Rather than intentionally burnish the base to create a shiny surface, the patchy sheen results from trimming and thinning the bottom. Nor was the burnish an effective procedure to reduce porosity.[14] The lamp was probably first thrown from a cone or hump of clay and left with a thick base that was thinned while it was held in the hand, thereby creating unintentional burnish strokes by compacting and compressing clay that had already dried slightly. Inclusions are black basalt, white rounded, rectangular voids of organic material, and very little, if any, grog. Voids of organics are so large that one can discern the regular striations of the fibers. Lamp 4185 (*Bethsaida* 1, pl. XVI:2), also probably thrown from a cone, is a nicer lamp with a smaller, tighter pinch than the previous. The bottom is uneven, yet less so than the other, and the base shows the fine concentric striations of a smoothing cloth.

## Mold manufacture

Produced with the help of a mold, cooking pot P38 perpetuates a Late Bronze and Iron Age I obsolescent tradition at Bethsaida. With the subsequent switch to a noncarbonaceous or powder-fine carbonaceous tempering material, potters could begin to fabricate cooking wares without a mold, first using coils and then with the help of a mobile work surface before throwing became possible. With 90 percent calcite and no basalt nonplastics, an elongated rim form, a wide vessel body, and a differentiated darkened core, cooking pot P38 contrasts with the red firing basalt-tempered cooking pots in form, fabric, fabrication, and firing. The vessel wall measures 4 mm at its thinnest point and 9 mm at the thickest point, which is found immediately above the point of carination. The lower body of this round-bottomed cooking pot was made in a mold, as is discernible in the bits of extra clay at the join of the mold and the first coil placed for the upper body. When the pot was made in a mold, the potter had control over the thickness of the lower body, which is quite thin here. It was more difficult to control the upper body thickness, which in this instance measures 5 mm more than the base. Smudging from cooking is still seen on the pot below the point of carination.

COIL MANUFACTURE

COOKING POTS. For cooking pot 4201 (*Bethsaida* 1, pl. IX:1) with a plain, simple rim from which two handles rise to the shoulder, there is a slight ridge on the neck, but no grooves. The gray core contains abundant black basalt inclusions, white gray angular fragments, and rectangular as well as oval (seed) voids of organic inclusions. The rounded base broke radially from the midpoint, then breaks as if one coil and another two coils were added up to the lower handle, followed by another coil, then one more coil until fifth was added for the rim. Coiled cooking pots tempered with basalt represent the local version of a noncalcite, nonmold made cooking pot.

## FIRING

Most shards have a darkened core area which is sandwiched by terra cotta colors. When firing pottery, organic material in the clay causes an initial dark color early in the firing. As the firing continues, the interior and exterior surfaces become lighter, but the gray, brown, or black cores remain when there is not a fully oxidized kiln atmosphere long enough for the oxygen to escape from the vessel wall. Had the potters fired their wares longer, had the kiln reached higher temperatures, and had the potters used more fuel, the cores would have disappeared resulting in a vessel wall of uniform color. Other considerations that determine the appearance of the darkened core are the amount and type of organic material, the vessel wall porosity, and the bond relation to the surfaces of the clay particles.[15] However, given the nature of the raw materials and the preferred surface appearance, a fully oxidized, "well-fired pot" was not necessarily desirable nor was it the ultimate goal. At times ancient potters may have aspired to create partially oxidized wares. More important than eliminating the dark core was the overall surface appearance, the nature of the nonplastics, and moderate use of fuel. There are two categories of pottery that would have suffered greatly from a fully oxidized kiln atmosphere: burnished wares and cooking pots tempered with carbonates, such as calcite or limestone. The Bethsaida Iron Age assemblage includes both of these vessel categories as do most contemporaneous pottery collections. A third consideration related to firing ceramics is the abundance and availability of fuels.

BURNISHED WARES

Various tools rubbed or pressed on a clay surface that has reached a certain stage of dryness, yet is not overly dry, can result in burnishing. Almost any solid, but not-too-hard object, such as a shell, will suffice for a tool. One result of pressing or rubbing the tool on the almost dry surface is the alignment of the clay particles in such a way that they will reflect light and appear to have a sheen after firing. Surfaces are intentionally burnished once a potter finishes forming the shape. In such instances the burnishing can be rendered by the potter, an apprentice, or a child. In contrast, an unintentional source of burnishing results from a stage in the manufacturing of the pot known as "turning" or "trimming" a pot made on a mobile work surface that normally lacks momentum. Although the primary goal of the operation is to thin the vessel wall, the effect is a burnished surface. For example, as a potter scrapes away the excess clay of a lamp base or the lower body of a bowl, the tool presses and compacts the clay particles in a manner similar to intentional burnishing. To fabricate many of the Iron Age bowls, potters used a turntable to help form the bowl, and initially left a thick rough base. In contrast, during this first stage of the work, the rim achieved its final form. After a brief period to allow the rim to dry sufficiently, the bowl would be repositioned on the turntable upside-down. In this position, the potter scraped or turned away unwanted clay from the lower half of the exterior wall to create a disc base of an appropriate thickness for a bowl. Potters could then add a clay coil to create a ring base. Since the upper part of the bowl was already thin enough, it required no trimming or turning. As a result, the burnish sheen is unevenly distributed over the vessel: It appears on the lower exterior wall, but not on the upper body nor the base, which was carved from clay that was still wet enough to trim yet too dry to become shiny.[16] One consequence for the archaeologist is difficulty in accurately describing the surface treatment of a vessel for which shards alone are present.

After the bowl dried, firing time proved to be critical for the final appearance of the vessel. The lower exterior retains a burnish sheen only if the kiln temperature did not exceed the point at which the burnish sheen fades. This applies for intentionally burnished pottery as well. Given the large percentage of burnished Iron Age pottery, potters would have taken care to avoid a fully oxidizing kiln atmosphere. They settled for a darkened core that still contained some organic material rather than risk losing the burnish sheen desired by their clients. Therefore, there is a direct connection between the presence of a burnished surface and the darkened cores. Evidence abounds that Iron Age potters were not always in full control of the kiln temperature. If potters lost the sheen, then only the slight indentations of the burnish or trimming tool remain as witness to the surface treatment, intentional or not.[17]

## Cooking Ware and Darkened Cores

The cooking vessel is another category of ware for which less firing can be better than more. For millennia, cooking pots were tempered with large calcite inclusions that were intentionally added to the clay because such inclusions allowed the pot to more easily withstand the stress of repeated heating and cooling, both during normal cooking and when in direct contact with heat. However, these same inclusions cannot withstand an initial firing temperature so high that the core disappears. Before that can happen the calcite disintegrates. Carbonate tempering materials, such as chalk, limestone, and calcite, experience thermal decomposition at temperatures as low as 600 degrees Centigrade, based on studies of samples from nearby Tell Hadar.[18]

At Bethsaida, Iron Age cooking pots are noteworthy for differences in firing color, tempering material, and manufacturing technique as well as in rim and body form. Bethsaida petrographic sample P38 belongs to a cooking pot form reminiscent of the Iron Age I tradition in that it has an elongated rim flange and a large wide body. It contains abundant angular milky-white shiny inclusions readily visible with the unaided eye. Microscopic analysis reveals that the sample contains 90 percent calcite, no basalt, and a small quantity of grog (5 percent) tempering material. The rim shape of this pot belongs to an older tradition than those that lack calcite tempering and have shorter, more compact rim shapes and small bodies, e.g., P32, 39, 56, 58, and 60. Overall vessel form is the superficial trait of the older tradition, but both the tempering material and the firing are also revealing. Unlike the red, brown, or tan firing cooking pots that are tempered with basalt (P32, 39, 56, 58, 60), P38 has a gray core with reddish margins. Darkened cores do not exist or are far less prominent in the basalt-tempered cooking pots because the potters could fire them to higher temperatures in the absence of a carbonaceous inclusion. Given the distinct mineralogical component of this cooking pot, which coincides with a vessel form, rim shape, and manufacturing technique derived from an earlier tradition, we conclude that more than one tradition of cooking pots coexisted. In addition to a small quantity of basalt, the foraminifera identified in the shard imply that potters made this cooking pot (and others not illustrated here) close to the site. Those potters were able to identify, select, and modify clays and tempering materials suitable for cooking wares, which differ from the clays used for the bulk of the repertoire.

Calcite tempering figures prominently as an inclusion in ancient cooking pots from Israel and Jordan.[19] Carbonaceous materials are the preferred inclusion for cooking ware because they can withstand constant and abrupt temperature changes during cooking.[20] Potters chose calcite to make cooking pots heat and shock resistant. This solution for dealing with the stress of cooking solved one problem, but it restricted the manufacturing technology and thereby created another dilemma, which was resolved only when cooking pot producers replaced the relatively large carbonaceous inclusions with other inclusions. Cooking pots excavated by Kathleen Kenyon at Jerusalem illustrate this important change.[21] Among Iron Age II cooking wares, several technologies coexisted. One tradition in Jerusalem perpetuates the Late Bronze Age coil-built cookers, while another tradition mimics the Iron Age I type of mold-made cooking pots with elongated rims and calcite tempering. Another type, class *c*, which originated in Transjordan in the twelfth century, has been suggested as the predecessor of cooking pots found west of the Jordan River in the Iron Age II period. Initially, it too was mold-made and contains coarse calcite tempering material. Only later did finer quartz inclusions replace calcite. Coinciding with the use of quartz was a shift in manufacture. Eventually the elimination of the mold enabled the entire shape of the cooking pot to become higher, narrower, and smaller. These changes could also have accompanied a change in usage or in eating habits. The shift to a fine quartz tempering material allowed the potters to produce wheel-thrown cooking pots (classes *d* through *f* at Jerusalem). A change to noncarbonaceous tempering material coincided with a new manufacturing technique, new rim forms, and a new ability to fire the ware to higher temperatures than ever before. One further development was the absence of darkened cores in cooking wares made in the new tradition; at least cores are less likely to be present. Without a carbonaceous material imposing a limit on the firing time and temperature, potters were able to fire cooking pots to a higher temperature for a longer duration.[22] At Bethsaida (table 4) cooking pots with the elongated rims that are characteristic of the Iron Age I tradition of manufacture correlate with the dark terra rosa brown and orange colored surfaces, the presence of a darkened core, and a carbonaceous tempering material. The shorter, fatter, more compact rims of the smaller cooking pots without calcite display no core or are less likely to have a core sandwiched between bright red and orange firing walls.

## DIFFERENTIATED CORES AND FUEL CONSERVATION

Fuel conservation is the third reason that potters accepted a differentiated core rather than a single firing color. Even more important than the lack of trees for fuel, was the expense in terms of the time required to cut or collect trees, branches, leaves, bark, pine cones, or dung. It is also heavy, hard work to transport fuel from its origin to the firing site. Traditional potters who work in Cyprus, Jordan, and the Philippines mention the hardships involved in the gathering and transporting of fuel as well as the difficulty of keeping it dry until used. Rather than collect fuel and carry it back, workers prefer to dig and carry clay back to their workspaces to make more pots.[23] In addition, the longer the fire burns, the longer the smoke is in the air, producing the least favorable aspect of the ceramics industry. Therefore, potters learned to produce pottery suitable for use yet not fully fired, and thereby saved fuel and cut costs while keeping the pottery's surface sheen that was preferred by their customers.

## ORIGIN OF BETHSAIDA IRON AGE CERAMICS

### BASALT-TEMPERED WARES

Determining the origin of the Bethsaida Iron Age wares is not a goal of the petrographic analysis, but a few general statements are possible since basalt is the dominant inclusion. Although not limited to the northern region, basalt is especially abundant north of Nahal Harod near Beth Shan as well as in the Galilee and Golan Heights.[24] Since Bethsaida is situated in a basalt-rich area, one can assume that basalt-tempered pottery was made at, near, or within a short distance from the site, but within the limited area of basalt outcrops. Olivine basalt

Table 4. Bethsaida Iron Age Cooking Pots, Loci 601 and 417

| Sample | Reg. no. | Locus | Core | Color | Inclusions | Rim[a] | Diameter (cm) |
|--------|----------|-------|------|-------|------------|-----|---------------|
| P32 | 5811.14 | 601 | A | Red | Basalt | C | 8.5 |
| P38 | 5834.10 | 601 | P | Red | Calcite | E | 11.0 |
| P39 | 5834.4 | 601 | A | Brown | Basalt; grog | C | N/A |
| | 5815.3 | 601 | N/A | N/A | N/A | E | N/A |
| | 5811.4 | 601 | N/A | N/A | N/A | E | N/A |
| P60 | 5811.20 | 601 | A | Brown | Basalt | Straight | 8.0 |
| P49 | 5168.13 | 417 | N/A | N/A | N/A | C | Iron III |
| P56 | 5163.1 | 417 | A | Red | Basalt | C | 10.5 |
| P57 | 5163.2 | 417 | P | Red | Basalt; grog; plus | E | N/A |
| P58 | 5163.3 | 417 | A | Tan | Basalt; grog; quart; plus | C | N/A |
| | 5176.1 | 417 | P | Brown | Calcit | E | N/A |
| | 5165.3 | 417 | ? | N/A | N/A | N/A | 12 |
| | 5146.1 | 417 | P | Red | Basalt; white and gray | E | 16 |
| | 5168.6 | 417 | P | Brown | Basalt; gray | E | 18? |
| | 5176.7 | 417 | P | Brown | Calcite | E | fragment |
| | 5180.3 | 417 | P | Red | Calcite | E | 18 |
| | 5142.1 | 417 | P | Red | N/A | E | N/A |
| | 5142.2 | 417 | P | Red | N/A | C | N/A |
| | 5142.3 | 417 | P | Brown | Calcite | C | N/A |
| | 5142.4 | 417 | N/A | N/A | Basalt; calcite | C | 10 |
| | 5142.8 | 417 | N/A | N/A | Calcite | C | fragment |
| | 4201 | 365 | P | Gray | Basalt; calcite | C | 15 |

a. Abbreviations: A=absent; P=present; E=elongated rim; C=compact rim; fragment=fragmentary and too small to determine rim diameter. Not all shards were submitted for petrographic analysis. Only those submitted were drawn. The only cooking pot from locus 365 included here is a pot published in *Bethsaida*, vol. 1, pl. ix.1.

of the type identified here, especially in samples P56 and 60, precludes origin of the pottery in the basaltic deposits of southern Israel.[25] Other sites yielding basalt-tempered wares include Tell Sasa, Tell Hadar, Tell Deir 'Alla, Bab edh-Dhra', and Numeira.[26] Basalt-rich wares are found in northern Israel beginning early as the Chalcolithic period.[27] At Tell 'Amal, not far from Bethsaida, basalt-tempered wares of the Early Bronze Age that were examined petrographically are similar to Iron Age pottery.[28] The Bronze Age wares are characterized as follows:

> In all cases, carbonate-rich clay, usually containing numerous foraminifera, was used together with tempering sand which consists of basalt, limestone, chert and chalk fragments. Basalt fragments: These are defined as alkali olivine basalt. The basalt is usually holocrystaline, with alternation of the olivine into iddingsite. Detrital crystals of basaltic minerals, derived from such rocks, also occur. The later contain plagioclase with polysynthetic twinning, augite and olivine. (Goren 1991:129)

The Bethsaida basalt-tempered wares closely resemble this description. Although the size and frequency of the basalt vary substantially, local and/or regional manufacture for basalt-tempered wares excavated at Bethsaida characterizes much of the pottery. Petrographic wares 2 and 3 were altered as found in nature, which is evident from the upper size limit of the largest basalt fraction in these two wares. Ware 1, the basalt-rich ware, was perhaps processed to remove the very largest rock fragments, but without eliminating as much basalt as for the other two wares.

The use of grog is clear evidence that the potters altered the raw material by intentionally crushing pottery and then adding it as an inclusion, especially if it constitutes 80 percent of the nonplastics. Grog lowers the overall percentage of basalt, and as a result, it is plausible that originally the clays used for the three different basalt-tempered wares were identical or at least similar, but were treated and prepared differently to accommodate the needs of the potter. For finer wares, or those with thinner walls and decorated surfaces, potters apparently sifted the clay to remove basalt before they added the grog. Alternatively, the four basalt wares might represent different clay deposits which differed initially and were further differentiated by cleaning and adding grog. The four basalt-tempered ware groups could also represent four workshops or groups of potters, contemporaneous or not, each of whom specialized in different vessel types made from a specific type of clay. The basalt-rich ware characterizes large vessels and cooking pots. Medium basalt wares include small- and medium-sized open and closed containers as well as cooking pots. Pots made from the low basalt ware range from small- and medium-sized bowls and jugs along with the construction material. Both the medium and basalt-rich clays were suitable for manufacture of cooking pots. This is one piece of evidence to suggest that once potters learned to create cooking pots without crushed calcite, they were free to use diverse clays, thereby allowing more potters to make cooking pots instead of only small groups of potters with access to the precious calcite. As a result one might detect an increase in the variety of rim and body shapes as well as diversity of clay recipes.

NON-BASALT-TEMPERED WARES. In contrast to the basalt-tempered wares, there are the five shards that altogether lack basalt. The small sample size and the nature of the petrographic analysis does not allow us to comment further than to state that these wares, except for the cooking pot, were not made in the immediate area of Bethsaida. They include the smaller decorated pieces as well as the old-fashioned cooking pot, P38. Theoretically, potters could bring calcite to any location to make cooking pots. Foraminifera in P38, identified as Cretaceous carbonates in the Bethsaida area, suggest that potters made the pot near the site using clays suitable for cooking pot manufacture.

Petrographic analysis, although not designed to address the issue of provenience, does enable one to separate pottery into ware categories which can help provide answers to questions related to the organization of both the ceramics industry and trade. One can comment on which types of vessels were imported to the site in contrast to those made in the vicinity of Bethsaida and can characterize variation within the basalt-tempered wares found at one site. For the Iron Age Bethsaida assemblage, although the petrographic results demonstrate that certain smaller decorated wares were made at some distance from the site (i.e. beyond the basalt areas), another example of decorated pottery (P41) was made within the area of clay deposits that contained basalt. Not all slipped and painted wares were acquired from long-distance trade. In the Iron Age, the local ceramics industry was sufficiently versatile and the clay was suitable enough to accommodate both utilitarian wares that were used daily (such as cooking pots and table wares) and the finer category (large to small decorated pottery). The term "local" is ambiguous since it fails to stipulate whether the pottery was made at the site, nearby, within 5 kilometers' distance, or even farther away.[29] Despite this uncertainty, we differentiate between wares that contain basalt and those that have no basalt. The latter were carried to the site from some distance. Imports or artifacts of long-distance trade normally include pots imported for their contents, special qualities (such as a cooking pot), and their intrinsic value or beauty. In addition to differentiating basalt from nonbasalt wares, there are divergencies within the basalt tempered wares based on the quantity and size of the basalt inclusions that can be interpreted as indicative of different workshops, recipes, potters, or chronological age.

## Distribution of the Ware Types at Bethsaida

An analysis of the distribution of the ware groups within the site based on this small sample is not necessarily informative since the petrographic sample derives from two loci and is not a representative sample of the Iron Age material as a whole. Nevertheless, the current results suggest that ware 1, the basalt-rich ware, is found in both loci 601 and 417. The same is true for ware 2, but ware 3, the low basalt group, figures most prominently in locus 601 (P30, 31, 33, 35, 37, 40, 46). Ware 4, the calcite-tempered old-style cooking pot, comes from locus 601. Cooking pots with elongated rims and made from a clay body rich in calcite appear in both loci 601 and 417. Shortened compact rims on cooking pots made from a basalt tempered clay are found in each deposit.

## Organization of the Regional Pottery Industry

Based on the Bethsaida material, it appears that potters working in the Iron Age either specialized according to vessel size and surface finish or that there were workshops which produced almost the full repertoire of shapes (table 5). The diversity of shapes, especially large forms and cooking pots made of petrographic ware group 1, suggests some workshops produced a wide range of shapes. In contrast, there were workshops or potters who specialized in small slipped and burnished pieces, both open and closed forms, fabricated from wares 2 and 3. A separate group of potters with access to calcite produced the old-fashioned cooking pots. Nothing suggests domestic production. The availability of grog indicates an industry of craft specialists who produced a large enough inventory to have wasters which could regularly be crushed into grog to guarantee sufficient tempering material.

## Regular Repertoire

Workshops Producing the Full Repertoire. Potter's marks drawn into wet clay help to identify wares produced in a single workshop, but they are often reserved for large containers, for example, the exterior base of the large slipped jar P42. Although other pots lack any signature or mark, this jar belongs to petrographic ware group 1, the basalt-rich clay which characterizes a third of our sample (table 6). One can infer that the same potter and/or workshop responsible for the signed jar made other smaller pieces belonging to the same ware group. Perhaps because of its fairly large size and painted decoration it warranted a potter's mark. In contrast, all the smaller pieces are without marks. Iron Age wares in general lack potter's marks, except for large jars. In our sample, wares 1 and 2 were clays used for painted and plain surfaces. Some vessel types are found made of either wares 1 or 2; for example, bowls, craters, and cooking pots. Ware 2 was satisfactory for jugs and the strainer/incense burner.

We conclude that ware 1 was manufactured by craft specialists who worked in seasonally operated potteries where they made a large variety of shapes. Based on our sample, craft specialists working with ware 2 produced a repertoire of smaller vessels. A broader sample might invalidate this assessment if larger containers are found to have been made of this ware. Seasonal production is stipulated for the dry months given the weather patterns prevalent in the region. Pottery production requires ample sunlight for all phases of the work. It is easier to dig dry clay rather than rain-saturated clay. Sunlight and dry air are requirements to dry pottery, which is never drier than the air around it given the hygroscopic property of clay: it absorbs moisture from the air. Without dry air, potters resort to artificial means to dry pots, such as drying fires. Fuel must be dry to burn. Rain falling on a stoked hot kiln causes disaster. When the water comes into contact with the hot pots and kiln they burst. One method to avoid this is to cover the kiln. Pottery production in the dry season also coincides with a lull in agricultural activities, thus enabling people to find work year-round.

Table 5. Petrographic Ware Groups 1–5 (Iron Age)

| Group | Sample | Reg. no. | Locus | Vessel type |
|---|---|---|---|---|
| 1 | P32 | 5811.14 | 601 | Cooking pot with compact rim |
| | P39 | 5834.4 | 601 | Cooking pot |
| | P42 | 5834.5 | 601 | Jar, slipped |
| | P44 | 5834.9 | 601 | Bowl, hemispherical |
| | P47 | 5168.8 | 417 | Jar, holemouth, Early Bronze Age |
| | P48 | 5168.2 | 417 | Bowl, large |
| | P49 | 5168.13 | 417 | Cooking pot |
| | P50 | 5168.10 | 417 | Crater |
| | P56 | 5163.1 | 417 | Cooking pot |
| | P57 | 5163.2 | 417 | Cooking pot |
| | P60 | 5811.20 | 601 | Cooking pot |
| 2 | P36 | 5824.2 | 602 | Jug |
| | P42 | 5834.2 | 601 | Jug, painted |
| | P43 | 5834.3 | 601 | Bowl, large |
| | P52 | 5176.2 | 417 | Bowl |
| | P53 | 5176.3 | 417 | Chalice/bowl, burnished |
| | P54 | 5176.8 | 417 | Strainer/incense burner |
| | P58 | 5163.3 | 417 | Cooking pot |
| | P59 | 5854.1 | 601 | Crater |
| 3A | P31 | 5811.1 | 601 | Bowl, red slip and burnish |
| | P37 | 5834.1 | 601 | Bowl, red slip and burnish |
| 3B | P35 | 5811.9 | 601 | Juglet |
| 3C | P33 | 5811.5 | 601 | Jug |
| 3D | P30 | 5811.19 | 601 | Construction material |
| 4 | P38 | 5834.1 | 601 | Cooking pot |
| 5 | P34 | 5811.2 | 601 | Jug, red slip and burnish |
| | P45 | 5824.4 | 601 | Bowl, with paint |
| | P52 | 5176.6 | 417 | Bowl |
| | P55 | 5180.5 | 417 | Bowl, hemispherical |

SMALL SLIPPED AND BURNISHED VESSELS. Contemporaneous with the workshops that produced a broad spectrum of shapes and sizes were more specialized potters who worked with ware 3, characterized by its low basalt content and somewhat smaller inclusion size than wares 1 and 2. This less coarse clay, suitable for bowls and jugs, usually appears with a slipped and/or burnished surface. The implication is that small open and closed shapes covered with a slip or burnish were the reserve of a different set of potters than those who worked with wares 1 and 2 to produce the larger, more utilitarian shapes. Therefore, while potters responsible for the basalt-rich ware 1 clay vessels were capable and did make small pieces, based on our sample, the latter were normally

Table 6. Distribution of Iron Age Vessel Types According to Petrographic Ware Groups

| Ware | Bowl | Chal-ice | Crater | Jug | Juglet | Store Jar | Cook-ing Pot | Lamp | Strainer | Const. mat'l | Totals |
|------|------|------|--------|-----|--------|-----------|-----------|------|----------|-------------|--------|
| 1 | 1 | 0 | 2 | 0 | 0 | 1 | 6 | 0 | 0 | 0 | 10 |
| 2 | 1 | 1 | 2 | 2 | 0 | 0 | 1 | 0 | 1 | 0 | 8 |
| 3 (a–d) | 4 | 0 | 0 | 1 | 1 | 0 | 0 | 0 | 0 | 1 | — |
| 3a | 2 | 0 | 0 | 0 | 0 | 0 | 0 | 0 | 0 | 0 | 2 |
| 3b | 0 | 0 | 0 | 0 | 1 | 0 | 0 | 0 | 0 | 0 | 1 |
| 3c | 0 | 0 | 0 | 1 | 0 | 0 | 0 | 0 | 0 | 0 | 1 |
| 3d | 2 | 0 | 0 | 0 | 0 | 0 | 0 | 0 | 0 | 1 | 3 |
| 4 | 0 | 0 | 0 | 0 | 0 | 0 | 1 | 0 | 0 | 0 | 1 |
| 5 | 2 | 0 | 0 | 0 | 2 | 0 | 0 | 0 | 0 | 0 | 4 |
| Totals | 8 | 1 | 4 | 3 | 3 | 1 | 8 | 0 | 1 | 1 | 30 |

made by potters working with a finer clay, ware 2 but especially ware 3. The results imply that potters specialized according to vessel size and surface treatment.

IMPORTED VESSELS. We cannot comment on the organization of the ceramics industries responsible for the production of ware 5. Our sample of two bowls and two jugs is not representative of those work-shops. It is possible that ware 5 was reserved for small decorated forms. Alternatively, if ware 5 represents items of long-distance trade, it is plausible that only small shapes reached Bethsaida and that larger pieces can be found closer to the source.

COOKING POT PRODUCTION. During the era of calcite-tempered cooking wares, production was most likely the work of potters who specialized in their manufacture. The potters worked with our designated ware 4. Potters able to procure calcite monopolized the market until others learned to work with different clays. The end of the monopoly and evidence that cooking pot manufacture shifted to a larger number of potters is discernible in the great variety of rim shapes. Potters who made the regular repertoire may have also made cooking pots once calcite was no longer essential. Of the basalt-tempered cooking pots sampled, six belong to ware 1 and only one was made of ware 2. The cooking pot specialists were possibly itinerant potters who carried calcite wherever they worked. Support for this suggestion is the presence of a small amount of basalt tempering found along with the calcite. Cooking pot producers may have extracted as much basalt as possible from the clay to which they added large quantities of calcite.

## Date of the Iron Age Ceramic Assemblage

To establish a date for the Iron Age pottery based solely on typological considerations does not provide a necessarily appropriate time frame for the construction, use, or reuse of the architecture in which it was found, given the extensive disturbances and reuse of the area in subsequent eras.

### Cooking Pots

Typologically, there is evidence of cooking pots normally dated to the eleventh century (P38) as well as those of the tenth century (P32, 39, 56, 57, 58) and early ninth century (P49, 60). We associate the elongated rim type (P38) with the older Late Bronze and Iron Age I tradition of wide-bodied calcite-tempered pottery. Sample P38 resembles a cooking pot found in the old and new Beth Shan excavations, where they are dated to the eleventh century, and a pot from Tell Mevorakh VIII.[30] Although this cooking pot is from locus 601, which could represent a prepalatial phase, cooking pots with short, thickened, compact rims characteristic of tenth- and ninth-century material are also found in locus 601, for example P32, with a ridge or step, and P39, with a short compact triangular rim, all of which are basalt tempered. Sample P32 exemplifies the new Iron Age II tradition of cooking pots that lack white inclusions among the plethora of small black inclusions in a red firing ware. Sample P39, with a shorter triangular rim than the Iron Age I tradition, lacks a groove under the rim and is similar to those from Beth Shan level IV and Tell Mevorakh VII.[31] The two handles are another feature of Iron Age II cooking pots. Short, squat bodies accompany these rims. Another rim type, which stands vertical with ridges and belongs to a short globular cooking pot (P60) and usually dates to the ninth and tenth centuries, is known from Tell 'Amal IV as well as Tell Mevorakh VII of the tenth century.[32]

Other cooking pot shards that display elongated rims typical of the earlier tradition are present in locus 601 (e.g. 5815.3, 5811.4) and in locus 417 (5180.3, 5142.3, 5142.8). These are calcite tempered and have differentiated cores. Although statistics on the percentages of old versus new cooking pots in each locus are not meaningful given the small sample size, the coexistence of at least two techniques and possibly three, is readily apparent in the nature of the inclusions as well as the precise vessel and rim forms. Vessels of the newer tradition tend to be smaller, lack calcite, contain basalt inclusions, fire without a darkened core, and they have smaller compact rims and squatter bodies. The onset of a new tradition does not irrevocably eradicate an earlier tradition. A possible experimental phase during which time potters used basalt-tempered clays while continuing to use molds and coils remains speculation. From locus 417, cooking pot 5180.3 displays a compact, short triangular rim with an undergroove characteristic of Iron Age II, yet it contains abundant fine white inclusions in a thin-walled red firing clay with a thick gray core. The estimated diameter is 10 cm, which would place it in the size category of the small cooking pots. This could be an example of another trend in cooking pot manufacture: the use of powdered or finely ground carbonaceous material which can withstand higher kiln temperatures than coarse-grained angular calcite fragments.

One consequence of a wider cooking pot production, facilitated by the use of noncarbonaceous inclusions, might be an increased variety of rim and body shapes. This has the potential to mitigate the chronological significance which is normally associated with changes or differences in rim and body forms found at different but contemporaneous sites.[33] By the ninth or eighth century, localized cooking pot production made possible by noncarbonaceous inclusions would contribute to the rise in regionalism of pottery production, thereby limiting the chronological significance of comparisons or the presence or absence of specific forms between sites and regions.

To consider the chronological significance of the presence of the cooking pot traditions also requires an assessment of the useful life of pottery. The obsolescent mold-made cooking pots with calcite tempering at Bethsaida could represent older pots still in use but no longer manufactured, possibly at the end of their production. Or they might

*Gloria London & Robert Shuster*

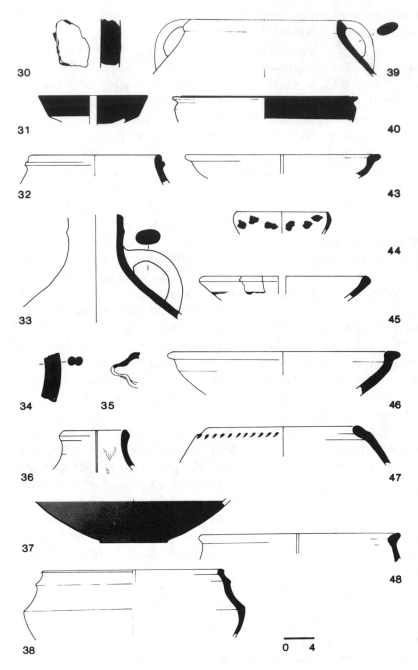

Plate I. Petrographic samples P30–P48.

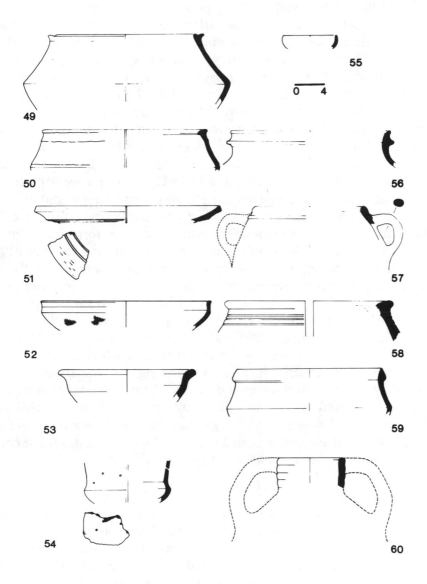

Plate II. Petrographic samples P49–060

have been stored and used for special occasions since they are larger than the newer shapes. Another explanation for their presence, considering the relatively short life span of cooking wares based on ethnoarchaeological data, is that specialized potters perhaps continued to produce and market calcite-tempered wares and overlapped with the newer tradition for as long as they could find customers.[34] Nostalgia for meals prepared by previous generations in pots identical to those used by parents and grandparents could have helped to maintain the market until it was overshadowed by quickly made wheel-thrown cooking pots.[35] Since wheel-thrown wares are made faster than others, these vessels would have become less expensive than the traditional form and eventually replaced all others. Alternatively, the earlier tradition had already ended by the time loci 417 and 601 were deposited, but some shards became mixed with those of the newer tradition.

Rims characteristic of cooking pots excavated in locus 417 include compact short shapes, P58 with a triangular form, P56 with a ridge or forked, as P49. Basalt tempering is a common feature: P49, P56, and P57 belong to petrographic ware group 1 and P58 falls in ware group 2 with significant grog inclusions. A short, squat globular body, as on P57, with two handles extending not from the rim but from the ridge, resembles an Iron Age II form from Hazor VIII and P56 is similar to pots from Tell Qiri and Beth Shan IV, as is P49.[36] In contrast, a cooking pot in locus 417 has carbonaceous inclusions: 5180.3 has a compact rim with a deep groove running underneath made of a red firing clay with a thick gray core and abundant but small white inclusions as well as the voids of organic material. An unpublished fragmentary cooking pot, 5176.7, which has an elongated rim and flange above a deep groove is made of a clay lacking calcite and resembles a small Iron Age II cooker from Hazor IX.[37]

SMALL BOWLS. An extremely shallow bowl, P51, perhaps belongs to the category of wares designated as Samaria ware. The sharp carination of this bowl resembles a vessel from Samaria.[38] Our sample lacks basalt altogether, which suggests that it was brought from elsewhere to the site. The clay contains mostly grog and quartz. There are two rows of double grooves on the exterior surface which appears not to be slipped but is burnished on both sides. Drag lines discernible on the exterior result in a rough finish not uncommon on Samaria ware shards. The special treatment of the exterior base, the burnish and the pattern of incised grooves as well as the overall vessel forms of the thin-walled Samaria ware hint at their double purpose and use: as drinking bowls and as lids for jars.[39]

A thin-walled bowl, P31, made of a light-colored ware exotic to Bethsaida, displays fine concentric burnishing on the exterior down to the point of carination and on the entire interior; it most resembles the Samaria ware vessels.[40] In addition to a trace of basalt, the matrix is 80 percent fine rounded calcite. The presence of Samaria or Samaria-like ware can imply a date as early as the tenth century for P31 from locus 601 and for P51 from locus 417.

Bowls with rounded bodies and a slight carination with rims showing a small flange or ledge sloping inward and thickening on the exterior (P43) are similar to a bowl from Hazor VB and Tell Yoqne'am where they are not common in the early Iron Age. Bowls with a rim flat on the top and thickening on the outside (P46) typical of Iron Age III are similar to Tell Beit Mirsim A, Beth Shan IV, and Tell Yoqne'am bowls.[41] A small hemispherical bowl, P44, with traces of slip on both sides resembles pots from Beth Shan level IV and in the same level is a match for a carinated bowl, P52.[42] With the remains of a band of red paint, P45 can be compared with a red slipped bowl from Tell Qiri VI.[43]

CHALICE. Burnished on the interior and exterior, but lacking evidence of a slip, the rim of P53 is similar to chalices from tenth century Tell 'Amal IV, a Beth Shan piece with interior and exterior red wash, a chalice from Tel Abu Hawam III, and a Tell Qiri chalice.[44] Our piece lacks evidence of a high base, but the rim stance suggests it belongs to a chalice.

CRATERS. A crater from locus 601 (P59) has a thickened T-shaped rim and ridges incised into the neck. It is reminiscent of an Iron Age II crater with a pronounced carination from Hazor X.[45] Another T-shaped rim belongs to a thinner-walled crater (P50) from locus 417, which resembles forms from Beth Shan IV, Tell 'Amal III, and Tell Qiri.[46] The same deposit yielded a crater (P48) with a more simple sloping rim thickened on the inside similar to a Beth Shan undeco-rated piece, two Tell Qiri craters, and a red slipped crater from Hazor VA of the Iron Age IIC period, but we lack evidence of handles. [47]

Jugs. Double-handled red burnished jugs characteristic of 'Akhziv Ware' could be a good match for our sample P 34 from locus 601, thus implying a tenth or ninth century date. This nonbasalt ware was most likely made outside the immediate region of Bethsaida.[48] Most of the other shards are fragmentary or of minimal chronological significance. Jugs have handles that extend to the shoulder from the rim, from a ridge on the neck, and from below the neck ridge.

Locus 365. Most of the Iron Age pottery at Bethsaida resembles material dated elsewhere to the tenth and ninth centuries. Postdepositional disturbances to the site caused considerable mixing of the remains. As a result, it is not prudent to attempt to draw conclusions based on the juxtaposition of shards found in each locus. Only locus 365 presents a viable primary assemblage.

Closed vessels from locus 365 include jug 4149 (*Bethsaida* 1, pl. XI:1) with a ridged rim similar to jugs from Beth Shan IV and tenth-century Tell 'Amal IV.[49] Juglet 4202 (*Bethsaida* 1, pl. XII:2) resembles a Beth Shan IV juglet both in form and composition since the latter is described as containing black inclusions, which may have been basalt as in the Bethsaida example.[50] A red slipped and burnished jug, 4201 (*Bethsaida* 1, pl. XII:1) displays features reminiscent of the Phoenician or "Akhziv" tradition in the surface treatment and the knob at the handle base. Around the bottom of the long conical neck are bands of plastic decoration. At the handle base is a small knob as seen on a jug designated as Cypro-Phoenician at Hazor VII.[51] Knobs at the base of handles on jugs and flasks imitate metallic vessels as known from Phoenician pottery found in tombs at Amathus and Episkopi among others in Cyprus. In shape, the long conical neck resembles a jug with a knob at the handle base from Megiddo.[52]

Having posited that the Iron Age assemblage contains a small number of cooking pots derived from the eleventh-century tradition, the obvious question concerns the dearth of other eleventh-century forms. However, cooking pots differ from all other vessel types in that until the Iron Age II/III eras, they were made from clays and tempering materials unique and distinct from the rest of the ceramic assemblage. They were probably made by potters who specialized in cooking vessels rather than the full repertoire and as such did not follow the same trends as the other shapes. There were different constraints and limitations imposed on cooking pots deriving from the fabric itself. Cooking pot shape and appearance did not vary at the whim of the clientele nor were they determined by aesthetic appeal. This pot, more than others, had to meet specific functional requirements which were less easy and therefore less likely to change with the rest of the repertoire. Undoubtedly there was some overlap between potters who produced the regular repertoire and the cooking pots, but there appears to have been little influence in the overall cooking pot form. Older cooking pot traditions may have continued longer than any other aspect of the ceramic repertoire. For this reason, it is plausible that in the absence of any other reminder of the eleventh-century ceramic tradition, the cooking pot remains, albeit rare. Other aspects of the pottery presented here, such as the overall vessel forms, and the presence of Samaria and "Akhziv" tradition wares, point toward tenth- and ninth-century ceramics. The mixing of the deposits and the postdepositional disturbance make it difficult to draw sharp distinctions in the chronological significance of the deposits.

## CONCLUSION

The Iron Age pottery at Bethsaida is a collection of locally made and imported wares with an emphasis on normal rather than luxury vessels. Basalt tempered wares made within the region include red burnished and slipped vessels as well as undecorated pottery and cooking pots. There are three types of cooking wares which can be differentiated by their clay bodies and/or their technique of manufacture and overall vessel shape. Diversity of the cooking pot forms and wares suggests a period of transition and experimentation in the local production of noncalcite tempered pots while the older tradition with calcite continues. The upright rims of the smallest cooking pots with rounded bodies represents the culmination of the experiment: a new ware with basalt rather than the large, angular calcite inclusions, a new manufacturing tradition made possible by the small size of the basalt inclusions, and a new shape quickly fashioned on the wheel.

Regarding the organization of the seasonally active ceramic industry, we infer from the distribution of the shapes, surface treatments, and wares that while there were those potters who produced the full repertoire, other potters and/or workshops specialized in slipped and burnished bowls and jugs and finally cooking pot producers. All of these sets of potters/workshops coexisted in the region.

Nothing can be said about the potters or workshops responsible for the imported vessels.

Luxury artifacts made of clay, if once used in the Bit Hilani, are not well represented in the deposits, which suffered at the hands of later occupants. Given the postdepositional disturbances, a date for the architecture based on the ceramics alone is elusive.

APPENDIX
DEFINITIONS OF SELECTED CERAMICS TERMS USED BY
ARCHAEOLOGISTS

APLASTICS: *See under* inclusions.

BURNISH: the surface of partially dry pots was at times rubbed or pressed and compacted for various reasons resulting in a more closed, compacted, and at times shiny surface. Burnished surfaces often involve a pot which has been slipped first.

CLAY BODY: includes the clay minerals as well as the rocks and minerals either added intentionally or native to the clay.

HOLEMOUTH JAR: refers to a specific rim shape common to Early Bronze Age jars.

INCLUSIONS: rocks, minerals, and organic materials added to or present in the clay. After the seeds, dung, straw, or other organics to the clay burned away during the firing of the pottery, voids alone remain. In the literature, inclusions are also termed nonplastics, aplastics, tempering materials, or grits.

CRATER: very large bowl. Also spelled crater.

NONPLASTICS: *see under* inclusions.

PAINT: fine clay to which pigment has been added. Paint is applied in a pattern covering specific parts of the pot, in contrast to slip which covers large areas or the entire surface.

SLIP: the fine clay particles, with or without pigment, which is then applied to all or most of the interior and/or exterior surface. Can be applied with a brush, cloth, hand, or pot is dipped into it.

TEMPERING MATERIALS: *see* inclusions.

VOIDS: holes of organic nonplastics which burned out during the firing process; they vary in size, shape, sorting, frequency, and orientation.

## Chapter Notes

1. Arav and Freund (1995), 5.
2. Arav and Freund (1995), 25–52.
3. Arav and Freund (1995), 24.
4. Thanks are extended to Rami Arav and Richard Freund for enabling us to study the Bethsaida material. Claire Epstein, Nurit Feig, Yuval Goren, Naomi Porat, and Shlomo Shoval provided their expertise and discussed their work in progress. Dr. Jack Shroder examined and identified the foraminifera in our sample. DreAnna Hadash drew the shards published with this report. Shamim Neilson and Wendi Chiarbos provided technical assistance. In the field Sandra Fortner graciously provided valuable information about the excavation and recording system. We also acknowledge with thanks the cooperation and assistance of the Alon Museum for providing workspace and logistical support. J. P. Dessel kindly read the text.
5. Potters who add water only include those observed in Crete by Blitzer (1984), 148; in Africa by Krause (1985), 92; in Cyprus by London, Egoumenidou, and Karageorghis (1989), 59; and in the Philippines by London (1991b), 189.
6. Longacre (1981), 54, and London (1985), 200, document Filipino potters who add two clays together, which is also described by Blitzer (1984), 145, and Voyatzogloy (1973), 14, for two villages in Crete.
7. Crowfoot (1932) described the practice in the region.
8. There is some indication that the quartz might have been intentionally added based on the comparison with the Tel 'Amal petrographic analysis of Goren (1991).
9. For bricks from Lachish, Rosen (1986), 75, notes that straw serves to physically bind and chemically strengthen clay by contributing humic acid to the clay.
10. London (1989), 221, describes construction workers in Cyprus who erect structures of stone and brick, but add color to the buildings by scattering large shards among the stones. Brickmakers transport broken pots from the pottery producing village of Kornos to crush the shards into grog used to temper bricks. Thanks are extended to Alison McQuitty, Noor Mulder–Hymans, and Murray Eiland for their comments about traditional tannur raw materials in use throughout the Middle East today.
11. For diversity of manufacturing techniques in a single Early Bronze II assemblage from Tell Yarmut, see London (1988), 119; in Bronze and Iron Age pottery from Tall al–'Umayri, see London (1991), 383ff.
12. Franken and Steiner (1990), figs. 5–9, illustrate bowl manufacture.
13. Franken (1973).
14. Franken and Steiner (1990), 103, note that burnishing a lamp is not the most effective way to reduce porosity. For an illustration of lamp manufacture, see ibid., 92, figs. 5–7.
15. Matson (1971), 66.
16. Franken (1973).
17. Another example of the relationship between the color of fired pottery and the presence or absence of both darkened cores and burnish are the Early Bronze IV wares noted for their greenish and generally light colors. In this instance, the situation is reverse of the Iron Age pottery: EB IV wares tend to lack a differentiated darkened core (or it is a light color) and never have a burnished surface. For the relationship between Early Bronze Age II burnished surfaces and darkened cores, see London (1988),122.
18. Shoval et al. (1993a) demonstrate that impurities in the clay and the precise nature of the clay matrix contribute to the decarbonization at relatively low temperatures for the Tell Hadar material. They conclude that calcite is preferable to other carbon-

ates, such as chalk and limestone, or calcareous clays because greater stability characterizes calcite at higher firing temperatures than for the other carbonaceous substances. Matson (1971), 77, notes that temperatures as low as 600 to 700 degrees for 30 minutes result in decomposition.

19. Calcite tempering, the most common inclusion intentionally added to cooking pots for millennia, has been identified in cooking pots in Israel and Jordan from the Bronze Age through the Iron Age, for example as documented at Jerusalem by Franken and Steiner (1990), 106; at Bab edh–Dhra' by Beynon et al. (1986), 303; at Jericho by Franken and Kalsbeek (1974), 58; at Tell Hadar by Shoval et al. (1993), 23; at Tall al–'Umayri by London, Plint, and Smith (1991), 436; at Tall Deir 'Alla by Franken and Kalsbeek (1969),11 and 124; and at Tall es–Sa'idiyeh by Vilders (1993), 149.

20. Rye (1976), Stimmel, Heimann, and Hancock (1982), and Steponaitis (1984), 113, discuss the beneficial properties of calcite for cooking wares from elsewhere in the world.

21. Franken and Steiner (1990), 106.

22. For example, Franken and Kalsbeek (1974), 86–87, describe Jericho Iron Age II wheel-thrown cooking pots as containing fine-grained inclusions added as a powder to the clay in wares that fire darker than cooking pots tempered with large calcite inclusions.

23. G. London, personal observations.

24. Franken and London (1995), 218, discuss cores in Late Bronze and Early Iron Age pottery.

25. In a petrographic analysis of basalt bowls from the northern Negev, Amiran and Porat (1984), 14, characterize them as olivine basalt known from either the Golan–Galilee or Transjordan rather than basalt known from Makhtesh Ramon.

26. Franken (1992), 109, identifies basalt tempering in a Late Bronze Age ware from Tall Deir 'Alla. The closest basalt area is approximately 40 kilometers north of the site. For third millennium BCE wares from Bab edh–Dhra' and Numeira in Jordan, Beynon et al (1986), 302, describe angular basalt inclusions as intentionally crushed and added to the clay matrix since there is no other nonplastic present. Although Gilead and Goren (1989), 12, refer to olivine basalt exposures east of the Dead Sea, south of Teleilat Ghassul in the Wadi Zarka Maein, Wadi Mujib, and Gebel Shihan, there is no reason to seek a source so far away for the Bethsaida clay deposits. For the basalt components identified in Iron Age I pithoi from Tell Sasa, Cohen-Weinberger and Goren (1996), 80, suggest an origin in the basalt flows of the Neogene-Pleistocene in the Golan and Galilee. Shoval et al. (1993a) refer to basalt in Iron Age cooking pots from Tell Hadar.

27. Epstein (1992), 1. The authors thank Ms. Epstein for her discussions about the Chalcolithic material.

28. Tell 'Amal, originally excavated and published by Levy and Edelstein (1972), is currently under investigation by Feig (1991), who submitted Early Bronze IV shards to Goren (1991) for petrographic analysis. They include basalt-tempered wares similar in appearance to the Iron Age material from Tell 'Amal according to Feig.

29. London (1991a), 223.

30. James (1966), fig. 53:1; Mazar (1993), 220, fig. 14:3; and Yadin and Geva (1986), fig. 25:2, which contains white grits (Beth Shan). See also Stern (1978), fig. 20:6 (Tell Mevorakh VIII).

31. James (1966), fig. 69:20 (Beth Shan); Stern (1978), fig. 14:9, 17; fig. 13:5 (Tell Mevorakh VII). For Bethsaida sample P32 comparable cooking pots are in: Hunt

(1987), fig. 34:2 (Tell Qiri V/VI); Stern (1978), figs. 14:1 and 20:7 (Tell Mevorakh VII and VIII); and Levy and Edelstein (1972), fig. 10:5 (Tell 'Amal III).

32. Levy and Edelstein (1972), fig. 9:2 (Tell 'Amal IV); Stern (1978), fig. 13:15 (Tell Mevorakh VII).

33. Geva (1992), 141, notes that the increasing regionalism seen in eighth century BCE pottery in northern Israel results in contemporaneous assemblages which are not identical. Mazar (1995), when discussing pottery from Khirbet Marjameh, refers to the regional diversity of ceramics but also addresses a critical issue concerning comparative ceramic analyses. Whereas parallels for pots from his site can be found at Hazor and Megiddo, Mazar states that there is in fact little resemblance between the bulk of the bowls, in this instance, with Khirbet Marjameh. What does similarity of pottery signify and how similar is similar if it relies on form and finish alone? For the Bethsaida pottery, comparable forms are presented below, but at times there is more than one parallel from the same and different sites. While the shards look similar, until there is adequate discussion of the mineralogical composition and manufacturing technique, ceramic analysis remains a subjective study open to interpretation. Superficial similarities are important for establishing relative dating, but even for this purpose, studies of surface features alone limit the potential of comparing and contrasting assemblages from nearby sites.

34. Ordinarily cooking vessels are used and washed daily, perhaps by children. They are exposed to unpredictable heating, possibly approached and overturned by dogs and other pets. As a consequence, cooking pots tend to have a relatively short life span. Nelson (1989), 174, notes that of pottery studied in ethnoarchaeological contexts, cooking ware has the shortest life span, ranging from a few months to five years, depending on the specific community.

35. For example, in 1986, a man in his thirties visited the Kornos pottery in search of a cooking pot his mother used to prepare Cypriote delicacies. He sought a particular type of cooking pot, no longer made, for his wife to prepare food that tasted comparable to what he remembered as a child. Personal observation, G. London.

36. Parallels for P57 include: Yadin et al. (1960), pl. LVII:15 (Hazor VIII), and Stern (1978), fig. 13:13 (Tell Mevorakh VII). Parallels for cooking pot P56 are: James (1966), fig. 69:16 (Beth Shan IV); Hunt (1987), fig. 33:15 (Tell Qiri); Stern (1978), fig. 14:2 (Tell Mevorakh VII). P49 resembles James (1966), 69: 6 (Beth Shan IV). Levy and Edelstein (1972), fig. 14:9 (Tell 'Amal) resembles Bethsaida P59.

37. Yadin et al. (1961), pl. CCIX:1 (Hazor IX).

38. Our thanks to Joe Zias for access to pottery from Samaria stored at the Rockefeller Museum. Crowfoot, Kenyon, and Sukenik (1957), fig. 19:7.37 (Samaria).

39. Plat Taylor (1959), 79, pl. II:10, lists a Samaria dish from al Mina, as a lid.

40. For comparable forms, see Crowfoot, Kenyon, and Sukenik (1957), fig. 18:10 (Samaria); Levy and Edelstein (1972, fig. 15: 3 (Tell 'Amal III).

41. Yadin et al. (1960), pl. LXXIX:7 (Hazor VB), or a rim flat on the top and thickening on the outside (P46) typical of Iron Age III and similar to the following: Albright (1943), pl. 21:15 (Tell Beit Mirsim A); James (1966), fig. 67:26 (Beth Shan IV); and Hunt (1987), 189; fig. 37:12 (Yoqne'am).

42. James (1966), fig. 67:23, with red slip and polish on both sides similar to the Bethsaida piece P44. Another small bowl, from Beth Shan, ibid., fig. 67:22, is listed as containing small black grits, probably basalt. P44 from Bethsaida is one of the few small forms made of basalt-rich clay. There is a comparable bowl from the new excavation at Beth Shan, Yadin and Geva (1986), fig. 11:1. For examples of the carinated bowl P52, see James (1966), 67:5 and 27 (Beth Shan IV), which have black grits and

one has an orange-red polish. Our sample with basalt nonplastics has traces of a red slip and possibly burnish. P52 is similar to a red slipped and burnished bowl, dated to Iron Age I, Hunt (1987), fig. 37:18 (Tell Qiri VIII B).

43. Ben-Tor and Portugali (1987), fig. 9:1 (Tell Qiri).
44. Levy and Edelstein (1972), fig. 16:5 (Tell 'Amal III), and Hamilton (1935), p. 23 (Tell Abu Hawam III). Also James (1966), fig. 67:28 (Beth Shan) with black grits, probably basalt, as the Bethsaida specimen. Hunt (1987), fig. 41:6 of Iron Age II date (Tell Qiri VII A) and Ben-Tor and Portugali (1987), fig. 10:11, lacking slip and burnish (Tell Qiri VII C).
45. Yadin et al. (1961), pl. CCVII:6 (Hazor X). Levy and Edelstein (1972), fig. 14:9 (Tell 'Amal) resembles Bethsaida P59.
46. James (1966) fig. 68:17 and 19 (Beth Shan IV); Levy and Edelstein (1972), fig. 14:7 (Tell 'Amal III), and Hunt (1987), fig. 39: 8 (Tell Qiri IX B).
47. Yadin et al. (1960), pl. CCXXVII:4 (Hazor VA); Ben-Tor and Portugali (1987), figs. 18:1;19:2 (Tell Qiri); Yadin and Geva (1986), fig. 11:2 (Beth Shan), and Levy and Edelstein (1972), fig. 14: 7 and 8 (Tell 'Amal III).
48. Amiran (1969), pl. 92:5 and 6 (Akhziv and Hazor V).
49. James (1966), fig. 71:3 (Beth Shan IV), but ours displays a less elegant form overall; see also Levy and Edelstein (1972), fig. 11:7 (Tell 'Amal IV).
50. James (1966), fig. 70:12 (Beth Shan IV).
51. Yadin et al. (1960), pl. LVIII:25 and 27 (Hazor VII).
52. Bikai (1987), 375, Amathus tombs 28, 37, 40; Episkopi tomb 40; and Lamon and Shipton (1939), pls. 3, 83 (Megiddo, Strata IV–II).

## LITERATURE CITED

Albright, William F. 1943. *The Excavation of Tell Beit Mirsim, III,* annual of the American Schools of Oriental Research, nos. 21–22. New Haven, Conn.: American Schools of Oriental Research.

Amiran, Ruth. 1969. *Ancient Pottery of the Holy Land.* Jerusalem: Massada.

Amiran, Ruth, and Naomi Porat. 1984. The Basalt Vessels of the chalcolithic Period and the Early Bronze Age I, *Tel Aviv* 11:11–19.

Arav, Rami, and Richard A. Freund, eds. 1995. *Bethsaida: A City by the North Shore of the Sea of Galilee,* vol. 1. Kirksville, Missouri: Thomas Jefferson University Press.

Ben-Tor, Amnon, and Y. Portugali. 1987. *Tell Qiri: A Village in the Jezreel Valley.* Qedem, no. 24. Jerusalem: Hebrew University.

Beynon. D. E., J. Donahue, R. T. Schaub, and R. A. Johnston. 1986. Tempering Types and Sources for Early Bronze Age Ceramics from Bab edh–Dhra' and Numeira, Jordan. *Journal of Field Archaeology* 13:297–305.

Bikai, Patricia M. 1987. *The Phoenician Pottery of Cyprus.* Nicosia: Leventis Foundation.

Blitzer, H. 1984. Traditional Pottery Production in Kentri, Crete: Workshops, Materials, Techniques and Trade. Pp. 143–57 in *East Cretan White–on–Dark,* ed. P. P. Betancourt. University Museum Monographs, no. 51. Philadelphia: University Museum.

Cohen-Weinberger, Anat, and Yuval Goren. 1996. Petrographic Analysis of Iron Age I Pithoi from Tell Sasa. *'Atiqot* 28:77–83.

Crowfoot, G. 1932. Pots, Ancient and Modern. *Palestine Exploration Quarterly* 6:179–81.

Crowfoot, J. W., G. M. Crowfoot, and K. M.Kenyon. 1957. *Samaria-Sebaste III: The Objects.* London: Palestine Exploration Fund.

Dothan, Moshe. 1971. Ashdod II: The Second and Third Seasons of Excavation, 1963, 1965. *'Atiqot* 9–10.

Epstein, Claire. 1992. Chalcolithic 'Golan Pottery' in Galilee. *Eretz-Israel* 23:1–4. Jerusalem: Israel Exploration Society. (Hebrew).

Feig, Nurit. 1991. Burial Caves of the Early Bronze IV at Tell 'Amal. *'Atiqot* 20:119–28.

Franken, H. J. 1973. Ring Burnished Bowls from the 7th Century BC in Palestine. Pp. 144–48 in *Symbolae et Mesopotamicae Francisco Mario Theodoro de Liagre Bohl.* ed. M. A. Beek, A. A. Kampman, and C. Nijland. Leiden: Brill.

———. 1992. *Excavations at Tell Deir 'Alla: The Late Bronze Age Sanctuary.* Louvain, Belgium: Peeters.

Franken, H. J., and Jan Kalsbeek. 1969. *Excavations at Tell Deir 'Alla. A Stratigraphical and Analytical Study of the Early Iron Age Pottery.* Leiden: Brill.

———.1974. *In Search of the Jericho Potters: Ceramics from the Iron Age and from the Neolithicum.* Amsterdam: North-Holland.

Franken, H. J., and Gloria London. 1995. Why Painted Pottery Disappeared at the End of the Second Millennium BCE. *Biblical Archaeologist* 58:214–22.

Franken, H. J., and Margreet L. Steiner. 1990. *Excavations in Jerusalem 1961–1967.* Vol. 2. Oxford: Oxford University Press.

Geva, Shulamit. 1992. The Typology of "Kitchen Ware" in the Kingdom of Israel during the 8th Century BCE. *Eretz-Israel* 23:120–42. Jerusalem: Israel Exploration Society. (Hebrew.)

Gilead, Isaac, and Yuval Goren. 1989. Petrographic Analysis of Fourth Millennium BC Pottery and Stone Vessels from the Northern Negev, Israel. *Bulletin of the American Schools of Oriental Research* 275:5–14.

Goren, Yuval. 1991. Petrographic Examination of the Ceramic Assemblage from Tell 'Amal. *'Atiqot* 20:129–30.

Hamilton, Robert W. 1935. Excavations at Tell Abu Hawam. *Quarterly for the Department of Antiquities of Palestine* 4: 1–69.

Hunt, Melvin. 1987. The Pottery, pp. 139–223 in *Tell Qiri: A Village in the Jezreel Valley,* ed. Amnon Ben-Tor and Y. Portugali. Qedem, no. 24. Jerusalem: Hebrew University.

James, Frances W. 1966. *The Iron Age at Beth Shan.* Philadelphia: University Museum.

Johnston, R. H., and R. T. Schaub. 1978. Selected Pottery from Bab edh-Dhra', 1975, pp. 33–49 in *Preliminary Excavation Reports: Bab edh-Dhra', Sardis, Meiron, Tell el-Hesi, Carthage (Punic),* ed. D. N. Freedman. Annual of the American Schools of Oriental Research, 43. Cambridge, Mass: American Schools of Oriental Research.

Krause, Richard A. 1985. *The Clay Sleeps: An Ethnoarchaeological Study of Three African Potters.* University: University of Alabama Press.

Lamon, Robert S., and G.M.Shipton. 1939. *Megiddo I.* Chicago: University of Chicago Press.

Levy, Shalom, and Gershon Edelstein. 1972. Cinq années de fouilles à Tel 'Amal (Nir David). *Revue Biblique* 79:326–67.

London, Gloria Anne. 1985. *Decoding Designs: The Late Third Millennium B.C. Pottery from Jebel Qa'aqir.* Ann Arbor: University Microfilms.

———. 1988. The Organization of the Early Bronze Age II Ceramics Industry at Tel Yarmuth: A Preliminary Report, pp. 117–24 in *Yarmouth I,* ed. Pierre de Miroschedji. Paris: Éditions Recherche sur les Civilisations.

———. 1989. Past Present: The Village Potters of Cyprus. *Biblical Archaeologist* 52:219–29.

———. 1991. Aspects of Early Bronze and Late Iron Age Ceramic Technology at Tell el-'Umeiri. Pp. 383–419 in *Madaba Plains Project IIt: The 1987 Season at Tell el-'Umeiri and Vicinity and Subsequent Studies,* ed. L. Herr, L. T. Geraty, Ø. S. La Bianca, and R. W. Younker. Berrien Springs, Mich.: Andrews University Press.

———.1991a. Ethnoarchaeological Evidence of Variation in Cypriot Ceramics and Its Implications for the Taxonomy of Ancient Pottery, pp. 221–35 in *Cypriot Ceramics: Reading the Prehistoric Record,* ed. Jane A. Barlow, Diane L. Bolger, and Barbara Kling. Philadelphia: Leventis Foundation and University Museum.

———.1991b. Standardization and Variation in the Work of Craft Specialists, pp. 182–204 in *Ceramic Ethnoarchaeology,* ed. Wm. A. Longacre. Tucson: University of Arizona Press.

London, Gloria, Frosso Egoumenidou, and Vassos Karageorghis. 1989. *Traditional Pottery in Cyprus.* Mainz: Philipp von Zabern.

London, Gloria Anne, Heather Plint, and Jennifer Smith. 1991. Preliminary Petrographic Analysis of Pottery from Tell el-'Umeiri and Hinterland Sites, 1987. Pp. 429–449 in *Madaba Plains Project: The 1987 Season at Tell el-'Umeiri and Vicinity and Subsequent Studies,* eds. Larry Herr, Lawrence T.Geraty, Øystein S. LaBianca, and R. W. Younker. Berrien Springs, Mich.: Andrews University.

Longacre, William A., 1981, Kalinga Pottery: An Ethnoarchaeological Study, pp. 49–66 in *Pattern of the Past,* ed. I. Hodder, G. Issac, and N. Hammond. Cambridge: Cambridge University Press.

Matson, Frederick, R. 1971. A Study of Temperatures Used in Firing Ancient Mesopotamian Pottery, pp. 65–79 in *Science and Archaeology,* ed. Robert Brill. Cambridge, Mass.: MIT Press.

Mazar, Amihai. 1993. Beth Shean in the Iron Age: Preliminary Report and Conclusions of the 1990–1991 Excavations. *Israel Exploration Journal* 43, no. 4: 202–29.

————. 1995. Excavations at the Israelite Town at Khirbet Marjameh in the Hills of Ephraim. *Israel Exploration Journal* 45, nos. 2–3: 85–117.

Nelson, Ben A. 1991. Ceramic Frequency and Use-Life: A Highland Mayan Case in Cross–Cultural Perspective. Pp. 162–81 in *Ceramic Ethnoarchaeology,* ed. Wm. A. Longacre. Tucson: University of Arizona.

Plat Taylor, Joan du. 1959. The Cypriot and Syrian Pottery from Al Mina, Syria. *Iraq* 21: 62–92.

Rosen, Arlene M. 1986. *Cities of Clay.* Chicago: University of Chicago Press.

Rye, Owen S. 1976. Keeping Your Temper under Control: Materials and the Manufacture of Papuan Pottery. *Archaeology and Physical Geography in Oceania* 11: 107–37.

Shoval, Shlomo, P. Beck, E. Yadin, Y. Kirsh, and M. Gaft. 1993. The Ceramic Technology of Iron Age Cooking Pots, Tell Hadar. Annual Meeting of the Israel Geological Society, Arad. Ed. Ittai Gavrieli, p. 23.

Shoval, S., M. Gaft, P. Beck, and Y. Kirsh. 1993. Thermal Behavior of Limestone and Mono-crystalline Calcite Tempers during Firing and Their Use in Ancient Vessels. *Journal of Thermal Analysis* 40:263–73.

Steponaitis, Vincas P. 1984. Technological Studies of Prehistoric Pottery from Alabama: Physical Properties and Vessel Function. Pp. 79–122 in *The Many Dimensions of Pottery,* ed. Sander E. van der Leeuw and Alison C. Pritchard. Amsterdam: University of Amsterdam.

Stern, Ephraim. 1978. *Excavations at Tel Mevorakh, 1973–1976.* Qedem, no. 9. Jerusalem: Hebrew University.

Stimmel, C., R. B. Heimann, and R. G. Hancock. 1982. Indian Pottery from the Mississippi Valley: Coping with Bad Raw Materials. Pp. 219–28 in *Archaeological Ceramics,* ed. J. S. Olin and A. Franklin. Washington, D.C.: Smithsonian Institution.

Vilders, Monique M. E. 1993. Some Remarks on the Production of Cooking Pots in the Jordan Valley. *Palestine Exploration Quarterly* 125:149–56.

Voyatzogloy, M. 1973. The Potters of Thrapsano. *Ceramic Review* 24:13–16.

Yadin, Yigal, Yohanan Aharoni, Ruth Amiran, Trude Dothan, Moshe Dothan, Immanuel Dunayevsky, and Jean Perot. 1958, 1960, 1961. *Hazor I–IV.* Jerusalem: Magnes Press and Jerusalem Exploration Society.

Yadin, Yigal, and Shulamit Geva. 1986. *Investigations at Beth Shean: The Early Iron Age Strata.* Qedem, no. 23. Jerusalem: Hebrew University.

*Baruch Brandl*

# Two First-Millennium Cylinder Seals from Bethsaida (et-Tell)

D URING THE 1994 SEASON of excavations at Bethsaida two cylinder seals were found, one in Area A and one in Area C. Unfortunately, their archaeological contexts are mixed, but typologically and stylistically they are well dated and attributed; as such they could contribute to the reconstruction of the site's history.[1] The photographs, the drawings, and the reconstructions were made under the writer's guidance. The directions in the descriptions of the seal designs refer to the modern impressions. Since this study appears in a report, illustrations of the parallels are not incorporated. Therefore, sometimes several references are made to the same items with the hope that some of them are more accessible.

## NEO-ASSYRIAN CYLINDER SEAL

### DESCRIPTION
- *Israel Antiquities Authority no. 96-2226.*
- *Reg. no. 9531.*
- *Locus no. 961.*
- *Area:* C.
- *Material:* Carnelian.[2]
- *Dimensions:* Height, 20+ mm (estimated[3] 28 mm). Diameter, 14.5 mm. Circumference, 43 mm.
- *Method of manufacture:* Carving, polishing, drilling, and cutting.
- *Workmanship:* Good.

225

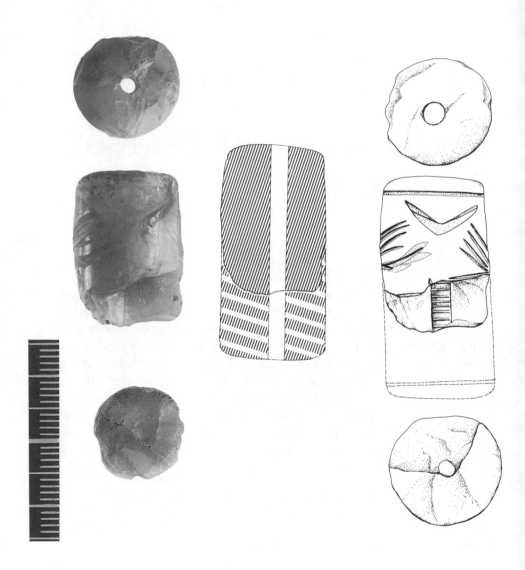

Fig. 1. Photo and drawing of the Neo-Assyrian cylinder seal. Israel Antiquities Authority no. 96-2226.

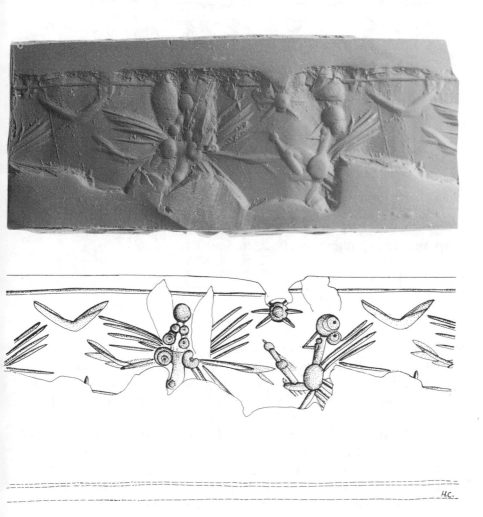

Fig. 2. Photo and drawing of the modern impression of the Neo-Assyrian cylinder seal. Israel Antiquities Authority no. 96–2226. Scale 4:1.

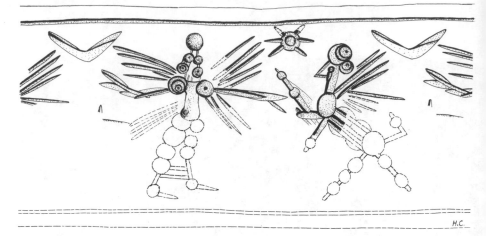

Fig. 3. Neo-Assyrian cylinder seal's impression, with partial reconstruction. Israel Antiquities Authority no. 96-2226. Scale 4:1.

- *Technical Details:* Perforated, drilled from one direction.
- *Preservation:* Broken, the whole lower third of the seal is missing.
- *Seal Design:* The seal is composed of a main scene and a terminal (or secondary scene) in a single register; above and below are borderlines.

   The main scene is composed of two imaginary or mythological creatures in combat. On the left is a standing bearded human-headed genie with four open stretched wings,[4] which is facing right and confronts a rampant winged sphinx. The genie grasps the sphinx with its stretched left hand, while its right bent hand most probably holds an unidentified weapon. The lower part of both figures was restored by comparison to a cylinder seal in the British Museum acquired by A. H. Layard ca. 1850.[5] Therefore, the lower wings of the genie have the same length as the upper.[6]

   The terminal consists of two astral signs, a six-horned star in front, and a recumbent crescent behind the figures' heads.[7]

   Three of the components were engraved in two techniques: by drills and by rotating cutting discs,[8] while the crescent was made only in the second technique.

## ICONOGRAPHY

The cylinder seal contains typical Mesopotamian figures and signs:

- The four-winged genie (or genius) appears in Assyrian monumental art in contexts of royal rituals[9] of a magical protective nature[10] and on minor art, especially on glyptic.[11]
- The winged sphinx is most probably a human-headed winged bull. It is a common motif from the Early Dynastic period to the Achaemenid period. Monumental sculptures of it were common in both the Neo-Assyrian and Achaemenian palaces as gateway guardians.[12]

   In the Neo-Assyrian glyptic the combat between a genie and a sphinx is a common motif.[13]
- The recumbent crescent of the moon is known in Mesopotamia as a religious symbol from its prehistoric period down to the Neo-Babylonian period. On the basis of related inscriptions, we know that it had functioned consistently as the symbol of the moon god Sin at least since the Old-Babylonia period.[14]
- The eight-horned star is known in Mesopotamia during the same periods as the recumbent crescent. On the basis of related inscriptions we know that since the Old-Babylonian period it was the symbol of the goddess of love and war Inana/Istar. The six-horned star appeared simultaneously, but its significance is unknown.[15]

   Both the crescent and the six-horned star appear together many times on cylinder seals.[16]

## TYPOLOGY

On the basis of all its iconographic components, the cylinder seal should be classified generally as a Neo-Assyrian product.

## STYLE

It seems, if we follow Edith Porada's stylistic classification for the first millennium Mesopotamian glyptic, that this seal was carved in an eclectic style. The components made by drills belong to the Neo-Assyrian Early Drilled-Style,[17] while those made by rotating cutting discs belong to the Neo-Babylonian[18] (or Neo-Assyrian[19]) Early Cut style.

- The first carving style is represented in the genie's head and torso; the hair, torso, and forelegs of the sphinx; and the star's center.

- The second carving style is represented mainly in the sphinx's prominent face, the weapon held in the hand of the genie, and the crescent.[20]

  Since the number of such seals is growing, there is a possibility that they belong to a separate group manufactured in a different workshop or even in several workshops within the territory of the Neo-Assyrian Empire.

### DATE

The seal should be dated on the basis of its combined carving style. The combination of the Neo-Assyrian Early Drilled style with the Neo-Babylonian (or Neo-Assyrian) Early Cut style could have been executed in the late eighth century BCE,[21] most probably from the days of Tiglath-Pileser III and on.

### ARCHAEOLOGICAL CONTEXT

The cylinder seal was found in sifting of locus 961. That locus is mixed and contained material from the Iron Age up to the very beginning of the twentieth century CE. Therefore, the dating of the seal is not based on stratigraphy.

### ACHAEMENIAN CYLINDER SEAL

### DESCRIPTION

- *Israel Antiquities Authority no.* 96-2227.
- *Reg. no.* 2823.
- *Locus no.* 813.
- *Area:* A.
- *Material:* Ceramic(?) sintered quartz(?).[22]
- *Dimensions:* Height, 21.5 mm. Diameter, 11 mm. Circumference, 36mm.
- *Method of manufacture:* Molding.[23]
- *Workmanship:* Very good.
- *Technical Details:* Made in a bivalve mold.[24] Perforated off-axis, since the string that created the perforation had passed through one of the valves.
- *Preservation:* Complete.
- *Seal design:* Organized exceptionally in two vertical and equal registers,[25] each register is limited by a double line on the sides, while

the upper and lower borderlines are the result of the bivalved mold.

Depicted in each register, facing to the right side, is an imaginary or mythological figure: In the upper[26] register is a walking winged bull. In the lower register is a bearded fish-man wearing a double plumed helmet, with his right hand in a blessing pose and his left hand holding a treelike staff.

ICONOGRAPHY

The cylinder seal contains typical Mesopotamian motifs:

* The winged bull is a common motif from the mid-second millennium onwards,[27] mainly in the Middle Assyrian and both the Second and Third Kassite glyptic.[28] During the beginning of the first millennium it is depicted on North Syrian orthostats from Tell Halaf,[29] dated to the ninth century BCE.[30] In Neo-Assyrian art it appears inter alia on bas reliefs,[31] ivories,[32] and cylinder seals,[33] mainly at Nimrud. Some metal objects dated to the eighth through seventh centuries BCE from pre-Achaemenian Iran also have it.[34] In the Achaemenian art it appears on enameled bricks at Susa,[35] on metal objects such as a belt and a goldsmith's stone die,[36] as well as on various types of seals.[37]
* The fish-man (or merman) is also a common motif and appeared since the Old Babylonian period onwards to the Seleucid period.[38] During the second millennium it appeared on both First and Second Kassite glyptic.[39] Like the previous motif, this motif appears on a North Syrian orthostat at Tell Halaf that is dated to the ninth century BCE.[40] In the Neo-Assyrian art, where it is known as *kulullu*, it appears on a monumental stone relief from Khorsabad[41] and on a fragment of bronze door plaque from the same site.[42] Clay figurines with its shape were found in the city of Assur in brick boxes buried in the foundations for protective magic.[43] In the Neo-Assyrian glyptic it appears on both, cylinder seals,[44] and various shapes of stamp seals or their impressions.[45] The same figure is found also on Neo-Babylonian cylinder seals.[46] This motif appears also on a Phoenician seal from the seventh to sixth centuries BCE.[47] This motif was found in the city of Nippur among the sealings in the Murasu archive that is dated to the fifth century BCE.[48] It seems that after the fifth century BCE the Mesopotamian fish-man motif was superseded in Phoenicia and

Fig. 4. Achaemenian cylinder seal and its modern impression. Israel Antiquities Authority no. 96-2227.

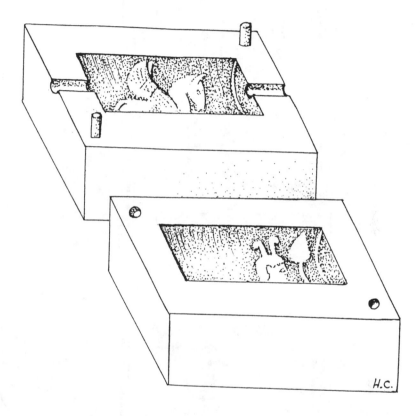

Fig. 5. A suggested reconstruction of the bivalve mold used during the manufacture of the Achaemenian cylinder seal.

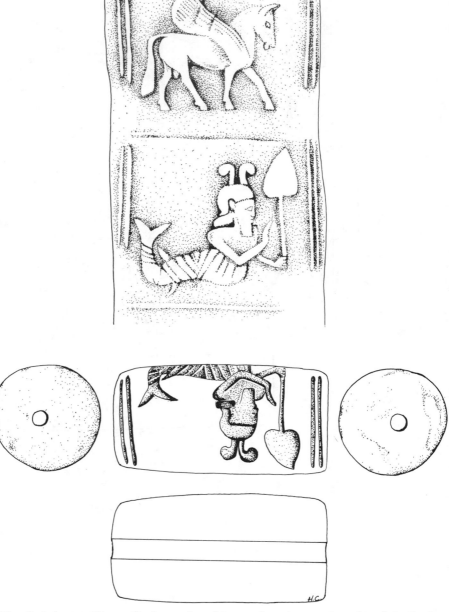

Fig. 6. Achaemenian cylinder seal and its modern impression. Israel Antiquities Authority no. 96-2226. Scale 4:1.

Palestine by the Greek style Triton,[49] as seen also on seals from Sardinia and Carthage.[50]

## TYPOLOGY

The cylinder seal should be classified as an Achaemenian product on the basis of the shape of the bull's wings. The curved wings, often depicted with a very concave upper edge, are so characteristic to Achaemenian art that they are now a hallmark of it.[51]

The seal reflects two different centers of influence: the Mesopotamian (mainly Assyrian) and the Phoenician. The Mesopotamian background is described above (p. 231), while the Phoenician flare is expressed in the Fish-man's plumed helmet and the treelike staff in his hand.[52]

## STYLE

The Bethsaida seal belongs to a new and small group of Achaemenian cylinder seals within the wider "Court" style,[53] which are characterized by the existence of two separated but equal motifs on them.

It seems that the original reason for this arrangement derived from the production technique—molding in a bivalve mold. The only other mold-made cylinder seal known to me from that group is from the ex-Moore Collection that was exhibited in the Metropolitan Museum of Art for thirty-five years.[54] This style was later adopted on cylinder seals made of hard stones, such as the seals from Susa and Borsippa.[55]

Most of these cylinder seals have a common peculiarity: They seem to display both eastern (Achaemenian) and western (Phoenician and Greek) motifs in equal prominence,[56] which reflects the political and cultural integration within the territory of the Persian Empire.

## DATE

The seal should be dated to the late sixth to fifth centuries BCE on the basis of the following:

- Its typological parallel that was produced by the same technique, i.e. in a bivalve mold, was dated by the later publisher to ca. 540–400 BCE.[57]
- The Mesopotamian and especially the Assyrian influence on the Achaemenian cylinder seals is more common on the earlier ones.[58]

- The Phoenician components (plumed helmet and treelike object) point, as well, to an early stage in Achaemenian art.

### Archaeological Context

The cylinder seal was found in a fill of rocks and loose soil. Locus 813 is mixed and contained material from the Iron Age up to the medieval period. Therefore, the dating of the seal is not based on stratigraphy.

### Summary and Conclusions

One of the two cylinder seals from Bethsaida is characterized by the carving style of its motifs, the other is characterized by its production technique. Both contain mythological motifs of Mesopotamian origin that reflect its long tradition.

The quality of the seals seems to indicate that they were made in central workshops within the Neo-Assyrian and the Achaemenian empires.[59]

If the distribution of these finds was by means other than trade or a later "migration,"[60] then these seals are the first local evidences for the presence of Assyrians and Persians at Bethsaida. As such, they contribute to the reconstruction of the site's history during the eighth and the fifth centuries BCE.

## Chapter Notes

1. These finds were represented first in the Bethsaida session during the 13th International Meeting of the Society for Biblical Literature (Brandl 1995a). Another find from that representation was published in the first volume of Bethsaida reports (Brandl 1995b).
2. For its definition and use, see: Tosi (1976–80); Collon (1987) 102, (1990) 32, 35, and Porada (1981) appendix IV.
3. The estimated height of this cylinder seal is based on two factors: the area needed for the reconstructions of the main figures and the heights of some Neo-Assyrian cylinder seals with the same diameter. Among them are Moortgat (1940) no. 733, Kühne et al. (1980) no. 86, and Collon (1987) no. 349, (which also served as the main source for restoration; see n. 5).
4. The reconstruction of the fourth wing is based on the appearance of the third wing.
5. Wiseman (1959) seal no. 59 = Collon (1987) no. 349.
6. Contrary to the general distinction that in Assyria the upper wings are shorter than the lower; Collon (1987) 77.
7. There is a possibility that two more signs were in the missing lower part, under the upper ones; cf. Moortgat (1940) pl. 86:733.
8. Porada (1948) 88.
9. S.v. "genies" in: Black, Green, and Rickards (1992) 65 (fig. 53) 86–88.
10. Paley (1992).
11. For a four-winged genius in glyptic, see an impressed docket from Nimrud; Parker (1962) 37 (ND 7070) fig. 5, pl. 20:4.
12. S.v. "bulls and lions with human head" in: Black, Green, and Rickards (1992) 50–51.
13. For example on a cylinder seal from Assur, see Moortgat (1940) 150, no. 733, pl. 86:733.
14. S.v. "crescent" in: Black, Green, and Rickards (1992) 54; Collon (1992).
15. S.v. "star (symbol)" in: Black, Green, and Rickards (1992) 169–70.
16. For example, Porada (1981) no. 1216; Collon (1987) no. 366.
17. Porada (1948) 83–85.
18. Porada (1947) 157–62; (1948) 88–89, nos. 724–33.
19. The appearance of an Early Cut-style cylinder seal in Hasanlu Stratum IVB, Winter (1977) 376, pl. 25, ill. 16 = (1980) 22, 89 fig. 57 = Marcus (1988) 264, 295–97 no. 59 = Marcus (1996) 44, 115–16 (no. 59) that was destroyed ca. 800 BCE, and the identification of it as Neo-Assyrian, had affected also Porada's original definition; see Porada (1981) 230 (no. 1216). There is a possibility that part of the seals related to this style were produced in the North Syrian centers that were annexes to the Assyrian Empire already in the ninth century BEC. One seal of that style was most probably found at Tell Halaf; see von Oppenheim and Hrouda (1962) 31, 35 pl. 25:32; three were bought near Carchemish; see Buchanan (1966) nos. 648, 650–51, and several from the market are in the Adana Museum; see Tunca (1979) 19 (nos. 103–6).
20. Cf. Porada (1948) nos. 727–31, 33; Moortgat-Corens (1968) no. 126; Kühne et al. (1980) no. 87; Porada (1981) no. 1216.
21. Cf. Porada (1947) 161–62; Buchanan (1966) 116 (nos. 656–59); Teissier (1984) 42, (no. 266).
22. The first option is based on the material of a seal made in the same technique that will be discussed below; Williams Forte (1976) no. 28. For the second option and its equivalents, see Collon (1987) 102 (period V).

23. Contrary to those of the middle of the second millennium that were cut; cf. Collon (1987) 102 (period V).
24. This could be deduced from the fragmentary double border lines of the cylinder seal.
25. Very few cylinder seals have vertical or perpendicular registers; see Frankfort (1939) pl. 10:a; Porada (1948) no. 955 = Collon (1981) no. 20. For mixed directions see: Porada (1948) no. 370; Amiet (1992) no. 222.
26. The registers are alternating if the cylinder seal is rolled several times. However, they are described in this order in accordance with the nature of the figures depicted on them.
27. Moorey (1967) 92.
28. Matthews (1990) 82 n. 306. (No. 211 = also Frankfort [1939] pl. 32:c.)
29. von Oppenheim, Opitz, and Moortgat (1955) 89–90, pls. 91b, 92a = Strommenger (1985) 362 (no. 181).
30. For its date, see Winter (1989).
31. Harden (1962) pl. 48 = Brentjes (1967) 119–21, fig. 13 = Reade (1995) 105; Frankfort (1954) 103–4, fig. 41.
32. Mallowan (1966) 270–71, fig. 253 (= Harden [1962] 185, pl. 68), 588–90, fig. 567.
33. Frankfort (1939) pl. 35:h, k (= 1954, pl. 119:B); Porada (1948) nos. 620, 753, 756; Collon (1987) nos. 337, 656 (= [1995] nos. 186, 188 respectively). A provincial Assyrian cylinder seal was found at Tel Dor; see Stern (1987) 69 = Collon (1987) no. 392 = Ornan (1990) 34–35, no. 23 = Keel and Uehlinger (1992) no. 283 = Stern (1993) 111–12, fig. 1:1 = (1994a) 135–36, fig. 1:1 = (1994b) 52–53, 59, fig. 1:a.
34. Moorey (1967) 93; Muscarella (1988) 192–202.
35. Ghirshman (1954) 166–67 = von der Osten (1956) pl. 42 lower.
36. Moorey (1967) 92–93, pls. 3a–4; Culiacan (1965) 152–53, pl. 64.
37. Delaporte (1910) no. 501 (= Bordreuil [1986] no. 129); Boardman (1970) pls. 835, 994; Bordreuil (1986) no. 127; Invernizzi (1995) 39–42, figs. 1, 3. A scaraboid with a crowned Persian figure grasping a winged bull was found at Tell Keisan; see Keel (1980) no. 21 = (1990) no. 21 = Keel and Uehlinger (1992) 433–34, fig. 360b. A clay bulla depicting a winged bull in "flying gallop" is said to come from a hoard in the vicinity of Samaria; see Stern (1992) 11, 24 fig. 1:4, 28 pl. I:4.
38. S.v. "merman and mermaid" in: Black, Green, and Rickards (1992) 131–32.
39. Matthews (1990) 60n47, seals no. 3, 129, 135, 137, 140, 141.
40. von Oppenheim (1931) 175–76, pl. 35b = von Oppenheim, Opitz, and Moortgat (1955) 91, pl. 94a.
41. Black, Green, and Rickards (1992) 131, ill. no. 107.
42. Loud and Altman (1938) 43–44, 59, 96 pl. 49:20 (while plaque 21 in the same plate has only a regular bull without wings).
43. Stucky et al. (1979) no. 141; Black, Green, and Rickards (1992) 92, ill. 70 lower.
44. Delaporte (1910) 219, pl. 27:392; Moortgat (1940) 73, pl. 85:725.
45. Layard (1853) 292–95; Delaporte (1910) 302–3, pl. 35:543a; (1920) 74, pl. 54 12a (D.81); von der Osten (1936) no. 140; Parker (1962) 37, fig. 2, pl. 20:1 (= Herbordt [1992] 112–13, pl. 15:14); Buchanan and Moorey (1988) no. 369; Collon (1995) 188 (no. 193).
46. Frankfort (1939) 219, fig. 68 = Brentjes (1967) 116, fig. 7:b; Porada (1948) no. 785.
47. Munn-Rankin (1959) 35–36, no. 73 = Bordreuil and Gubel (1987) 311, fig. 2.
48. Bregstein (1993) 891 [seal no. 487], 941–43 [seals no. 537–39]. For the time span of the Murasu archive see also Zettler (1979) 258n7.

49. Petrie (1927) 18, pl. 14:209; Ridder (1911) 490–91, pl. 16 [no. 2507] = Bordreuil (1986) no. 28; Murray (1953) 365, 372, pl. 44:123; Barak and Amorai-Stark (1989) 334–35, fig. 28.1.3, pl. 73:3; Tubb, Dorrell, and Cobbing (1996) 22, 25 fig. 12:1; also cf. Boardman (1970) no. 276.
50. Walters (1926) 48, pl. 7: 396–397; Harden (1962) 216, pl. 108:h = Buchanan and Moorey (1988) 73, pl. 16:489; Vercoutter (1945) 231, pl. 16:61; 244, pl. 19:673.
51. Munn-Rankin (1959) 34 [no. 65]; Moorey (1967) 93; Invernizzi (1995) 40.
52. A figure with plumed helmet (?) holding a fanlike staff in its hand is depicted on a seventh-century-BCE silver bowl from Idalion; Harden (1962) pl. 47 = Markoe (1985) 154–55, 170–71, 244–45 [Cy2] = Gubel (1993) 108, fig. 18. A figure holding a treelike staff is depicted on the *"lgrsd"* scarab; Levy (1869) pl. 2:9 = Bordreuil (1986) no. 26, Avigad and Sass (1997) no. 736, on two scarabs from Bothros 1 in Kition; Clerc (1976) 53–54 [Kit. 505], 84–85 [Kit. 995], and on a Phoenician scaraboid from Ibiza; Culican (1962) 43–44, pl. I, fig. Ia = (1976) 57, pl. 8:1 = Fernandez (1983) 121 = Gubel (1986).
53. Cf. Boardman (1970) 305–9.
54. Eisen (1940) no. 103 = Williams–forte (1976) no. 28 = Sotheby's, sale 6256, no. 86..
55. For Susa, see Delaporte (1920) 79, pl. 52:18 [D.142]; for Borsippa, see Frankfort (1954) pl. 190:B–C = Wiseman (1959) no. 105 = Collon (1987) no. 428.
56. On the ex-Moore Collection seal are depicted Median and Greek warriors; cf. Wiseman (1959) no. 117; on the Borsippa seal are a Persian crowned figure and a Greek hero in contest with a lion and a bull, respectively, while on the Susa cylinder seal are Neptune with his trident and an eastern figure lying on a bed.
57. Williams-Forte (1976) no. 28.
58. Cf. Boardman (1970) 304.
59. For a locally made cylinder seal, see Aharoni (1996).
60. Tadmor and Tadmor (1995) 352–55.

## LITERATURE CITED

Aharoni, M. 1996. An Iron Age Cylinder Seal. *Israel Exploration Journal* 46:52–54.

Amiet, P. 1992. *Corpus des cylindres de Ras-Shamra-Ougarit II: Sceaux cylindres en hématite et pierres diverses*. Ras Shamra-Ougarit 9. Paris: Editions Recherche sur les Civilisations.

Avigad, N., and B. Sass. 1997. *Corpus of West Semitic Stamp Seals*. Jerusalem.

Barak, M., and S. Amorai-Stark. 1989. Seals and Seal Impressions. Chap. 28a, pp. 333–38, in: *Excavations at Tel Michal, Israel,* ed. Z. Herzog, G. Rapp Jr., and O. Negbi. Publications of the Institute of Archaeology, 8. Minneapolis University of Minnesota Press / Tel Aviv: Sonia and Marco Nadler Institute of Archaeology.

Black, J., A. Green, and T. Rickards. 1992. *Gods, Demons and Symbols of Ancient Mesopotamia: An Illustrated Dictionary*. London: British Museum / Austin: University of Texas Press.

Boardman, J. 1970. *Greek Gems and Finger rings: Early Bronze Age to Late Classical*. London: Thames and Hudson.

Bordreuil, P. 1986. *Catalogue des sceaux ouest-sémitiques inscrits de la Bibliothèque nationale, du Musée du Louvre et du Musée biblique de Bible et Terre Sainte*. Paris: La Bibliothèque.

Bordreuil, P., and E. Gubel. 1987. *Bulletin d'Antiquités Archéologiques du Levant Inédites ou Méconnues* (BAALIM) 4, *Syria* 64: 309–21.

Brandl, B. 1995a. History of Iron Age et-Tel (Bethsaida) through Its Small Finds (abstract). In: *Society of Biblical Literature Thirteenth International Meeting. Kulturinov / Center for Cultural Innovation*. Budapest, Hungary, 23–26 July 1995: 44.

———. 1995b. An Israelite Bulla in Phoenician Style from Bethsaida (et-Tell). In: *Bethsaida: A City by the North Shore of the Sea of Galilee*. Vol. 1. Ed. R. Arav and R. A. Freund. Kirksville, MO: Thomas Jefferson University Press, 141–64.

Bregstein, L. B. 1993. *Seal Use in Fifth Century B.C. Nippur, Iraq: A Study of Seal Selection and Sealing Practices in the Murasu Archive*. Ph.D. dissertation, University of Pennsylvania, Philadelphia.

Brentjes, B. 1967. Maritime säugetiere in den Kulturen des Alten Orient. *Zeitschrift für Säugetierkunde* 32: 114–25.

Buchanan, B. 1966. *Catalogue of Ancient Near Eastern Seals in the Ashmolean Museum*. Vol. 1, *Cylinder Seals*. Oxford: Clarendon Press.

Buchanan, B., and P. R. S. Moorey. 1988. *Catalogue of Ancient Near Eastern Seals in the Ashmolean Museum*. Vol. 3, *The Iron Age Stamp Seals (c. 1200–350 BC)*. Oxford: Clarendon Press.

Clerc, G. 1976. Scarabées, Amulettes et Figurines. In: G. Clerc, V. Karageorghis, E. Lagarce, J. I. Leclant. *Fouilles de Kition*. Vol. 2: *Objets égyptiens et égyptísants*. Nicosia, 19–165.

Collon, D. 1981. The Alepo Workshop: A Seal-Cutter's Workshop in Syria in the Second Half of the 18th Century BC. *Ugarit-Forschungen* 13:33–43.

———. 1987. *First Impressions: Cylinder Seals in the Ancient Near East*. London: British Museum.

———. 1990. *Near Eastern Seals*. Berkeley: University of California Press / London: British Museum.

———. 1992. The Near Eastern Moon God. In: D. J.W. Meijer, ed., *Natural Phenomena: Their Meaning, Depiction and Description in the Ancient Near East*. Amsterdam: Royal Netherlands Academy of Arts and Sciences, 19–37.

———. 1995. Seals and Sealings. Chap. 8 in: J. E. Curtis and J. E. Reade, eds., *Art and Empire: Treasures from Assyria in the British Museum*. New York: Metropolitan Museum of Art, 179–89.

Culiacan, W. 1962. Melquart Representations on Phoenician Seals. *Abr-Nahrain* 2:41-54.
———. 1965. *The Medes and Persians*. London: Thames & Hudson / New York: Praeger.
———. 1976. Baal on Ibiza Gem. *Rivista di Studi Fenici* 4:57-68.
Delaporte, L. 1910. *Catalogue des cylindres orientaux et des cachets assyro-babyloniens: perses et syro-cappadociens de la Bibliothèque Nationale*. Paris: Leroux.
———. 1920. *Musée du Louvre: Catalogue des cylindres cachets et pierres gravées de style oriental*, vol. 1: *Fouilles et missions*. Paris.
Eisen, G. A. 1940. *Ancient Oriental Cylinder and Other Seals with a Description of the Collection of Mrs. William H. Moore*. University of Chicago Oriental Institute Publication 47. Chicago: University of Chicago Press.
Fernandez, J. H. 1983. *Guia del Museo Monographico del Puig de Molins*. Trabajos del Museo Arquelogico de Ibiza 10. Madrid.
Frankfort, H. 1939. *Cylinder Seals: A Documentary Essay on the Art and Religion of the Ancient Near East*. London: Macmillan.
———. 1954. *Art and Architecture of the Ancient Orient*. 2d rev. ed., 1958 impression. New York: Penguin
Flinders Petrie, W. M. *See* Petrie, W. M. Flinders.
Ghirshman, R. 1954. *Iran: From the Earliest Times to the Islamic Conquest*. New York: Penguin.
Gubel, E. 1986. The Iconography of the Ibiza Gem MAI 3650 Reconsidered. *Aula Orientalis* 4:111-18.
———. 1993. The Iconography of Inscribed Phoenician Glyptic. In: B. Sass and Ch. Uehlinger, eds. *Studies in Iconography of Northwest Semitic Inscribed Seals: Proceedings of a Symposium Held in Fribourg on April 17-20, 1991*. Orbis Biblicus et Orientalis 125. Freiburg/Schweiz: University Press / Göttingen: Vandenhoeck & Ruprecht, 101-29.
Harden, D. 1962. *The Phoenicians*. London: Thames & Hudson.
Herbordt, S. 1992. *Neuassyrische Glyptic des 8.–7. Jh. v. Chr. unter besonderer Berücksichtigung der Siegelungen auf Tafeln und Tonverschlüssen*. Helsinki: Neo-Assyrian Text Corpus Project.
Invernizzi, A. 1995. Seal Impressions of Achaemenid and Graeco-Persian Style from Seleucia on the Tigris. *Mesopotamia* 30:39-50.
Keel, O. 1980. La glyptique. Chap. 14, in: J. Briend, J.-B. Humbert, et al., *Tell Keisan (1971-1976): Une cité phénicienne en Galilée*. Orbis Biblicus et orientalis, Series Archaeologica 1. Fribourg: Editions Universitaires / Göttingen / Paris, 257-295.
———. 1990. IV: La glyptique de Tell Keisan (1971-1976). Pp. 163-260, 298-321 in: Keel, O.; M. Shuval; and Ch. Uehlinger. Studien zu den Stempelsiegeln aus Palästrina/Israel III: Die frühe Eisenzeit, ein Workshop. Orbis Biblicus et Orientalis 100. Freiburg, Schweiz, u. Göttingen: Universitätsverlag; Vandenhoeck & Ruprecht.
Keel, O., and Ch. Uehlinger. 1992. *Göttinnen, Götter und Gottessymbole: Neue Erkenntnisse zur Religionsgeschichte Kanaans und Israels aufgrund bislang unerschlossener ikongraphischer Quellen*. Fribourg, Basel und Vienna: Herder.
Kühne, H, et al. 1980. *Das Rollsiegel in Syrien: Zur Steinschneidekunst in Syrien zwischen 3300 und 330 vor Christus*. Tübingen: Altorientalisches Seminar der Universität Tübingen.
Layard, A. H. 1853. *Discoveries among the Ruins of Nineveh and Babylon, with Travels in Armenia, Kurdistan and the Desert: Being the Result of a Second Expedition, undertaken for the Trustees of the British Museum*. New York: Harper & Bros.

Levy, M. A. 1869. *Siegel und Gemmen mit aramäischen, phönizischen, althebräischen, himjarischen, nabathäischen und altysyrischen Inschriften.* Breslau: Schletter'schebuchh.

Loud, G., and C. B. Altman. 1938. *Khorsabad.* Part 2: *The Citadel and the Town.* University of Chicago Oriental Institute Publications 40. Chicago: University of Chicago Press.

Mallowan, M. E. L. 1966. *Nimrud and Its Remains I–II.* London: Collins. [Emended impression, with 6 pp. of addenda and corrigenda, 1975]

Marcus, M. I. 1988. The Seals and Sealings from Hasanlu IVB, Iran. Ph.D. Dissertation, University of Pennsylvania.

————. 1996. *Emblems of Identity and Prestige: The Seals and Sealings from Hasanlu, Iran: Commentary and Catalog.* Hasanlu Special Studies III: University Museum Monograph 84. Philadelphia: University of Pennsylvania Press.

Markoe, G. 1985. *Phoenician Bronze and Silver Bowls from Cyprus and the Mediterranean.* University of California Classical Studies 26. Berkeley: University of California Press.

Matthews, D. M. 1990. *Principles of Composition in Near Eastern Glyptic of the Later Second Millennium B.C.* Orbis Biblicus et Orientalis Series Archaeologica 8. Freiburg /Schweiz: University Press / Göttingen: Vandenhoeck & Ruprecht.

Moorey, P. R. S. 1967. Some Ancient Metal Belts: Their Antecedents and Relatives. *Iran* 5:83–98.

Moortgat, A. 1940. *Vorderasiatische Rollsiegel: Ein Beitrag zur Geschichte der Steinschneidekunst.* Berlin: Gebr. Mann.

Moortgat-Corens, U. 1968. Die Ehemalige Rollsiegel-Sammlung Erwin Oppenländer. *Baghdader Mitteilungen* 4:233–89.

Munn-rankin, J. M.1959. Ancient Near Eastern Seals in the Fitzwilliam Museum, Cambridge. *Iraq* 21:20–37.

Murray, M. A. 1953. Hieroglyphic and Ornamental Seals. Chap 11 in: O. Tufnell, M. A. Murray, and D. Diringer, *Lachish III (Tell ed-Duwier): The Iron Age.* London: Oxford University Press, 360–73.

Muscarella, O. W. 1988. *Bronze and Iron: Ancient Near Eastern Artifacts in the Metropolitan Museum of Art.* New York: Metropolitan Museum of Art.

Oded, B. 1993. Ahaz'a Appeal to Tiglath-Pileser III in the Context of the Assyrian Policy of Expansion. Pp. 63–71 in: *Studies in the Archaeology and History of Ancient Israel, in Honour of Moshe Dothan.* Ed. M. Heltzer, A. Segal, and D. Kaufman. Haifa: University of Haifa.

von Oppenheim, M. F. 1931. *Tell Halaf: A New Culture in Oldest Mesopotamia.* Trans. from the 1931 German edition by Gerald Wheeler. London and New York: G. P. Putnam's Sons.

von Oppenheim, M. F., D. Opitz, and A. Moortgat. 1955. *Tell Halaf.* Vol. 3, *Die Bildwerke.* Berlin: De Gruyter.

von Oppenheim, M. F., and B. Hrouda. 1962. *Tell Halaf,* vol. 4, *Die Kleinfunde aus historischer Zeit.* Berlin: De Gruyter.

Ornan, T. 1990. Studies in Glyptics from the Land of Israel and Transjordan: Assyrian, Babylonian and Achaemenid Cylinder Seals from the 1st Half of the 1st Millennium BCE. Unpublished M.A. thesis, Hebrew University, Institute of Archaeology, Jerusalem. [Hebrew.]

von der Osten, H. H. 1936. *Ancient Oriental Seals in the Collection of Mrs. Agnes Baldwin Brett.* University of Chicago, Oriental Institute Publication 37. Chicago: University of Chicago Press.

————. 1956. *Die Welt der Perser.* Groskulturen der Frühzeit. Stuttgart: Kilpper.

Parker, B. 1962. Seals and Seal Impressions from the Nimrud Excavations, 1955–1958. *Iraq* 24:26–40.

Paley, S. M. 1992. The Assyrian *Winged Genius* in the Middlebury College Museum of Art. *Middlebury College Museum of Art 1992 Annual Report*. Middlebury, 13–31.

Petrie, W. M. Flinders. 1927. *Objects of Daily Use, with over 1800 Figures from University College*. London: British School of Archaeology in Egypt.

Porada, E. 1947. Suggestions for the Classification of Neo-Babylonian Cylinder Seals. *Orientalia* 16:145–65.

———. 1948. *Corpus of Ancient Near Eastern Seals in North American Collections*. Vol. 1, *The Collection of the Pierpont Morgan Library*. Washington, D.C.: Pantheon.

———. 1981. Stamps and Cylinder Seals of the Ancient Near East. In: *Ancient Bronzes, Ceramics and Seals*. Ed. G. Markoe. Los Angeles: Los Angeles County Museum of Art, 187–234, 268–69.

Reade, J. E. 1995. Palaces and Temples. Chap. 2 in: J. E. Curtis and J. E. Reade, eds. *Art and Empire: Treasures from Assyria in the British Museum*. New York: Metropolitan Museum of Art, 92–108.

Ridder, A. 1911. *Collection de Clercq, Catalogue … Tome VII: 2me Partie: Les Pierres gravées*. Paris: Leroux.

Sotheby's. Sale 6256: *The Ada Small Moore Collection of Ancient Near Eastern Seals*. New York, 12 December 1991.

Stern, E. 1987. Excavations at Tel Dor: A Canaanite-Phoenician Port-City on the Carmel Coast. *Qadmoniot* 20 (79–80): 66–80 [Hebrew.]

———. 1992. A Hoard of Persian Bullae from the Vicinity of Samaria. *Michmanim* 6:7–30 [Hebrew.]

———. 1993. Notes on the Development of Stamp Glyptic Art in Palestine during the Assyrian, Babylonian and Persian periods. In: M. Heltzer, A. Segal, and D. Kaufman, eds. *Studies in the Archaeology and History of Ancient Israel, in Honour of Moshe Dotham*. Haifa: University of Haifa, 111–22. [Hebrew.]

———. 1994a. Notes on the Development of Stamp Glyptic Art in Palestine during the Assyrian and Persian periods. Pp. 135–146 in: L. M. Hopfe, ed. *Uncovering Ancient Stones: Essays in Memory of H. Neil Richardson*. Winona Lake, IN: Eisenbrauns.

———. 1994b. Assyrian and Babylonian Elements in the Material Culture of Palestine in the Persian Period. *Transeuphratène* 7:51–62.

Strommenger, E. 1985. Small orthostat [181]. In: H. Weiss, ed. *Ebla to Damascus: Art and Archaeology of Ancient Syria*. Washington, DC: Smithsonian Institution Traveling Exhibition Service, 362.

Stucky, R, et al. 1979. Objects 134–209. In: *Sumer Assur Babylone: 7000 ans de culture et d'art sur le Tigre et l'Euphrate: Exposition Neue Galerie. Sammlung Ludwig: à Aix-la-chapelle, 1er Juin–Août 1979*. Museum für Vor- und Frühgeschichte der Staatliche Museen Preussischer Kulturbesitz, Berlin.

Tadmor, H., and M. Tadmor. 1995. The Seal of Bel-Asharedu: A Case of "Migration." In: K. van Lerberghe and A. Schoors, eds., *Immigration and Emigration within the Ancient Near East: Festschrift E. Lipiński*. Orientalia Lovaniensia Analecta 65. Leuven, 345–55.

Teissier, B. 1984. *Ancient Near Eastern Cylinder Seals from the Marcopoli Collection*. Berkeley: University of California Press.

Tosi, M. 1976–80. S.v. "Karneol," *Reallexikon der Assyriologie und Vorderasiatischen Archäologie* 5:448–52. Berlin.

Tubb, J. N., P. G. Dorrell, and F. J. Cobbing. 1996. Interim Report on the Eighth (1995) Season of Excavations at Tell es-Sa°idiyeh. *Palestine Exploration Quarterly* 128:16–40.

Tunca, Ö. 1979. Catalogue des sceaux-cylindres du Musée Régional d'Adana. *Syro-Mesopotamian Studies* 3/1:1–27.

Vercoutter, J. 1945. *Les objets égyptiens et égyptisants du mobilier funéraire carthaginois.* Paris: Paul Geuthner.

Walters, H. B. 1926. *Catalogue of the Engraved Gems and Cameos Greek Etruscan and Roman in the British Museum.* London: Bernard Quaritch and Humphrey Milford.

Williams-Forte, E. 1976. *Ancient Near Eastern Seals: A Selection of Stamp and Cylinder Seals from the Collection of Mrs. William H. Moore.* New York: Metropolitan Museum of Art.

Winter, I. J. 1977. Perspective on the "Local Style" of Hasanlu IVB: A Study in Receptivity. Pp. 371–386 in: *Mountains and Lowlands: Essays in the Archaeology of Greater Mesopotamia.* Ed. L. D. Levine and T. C. Young, Jr. Bibliotheca Mesopotamica, 7. Malibu, CA: Undena Publications, 371–86.

————. 1980. *A Decorated Breastplate from Hasanlu, Iran: Type, Style, and Context of an Equestrian Ornament.* Hasanlu Special Studies, 1: University Museum Monograph, 39. Philadelphia: University of Pennsylvania Press.

————. 1989. North Syrian Ivories and Tell Halaf Reliefs: The Impact of Luxury Goods upon "Major" Arts. In: *Essays in Ancient Civilization Presented to Helene J. Kantor.* Ed. A. Leonard, Jr., and B. B. Williams. Studies in Ancient Oriental Civilization, 47. Chicago: University of Chicago Press, 321–32.

Wiseman, D. J. 1959. *Cylinder Seals of Western Asia.* London: Batchworth Press.

Zettler, R. L. 1979. On the Chronological Range of Neo-Babylonian and Achaemenid Seals. *Journal of Near Eastern Studies* 38:257–70.

## ACKNOWLEDGMENTS

Thanks are due to Dr. Michelle Marcus for clarification of some points in her last publication; to Dr. Benjamin Sass for making the modern impressions; to Mr. Ilan Sztulman and Mr. Eran Kessel of Sztulman-Kessel Photographic Services, Ltd., for the photographs; and Mrs. Carmen Hersch for the drawings and reconstructions.

*Arie Kindler*

# The Coins of the Tetrarch Philip and Bethsaida

T HE TETRARCH PHILIP (4 BCE–34 CE), the son of Herod the Great, who ruled the territories in the north of the country, including Trachonitis, Auranitis, Batanaea, and Gaulanitis, issued a rather long series of coins, most of them *semis* of one particular design. On their obverses usually appears the portrait of the emperor (Augustus or Tiberius); on their reverses usually appears a depiction of the temple of Augustus which Philip's father Herod had erected in Panias before Philip made that city his capital. During the first years of his rule, Philip even issued a limited number of coins which bear his own portrait.[1]

However, in the thirty-fourth year of his reign (30/31 CE), for the first time he issued a series of three coins, a series that differs from his former issues by two of its types and denominations: *semis, quadrans,* and half-*quadrans.* Here follows their descriptions.

1. AE.
Denomination: *semis*
      Weight: 5.16–6.51 gr
        Size: 17–20 mm
   Obverse: Portrait of Tiberius to right
            Olive spray in front to head
            Dotted border
            Legend (around from left below); ΤΙΒΕΡΙΟΥ ϹΕΒΑϹΤΟϹ ΚΑΙϹΑΡ
   Reverse: Tetrastyle temple with triangle-shaped pediment, within which is a
            dot
            At base of the temple, three lines (stairs?)
            Dotted border
            Legend (around from left below, reading outwardly to the right): ΕΠΙ
            ΦΙΛΙΠΠΟΥ ΤΕΤΡΑΡΧΟΥ ΚΤΙϹ (τζs) (= by Philip the tetrarch,
            the founder)
            Between the columns of the temple, the date of issue: ΛΛΔ = year of
            Philip 34 (30/31 CE)[2]

The olive spray on the front of the emperor's portrait expresses an act of celebration. The legend on the obverse ends with the word ΚΤΙϹ(τζs), "founder." To date, scholars have not offered any sound explanation for the appearance of this word on this coin.

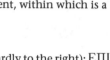

2. AE.
Denomination: *quadrans*
      Weight: 3.00 gr
        Size: 15.4 mm
   Obverse: Portrait of Livia to right, draped
            Dotted border
            Legend (around from left below): ΙΟΥΛΙΑ ϹΕΒΑϹΤΗ
   Reverse: A hand to the left, holding three ears of barley
            Dotted border
            Legend (in semicircle from left to right, reading outwardly): ΚΑΡΠΟ-
            ΦΟΡΟϹ
            in field above, the date of issue: ΛΛΔ = year 34 (30/31 CE)[3]

This type has recently been connected to Philip.[4] As a matter of fact, the legend of this coin does not directly refer to Philip or to the city of Panias. It was, however, related to Philip because of the date of issue (year 34), and to the city of Panias because of the Karpophoros type, represented by the hand holding the ears of barley. This type reappears twice: (a) on a coin struck for Kypros, the wife of Agrippa I[5] and

(b) on the coins of Agrippa II struck in his eleventh year of reign,[6] a year in which Panias was doubtless Agrippa's capital. Another indication that this coin belongs to the series of coins of Philip is, besides the date of issue, the fact that the legend reads outwardly, a *modus* common on the coins of Philip. It is likely that the Karpophoros is meant to express the abundance of grain in the territories ruled by Philip.

3. AE.
Denomination: half-*quadrans*
          Weight: 1.46–1.75 gr
             Size: 10–12 mm
        Obverse: Portrait of Philip to right, draped, bareheaded
                    Dotted border
                    Legend (around from left below): ΦIΛIΠΠOΥ
        Reverse: Wreath, tied at bottom
                    Legend (within the wreath in one line is the date of issue): LΛΔ = year 34 (30/31 CE)[7]

A similar series was issued by Philip a second time in the thirty-seventh and last year of his reign, 33/34 CE. However, only in the thirty-fourth year of his rule does the title KTIC(τζs), "founder," appear. This fact doubtless hints at an extraordinary event which occurred in that year (30/31 CE), in the tetrarchy of Philip. This event seems to have provided an impetus for him to leave his numismatic routine and issue a more complicated series, different from the monotonous series of coins he had issued during most of the other years of his reign.

In view of the indirect numismatic evidence provided by the three aforementioned coin types it is well to review the relevant evidence found in Josephus's *Antiquities*,[8] according to which the village called Bethsaida was renamed Julias by Philip in honor of Julia, the daughter of Augustus. Almost by necessity, the renaming of Bethsaida would have had to occur before 2 BCE, for in that year Julia was exiled by her father to the island of Pandateria. Josephus does not give this information in chronological order. He reports first the liquidation of Archelaus's properties by Quirinius, the governor of Syria, during the thirty-seventh year of reign of Augustus (6 CE). Then he goes back ten years, to report that the two other sons of Herod, Antipas and Philip, were given their tetrarchies; Antipas named Betharamphtha Julias after Livia, Augustus's wife; Philip named Bethsaida Julias after Julia, Augustus's daughter. The mention of the renaming of both these cities in one sentence is curious. The daughter of Augustus was, as mentioned above, banned in 2 BCE, while Livia, his wife, was given the name Julia only some sixteen years later, according to the will of Augustus. Josephus discusses the same matter in a different way in his *Bellum Judaicum*, and it seems that in this case he was more careful about chronology:

> On the death of Augustus ... the empire of the Romans passed to Tiberius, the son of Julia. On his accession, Herod (Antipas) and Philip continued to hold their tetrarchies and respectively founded cities: Philip built Caesarea near the sources of the Jordan, in the district of Panias, and Julias in lower Gaulanitis; Herod built Tiberias in Galilee and a city which also took the name of Julias, in Peraea.[9]

The era of the coins of the city of Panias starts in 3 BCE, namely one year after Philip received his tetrarchy. It is unlikely that the foundation of Panias (which was also called Caesarea Philippi) should be mentioned on Philip's coins, arbitrarily, some thirty years later. Based on coin no. 2 on which Livia/Julia is depicted, I would suggest that the event of foundation mentioned on coin no. 1 refers to the foundation of Bethsaida as Julias. Livia, Augustus's wife, was adopted into the Julian *gens*, according to Augustus's will, in 14 CE and died in the year 29. Since these coins were issued in 30/31, it is appropriate that the two cities (Bethsaida and Betharamphtha) should be renamed in honor of the mother of Tiberius,[10] rather than in honor of Augustus's daughter.

If this suggestion is accepted, it follows that Bethsaida was founded anew in the year 34 of Philip's rule, namely in 30/31 CE. Whether the Julias of Philip was renamed before Antipas gave the same name to Betharamphtha remains, for the time being, an open question. If, however, one can compare the relationship between the renaming of the two cities and the behavior of Antipas towards King Agrippa I (a behavior guided by the jealousy of his wife, Herodias), one may imagine that it was Antipas who followed after Philip, to please Emperor Tiberius. Thus it is likely that Betharamphtha was renamed Julias after 30/31 CE.

## Chapter Notes

1. Kindler (1971) 161–63, pl. 32.
2. Maltiel-Gerstenfeld (1989) p. 148, no. 119; p. 198. Meshorer (1982) p. 246, no. 11, pl. 8, no. 11. This coin type was also issued in the year 37 of Philip's rule, using the same portrait of Tiberius as depicted on the issue of year 34; cf. Meshorer (1982) pl. 8, no. 14.
3. Cf. Maltiel-Gerstenfeld (1982) p. 148, no. 190 and Rosenberger (1977) p. 38, no. 4; cf. also Meshorer (1982) supplement 3, p. 278, no. 1.
4. Maltiel-Gerstenfeld (1982) p. 148, no. 120.
5. Maltiel-Gerstenfeld (1982) p. 157, no. 143; Meshorer (1982) p. 250, no. 6, pl. II.6.
6. Maltiel-Gerstenfeld (1982) p. 149, no. 121; Meshorer (1982) p. 246, no. 12, pl. 8, no. 12.
7. Josephus, *Antiquities* 18.28.
8. Josephus, *Bellum Judaicum* 2.168.
9. Tacitus, *Annals* 1.8: "On the first day of the Senate he (Tiberius) allowed nothing to be discussed but the funeral of Augustus, whose will was brought by the Vestal Virgins. He named as his heirs Tiberius and Livia. The latter was admitted into the Julian *gens* with the name of Augusta."
10. And this in spite of the fact that Tiberius hesitated to perpetuate her memory; cf. Tacitus, *Annales, 5.2.*

## Literature Cited

Kindler, A. 1971. A Coin of Herod Philip—the Earliest Portrait of a Herodian Ruler. *Israel Exploration Journal* 21:162–63.
Josephus, Flavius. [*Works*, English & Greek, 1958–]. Loeb Classical Library. 9 vols. Cambridge, Mass.: Harvard University Press; London: W. Heineman, 1958–1965.
Maltiel-Gerstenfeld, J. 1989. *260 Years of Ancient Jewish Coins*. Tel-Aviv: Kol Printing Service, Ltd.
Meshorer, Ya'a'kov. 1982. *Ancient Jewish Coinage*, 2 vols. Vol. 1, *Persian Period through Hasmoneans*, Vol. 2, *Herod the Great through Bar Cochba*. Dix Hills, N.Y.: Amphora Books.
Rosenberger, M. 1977. City Coinage of Palestine, III, Jerusalem. Jerusalem: Rosenberger.
Tacitus, Cornelius. 1989. *Annals*. Book IV. Ed. A. J. Church and W. J. Brodribb. New York: Columbia University Press.

## Acknowledgments

This chapter, based on a lecture presented by the author in a congress on Herod at Haifa University on 9–10 April 1986, was published in *Cathedra for the History of Eretz Israel and Its Yishuv* 53 (Jerusalem, Sept. 1989 [Hebrew]).

*Arie Kindler*

# The Coin Finds at the Excavations of Bethsaida

D URING THE EXCAVATIONS CONDUCTED AT BETHSAIDA by R. Arav and his staff, some 220 coins were discovered up to March 1996. These can be divided into the following groups and periods:

| Group | Period |
|---|---|
| Persian | ca. 450–330 BCE |
| Hellenistic | ca. 260–125 BCE |
| Jewish coins | ca. 128 BCE–84/85 CE |
| Palestinian city coins | ca. 100–300 CE |
| Late Roman and Byzantine coins | ca. 310–578 CE |
| Islamic coinage | ca. 900–1400 CE |
| European coins | ca. 1556–1728 CE |
| Ottoman coins from Ahmet III to Abdul Hamid II | 1703–1879 CE |

The finds of the Persian period (ca. 450–330 BCE) are scarce; we have only one Athenian tetradrachm that can be dated to approximately 450 BCE and two silver coins of the city of Tyre (ca. 400–330 BCE).

The Hellenistic period is represented by twenty-six Ptolemaic bronze coins of Ptolemy II and III, which compose about 12 percent of the entire find. These are followed by a rather large number of Seleucid coins: Those of Antiochus III the Great, who conquered Palestine from the Ptolemies with the battle of Paneas in 200 BCE (seventeen), followed by coins of Antiochus IV Epiphanes (four), Demetrius I (three), Antiochus V (three), Antiochus VII Sidetes (four), Demetrius II (nine),

250

and some unidentifiable Seleucid coins (twenty-three), for a total of sixty-four specimens, which are about one-third of the entire find.

The group of Jewish coins can be subdivided into Hasmonean and Herodian groupings. The Hasmonean group is composed of the coins of John Hyrcanus I (five), Alexander Jannaeus (four), Aristobulus II (four); the Herodian group is composed of the coins of Herod I (one), Archelaus (one), Antipas (one), Philippus (three), Agrippa I (one), and Agrippa II (two), altogether twenty-two specimens, or 10 percent of the find.

The city coins are few. The cities represented are Bostra (one), Damascus (two), Diocaesarea (one), Tiberias (three), and Tyre (five).

The dominant mint from the Hellenistic period is that of the city of Tyre with forty-three specimens, Seleucid issues of the second century BCE. This is not surprising, at least for the northern part of the country.[1] The other mints of that period are Alexandria with nineteen specimens; Salamis, Cyprus, with four; and Sidon with one specimen.

There are only two Late Roman coins and three Byzantine coins that were struck under Justinus II (565–578 CE).

The Islamic coins range from the eighth to the fourteenth centuries with twenty-two specimens, twenty-one of which are Mamluk.

Quite a few Ottoman coins were discovered, thirteen of which come from tomb no. 3. All these are pierced and seem to have formed part of a headgear.

The finds close with some modern Syrian coins issued in 1947 and 1965 respectively.

It is quite astonishing that only two Late Roman and three Byzantine coins were discovered—astonishing because in almost all other excavations in the region, the Late Roman coins are quantitatively dominant. Their absence in Bethsaida could point to a gap in the occupation of Bethsaida between the late fourth and the early eighth centuries, although also the Ummayad (early Arab issues ca. 650–750 CE) coin find includes only two specimens.

Two European coins, one of the Venetian doge Lorenzo Priuli (1556–59) and the other of Philippus V, king of Spain (1724–46), came to light as well and were probably found here as a result of commercial relations between the Ottoman empire and Europe. Since both specimens are pierced, they were in secondary use and probably also formed part of an Arab woman's headgear.

*Arie Kindler*

## COIN FINDS AT BETHSAIDA EXCAVATION

| | Ruler | Type[a] | Mint | Area | Locus | Basket | Remarks |
|---|---|---|---|---|---|---|---|
| **AREA A** | | | | | | | |
| 1. | Athens | A | Athens | A | 790 | 2550 | ca. 450 BCE, tetradrachm |
| | | | | | | | |
| 2. | Tyre | C | Tyre | A | 303 | 1224 | silver sheqel |
| 3. | Ptolemy II or III | D | Alexandria | A | 46/90 | 1941 | Tetradrachm, copper core |
| 4. | Ptolemy II or III | E | Salamis, Cyprus | A | 585 | 1929 | ca. 287–241 BCE |
| 5. | Ptolemy II or III | E | Salamis, Cyprus | A | 551 | 1762 | |
| 6. | Ptolemy II or III | E | | A | 502 | | |
| 7. | Ptolemy II or III | E | Tyre | A | 767 | 2377 | |
| 8. | Ptolemy II or III | E | Alexandria | A | | 1951 | surface find |
| 9. | Ptolemy II or III | E | Alexandria | A | 773 | 2413 | |
| 10. | Ptolemy II or III | E | Alexandria | A | 817 | 2831 | |
| 11. | Ptolemy II or III | E | Alexandria | A | 818 | 2851 | |
| 12. | Ptolemy II or III | E | Alexandria | A | 818 | 2859 | completely corroded |
| 13. | Ptolemy II or III | E | Alexandria | A | 825 | 2918 | |
| 14. | Ptolemy II or III | E | Alexandria | A | 830 | 2982 | |
| 15. | Antiochus III | G | | A | 830 | 2936 | 222–187 BCE |
| 16. | Antiochus III | G | | A | 831 | 2973 | |
| 17. | Demetrius I | H | Tyre | A | 818 | 2862 | 162–150 BCE (162) |
| | | | | | | | |
| 18. | Demetrius II | H | Tyre | A | 828 | 2959 | 130–125 (2nd reign) |
| 19. | Demetrius or Antiochus | H | Tyre | A | | 2801 | |
| | | | | | | | |

| | Ruler | Type[a] | Mint | Area | Locus | Basket | Remarks |
|---|---|---|---|---|---|---|---|
| 20. | Seleucid | I | Tyre | A | 747 | 2274 | |
| 21. | Alexander Jannaeus | N | Jerusalem | A | 817 | 2848 | 103–76 BCE |
| 22. | Alexander Jannaeus | O | Jerusalem | A | 831 | 2945 | (78) |
| 23. | Aristobulus II | N | Jerusalem | A | 818 | 2857 | 67–63 BCE |
| 24. | Herod I | P | Jerusalem | A | 859 | 8429 | 37–4 BCE |
| 25. | Antipas | Q | Tiberias | A | 858 | 8384 | 4 BCE–39 CE (33) |
| 26. | Philippus | R | Paneas | A | 784 | 2479 | 4 BCE–34 CE |
| 27. | Elagabalus | Z | Tyre | A | | 2944 | 218–222 CE |
| 28. | Elagabalus | | | A | 830 | 2960 | city coin; reverse blank |
| 29. | Severus Alexander | Ab | Bostra | A | 825 | 2919 | |
| 30. | ? | | | A | 829 | 2928 | probably city coin |
| 31. | Constantine I | Ak | | A | 734 | 2223/ 1992 | 308–337 CE |
| 32. | Crispus | Al | Arelatum | A | 787 | 2532 | 317–326 CE |

| | Ruler | Type[a] | Mint | Area | Locus | Basket | Remarks |
|---|---|---|---|---|---|---|---|
| 33. | Justinus II | Am | | A | 818 | 2832 | 565–578 CE. M = follis |
| 34. | Justinus II | An | | A | | | K = 1/2 follis |
| 35. | Ummayad or Abassid | Ao | | A | 784 | 2502 | gold dinar |

| | Ruler | Type | Mint | Area | Locus | Basket | Remarks |
|---|---|---|---|---|---|---|---|
| 36. | Mameluk | Ao | | A | tomb 63, 1733 | | |
| 37. | Mameluk | | | A | 46/90 | 1952 | coin-shaped piece of copper |
| 38. | Mameluk | blank | | A | 818 | 2843 | |
| 39. | Mameluk | blank | | A | 831 | 2962 | |
| 40. | Lorenzo Priuli | Aq | Venice | A | 788 | 2537 | 1556–1559; 4 soldi, copper |
| 41. | Philippus V | Ar | Spain | A | 850 | 8517 | 1724–1746 (1728) |

| | Ruler | Type | Mint | Area | Locus | Basket | Remarks |
|---|---|---|---|---|---|---|---|
| 42. | Token | At | Germany | A | | | Rechenpfennig |
| 43. | ? | | | A | 818 | 2528 | |
| 44. | ? | | | A | 817 | 2830 | completely corroded |
| 45. | Ahmed III | As | Egypt | A | 818 | 2343 | 1703–1730 |
| 46. | Osman III | As | Constanti-nople | A | 858 | 8379 | 1754–1757 |
| 47. | Mahmud II | As | Constanti-nople | A | 858 | 8401 | 1808–1839 (1811) |
| 48. | Mahmud II | As | Constanti-nople | A | 858 | 8397 | (1819) |
| 49. | Mahmud II | As | Constanti-nople | A | 791 | 2638 | (1826–1830) |
| 50. | Abdul Medjid | As | Constanti-nople | A | 858 | 8380 | 1839–1861 (1841) 20 Paras |
| 51. | Abdul Medjid | As | Constanti-nople | A | 858 | 8398 | (1843) 20 Paras |
| 52. | Abdul Medjid | As | Constanti-nople | A | 850 | 8363 | (1843) 20 Paras |
| 53. | Abdul Medjid | As | Constanti-nople | A | Tomb 62 | 1676 | (1854) 5 Paras |
| 54. | Abdul Medjid | As | Constanti-nople | A | 181 | 2528 | |
| 55. | Abdul Medjid | | Constanti-nople | A | 787 | 2535 | effaced |
| 56. | Abdul Hamid II | As | Constanti-nople | A | 790 | 2575 | 1876–1909 10 Paras |

| | Ruler | Type[a] | Mint | Area | Locus | Basket | Remarks |
|---|---|---|---|---|---|---|---|
| 57. | Abdul Hamid II | As | Constanti-nople | A | 858 | 8385 | (1879) 5 Paras |
| 58. | Ottoman | | | A | 818 | 2851 | |
| 59. | Ottoman | | | A | 790 | 2579 | |
| 60. | ? | | | A | 858 | 8406 | unclear fragment of a coin |

## AREA B

| | Ruler | Type[a] | Mint | Area | Locus | Basket | Remarks |
|---|---|---|---|---|---|---|---|
| 61. | Ptolemy II or III | E | Tyre | B | 364 | 4146 | |
| 62. | Ptolemy II or III | D | Alexandria | B | | 2062 | Tetradrachm on copper core; surface find |
| 63. | Ptolemy II or III | E | Alexandria | B | 362 | 4152 | |
| 64. | Ptolemy II or III | E | Tyre | B | 371 | 4212 | |
| 65. | Ptolemy II or III | E | Alexandria | B | 450 | 5485 | |
| 66. | Ptolemy II or III | E | Alexandria | B | | | found by a Bedouin |
| 67. | Antiochus III | G | | B | 312 | 3064 | 222–187 BCE |
| 68. | Antiochus III | G | | B | 369 | 4169 | |
| 69. | Antiochus III | G | | B | 448 | 5511 | |
| 70. | Antiochus III | G | | B | 493 | 5745 | |
| 71. | Antiochus III | G | | B | 603 | 5838 | |
| 72. | Antiochus III | G | | B | 622 | 5947 | |
| 73. | Antiochus III | G | | B | 626 | 6070 | |
| 74. | Antiochus III | G | | B | 674 | 6176 | |
| 75. | Antiochus III | | | B | 676 | 6183 | |
| 76. | Antiochus III | G | | B | 689 | 6336 | |
| 77. | Antiochus III | J | | B | | 2062 | survey find |
| 78. | Antiochus IV | I | | B | 672 | 6127 | 175–164 BCE |
| 79. | Antiochus IV? | K | | B | 42-601 | 5862 | |

| Ruler | Type[a] | Mint | Area | Locus | Basket | Remarks |
|---|---|---|---|---|---|---|
| 80. Antiochus V | H | Tyre | B | 408 | 5049 | 163–162 BCE |
| | | | | | | |
| 81. Antiochus or Demetrius | H | Tyre | B | 42-601 | 5872 | |
| 82. Antiochus IV or Demetrius I | J | Tyre | B | 626 | 5615 | |
| | | | | | | |
| 83. Demetrius I | H | Tyre | B | 493 | 5731 | 162–150 (152) |
| 84. Demetrius I | H | Tyre | B | 672 | 6138 | |
| 85. Demetrius I(?) | J | Tyre | B | 612 | 5990 | |
| | | | | | | |
| 86. Antiochus VII | H | Tyre | B | 316 | 3093 | 138–129 BCE |
| | | | | | | |
| 87. Antiochus VII | J | Sidon | B | 496 | 5825 | |
| | | | | | | |

| | Ruler | Type[a] | Mint | Area | Locus | Basket | Remarks |
|---|---|---|---|---|---|---|---|
| 88. | Antiochus VII | H | Tyre | B | 626 | 5875 | |
| 89. | Demetrius II | E | Tyre | B | 313 | | silver didrachm |
| 90. | Demetrius II | E | Tyre | B | 313 | | |
| 91. | Demetrius II | E | Tyre | B | 367 | | 1st reign 145–139 BCE |
| 92. | Seleucid | H | Tyre | B | 252 | | |
| 93. | Seleucid | H | Tyre | B | 499 | 5804 | |
| 94. | Seleucid | H | Tyre | B | 499 | 5803 | |
| 95. | Seleucid | H | Tyre | B | 587 | 6712 | |
| 96. | Seleucid | H | Tyre | B | 619 | 5917 | |
| 97. | Seleucid | H | Tyre | B | 668 | 6115 | |
| 98. | Seleucid | H | Tyre | B | 672 | 6151 | |
| 99. | Seleucid (?) | K | | B | H36 | 2001 | |
| 100. | Hyrcanus I | N | Jerusalem | B | 369 | 4143 | 135–104 BCE |
| 101. | Hyrcanus I | N | Jerusalem | B | 612 | 5922 | |
| 102. | Hyrcanus I | N | Jerusalem | B | | 6331 | surface survey |

| Ruler | Type[a] | Mint | Area | Locus | Basket | Remarks |
|-------|---------|------|------|-------|--------|---------|
| 103. Alexander Jannaeus | N | Jerusalem | B | 314 | | 103–76 BCE |
| 104. Alexander Jannaeus | O | Jerusalem | B | 524 | 1643 | |
| 105. Aristobulus II | N | Jerusalem | B | 303 | 1290 | 67–63 BCE |
| 106. Aristobulus II | N | Jerusalem | B | 302 | 1217 | |
| 107. Hasmonaean | N | Jerusalem | B | 301 | 1208 | |
| 108. Archelaos | P | Jerusalem | B | 424 | 5200 | 4 BCE -6 CE |
| 109. Philippus | S | Paneas | B | 550 | 1738 | 4 BCE–34 CE |
| 110. Philippus | S | Paneas | B | 301 | 1235 | |
| 111. Agrippa I | T | Jerusalem | B | L-43 494 | 5755 | 37–44 CE |

| Ruler | Type[a] | Mint | Area | Locus | Basket | Remarks |
|---|---|---|---|---|---|---|
| 112. Agrippa II | R | Tiberias | B | 491 | 5732 | ca. 50–100 CE |
| 113. Agrippa II | Ra | Paneas (?) | B | 436 | 5320 | (84/5 CE) |
| 114. Trajanus | U | Rome | B | 451 | 5467 | 98–117 CE |
| 115. Trajanus | V | Tiberias | B | 604 | 5830 | |
| 116. Trajanus | W | Tiberias | B | 494 | 5738 | |
| 117. Trajanus | X | Tiberias | B | 493 | 5750 | |

| Ruler | Type[a] | Mint | Area | Locus | Basket | Remarks |
|---|---|---|---|---|---|---|
| 118. Antoninus Pius | Y | Diocae-sarea | B | 492 | 5729 | |
| 119. Julia Mamaea | Ya | Tyre | B | 503 | 1885 | |
| 120. Salonina | Ad | Tyre | B | 526 | 1704 | |
| 121. Valerianus | Ae | Tyre | B | 586 | 1925 | |
| 122. Otacilia Severa | Af | Damascus | B | 558 | | |
| 123. Otacilia Severa | Ag | Damascus | B | | | |
| 124. Unidentified city coin | Af | | B | 610 | 5896 | |
| 125. Unidentified city coin | Ai | | B | 619 | 5923 | |
| 126. Ummayad | Ao | | B | 574 | 6462 | |
| 127. Ummayad | Ap | | B | 681 | 6292 | |
| 128. Al-Malik al Adil Nur al-Din Mahmud | Ao | Damascus | B | 1146–1174 | | fils Atabeg of Haleb Zandjid dynasty |
| 129. Al-Malik al Adil Nur al-Din Mahmud | Ao | Damascus | B | 1146–1174 | | fils Atabeg of Haleb Zandjid dynasty |
| 130. Maml. Al-Salih Imad al-din Ismail | Ao | " | B | 303 | | fils |
| 131. Maml. Al-Salih Imad al-din Ismail | Ao | | B | 405 | | fils |
| 132. Maml. Al-Salih Imad al-din Ismail | Ao | | B | 608 | | fils |
| 133. Mameluk (?) | | | B | 329 | | fils |
| 134. Mameluk (?) | | | B | | | fils; blank |
| 135. Mameluk (?) | Ao | | B | 302 | 3000 | |
| 136. Mameluk (?) | Ao | | B | 350 | 4056 | |
| 137. Mameluk (?) | Ao | | B | 438 | 5639 | blank |

| Ruler | Type[a] | Mint | Area | Locus | Basket | Remarks |
|---|---|---|---|---|---|---|
| 138. Mameluk (?) | Ao | | B | 614 | 6049 | |
| 139. Mameluk | | | B | | 6146 | blank |
| 140. Al-Ashraf Abu al-Nasr Qa'itbay | Ao | | B | 302 | | fils |
| 141. Al-Ashraf Abu al-Nasr Qa'itbay | AN | Persia | B | | | copper |
| 142. Mahmud II | As | Constanti-nople | B | 421 | | 20 Paras 1826 |
| 143. Mahmud II | As | Constanti-nople | B | | | Uclik 1834 |
| 144. Mahmud II | As | Constanti-nople | B | 311 | | 1837 |
| 145. Mahmud II | As | | B | 589 | | Para |
| 146. ? | As | | B | 303 | | |
| 147. ? | As | | B | 301 | | Para |
| 148. ? | As | | B | 301 | | Para |
| 149. ? | As | | B | 302 | | Para pierced |
| 150. ? | As | | B | 302 | | Para pierced |
| 151. ? | As | | B | 302 | | Para pierced |
| 152. ? | As | | B | 302 | | Para pierced |
| 153. ? | | | B | 301 | ..32 | silver fragments |
| 154. Syria | | | B | 641 | 6040 | modern coin 1947 |
| 155. Syria | | | B | | | modern coin 1947(50 Piastre) |
| 156. | | | B | 585 | | effaced |
| 157. Medal or token, modern, pierced. | | | | | | |

## Area C

| Ruler | Type[a] | Mint | Area | Locus | Basket | Remarks |
|---|---|---|---|---|---|---|
| 158. Tyre | B | Tyre | C | | 9094 | silver obol |
| 159. Ptolemy II | F | Alexandria | C | 952 | 9554 | 285–247 BCE |

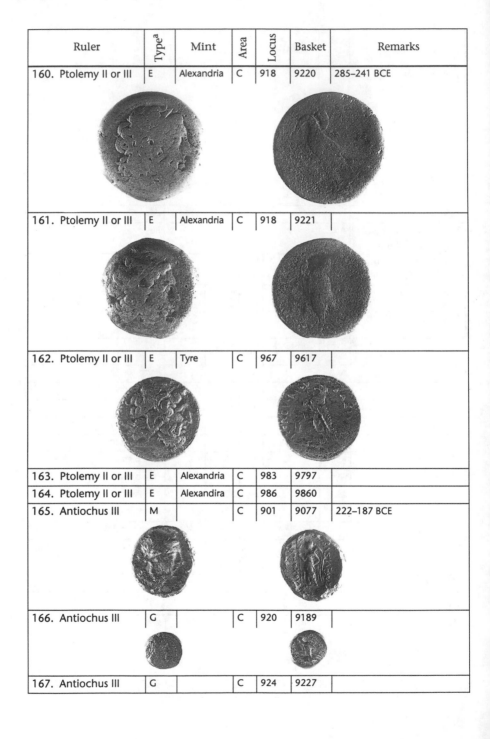

| Ruler | Type[a] | Mint | Area | Locus | Basket | Remarks |
|-------|---------|------|------|-------|--------|---------|
| 160. Ptolemy II or III | E | Alexandria | C | 918 | 9220 | 285–241 BCE |
| 161. Ptolemy II or III | E | Alexandria | C | 918 | 9221 | |
| 162. Ptolemy II or III | E | Tyre | C | 967 | 9617 | |
| 163. Ptolemy II or III | E | Alexandria | C | 983 | 9797 | |
| 164. Ptolemy II or III | E | Alexandira | C | 986 | 9860 | |
| 165. Antiochus III | M | | C | 901 | 9077 | 222–187 BCE |
| 166. Antiochus III | G | | C | 920 | 9189 | |
| 167. Antiochus III | G | | C | 924 | 9227 | |

| Ruler | Type[a] | Mint | Area | Locus | Basket | Remarks |
|-------|---------|------|------|-------|--------|---------|
| 168. Antiochus III | G | | C | 943 | 9329 | |
| 169. Antiochus IV | H | Tyre | C | 901 | 9089 | 175–164 BCE |
| 170. Antiochus V | H | Tyre | C | 967 | 9640 | 164–162 BCE |
| 171. Antiochus VII | H | Tyre | C | 977 | 9709 | 138–129 BCE |
| 172. Demetrius II | H | Tyre | C | 911 | 9114 | 130–125 BCE |
| 173. Demetrius II | H | Tyre | C | 901 | 9018 | |
| 174. Demetrius II | H | Tyre | C | 917 | 9181 | |
| 175. Demetrius II | E | Tyre | C | 907 | 9064 | silver tetradrachm |
| 176. Seleucid | H | Tyre | C | 901 | 9108 | |
| 177. Seleucid | H | Tyre | C | 909 | 9042 | |
| 178. Seleucid | H | Tyre | C | 915 | 9150 | |
| 179. Seleucid | H | Tyre | C | 917 | 9173 | |
| 180. Seleucid | H | Tyre | C | 917 | 9159 | |

| Ruler | Type[a] | Mint | Area | Locus | Basket | Remarks |
|---|---|---|---|---|---|---|
| 181. Seleucid | H | Tyre | C | 917 | 9168 | |
| 182. Seleucid | H | Tyre | C | 918 | 9226 | |
| 183. Hellenistic | (?) | | C | 951 | 9502 | completely effaced |
| 184. Probably Phoeni-cian | | | C | 901 | 9109 | traces of striking |
| 185. Hyrcanus I | N | Jerusalem | C | 911 | 9100 | 135–104 BCE |
| 186. Justinus II | A | Constanti-nople | C | 917 | 9182 | 565–578 CE |
| 187. Mameluk | | | C | 961 | 9532 | |
| 188. Mameluk | App | | C | 963 | 9558 | |
| 189. Mameluk | App | | C | 964 | 9597 | |
| 190. Mameluk | | | C | 964 | 9598 | blank |
| 191. Mameluk | A | | C | H/39 | | |
| 192. Abdul Medjid | As | Constanti-nople | C | 953 | 9435 | 1839–1861 |
| 193. Syria | | | C | 969 | 9708 | modern coin (1965) |

MISCELLANEOUS

| Ruler | Type[a] | Mint | Area | Locus | Basket | Remarks |
|---|---|---|---|---|---|---|
| 194. Ptolemy II | E | Salamis, Cyprus | | 150 | 2524 | 285–247 BCE |
| 195. Ptolemy II | E | Salamis, Cyprus | | 150 | 2524 | |
| 196. Ptolemy II | E | Alexandria | | 46/90 | 1951 | |
| 197. Ptolemy III | E | Alexandria | | T64 | | 247–222 BCE |
| 198. Antiochus IV | J | Tyre | | | | 175–164 BCE |

| Ruler | Type[a] | Mint | Area | Locus | Basket | Remarks |
|---|---|---|---|---|---|---|
| 199. Antiochus V | M | | | 977 | 9732 | 164–162 BCE |
| 200. Demetrius II | H | Tyre | | 598 | 6474 | 145–139 BCE 1st reign |
| 201. Seleucid | H | Tyre | | 401 | 8393 | |
| 202. Hyrcanus I | N | Jerusalem | | 588 | 6412 | 135–104 BCE |
| 203. Aristobulus II | N | Jerusalem | | 150 | 2521 | 67–63 BCE |
| 204. Elagabalus | Aa | Tyre | | 150A | 2522 | 218–222 CE |
| 205. Mameluk | | | | 853 | 8535 | blank |
| 206. Mameluk | | | | | | blank |
| 207. Mahmud II | As | Constanti-nople | | 524 | 1663 | 1808–1859 |
| 208. Mahmud II | As | Constanti-nople | | | | (1836) |
| Tomb 3 (Bedouin) | | | | | | |
| 209. Mahmud II | As | Constanti-nople | | 1252 | 1808–1839 | 10 Paras |
| 210. Mahmud II | As | Constanti-nople | | 1252 | | 10 Paras |
| 211. Mahmud II | As | Constanti-nople | | 1252 | | 20 Paras |

*Arie Kindler*

| Ruler | Type[a] | Mint | Area | Locus | Basket | Remarks |
|---|---|---|---|---|---|---|
| 212. Mahmud II | As | Constanti-nople | | 1252 | | 20 Paras |
| 213. Mahmud II | As | Constanti-nople | | 1252 | | 20 Paras |
| 214. Mahmud II | As | Constanti-nople | | 1252 | | 20 Paras |
| 215. Mahmud II | As | Constanti-nople | | 1252 | | 20 Paras |
| 216. Abdul Medjid | As | Constanti-nople | | 1252 | 1839–1861 | |
| 217. Abdul Medjid | As | Constanti-nople | | 1252 | | 10 Paras |
| 218. Abdul Medjid | As | Constanti-nople | | 1252 | | 20 Paras |
| 219. Abdul Medjid | As | Constanti-nople | | 1252 | | 20 Paras |
| 220. Abdul Hamid II | As | Constanti-nople | | 1252 | (1879) | 5 Paras |
| 221. | | | | 1252 | blank, coin-shaped silver pendant | |

a. See Key to Types on next page.

| | Key to Types |
|---|---|
| A | Head of Pallas Athene/Owl |
| B | Dolphin/Owl |
| C | Melqarth riding hippocamp/Owl |
| D | Head of Ptolemy I/Eagle |
| E | Head of Zeus Ammon/Eagle |
| F | Head of Hercules–Alexander/Eagle |
| G | Head of Antiochus III/Apollo standing |
| H | Head of King/Palm-tree |
| I | Head of King/Apollo seated on Omphalos |
| J | Head of King/War-galley |
| K | Head of King/standing figure |
| L | Head of Apollo/Female figure standing |
| M | Head of Apollo/Nike standing |
| N | Double cornucopiae/Legend surrounded by wreath |
| O | Star/Anchor |
| P | Anchor/Double cornucopiae |
| Q | Palm-branch/Legend surrounded by wreath |
| R | Head of Augustus/Tetrastyle temple |
| Ra | Bust of Domitian/Nike standing |
| S | Head of Tiberius/Tetrastyle temple |
| T | Umbrella-shaped canopy/Three ears of barley |
| U | Head of Hercules/Boar walking |
| V | Head of Trajanus/Tyche standing |
| W | Head of Trajanus/Palm-branch between double cornucopiae |
| X | Head of Trajanus/Anchor |
| Y | Bust of Antoninus Pius/Temple of Tyche |
| Z | Bust of Elagabalus/Temple of Tyche |
| Aa | Bust of Elagabalus/Tyche standing, etc. |
| Ab | Bust of Severus Alexander/Bust of Tyche |
| Ac | Bust of Julia Mammaea/Ovoid baetyl |
| Ad | Bust of Salonina/Victoria standing |
| Ae | Bust of Valerianus/Roma seated |
| Af | Bust of Otacila Severa/She-wolf suckling twins |
| Ag | Bust of Otacila Severa/Scene of sacrifice |
| Ah | Figure standing |
| Ai | Figure standing/Palm-tree |
| Aj | Head of Tyche |
| Ak | Bust of Constantinus I/Jupiter standing |
| Al | Bust of Crispus/Legionary in fighting attitude |
| Am | Justinus and Sophia seated/M |
| An | Justinus and Sophia seated/K |
| Ao | Legend/Legend |
| Ap | Legend/Chalice-shaped object |
| App | Star of David/Star of David |
| Aq | Doge and Maria/Lion of St. Marcus |
| Ar | Heraldic symbol of Spain/Castilia and Leone |
| As | Tughra/Legend |
| At | German Rechenpfenning |

## CHAPTER NOTES

1.   Kindler (1967) pl. 46.s

## LITERATURE CITED

Kindler, Arie. 197. The Mint of Tyre: The Main Supplier of Silver Coinage in Antiquity in Eretz Israel [Hebrew]. *Eretz Israel* 8:318–324 [English summary, p. 29.

*Sandra Fortner*

# The Fishing Implements and Maritime Activities of Bethsaida-Julias (et-Tell)

T HE PURPOSE OF THIS CHAPTER is to present material evidence that one of the occupations of the citizens of Bethsaida-Julias (et-Tell) was fishing in the Sea of Galilee. Geological and geographical evidence for such activity was well established by John J. Shroder and Moshe Inbar in volume 1 of this series. A comprehensive analysis of the fishing implements that were found at the site of Bethsaida-Julias will be part of this author's doctorate theses about the Hellenistic and Early Roman Period at Bethsaida-Julias. In this chapter a small selection of fishing implements and anchors are presented to establish evidence of fishing at Bethsaida-Julias.

All three areas excavated at Bethsaida-Julias have yielded fishing implements. There is no concentrated accumulation in any particular area or building. The items are fairly equally distributed throughout the site on top of the mound in Hellenistic and Early Roman find contexts and in survey finds.

These implements were used in several ways: as weights on throw-nets, drag-nets, and hook-and-line fishing implements; as tools to repair nets; and as anchors for boats. They are separated into two main categories, metal (which includes lead net weights, iron hooks, and iron and bronze needles) and stone (which includes basalt weights, limestone weights, and basalt anchors), described below.

269

## Metal Fishing Implements

### Lead Weights

Four forms of lead net weights have been identified so far: a folded bar around the string of the net (figs. 1:1–3), a hemispherical weight (fig. 1:4), a disc-shaped weight (fig. 1:5), and a cube weight (fig. 1:6).

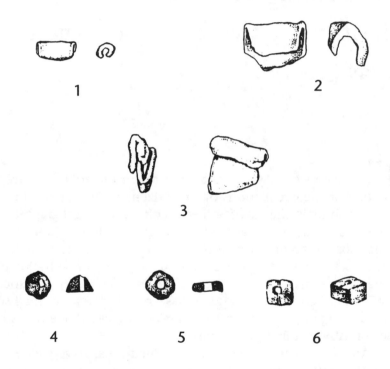

Fig. 1. Four types of lead net weights found at Bethsaida-Julias through 1996. Scale 1:2.*

*Catalog numbers correspond to illustration numbers.

So far, twenty-seven folded lead weights, used as net sinkers, were discovered. The lengths of these lead weights range between 2.2 and 4.3 cm; the diameter of the openings created by the folding of the lead around the string of the nets ranges between 0.1 and 1.0 cm, which might indicate the diameter of the string used. The folded type of lead weight was made when molten lead was poured into flat sheets, cut into strips about 2 x 6 cm, and then folded over. Two examples for a molded half-round and disc-shaped lead weight with one opening in the center for the string 0.6 to 0.9 cm in length, with a diameter of 1.5 cm, were found. A cubic molded lead weight is thus far unique at the excavations of Bethsaida-Julias.

## Hooks

Hooks used for fishing appear less frequently than the lead weights; however, they are fairly represented. Thirteen iron hooks, ranging from 3.1 to 6.1 cm in length and with different designs, were uncovered and are usually made from a once-bent, almost flat rod or from a bar with a rectangular section (fig. 2:7). One elaborately worked hook with a flat-hammered middle section is an exception (fig. 2:8). Also unique at Bethsaida-Julias is a bronze hook made from two wires that are intertwined (fig. 2:9).

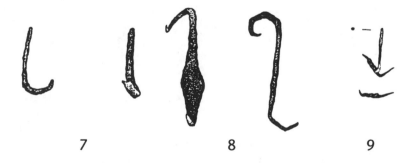

7          8          9

Fig. 2. Iron hooks, nos. 7 and 8; bronze, no. 9. Scale 1:2.

NEEDLES

Seven examples of bronze and iron needles that were used to repair
nets or sails measure between 12 and 15 cm in length. One slightly
bent example with a large eye is made of bronze (fig. 3:10). Another
form, with a large broken loop, consists of iron (fig. 3:11). Both shapes
were supposedly used for repairing nets or sails, since the eye and loop
(1.0 cm) are wider than the diameter of the rope. (Compare the diameter of lead weight holes, which are between 0.2 and 0.4 cm.)

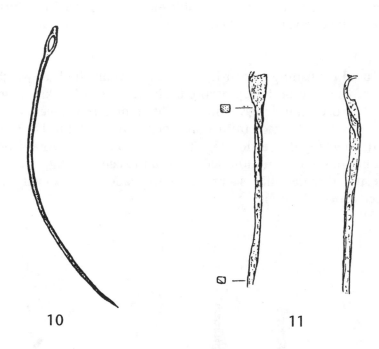

10                                                        11

Fig. 3. Examples of bronze (no. 10) or iron (no. 11) needles found at Bethsaida-
Julias. Scale 1:2.

STONE FISHING IMPLEMENTS

With the predominance of basalt rock in the vicinity it is not surprising that a large number of basalt fishing implements have been found
at Bethsaida-Julias. Examples from basalt include medium-sized ring
weights (perhaps for nets) and large anchors for boats. A smaller
number of limestone net weights have also been discovered.

## BASALT WEIGHTS

Two types are to be distinguished: Naturally shaped basalt rocks, which have only a drilled hole, or elaborately dressed round basalt rocks in different sizes, so-called ring weights. So far fifteen ring weights (figs. 4:12, 13) and three naturally shaped weights/sinkers with a natural opening (figs. 5:14, 15) or dressed groove (fig. 6:16) were found. The large ring weights have holes from 2.0 to 3.0 cm, and might have been used as net weights. Small ring-shaped weights of 2.6 to 4.3 cm in diameter for a net are relatively rare. Only three could be identified so far (figs. 7:17,18).

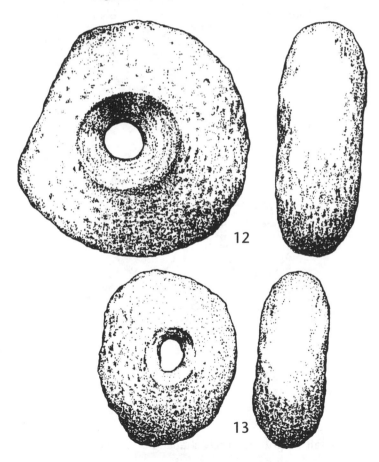

Fig. 4. Basalt weights. Scale 1:2.

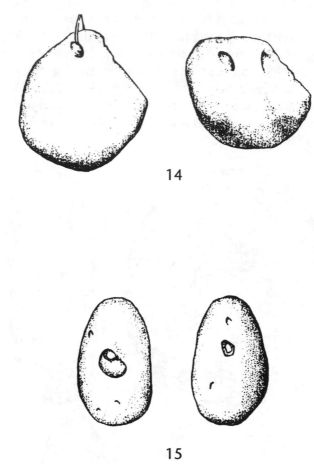

Fig. 5. Basalt weights, naturally shaped but drilled. Scale 1:2.

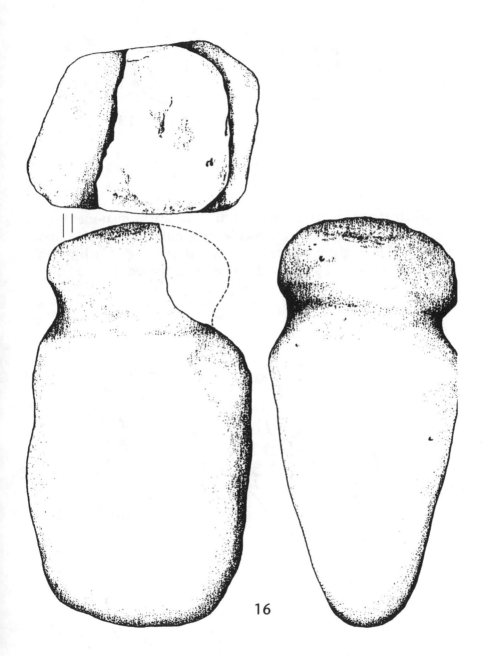

16

Fig. 6. Basalt weight/anchor. Scale 1:2.

17                    18

Fig. 7. Small basalt ring weights. Scale 1:2.

LIMESTONE WEIGHTS

Irregularly shaped limestone rocks with a natural or man-made opening of about 2.5 cm, through which a rope could pass, are also among the finds that might have been used for fishing. Eight such weights, between 9.0 and 12.3 cm wide, have been uncovered (fig. 8:19).

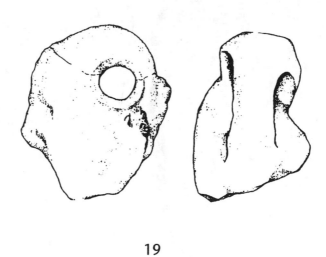

19

Fig. 8. Limestone weights. Scale 1:2.

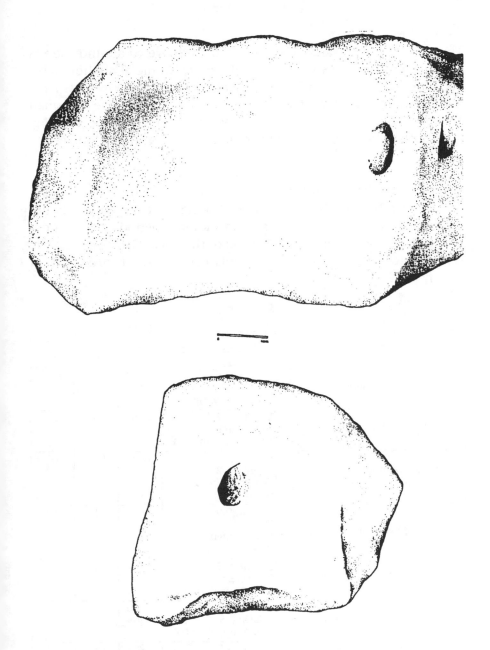

Fig. 9. Basalt anchor (illustration truncated). Scale 1:2.

BASALT ANCHORS

The anchors of Bethsaida-Julias and those discovered around the Sea of Galilee so far are usually made of basalt. No metal anchors have been found. The irregularly shaped basalt anchors and weights have two different means for attaching ropes. A few of both large and small anchors and weights have grooves around which a rope was tied (fig. 6:16). Others have holes drilled through one corner (fig. 9:20).

CONCLUSION

In total, more than one hundred items connected to fishing have been found so far. This clearly indicates that fishing was one of the activities of the populace in the Hellenistic and Roman period at Bethsaida-Julias. The question about the position of the Sea of Galilee during the Hellenistic and Early Roman periods is discussed thoroughly in volume 1 of this series.

Catalog

| | Description | Dimensions (cm) | Weight | Inv. No. | Fig. No. |
|---|---|---|---|---|---|
| 1. | Folded lead weight | Length: 2.2<br>Width: 0.9<br>Dia. of opening: 0.2 | 7.93 gr | 801 | 1:1 |
| 2. | Folded lead weight | Length: 3.8<br>Height: 0.6<br>Dia. of opening: 0.1 | 33.89 gr | 804 | 1:2 |
| 3. | Lead weight made of two intersecting folded bars | Length 3.3<br>Height: 3.2<br>Dia. of opening: 0.2–0.4 | 51.00 gr | 812 | 1:3 |
| 4. | Hemispherical lead weight | Height: 0.9<br>Diameter: 1.5<br>Dia. of opening: 0.2–0.4. | 9.00 gr | 817 | 1:4 |
| 5. | Disc-shaped lead weight | Height: 0.5<br>Diameter: 1.5<br>Dia. of opening 0.4 | 7.00 gr | 806 | 1:5 |
| 6. | Cube-shaped lead weight | Height: 1.0<br>Width: 1.5<br>Dia. of opening: 0.4. | 20.00 gr | 816 | 1:6 |
| 7. | Simple iron hook, heavily corroded | Height: 3.7<br>Width 0.7 | | 852 | 2:7 |
| 8. | Iron hook with flat rhombic middle section | Height: 6.1<br>Width: 0.9 | | 851 | 2:8 |

## Catalog

| | Description | Dimensions (cm) | Weight | Inv. No. | Fig. No. |
|---|---|---|---|---|---|
| 9. | Bronze hook made of two round thin entwined wires. One sharp, pointed tip. Upper part for fixing the hook to the string is broken off | Height: 2.5<br>Dia. of wire: 0.15 | | 861 | 2:9 |
| 10. | Bronze needle with large eye. Round section, sharp point. | Length: 15.0<br>Length of eye: 1.0<br>Diameter: 0.4 | | | 3:10 |
| 11. | Iron needle with broken loop and broken tip. Rectangular section. Below-looptorsion of upper part of needle. | Length: 12.1<br>Diameter: 0.2–0.4 | | 875 | 3:11 |
| 12. | Basalt ring weight with worked surface and drilled hole | Height: 4.7<br>Diameter: 12<br>Dia. of opening: 5.4 –2.0 | | 931 | 4:12 |
| 13. | Basalt ring weight with worked surface and drilled hole | Height: 3.8<br>Diameter: 9.2 x 7.1<br>Dia. of opening: 2.7 –1.2 | 0.402 kg | 953 | 4:13 |
| 14. | Basalt weight, naturally shaped, with a pierced opening | Height: 8.0<br>Width: 7.0<br>Diameter: 67.0<br>Dia. of openings: 1.0 | 0.400 kg | 932 | 5:14 |
| 15. | Basalt weight, naturally shaped, with a pierced opening | Height: 7.5<br>Width: 4.5<br>Dia. of opening: 1.0–2.0 | 0.103 kg | 933 | 5:15 |
| 16. | Basalt sinker anchor with one worked groove in the upper part to tighten a rope. Perhaps used for measuring the depth of water | Height: 22.5<br>Width in middle: 11.5<br>Width of groove: 8.2 | | 992 | 6:16 |
| 17. | Basalt net ring weight, worked with drilled hole | Height: 1.8<br>Diameter: 2.7<br>Dia. of opening: 0.9 | 0.015 kg | 952 | 7:17 |
| 18. | Basalt net ring weight, worked with drilled hole. | Height: ca. 2.9<br>Diameter: 4.3<br>Dia. of opening: 1.1–1.9 | 0.065 kg | 951 | 7.18 |
| 19. | Limestone weight with drilled opening | Height: 8.0<br>Width: 5.0<br>Dia. of opening: 1.9 –3.0 | 0.315 kg | 981 | 8.19 |

## Catalog

| Description | Dimensions (cm) | Weight | Inv. No. | Fig. No. |
|---|---|---|---|---|
| 20. Basalt anchor, irregular shape, partly dressed, with drilled opening at one edge | Height: 24.0<br>Width: 24.0<br>Dia. of opening: 3.0 | | 901 | 9.20 |

### ACKNOWLEDGMENTS

I am grateful to my colleagues Fred and Gloria Strickert for their help during the preparation of this chapter to collect the material from the storage rooms and field diaries as well as for discussions relating to this chapter. I am also indebted to John T. Greene and Wendi Chiarbos for proofreading the draft version, and to DreAnna Hadash for the drawings.

# Part 2

# Literature of Bethsaida

*Heinz-Wolfgang Kuhn*

# An Introduction to the Excavations of Bethsaida (et-Tell) from a New Testament Perspective

I N THIS SECOND VOLUME of the Bethsaida Excavations Project series I summarize recent developments from the perspective of a New Testament scholar in five points.[1] This paper has been checked with the development of the excavations through the end of 1996.[2]

1. The possibility that the ancient Bethsaida was situated directly on what is now the northern shore of the Sea of Galilee, namely in el-Araj and/or el-Mesadiyeh, as was recently again suggested by the Israeli historian and archaeologist Dr. Dan Urman of Ben-Gurion University of the Negev,[3] can certainly now be excluded on the basis of geological research.

Urman leaves open the question of which of the three sites—el-Araj, el-Mesadiyeh, or et-Tell (our excavation site)—contains the remains of Bethsaida-Julias. The research of Prof. Dr. John F. Shroder, Jr., chair of the Department of Geography and Geology at the University of Nebraska at Omaha, and his team, which also included Prof. Dr. Moshe Inbar of the University of Haifa, has already demonstrated[4] that due to a massive slope failure about 9 km north of et-Tell a catastrophic flood took place between about 1,600 and 2,000 years ago. This flood, presumably linked to an earthquake in 363 CE,[5] dragged rocks and debris in its wake, must have substantially enlarged the plain between et-Tell and the northern end of the Sea of Galilee, thereby creating the present-day distance of about 2 km between et-Tell and the lake and making the old port of Bethsaida unusable (the port was situated at the foot of the hill in the southwest and may have been linked to the lake, e.g., by an estuarine channel). The sites of el-Araj and el-Mesadiyeh were probably still under water in New Testament times. Excavations of these sites have so far yielded only architectural remnants of the Byzantine period. The mere presence of shards from the Hellenistic/Early Roman period, which have been ascertained for both sites on several occasions, proves nothing, as these may have been carried to the site by flood waters.[6]

2. It is certain that Bethsaida-Julias was still settled after the Jewish-Roman war (66 to c. 74 CE). I cannot recognize any evidence, either of an archaeological nature or in Josephus's works, that Bethsaida was destroyed in the course of the Jewish-Roman war,[7] or even that the city was abandoned about the year 67 CE. The facts (1) that Bethsaida is mentioned in the Rabbinic literature (e.g. as צייד in the Jerusalem Talmud in tractate Sheqalim 6.50a and Midrash Qohelet Rabbah at 2.8),[8] (2) that a large number of coins was found from the period between the second and the fourth centuries CE,[9] and—a crucial factor—(3) that pottery dates from this time,[10] all point towards a settlement up until the period between 300 and 400 CE. It is likely that the final end of Bethsaida was connected to the earthquake and catastrophic flood mentioned under paragraph number 1.

3. The following can be said about the Iron Age (mainly from Iron Age IIA onwards, i.e. c. 1000–925 BCE), which has dominated the excavation in the recent past:

(a) According to Arav, the settlement on the mound as a whole during the Iron Age had the following layout: The upper city (including a palace in the center) was situated on the northeast part of the hill, while the lower city, which has hardly been excavated, was spread out along the southern and western slopes of the hill.

(b) The excavation of the public building in Area B shows that squares G–M 41–44 apparently contain an Iron Age palace of the same type as north Syrian palaces, such as in Tell Tainat (Kinalua?), a good parallel to the Bethsaida palace in the Iron Age. There is also a similarity to the north Syrian palaces of Tell Ḥalaf (Guzana) and Zincirli (Samal) that date from the Iron Age and the North Syrian palace in Tell Açana (Alalakh) that dates from the Late Bronze Age.[11] I will not comment on the usual designation of these buildings as palaces of the Bit Hilani type[12] nor on the parallel that is often drawn between the unity of palace (of the north Syrian type) and temple in Tell Tainat and the Salomo temple (1 Kings 6–7).[13] In the building in Bethsaida, which consists of an entrance with apparently two subdivisions (the base for the west pillar has been excavated), a vestibule, a main hall (which Arav also refers to as the throne room[14]), and several adjacent rooms, the Egyptian figurine of a Pataekos was found in the main hall (square L 42)[15]—possibly the most beautiful found in Israel/Palestine up till now. The palace, which dates from Iron Age IIA, was modified and built over the first still during the Iron Age period and then in the Hellenistic/Early Roman era. Of particular interest for the New Testament scholar is that in the course of these structural modifications two rooms were built into the nearby Iron Age city wall, probably in the Roman period until the second century CE.

(c) The remnants of a city wall in Area C in squares 19–21, which earlier were assumed to date from the Early Bronze Age (3200–2200 BCE), have now almost completely been dated to Iron Age II. However, a number of smaller remnants from the Early Bronze Age have been discovered so far at et-Tell.

(d) The most important discovery in the summer of 1996 was the Iron Age city gate of enormous size in the eastern part of the city wall in Area A (squares I–N 51–57); there are two chambers on each side of the paved passageway. The gate is not yet fully excavated. The width (roughly from north to south) is about 30 m (the exact southern end has not yet been determined); the depth at the north front is about 17 m. Very parallel in size and especially in form is the Iron Age gate of level IVA in Megiddo. While this Megiddo gate is smaller (25 x 15.50 m), the main gate of Dan[16] (also from the Iron Age)—the largest gate with two chambers on both sides, so far as I know, in Israel/Palestine (29.50 x 17.80 m)—is about the same size as the Bethsaida gate. In Syria one finds a close parallel for an Iron Age gate with four chambers in the west gate of the outer city of Cerablus (Carchemish) (27 x 18 m).[17] The question of a more exact dating of the Bethsaida gate and the other Iron Age gates cannot be discussed here.

4. From November 1995 to February 1996, particularly the two courtyard houses from the Hellenistic/Early Roman period were conserved and reconstructed by the Israel Antiquities Authority. With the marking of the reconstruction after Passover 1996, the work has been

completed for the time being.

5. Finally I mention a few finds and excavation results (a thorough examination of the ceramics from the Hellenistic period onwards, conducted mainly by the Munich archaeologist Sandra Fortner, is still in progress[18]).

(a) A shard of pottery with a cruciform motif was found on May 13, 1994, in a northern room of the courtyard house in Area C, more exactly in square F 29 in the very southeast corner (locus 924).[19] Three explanations for this marking are possible (I do not go into detail here but mention only a few relevant references[20]):

(i) It could be merely a marking as can be found on some ossuaries in Israel/Palestine, which was widespread there in the period between the first century BCE and the first half of the second century CE.

(ii) Cross-shaped marks could be explained either in terms of the Hebrew letter *taw* or the Greek *chi*. An explanation in terms of the Hebrew *taw* again allows for various interpretations. In particular, a religious use of the letter *taw* springs to mind: The letter means "sign" and in its ancient Hebrew form looked like a cross either upright or lying on its side (T, X). There are references to this *taw* in texts from Ezekiel (9:4–9) to the Song of Solomon (15:6), the Qumran texts (CD XIX 9–13) up until the Rabbinic literature (Babylonian Talmud, Shabbat 55a). It is often assumed that this explains some use of cross-shaped marks, especially on ossuaries, in early Judaism. For the cross-shaped mark on a jug at Masada an explanation in terms of the word *terumah* ("the priest's share") has been considered. The cross-shaped mark on coins of Herod the Great has been partly explained in terms of the Greek letter *chi* (X).

(iii) The cross-shaped mark found in Bethsaida points to a third possible explanation. The decisive factor is the inner circle from which the four apparently equal long arms are drawn (the lower arm has been corrected so as to be of equal length as the left and right ones; the length of the upper arm has not been preserved). As far as I can see, there is no real parallel to the cross-shaped mark found in Bethsaida in the Hellenistic/Early Roman period in Israel/Palestine or outside. The closest possible parallel, mentioned cautiously by Dr. Denny Clark at the Bethsaida Conference in Omaha in April 1996 in his lecture, is a cross-shaped mark with a kind of black dot in the middle (on an ossuary from the vicinity of Jerusalem), but this does not appear to me to be a true parallel.[21] The closest parallels to my knowledge of such cross-shaped marks are, as I said at the conference, to be found in other parts of the Middle East. A good example can be seen on stelae of the Neo-Assyrian king Assurnasirpal II (883–859 BCE), which show him wearing an amulet that has a cross with an inner circle.[22] This circle is essential when looking for a parallel to the "Bethsaida cross."[23] The cross-shaped mark on the stela is explained as being a symbol for the sun god Shamash, so that the structure of this sign obviously represents the disk of a sun with sun rays.[24] The shard with the cross-shaped mark found in Bethsaida in Area C in a room north of the courtyard has the following context: According to the field diary, locus 924 at the level of the find (-166.96 m) and above and below it is almost exclusively Hellenistic and hardly Iron Age (22 cm above, a coin of Antiochus III, 223–187 BCE, was discovered; even at the closing of the locus, 28 cm below, many Hellenistic shards were found). I have not been able to explain the discrepancy between the time frame given by the context of the find and the existing parallels in the Middle East region.

(b) There are four coins among the Bethsaida finds from the rulers who reigned over Galilee and the Gaulanitis during the time Jesus was active there. Three coins of Philip, the son of Herod the Great, who ruled over the Gaulanitis and the bordering territories from 4 BCE to 33/34 CE, have been found—the last one in May 1994. This coin, which is of the undated type and which has not yet been published, shows on the obverse the jugate heads of Augustus and Livia-Julia (to right). On the reverse the shape of a tetrastyle temple is still recognizable; this probably depicts the temple built in honor of Augustus in Caesarea Philippi.[25] On the Philip coin found in 1990, as the second of the coins (obverse: head of Tiberius to right; reverse: again traces of the tetrastyle temple), the year 33 can be read, which means about 29/30 CE.[26] The best-preserved coin was found as early as 1988 and shows on the obverse a head which is obviously that of Tiberius and on the reverse again what is presumably the Augusteum of Caesarea Philippi.[27] One coin has been discovered of Antipas, another son of Herod the Great, who ruled over the Galilee from 4 BCE to 39 CE.

(c) Worth mentioning in connection with the two court-yard houses from the Hellenistic/Early Roman period in Areas B and C (the one in Area B contained many fishing implements) is the discovery of a storage cellar (especially a wine cellar) on the east side of the courtyard house in Area C in which were found a large casserole and four large jars, which were intact or could be restored.

(d) Regarding a find that had been thought to be a strigilis (see also my contribution in *Bethsaida* 1:45), another suggestion has been made: this item is thought to be a weaving shuttle[28] from the Hellenistic/Early Roman period.

(e) Of great interest for the New Testament scholar is the discovery in the spring of 1996 of a short-handled bronze shovel from a pit on which probably incense or perfumes were burned over coals.[29] The shovel has a very close parallel in one of the four so-called incense shovels from the finds of the Bar Kokhba revolt (132–135 CE), which Y. Yadin and his team discovered in 1960 and 1961 in Nahal Hever southwest of En-gedi on the western shore of the Dead Sea, in the so-called Cave of Letters.[30] This one is the smallest of the three so-called incense shovels found in a basket in 1960 (shovel no. 5),[31] and is almost identical to the Bethsaida shovel in terms of the pan (including five concentric circles, one in the center and four in the corners), the handle (in form of a column with Corinthian capital), and the four feet, and also in terms of the size of the shovel.[32] The New Testament mentions in Rev. 8:3, 5 in a scene of a heavenly cult a golden incense shovel or pan (λιβανωτός in these verses means not only "incense," but an incense shovel or pan) which becomes filled with fire for throwing it on the earth (here we have one and the same instrument which has to do with incense—it is even called λιβανωτός, i.e. incense instrument—and which can carry coals).[33] A high degree of similarity with the Bethsaida shovel can also be found in the shovels discovered in Pompeii or Herculaneum,[34] which means that they date from before 79 CE. The same is true of five more short-handled shovels that were on exhibition during my visit in Jerusalem in September 1996 in the Rockefeller Museum (2 shovels)[35] and in the Israel Museum (3 shovels in addition to all 4 shovels of the Bar Kokhba find in the Shrine of the Book; another short-handled shovel can be found in the Bible Lands Museum). I mention also, e.g., a shovel of this kind, which apparently originates from Gaul and which G. Faider-Feytmans dates to the first century CE.[36] Further comparable objects must surely or probably come from Israel/Palestine[37] and Syria (including three shovels probably from the Hauran, one of which is very similar to the Bethsaida shovel[38]).[39] According to Yadin, this type of shovel "came into use in the first century A.D., at the latest."[40]

Unfortunately, it is questionable whether an exact dating is possible for the Bethsaida shovel, and especially whether the shovel can be dated as early as the first half of the first century CE. Only in this case could one perhaps assume that Bethsaida was a much more pagan place already in Jesus' time than was thought up to now; Caesarea Philippi, the capital of the tetrarchy of Philip, was in any event primarily pagan. While the corresponding Bar Kokhba finds consist of implements probably of originally Roman ownership (possibly items of booty),[41] our shovel may have been a cult object connected to an alleged imperial cult in Bethsaida. However, a further uncertainty affects the find since ancient Jewish usage of incense outside of the temple area is documented in private houses (see Berakoth 6.6 with Babylonian Talmud, Berakoth 43a, b[42]; compare also Tobit 6:17–18; 8:1-2);[43] even a purely noncultic or nonmagical use, e.g. in wealthier homes, cannot be excluded.[44] A private use seems to be probable in the case of a third shovel of the Rockefeller Museum which was not on exhibition in September 1996; it bears the inscription "good luck to the purchaser" (εὐτυχίτω ὁ ἀγοράσας).[45] The question is whether the context of the find in Bethsaida will enable a more precise classification in terms of dating and history of religion. We need a monograph that collects all so-called incense shovels together with critical research from the perspectives of archaeology, history of religion, and history and takes into account Hebrew/Aramaic, Greek, and Latin sources. Hitherto I am not sure about a building discovered in the summer of 1996 in Area A, which is about 9 m away from the place where the shovel was found and which is suggested to be a small Early Roman temple (with antae on both small sides and a column discovered at the entrance). The question whether we can speak of a Roman imperial cult at Bethsaida-Julias is still open.

I close this paper with the following summary: Bethsaida is an archaeological site most interesting for those working in the field of Near Eastern Archaeology with emphasis on the Iron Age from about 1000 BCE on and also especially for New Testament scholars, since Bethsaida is one of the three places (next to Capernaum and Chorazin) where with a high degree of historical probability[46] Jesus was active.

CHAPTER NOTES

1. The following is partly a short summary of my lecture "Keynote for the Conference: An Introduction to Bethsaida from the Viewpoint of a New Testament Scholar" given on April 19, 1996, at the conference on the excavations of Bethsaida at the University of Nebraska at Omaha. Especially important for me were the conversations with the archaeological director of the site, Prof. Dr. Rami Arav, who also made plans and drawings available to me. I also had access to the identification of Bethsaida coins, which the leading numismatist of the Ha'aretz Museum in Tel Aviv, Dr. Arie Kindler, had carried out for us and to his paper on the Bethsaida coins in this volume. Cf. also Arav (1997), where the excavations are summarized until 1995, and his statements in this volume. Systematic data from the Bethsaida excavtions are stilllacking in recent literature. Witness the article on Bethsaida in *Der neue Pauly* which does not say anything about the excavations that were begun ten years ago: Colpe (1997). For the basic translation of my paper I have to thank Almut Köster, Munich.
2. Cf. also Kuhn (1998).
3. Urman (1995) 519–527. His response to the archaeological lectures on Bethsaida at the Society of Biblical Literature International Meeting in July 1997 at Lausanne, Switzerland, brought no new insights.
4. I refer mainly to Shroder and Inbar (1995) and to the more detailed videotape, containing lectures by Shroder and Michael Bishop, which was shown in July 1995 at the Society of Biblical Literature International Meeting in Budapest and a copy of which was made available to me; I refer also to the contributions of Shroder, Bishop, and K. J. Cornwell at the above-mentioned Bethsaida Conference at Omaha and to conversations that I had there with Shroder. See the most recent update of the arguments in this volume.
5. Regarding the earthquake dated May 19, see Amiran, Arieh, and Turcotte (1994) 265: "Strong earthquake affecting most of Palestine and Jordan. Severe damage at Banias, Capernaum, Tiberias...." Cf. also Amiran (1996). Damage from earthquakes can be seen clearly on buildings that date from the late Hellenistic/Early Roman period in Bethsaida in Area B in the east of the courtyard house (in square J 39) and south of the palace (in squares I–J 44) and also in Area A (in square I 52).
6. With what I have said under paragraph no. 1, I make a correction of my sentence in Kuhn (1995) 244 under no. 3: "A smaller place on today's shore, which also bore the name Bethsaida, would be possible."
7. Prof. Dr. John T. Greene rightly pointed this out in his talk "The Roman War against the Jews at Bethsaida and Gamla" at the Bethsaida Conference in Omaha in April 1996; Greene kindly made his manuscript available to me; cf. also Greene (1995). An updated version of this talk is included in this volume.
8. Cf. Kuhn, in Kuhn and Arav (1991) 82; Urman (1995) 520–21; Freund (1995) 267–311.
9. Most of them are from the second and third centuries CE.
10. Cf. this paper at the beginning of paragraph no. 5.
11. One may refer also to Tell Meskéné (Emar), where the interpretation of the excavation is more difficult.
12. Cf. Hrouda (1972–1975).
13. Cf., e.g., Otto (1980) 55 (fig. 6 shows Tell Tainat). For earlier discussions in relation to Bethsaida see Kuhn (1994) 23.
14. Arav (1995a) 24. The size of the main hall is about 20 x 4.5 m, the size of the palace about 28.5 x 15 m. For more information on the palace see the chapter by Arav in

this volume, and by Arav and Bernett on Syrian-Palestinian palaces during Iron Age II (forthcoming in *IEJ*).

15. Shown on the cover of *Biblical Archaeology Review* 21/1 (1995) with a brief description by Arav on p. 44. An article by Arav and Bernett about this Pataekos appeared in the *Israel Exploration Journal* 47 (1997), 198–213 (in fig. 1 the western part of the public building is missing, though the size of the palace and the number of surrounding rooms are given correctly on 201).

16. See Biran (1994) esp. 236 (illus. 194, no. 3).

17. For gates in Israel/Palestine and in the neighboring countries see Herzog (1986).

18. Cf. Fortner (1995) and Tessaro (1995).

19. A photograph of the shard is found, e.g., on the front cover of the paperback edition of Arav and Freund (1995).

20. I plan to publish more about it.

21. A reproduction of this "cross," with the word יהוה above it, can be found, e.g., in Goodenough (1953) 3, no. 227, and Finegan (1992) 300. What appears to be a dot in the middle is apparently only damage to the surface of the ossuary such as can also be found on the letters י and ו.

22. A reproduction of the stela from the royal palace in Nimrud can be found, e.g., in Black and Green (1992) 31. A similar image from this palace is to be found on a stela to the left of the face of the ruler; the inscription on this stela makes reference to the inauguration of the palace in 879 BCE. A similar amulet can also be seen, e.g., on a set of reliefs of this king in the same palace; for the last two images see the descriptions and reproductions in Hrouda (1991) 125–26.

23. Regarding this point, I agree with Clark in his lecture at Omaha in April 1996 on "A First Century Cross at Bethsaida."

24. Cf., e.g., Black and Green (1992) 54–55 (s.v. "cross"). See also the "cross" and what are obviously sun rays on the reproduction in Hrouda (1991) 125 (top left), mentioned in n. 23 above.

25. The description of the type is based on a comparison with two coins in Meshorer (1982), vol. 2, pl. 7, nos. 6 and 6a (see also ibid., pp. 42–49, 245), one coin in Maltiel-Gerstenfeld (1987) 78, no. 126 (see also p. 75), and a further coin of this type that was found in the context of the "Galilean boat" of 1986; see Gitler (1990) 104 and fig. 14.1, no. 22. As the inscription Σεβαστῶν on this type of coin suggests, it depicts Augustus and not Tiberius with Julia (different from Gitler, but in agreement with Kindler for the Bethsaida Excavations Project), even if the coin was not minted until the reign of Tiberius; see Ollendorff (1926) 37–48, 917. A further reproduction of this coin type, from the private collection of Meshorer, can be found, e.g., in Strickert (1995a) 179 (see the acknowledgment, 189); a drawing of this coin type can also be found here and in Strickert (1995b) 49.

26. .Preliminary publication by Meier (1995) 58 no. 43 (the reproduction of the obverse needs to be turned slightly to the left; the year should read: AΓ).

27. Preliminary publication by Arav, in Kuhn and Arav (1991) 97 (in Arav's note on the two coins of Philip of 1988 and 1990: "one dates clearly to 29/30 CE [Meshorer type 10, illustration 1]," only "illustration 1" refers to the 1988 coin depicted in the illustration, while the preceding text refers to the dated coin of 1990, which has no illustration here) and by Meier (1995) 58, no. 44 (here the reverse is shown upside down). Regarding this coin, see also Kuhn, in Kuhn and Arav (1991) 90.

28. See the "Errata and Corrigenda" (to p. 34, fig. 22) appended to Arav and Freund (1995).

29. Found in Area A in square G 54 (in the balk between squares F and G). I am grateful to Arav for letting me know of the discovery via two faxes in May 1996 and for supplying me with three 1:1 drawings (the shovel was found on May 7). In September 1996 I had the chance to see the shovel, to take photographs, and to receive further drawings of it. My formulations here are checked against a paper of Freund on incense shovels which he gave at the Society of Biblical Literature International Meeting at Lausanne in July 1997. A complete chapter by Freund on an interpretation of the shovel is found in this volume.

30. Yadin (1963) fig. 14 and pl. 16 (top).

31. Yadin (1963) 48–58, and the corresponding plates; see also Yadin (1971) in both versions 92–104.

32. Only the "ears" at the bottom corners of the rectangular shovel in the Bethsaida find are somewhat different; even the size of the two shovels is almost the same: the Bethsaida shovel is (from the middle of the end of the pan to the middle of the end of the handle) almost exactly 20 cm long, while the shovel in the Bar Kokhba find, according to Yadin (1963) 51, measures 23 cm. "Ears" such as the ones on the Bethsaida shovel can, however, be found on the Bar Kokhba shovel no. 4; see Yadin (1963) fig. 13 and pl. 15 (bottom).

33. Though there are problems with the exegesis of Rev. 8:3–5, what is said above seems to be sure. Cf. also *vatillum* in Horace, *Satires* 1.5: 36 (*prunaeque vatillum* "and a pan of charcoal" which belongs to the gew-gaws of a chief official). Very clear is the function of a shovel or pan, e.g., in Num. 17:11 (מחתה/πυρεῖον).

34. Cf. Yadin (1963) 54 with pl. 28 (top).

35. According to a copied guide lent to visitors and a description in the archives of the museum one of two shovels, which originates apparently from the vicinity of Hebron, is said to have been found together with a coin struck by a Roman governor in the first half of the first century CE (I thank Munich archaeologist Sandra Fortner for letting me see the internal description she received from the museum). For information about a third shovel of the museum, see below.

36. Faider-Feytmans (1952) 174 with pl. 61 (F. 25); cf. Yadin (1963) 54 with n. 25.

37. Cf. Yadin (1963) 55–56 with n. 29–33.

38. See Richter (1915) 235–236 (nos. 658–60); cf. Yadin (1963) 55 (no. 660): "most similar to our No. 5."

39. Cf. Yadin (1963) 55 with nn. 26, 27.

40. Yadin (1963) 57.

41. Yadin (1993) 830a ("It appears that Bar-Kokhba's soldiers … either acquired them before the revolt or took them as booty from a Roman unit at the beginning of the war"); Yadin (1971): in both versions 99–104; cf. Yadin (1963) 58.

42. "Here [in the Babylonian Talmud] is direct evidence that incense was blessed and burned in homes," Goodenough (1954) 4:202.

43. Cf. Goodenough (1954) 4:195–208 and the corresponding figures in vol. 3 (1953).

44. Cf. Pfister (1914) 275, 278.

45. Iliffe (1933) 123 with pl. 46a (the provenance is unknown; the date given here is about 3d century CE); cf. Yadin (1963) 57 with n. 35.

46. See Kuhn, in Kuhn and Arav (1991) 77–79.

## LITERATURE CITED

Amiran, D. H. K. 1996. Location Index for Earthquakes in Israel since 100 BCE, *Israel Exploration Journal* 46: 120–30.

Amiran, D. H. K., E. Arieh, and T. Turcotte. 1994. Earthquakes in Israel and Adjacent Areas: Macroseismic Observations since 100 BCE, *Israel Exploration Journal* 44: 260–305.

Arav, R. 1991 (*s.v.* Kuhn and Arav).

———. 1995a. Bethsaida Excavations:Preliminary Report, 1987–1993. With Appendix to chapter 1 (appendix of coins) by C. Meier, pp. 3–63 (appendix, 53–61) in: Arav and Freund (1995) (q.v.).

———. 1995b. An Iron Age Amulet from the Galilee. *Biblical Archaeology Review* 21/1:44 (and cover 1).

———. 1997. Bethsaida. *The Oxford Encyclopedia of Archaeology in the Near East,* vol. 1: 302–5.

Arav, R., and R. A. Freund, eds. 1995. *Bethsaida:A City by the North Shore of the Sea of Galilee.* Bethsaida Excavations Project, vol. 1. Kirksville, Mo.:Thomas Jefferson University Press.

Biran, A. 1994. *Biblical Dan.* Jerusalem:Israel Exploration Society.

Black, J., and A. Green. 1992. *Gods, Demons and Symbols of Ancient Mesopotamia:An Illustrated Dictionary,* illustrations by T. Rickards. London:British Museum Press.

Colpe, C. 1997. Bethsaida, *Der Neue Pauly: Enzyklopädie der Antike* 2: 596–97.

Faider-Feytmans, G. 1952. Antiquités Gallo-Romaines, pp. 163–81 with pls. 59–63 in: *Les Antiquités Égyptiennes, Grecques, Étrusques, Romaines et Gallo-Romaines du Museé de Mariemont.* Brussels:Éditions de la Librairie Encyclopédique.

Finegan, J. 1992. *The Archeology of the New Testament:The Life of Jesus and the Beginning of the Early Church.* Rev. ed. Princeton:Princeton University Press.

Fortner, S. 1995. Hellenistic and Roman Fineware from Bethsaida, pp. 99–126 in: Arav and Freund (1995) (q.v.).

Freund, R. A. 1995. The Search for Bethsaida in Rabbinic Literature, pp. 267–311 in: Arav and Freund (1995) (q.v.).

Galling, K. 1953. Archäsologisch-historische Ergebnisse einer Reise in syrien und Libanon im Spätherbst 1952. *Zeitschrift des Deutschen Palästina-Vereins* 69: 181–87, with pl. 6.

Gitler, H. 1990. The Coins, pp. 101–6 in: Wachsmann, S., *The Excavations of an Ancient Boat in the Sea of Galilee (Lake Kinneret).* With contributions by J. R. Steffy, et al. 'Atiqot, English Series, 19. Jerusalem:Israel Antiquities Authority, 101–6.

Goodenough, E. R. 1953 and 1954. *Jewish Symbols in the Greco-Roman Period III and IV.* New York:Pantheon Books.

Greene, J. T. 1995. Bethsaida-Julias in Roman and Jewish Military Strategies, 66–73 CE, pp. 203–7 in: Arav and Freund (1995) (q.v.).

Herzog, Z. 1986. *Das Stadttor in Israel und in den Nachbarländern, übersetzt von M. Fischer.* Mainz:Philipp von Zabern.

Hrouda, B. 1972–1975. Hilāni, bet:B. *Archäologisch, Reallexikon der Assyriologie und der Vorderasiutischen Archäologie* 4:406–9.

———. 1991. *Der Alte Orient. Geschichte und Kultur des alten Vorderasien,* mit Beiträgen von J. Bottéro, et al. München:C. Bertelsmann.

Iliffe, J. H. 1933. Greek and Latin Inscriptions in the Museum, *The Quarterly of the Department of Antiquities in Palestine* 2: 120–26, with pls. 44–46.

Kuhn, H.–W. 1994. et-Tell (Betsaida): Ausgrabung einer Wirkungsstätte Jesu, besiedelt seit der Frühen Bronzezeit. In: *72. Jahresbericht 1993*. Gesellschaft von Freunden und Förderern der Universität München: 22–24.

——. 1995 Bethsaida in the Gospels: The Feeding Story in Luke 9 and the Q Saying in Luke 10. Pp. 243–56 in: Arav and Freund (1995) (q.v.).

——. [1997]. et-Tell (Betsaida): 10 Jahre Ausgrabung einer Wirkungsstätte Jesu. In: *75. Jahresbericht 1996*. Gesellschaft von Freunden und Förderern der Universität München: 24–26 (and cover).

Kuhn, H.–W., and R. Arav. 1991. The Bethsaida Excavations: Historical and Archaeological Approaches. Pp. 77–91 (Kuhn) and 91-106 (Arav) in: *The Future of Early Christianity*. Ed. B. A. Pearson, et al. Minneapolis: Fortress Press.

Maltiel-Gerstenfeld, J. 1987. *New Catalogue of Ancient Jewish Coins*. Tel Aviv: Minerva Associated.

Meier, C. 1995 (s.v. Arav [1995a]).

Meshorer, Y. 1982. *Ancient Jewish Coinage*. Vol. 2, *Herod the Great through Bar Cochba*. Dix Hills, N.Y.: Amphora Books.

Ollendorff, L. 1926. Livius (Livia): 37. Livia Drusilla. *Paulys Realencyclopädie der classischen Altertumswissenschaft* 13.1: 900–924.

Otto, E. 1980. *Jerusalem—die Geschichte der Heiligen Stadt*. Urban-Taschenbücher 308. Stuttgart, et. al.: W. Kohlhammer.

Pfister, F. 1914. Rauchopfer. *Paulys Realencyclopädie der classischen Altertumswissenschaft* 1A.1: 267–86.

Richter, G. M. A. 1915. *Greek, Etruscan and Roman Bronzes*. New York: Metropolitan Museum of Art.

Strickert, F. 1995a. The Coins of Philip. Pp. 165–89 in: Arav and Freund (1995) (q.v.).

——. 1995b. The Founding of Bethsaida-Julias: Evidence from the Coins of Philip, *Shofar* 13:40–51.

Shroder, J. F., and M. Inbar. 1995. Geologic and Geographic Background to the Bethsaida Excavations. Pp. 65–98 in: Arav and Freund (1995) (q.v.).

Tessaro, T. 1995. Hellenistic and Roman Ceramic Cooking Ware from Bethsaida. Pp. 127–39 in: Arav and Freund (1995) (q.v.).

Urman, D. 1995. Public Structures and Jewish Communities in the Golan Heights. Pp. 373–617 (on Bethsaida, 519–27) in: *Ancient Synagogues: Historical Analysis and Archaeological Discovery* 2. Ed. D. Urman and P. V. M. Flesher. Studia Post-Biblica 47.2. Leiden et al.: Brill.

Yadin, Y. 1963. *The Finds from the Bar Kokhba Period in the Cave of Letters*. Jerusalem: The Israel Exploration Society.

——. 1971. *Bar-Kokhba: The Rediscovery of the Legendary Hero of the Last Jewish Revolt against Imperial Rome*. London and Jerusalem: Weidenfeld and Nicolson. (German version: 1971. *Bar Kochba: Archäologen auf den Spuren des letzten Fürsten von Israel*. Hamburg: Hoffmann und Campe).

——. 1993. Cave of the Letters (in: Judean Desert Caves). *The New Encyclopedia of Archaeological Excavations in the Holy Land* 3: 829–32.

*Ketziah Spanier*

# The Two Maacahs

S EVERAL SEASONS AGO sections of a substantial city wall and remnants of a large structure, which may have been a palace or administrative building, were discovered at the Bethsaida excavation. They were dated to the Iron Age IIA period, around 1000 BCE. This indicates that a city of some considerable size existed on this site during the period of the rise of the Davidic kingdom. Bethsaida's strategic location within the territory of the ancient kingdom of Geshur suggests that it might have been the ancestral home of David's wife Maacah.

Royal marriages attested in the Bible and other ancient Near Eastern cultures were usually motivated by political, economic, and strategic considerations. In the polygamous royal household some native women achieved primary status because they belonged to prominent families that represented powerful factions within the state, while foreign royal women were brought into the court as a result of diplomatic marriages that constituted a part of comprehensive treaty agreements. The status of each woman within the household was determined by the terms of her marriage agreement and the balance of power between her ancestral home state and that of her husband. One of these women was designated as the chief, or favorite, wife. This title not only afforded her a superior position in her husband's court, but brought about the selection of her son as the heir apparent to the throne, sometimes without regard to his chronological placement among his agnatic brothers. This woman came into her full power following her husband's death and the subsequent corona-

tion of her son. She usually retained her position either for her lifetime or, if her son predeceased her, for the duration of his reign.

Two royal wives in the Davidic court bore the name Maacah.[1]
The first was the daughter of the Geshurite king Thalmai and the
mother of Absalom, one of the sons born to David at Hebron (2 Sam.
3:3). Two generations later, this woman's descendant and namesake
appears as the daughter of Absalom, and favorite wife of Rehoboam (2
Chron. 11:21). She is listed as the mother of both Abijah and his son
Asa (1 Kgs. 15:2, 10). The textual information concerning these
women is terse and somewhat enigmatic. Yet, through an examination of the information provided concerning their patronyms and
places of origin it is possible to reconstruct the circumstances that
brought them into the Davidic court as well as the source and extent
of their power within it. Both these women's tenures were within periods of transition. The first Maacah arrived at Hebron shortly after
David had established his rule there and probably just before he
launched his successful bid to become ruler over the united tribal coa-
lition. The second Maacah came into the Judaean court just after the
division of the Solomonic kingdom, when Judah had been reduced to
a small landlocked state. In both cases, the fortunes of the Davidic
kingship depended, at least in part, upon these women's ancestral and
territorial connections.

Each of the six sons born to David at Hebron is mentioned with
a different matronym (2 Sam. 3:2–5). This indicates that the list is
hierarchal and represents the placement of the sons in the order of
succession and not in their chronological order of birth.[2] Each son's
position may then be assumed to have been determined by his
mother's relative importance within the household. Amnon, the son
of Ahinoam, received the title of בכור (firstborn);[3] Kileab, son of Abigail, is described as משנהו (his viceroy),[4] while Maacah's son Absalom is
השלשי (the third).

Ahinoam and Abigail were Israelite women who belonged to
prominent families within economically and strategically important
areas of the Saulide kingdom. David's marriages to these women
occurred during the course of his ongoing struggle against Saul's rule.[5]
Amnon's mother, Ahinoam, was a member of an important Jezreelite
family.[6] It is highly unlikely that her name was only coincidentally
identical with that of Saul's chief wife (1 Sam. 14:50).[7] The fertile
Jezreel valley formed the heartland of the kingdom of Saul[8] and was

the locus of a juncture of several important international trade and military routes. The city of Jezreel was a fortified stronghold and evidently a Saulide district capital and royal residence. The city's location was at the crossroads of the main routes from Megiddo and the Samarian hills to Beth Shean and the Galilee. Y. Aharoni suggests that when Saul had gained control over the central Jezreel valley he gained the capacity to close off the Via Maris against the Philistines.[9] The well at Jezreel was the mustering point of Saul's forces in his last battle (1 Sam. 29:1). It is mentioned as the place from which the news of the deaths of Saul and his heir apparent, Jonathan, came (2 Sam. 4:4) and as part of the territory over which Abner later anointed Saul's surviving son, Ishbaal, as king (2 Sam. 2:8 ff.). The economic and strategic advantages offered by Ahinoam's place of origin as well as her association with the Saulide throne, whether real or merely perceptual, were determining factors in the designation of her son as David's heir apparent.

Kileab's mother, Abigail, is referred to as "the wife of Nabal."[10] She was a native of Carmel (1 Chron. 3:1), a town within the Calebite area of the Judaean territory south of Hebron.[11] The Judaean population of this area was loyal to Saul,[12] who erected a stele there to commemorate his victory over the Amalekites (1 Sam. 15:12). Abigail's marriage to David brought about the pacification and support of the local population in the southern Judaean district and provided David with the base from which he would eventually gain control over the entire country. Through his marriages to Ahinoam and Abigail, David gained the advantage of close family ties to powerful elements in two important areas: the southern Judaean territory and the central region of the country. [13]

David's union with Absalom's mother, Maacah, took place soon after he had established his rule at Hebron. Maacah was the daughter of the king of Geshur and, as indicated by her name, had an ancestral matriarchal connection with the kingdom of that name.[14] G. W. Ahlstrom suggests that this marriage ratified a treaty that was intended to weaken Saul's heir's claim to the throne.[15] Having secured control over the southern and central Israelite territories, David sought to consolidate his power by outflanking and surrounding the northern Israelite tribes who remained loyal to the Saulides.[16] His marriage to the Geshurite princess also enhanced his reputation in the international sphere and engendered the goodwill of the neighboring Aramaean populations to the east and north, with which Geshur and Maacah were identified.[17] The strategic importance of the alliance was no doubt related to the geographical positions of Geshur and Maacah, which usually appear together in the biblical text. According to the territorial description at the time of the conquest these kingdoms were among those that remained unconquered by the Israelites (Deut. 3:14, Josh. 13:11). Their climate, soil conditions, and geographical positions facilitated the development of a flourishing agricultural system and the establishment of cities on the vital international trade routes.[18]

Geshur was situated on the western slopes of the Bashan plain (Josh. 12:5); the Yarmuk river, which flows into the Jordan, formed its southern border. Its territory extended north along the eastern shore of the Sea of Galilee (Kinneret) and continued up the Jordan river to the Huleh valley. This enabled Geshur to control the eastern sources of the river and the Kinneret.[19] The district of Maacah extended to the north and northwest of Geshur. Its territory at that time included the cities of Abel-Maacah, Ijon, and Dan, which were situated along the northern water sources of the Jordan river.[20] Sometime during David's reign these cities came under his rule and became an integral part of his domain.[21] David's marriage to Maacah was consistent with the practice of consolidating territorial alliances through familial ties. It enabled David to outflank the remnants of the Saulides and afforded him a measure of protection from attacks by neighboring states. In addition, it opened up trade routes with the Phoenicians and, through them, with other traders.

The position of the Geshurite princess in David's court was no doubt commensurate with these advantages and may have been a determining factor in her son's later claim to the throne.[22] The biblical account of the assassination of David's heir apparent, Amnon, portrays it as an act of revenge by Absalom for the rape of his sister, Dinah. The text does not specifically indicate what Absalom stood to gain from Amnon's death as the next in the line of succession;[23] some of the burden of guilt for the assassination is placed upon David, who had neglected to discipline his heir apparent. David later refused to acknowledge Absalom's claim as successor to the throne and threatened to have him killed (2 Sam. 13:39). Absalom fled to his maternal grandfather's territory and remained in Geshur for three years (v. 38) before being summoned back to Jerusalem (14:24). It is likely that he was given a member of the royal family as a wife during his sojourn in

Geshur.[24] Soon after his return to Jerusalem, convinced that David would not accept him as successor to the throne, Absalom launched an insurrection against his father. It was symbolically significant that he secured the allegiance of representatives of all the Israelite tribes at Hebron, his father's first capital (15:10–14).[25] The bitter civil war that ensued ended with Absalom's death.[26] This rift foreshadowed the later division of the united kingdom during the reign of Rehoboam. The exclusion of any further mention of Absalom's mother may have been an effort to obfuscate the important role she played in the struggle for succession to the Davidic throne.

Two generations later, a descendant and namesake of the Geshurite princess Maacah, daughter of Absalom,[27] is mentioned in the chronicler's report as the preferred wife of Rehoboam. Their marriage evidently took place following his accession to the throne.[28] The text indicates that because Rehoboam preferred this woman over all his other wives and concubines he designated her son Abijah as the heir apparent to the throne, without regard to Abijah's chronologically junior status among the king's progeny (2 Chron. 11:21–22). This Maacah later appears as the king's mother in the succession formula for the reign of Abijah's son Asa (1 Kgs. 15:10).

In order to understand these exceptions to the customary order of succession it is necessary to examine the political circumstances that brought them about. Solomon's long reign had been marked by a period of relative peace and prosperity that facilitated the expansion of a considerable commercial empire.[29] This expansion was not, however, devoid of negative consequences. Considerable discontent arose in the later years of Solomon's rule, particularly among the Israelite tribes, who may have paid the heavy cost of the expansion and were resentful of the disproportionate benefits that accrued to the Judaeans. Solomon's appointment of Jeroboam to the leadership of the house of Joseph may signal an effort by the crown to placate the Ephraimites, who represented that population (1 Kgs. 11:28). Apparently Solomon's strategy did not serve its intended purpose: The Bible reports that Jeroboam led a failed assassination attempt against the king and then fled to Egypt, where he remained until he received news of Solomon's death (v. 40).

Rehoboam was thus confronted with an insurrection at the inception of his reign (1 Kgs. 12:1–21). The biblical account suggests that Solomon's heir had surrounded himself with a partisan faction of courtiers during his tenure as heir apparent. Immediately following his accession to the throne, a conflict developed within the royal court between this faction and Solomon's advisors, who urged the new king to abate some of his father's burdensome decrees (vv. 6–7). In an effort to assert his independence Rehoboam refused to heed their counsel. He pursued a harsh policy that increased alienation among the populace (vv. 10–11). Jeroboam led the ensuing revolt, which ended with the secession of most of the tribes and the loss of the northern Israelite territory. The area under Judaean control was reduced to the traditional tribal boundaries of the Judahites and Benjaminites (vv. 12–20).

In his effort to stem the loss of territory, Rehoboam fortified several cities within his reduced borders, and he gained the support of Yahwistic cultic personnel who flocked to Jerusalem from their cities in the north (2 Chr. 11:1, 5–17). It was at this juncture that he also promoted Maacah to the position of favorite wife and declared that her son Abijah would be his heir apparent, disregarding the chronological line of succession to the throne (2 Chron. 11:18-22).[30] Maacah's ancestry and familial connections made her a particularly desirable wife. Her association with the kingdom of Geshur and the district of Maacah provided protection on the eastern border of Judah as well as a staging area for preemptive attacks along the northern reaches of the expanding Israelite kingdom.[31] In addition to the immediate strategic importance provided by Maacah's familial connections, a perceptual advantage existed in Abijah's ancestry. His genealogy included the two most important strains within the Davidic line: He was a descendant of Solomon through his father, and of Absalom through his mother.[32] This was an important element in the king's effort to retain not only the support of different factions within the Judaean kingdom, but also to convince those who had seceded to return to Davidic rule. [33]

Rehoboam and Abijah had spent most of their tenures battling the northern Israelite kingdom. The Judaean kingdom was steadily losing ground to the larger, more powerful northern kingdom, while the official tolerance of foreign cults, which had been established during the Solomonic era, continued under their rule. As Rehoboam's chief wife, and later queen mother, Maacah was actively involved in the sponsorship and promulgation of the cult of the Ashera in the Judaean court.[34]

The textual rendering of the familial relationships of Maacah, Abijah, and Asa is unclear. Abijah is listed as the father of Asa, and Maacah appears as the mother of both (1 Kgs. 15:2, 10; 2 Chron. 11:20; 15:16).[35] Abijah died after a three-year rule. Maacah remained in her official post during the first years of the reign of Asa, who may have been Abijah's son and who was probably chosen by the queen mother because of his extremely young age. The appellative "mother of the king" or *gebirah* was thus used to describe her official position rather than her actual maternity of Asa (2 Chron. 15:10–16).[36] This enabled her to assume the power of the throne on Asa's behalf for the period of his minority.[37]

In the fifteenth year of his reign, Asa decided to free himself of the queen mother's influence, to establish his own rule, and to distinguish himself through a radical departure from his predecessors' policies. He initiated a series of cultic reforms that were aimed at strengthening the exclusive worship of Yahweh in Jerusalem. This required the destruction of the foreign cults prevalent in the capital. The symbolic emblem of these reforms was the removal of Maacah from her position as queen mother and the destruction of the image of the Ashera that had been erected under her patronage (1 Kgs. 15:13; 2 Chron. 15:8–19). The manner of Maacah's banishment speaks eloquently to the great extent of her authority. She was confronted by the king on a ritual occasion and was formally ousted from her official post. Her cult was then ceremonially destroyed. This constituted the climax of a sweeping wave of political and cultic reforms and was followed by an upsurge in the power and prosperity of Judah.

## Chapter Notes

1. The name appears in the biblical text as an epicene personal name and as a place name. One of Nahor's sons by his concubine Reumah is listed as the eponymous ancestor of the Aramaeans who settled the territory of Maacah, which was located to the south and west of Aram Naharaim (Gen. 22:24). Several women by that name were affiliated with different tribal groups. One was the concubine of the Judaean Caleb (1 Chron. 2:48), another was the wife of the Manassehite Machir (1 Chron. 7:16), yet another was the mother of Gibeon the Benjaminite (1 Chron. 8:29, 9:35). Maacah is also the name of the father of Achish, king of Gath (1 Kgs. 2:39), as well as the name of the father of Hannan, one of David's heroes (1 Chron. 11:43), and the father of Shephatiahu the Simeonite (1 Chron. 27:16).

2. This was, most often, determined by benefits that accrued to the crown as a result of her association with it. With time, the importance of these benefits was altered as the political and strategic situation changed. Certain commitments, which were made at the time of the various marriages, had to be adhered to regardless of these changes. See for example Nugayrol (1956), 126–217.

3. The term 'firstborn' does not exclusively refer to primogeniture. In many cases it is the father's chosen heir apparent despite his junior place in the order of birth. See *Cassell's Latin Dictionary* and discussion in Koschaker (1933), 35–37. The term appears in several Nuzi adoption documents in connection with the ranking of the prospective adoptee within the family; see Harvard Semitic Series, vol. 5, no. 60, lines 8–11; vol. 5, no. 6, lines 14–15; and vol. 5, no. 67, lines 9–10, and several times in the biblical text (1 Chron. 5. 2, for example); see also comments by Stohlman (1971).

4. It should be noted that this term is often used as a military rank or hierarchal designation; see for example 1 Sam. 17:13, 23:17; 1 Chron. 16:5; and 2 Chron. 28:7.

5. This marriage, as well as the one to Abigail, evidently predates his association with Achish, king of Gath, and his taking up residence at Ziqlag (1 Sam. 27:6).

6. The mention of Jezreel in Josh. 15:56 together with the southern Maon and Carmel (southern locations associated with David's second wife, Abigail) has led Noth to assume that Ahinoam was also a native of the southern Judaean territory; see Noth (1958), 180.

7. It has been suggested that David actually possessed Saul's wife; see Levenson and Halpern (1980), 507–18. Another possibility is that David took another woman from that district and/or family and gave her the name of the mother of Saul's heir apparent in order to legitimize his rule.

8. Aharoni (1967) 21–22.

9. Aharoni (1967) 258.

10. Kileab is listed as Daniel in the chronologer's genealogical account of the sons of David (1 Chron. 3. 1).

11. Aharoni (1967) 257

12. This is evidenced by Nabal's response to David, which acknowledges loyalty to the reigning monarch (1 Sam. 25:10).

13. David's previous effort to legitimize his claim to the throne, through his marriage to Saul's daughter Michal had failed (1 Sam. 25:44

14. See the association of Geshur and Maacah in Deut. 3:14, Josh. 13:11, among others. See also Mazar (1961) 16–28, and Kochavi (1989) 1–15.

15. Ahlstrom (1993) 399–40.

16. Malamat (1963) 8.

17. Kochavi(1989) 3. According to tradition, Abraham's brother Nahor, father of Maacah, was an Aramaean (Gen. 24:10).
18. Mazar (1961) 22–23.
19. Aharoni (1967) 216, 264, and Issar(1990) 126.
20. Issar (1996) 125; see also Mazar (1961).
21. Following Absalom's usurpation attempt against David, the Wise Woman of Abel Maacah pointed out to Joab that her city was part of the Israelite territory (2 Sam. 20:18–19). Subsequent to the later division of the Solomonic kingdom, these cities were part of the Northern Israelite territory.
22. The mothers of the first two heirs represented the incorporation of territories that had belonged to Saul and were part of his power base. Maacah represented a foreign entity that would enable David to consolidate his rule and receive international backing for it.
23. The fate of Kileab/Daniel is not known since he is never mentioned except in the genealogical lists. The general scholarly assumption is that he died at a young age, making Absalom the heir immediately following Amnon in the order of succession; see Yeivin (1960a) 196–97 [Hebrew].
24. The name and patronym of Rehoboam's wife Maacah indicate that she was descended from this marriage.
25. The significance of Hebron should not be overlooked since it was there that David began his rule and from there that he proceeded to become ruler over all of Israel (2 Sam.5:1–4).
26. David's lament reflects his need to distance himself from the killing (2 Sam.15:1–8). It suggests that many of Absalom's supporters later harbored a resentment against David and against his chosen successor, Solomon.
27. Absalom was Maacah's significant ancestor rather than her biological father; see for example 1 Kgs. 15:3, 11, where David appears as the father of both Abijah and Asa.
28. Prior to taking over the throne, and probably under the direction of his father, Rehoboam had entered into marriages with members of the Davidic family. Mahalath, his first primary wife and the mother of several sons, is identified as the daughter of Jerimoth, who is said to have been related to David. She is also a descendant of Eliab, firstborn son of Jesse, father of David (2 Chron. 11:18).
29. Malamat (1963) 8–9.
30. The preference of the firstborn in matters of inheritance and succession is well attested in the Hebrew Bible and in other ancient Near Eastern literature. Exceptions, however, abound. In Akkadian the ternary *rabu* (chief son) is used in reference to the firstborn. In many documents, however, this term took on a legal meaning which was not necessarily synonymous with primogeniture. See Ras Shamra 14:16, and discussion by Thureau-Dangin (1951)174. Similarly, when Jacob adopted Joseph's two elder sons as his own, he gave Ephraim, who was the younger, the status of firstborn (Gen. 48:18–19). A marriage document from Nuzi includes a clause that provides for the bride's firstborn to become his father's chief heir. The context of this document makes it clear that this marriage was not the husband's first and that he had already fathered several sons by other women; see Harvard Semitic Series, vol. 9, no. 24.
31. Jeroboam's revival of Dan as a cultic center in the traditional district of Maacah may have represented his effort to overcome Maacah's influence in that area (1 Kgs. 12:26–30).
32. The chronicler's succession formula for the reign of Abijah mentions Micaiah, daughter of Uriel of Gibeah, as the king's mother (2 Chron. 13:2). This woman's

place of origin connects her to the Saulide capital at Gibeah. It is possible that this matronym was added in order to provide Rehoboam's successor with an ancestral connection to the Saulide Benjaminites, who also had a claim to the throne.

33. The chronicler's report accurately accounts for the shift of power within the court but attributes it to Rehoboam's personal preference rather than to political and strategic motives. He emphasizes that Maacah was not the first primary wife or the mother of the firstborn. He further states that the king "loved Maacah more than all his other wives and concubines," and as a consequence he made her son, Abijah, the heir apparent to the throne (2 Chron. 11:18–22).

34. Ackerman (1993) 385–401, Arbeli (1987) 165–178.

35. Andeasen (1983) 179–194, and Yeivin (1960) 236–39.

36. Maacah's tenure may be compared to those of several Hittite great ladies, including Tawananna, Danu-hepa, and Pudu-hepa as well as several queen mothers attested in the biblical text, including Jezebel, Athalia, Meshullemeth, and Hamutal, all of whom were involved with foreign cults, held their positions through two or more reigns, and whose removal involved a cultic reform; see Ben-Barak (1991) 23–34, Bin-Nun (1975) 185–97, Ahlstrom (1987) 57–58.

37. Bright (1990) 240, and Montgomery (1951) 274–75.

# LITERATURE CITED

Ackerman, S. 1993. The Queen Mother and the Cult in Ancient Israel. *Journal of Biblical Literature* 112:385–401.

Aharoni, Y. 1966. *The Land of the Bible: A Historical Geography.* Trans. from the Hebrew by A. F. Rainey. London: Burns & Oates.

Ahlstrom, G. W. 1963. *Aspects of Syncretism in Israelite Religion.* Horae Soederblomianae, 5. Lund: C. W. K. Gleerup.

———. 1993. *The History of Ancient Palestine.* 1st Fortress Press edition. Minneapolis: Fortress Press.

Andeasen, A-E. A. 1983. The Role of the Queen Mother in Israelite Society. *Catholic Biblical Quarterly* 45:179–94.

Arbeli, S. 1985. Maacah as the Queen Mother in the Reigns of Abijah and Asa and Her Removal from This Exalted Position [Hebrew], *Annual for the Study of the Bible and the Ancient Near East.* Ed. M. Weinfeld. 9:165–78.

Ben-Barak, Z. 1991. The Status and Right of the Gebira. *Journal of Biblical Literature.* 110:23–34.

Bin-Nun, S. R. 1975. *The Tawananna in the Hittite Kingdom.* Heidelberg: Winter.

Bright, J. 1981. *A History of Israel.* Philadelphia: Westminster Press.

Harvard Semitic Museum. 1929—. *Excavations at Nuzi conducted by the Semitic Museum and the Fogg Art Museum of Harvard University, with the cooperation of the American School of Oriental Research at Bagdad.* Vols. 5 and 9. Cambridge, MA: Harvard University Press.

Issar, A. S. 1990. *Water Shall Flow from the Rock: Hydrogeology and Climate in the Lands of the Bible.* New York: Springer Verlag.

Kochavi, M. 1989. The Land of Geshur Project. *Israel Exploration Journal,* 39:1–15.

Koschaker, P. 1933. Fratriarchat, Hausgemeinschaft und Mutterrecht in Keilschriftrechten. Zeitschrift fur Assyriologie no.41/n.f.VII:35–37.

Levenson, J. D., and B. Halpern. 1980. The Political Import of David's Marriages. *Journal of Biblical Literature.* 99/4:507–18.

Malamat, A. 1963. Aspects of the Foreign Policies of David and Solomon. *Journal of Near Eastern Studies,* 22:1–17.

Mazar, B. 1961. Geshur and Maacah. *Journal of Biblical Literature.* 80:16–28.

Montgomery, James A. 1951. *A Critical and Exegetical Commentary on the Book of Kings.* Edinburgh: T. & T. Clark.

Noth, M. 1958. *The History of Israel.* New York: Harper.

Nugayrol, J. 1956. *Palais Royal d'Ugarit.* Vol. 5. Paris: Imprimerie Nationale, Librairie C. Klincksiek.

Ras Shamra 14.16.

Simpson, D. P. 1979. *Cassell's Latin Dictionary.*

Stohlman, S. C. 1972. Real Adoption at Nuzi. Unpublished dissertation, Brandeis University.

Thureau Dangin. 1951. Six Textes de Ras Shamra, *Syria* 28:174.

Yeivin, S. 1960a. *Research in the History of Israel and Its Land* [Hebrew]. Tel Aviv: Newman Publications.

———. 1960b. Abijam, Asa & Maacah, Daughter of Abishalom. Pp. 236–39 in: *Research in the History of Israel and its Land* [Hebrew]. Tel Aviv: Newman Publications.

*John T. Greene*

# The Honorific Naming of Bethsaida-Julias

THERE IS NO MORE SINGULAR COMPLIMENT than to have someone or something named in one's honor. For example, newborn children named after fathers, mothers, or other relatives; buildings, ships, and aircraft after philanthropists, patrons, and pioneers of aviation; streets, boulevards, and even cities after politicians, martyrs, and members and benefactors of powerful families. Honorific namings— or renamings—occurred as often in ancient times as they occur nowadays. An ancient example of this honorific naming practice is the transformation of a former fishing village called Bethsaida (fisherman's house) into the polis Julias. This chapter examines, first, why the honorific renaming occurred and, second, who might have been extolled by the renaming.

The task of providing incontrovertible evidence that a particular archaeological site does indeed enshrine a suspected ancient site always plagues archaeological research teams. Moreover, regardless of how much hard evidence is supplied, there are always naysayers who lurk about to bark and nip at the heels of those who provide enough data to satisfy the most healthy skepsis. Those lurking, barking nippers are the motivation for this work.

The excavators of the Bethsaida Archaeological Excavations Project have faced two major challenges apart from those presented by the site itself: (1) ongoing questions about its claim of positive physical site identification and (2) the ancillary problem of precisely for whom Bethsaida was honorifically renamed. Thus far the project has provided geographical, geological, hydrological, archaeological, literary, and numismatic evidence that et-Tell, the site some 2.5 km northeast of Lake Kinneret, is indeed the Bethsaida of the New Testament Gospels and the Bethsaida-Julias about which Flavius Josephus wrote.

Morton Scott Enslin commented as follows on an account in Josephus' *Antiquities* 12.4.1 ff. that concerns the high-priesthood of Onias II and his suspected pro-Syrian–Seleucid leanings at a time when Palestine was a part of Egypt:

> The story is not without difficulties with regard to chronology and is also replete with gossip details which Josephus was wont to employ when his sources ran dry.[1]

Almost as if he were aware of this tendency of Hellenistic-era history writing, exemplified by Josephus, the Roman senator, observer of the times, and writer Tacitus wrote:

> ... a historian's foremost duty [is] to ensure that merit is recorded, and to confront evil deeds and words with the fear of posterity's denunciations.[2]

One might conclude prima facie, therefore, that Tacitus would have abhorred Josephus' historical writings, especially with respect to chronology and gossipy details that are used as fillers. In all fairness, however, we should remember that Tacitus emulated the style of Thucydides, who himself interrupted his famous narratives such as those in his unfinished *Peloponnesian War,* to insert well-written speeches or other fillers. Indeed, chronology and gossipy fillers in one specific Josephan account have necessitated our subscribing to Tacitus in a sustained manner in order to help determine for whom the polis Julias was honorifically named.

Flavius Josephus (*né* Yosef ben Mattitiyahu, son of a Jewish priest and a female descendant of the famous—and priestly—Maccabean/Hasmonean family) was an eyewitness to events of 37 to 93 CE that he recorded: He actively provided leadership to the Jewish rebel forces in the Galilee/Golan region during the outbreak of hostilities. Yet, his earliest work, *Wars of the Jews,* was not completed until the end of Vespasian's reign as emperor. This work, written in Aramaic and in the same spirit as Caesar's *Gallic Wars,* is a propaganda piece commissioned by the emperor. Fifteen years later (ca. 94/5 CE) Josephus published his *Antiquities of the Jews,* which he modeled on the *Roman Antiquities* of Dionysius of Harlicanassus. *Life,* Josephus' autobiography and a personal apology, appeared after 100 CE. Although an eyewitness to much, he could not have personally witnessed everything he recorded. Like Tacitus, especially in *The Annals of Imperial Rome* (which covers the period from the death of Augustus in 14 CE to that of Nero in 68 CE), Josephus provides sources for the period under study that are of limited assistance and must therefore be employed gingerly. The three works of Josephus mentioned above and the *Annals* of Tacitus contain information about the existence and activities of women in the imperial family named Julia as well as honors bestowed upon women of the same name.

In various parts of the Roman Empire emperor cults existed. Many client rulers appointed by Caesars Augustus and Tiberius were also desirous to demonstrate their gratitude as well as their loyalty to patrons. In what was ancient Greater Palestine, for instance, members of the client prince Herodian family (i.e., Herod the Great and his successors) signaled gratitude or loyalty by honorifically naming the cities of Caesarea Maritima, Caesarea Philippi (Paneas), Sebaste (Samaria), and Tiberias after these two emperors. To some, the existence of such places points to physical evidence of emperor cults in the eastern Mediterranean. This leads to thoughts about the existence of other cults formed around significant female members of the imperial family as well. Thus scholars who read Flavius Josephus' account of the upgrading of the village Bethsaida to the status of polis and the apparent renaming of it in honor of (one argues) Livia Julia, empress and wife of Caesar Augustus, tend to accept this action on the part of Philip as pointing in the same cult-oriented direction.

During the 1988 season, in Area A of the Bethsaida excavations, a bust of a small female figurine was found, and in 1996, Area A yielded a Roman-style temple. These two are described more fully in Rami Arav's archaeological reports in this series; the figurine is described in volume 1. During 1996, in close proximity to the Roman temple, there was found a bronze incense shovel similar to those found by Yigal Yadin in the Cave of Letters and associated by Yadin with Roman cult religion. The Roman style temple together with the incense shovel and the female figurine lead one to speculate on the meaning of the figurine and the type of Roman cult that occupied the temple. The head of the figure features long, wavy hair covered with what appears to be a scarf. Since this figure was discovered in such close proximity to a religious structure, speculation centers on (1) the figurine's being a representation of Livia Julia the Augusta, and (2) its presence demonstrating that her cult was in existence at Julias. These speculations may or may not be true. Several other interpretations of this artifact are possible. An investigation of the Augusta and at least one other woman of the imperial family named Julia must be the starting point for any attempt which hopes for success.

## THE FIRST ANCIENT LITERARY WITNESS: JOSEPHUS AND THE JULIAS

### THE PROBLEMS

Numerous Josephan passages in three of his copious writings mention a city called Julias, and one identifies Bethsaida as Julias.[3] Five specific Josephan passages refer to actions on the part of members of the Herodian family in honor of a member of the Roman imperial family named Julia. Two of these passages are contained in the *Antiquities* (18.2.1;18.4.6); the other three are contained in his *Wars of the Jews* (2.9.1; 3.3.5; 3.10.7; 4.8.2). These are discussed below.

An attending problem is this: There continue to be skeptics[4] who doubt whether New Testament Bethsaida[5] and the Bethsaida-Julias identified by Flavius Josephus[6] are both enshrined in et-Tell, a mound located some 2.5 km northeast of the Sea of Galilee. The archaeological objections have been adequately addressed by Rami Arav, chief archaeologist of the Bethsaida Excavations Project.[7] Yet, there lingers the attending problem of passages in two of the writings of Josephus that refer to Bethsaida's honorific renaming as Julias and when this renaming took place. One would tell the researcher much about the other. Let us cite them now:

### ANTIQUITIES 18.2.1

1. He [Herod Antipas] also built a wall round Betharamptha, which was itself a city also, and called it Julias, from the name of the emperor's wife.

2. He [Philip] also advanced the village Bethsaida, situate at the lake of Gennesaret, unto the dignity of a city [i.e., polis],[8] both by the number of inhabitants it contained and its other

grandeur, and called it by the name of Julias, the same name as Caesar's daughter.[9]

3. Salome [sister of King Herod] bequeathed to Julia, the wife of Augustus, both her toparchy and Jamnia, as also her plantation of palm trees that were in Phasaelis.

4. In addition, and after the ascension of Tiberius, son of Augustus and Julia, Philip built the city of Caesarea, at the fountains of the Jordan and in the region of Paneas; also the city Julias in the lower [i.e., western] Gaulanitis.

5. Herod [Antipas] also built another [city)] that was also called Julias.

To some readers the second of these renderings appears to contradict or conflict with the first and the fifth of these statements. In addition, Fred Strickert, one of the project's codirectors, has written that in 1 CE Philip began to mint coins, and he minted them seven more times before his death in 33 CE; "in both 30 and 33 CE, Philip issued a coin with the image of Livia/Julia."[10] Because these dates are later than the time of Julia III's banishment (ca. 2 BCE), some readers cast aspersions on the project's having firmly laid to rest all objections to et-Tell's being identified as the Bethsaida of the New Testament and the Bethsaida-Julias of *Antiquities* 18. They taunt, "Will the real Julia please stand and identify herself?"

While other authorities may prove helpful in unraveling some of this problem,[11] its genesis may without question be traced to the common practice of so-called history writing employed by Josephus. A few examples (which could be greatly multiplied) will suffice.[12] Others are found in Thucydides' *Peloponnesian War*. Writing about the Maccabean revolt, and especially about the number of forces under the command of the Hasmonean priest-king Alexander Jannaeus, Josephus' *Wars* 1.4.5 holds that he had 1,000 horsemen, 8,000 mercenaries on foot, and some 10,000 Jews who favored him. *Antiquities* 13.14.1 reflects that the mercenaries numbered 6,200 and that his Jewish admirers numbered 20,000 (i.e., twice as many).

Elsewhere in his account of the Hasmoneans this *Zweideutigkeit* approach adds opposing chatty episodes surrounding the brief reign of Aristobulus I. Josephus holds in *Antiquities* 13.11.1–2 that Aristobulus was cruel to his mother and brothers, and that he died in agony. This is immediately followed, however, by a thirdhand quotation of one Timagenes, whose characterization of Aristobulus paints him in glowing terms and calls him a man of candor (*Ant.* 13.11.3).

And while there is no intention to engage in unnecessary Josephus bashing, it is important to point out that concerning the military engagement near this city of Bethsaida-Julius, Josephus writes about it not in his famous *Wars,* but in his autobiography, *Life.* In essence, his attitude toward this city and the person after whom it was honorifically named appears to show him negligent and misdirecting. Given that accounts that mention Bethsaida in *Wars, Antiquities,* and *Life* were written at different times and for differently targeted audiences, modern researchers would expect some consistency in order to find his works useful. This need forces them to turn elsewhere.

Honorific (re)namings of locales in the name of imperial patrons was a common practice.[13] But locales were named after persons of lesser rank also.[14] One problem seems clear, however: In his numerous accounts of honorific namings of locales, Josephus is never as consistent as modern researchers wish him to have been. Thus witness:

1. *Ant.* 16.5.1 has the reader assume that an honorific naming has occurred when one reads: "About this time it was that Caesarea Sebaste, which he [Herod the Great] had built, was finished."

2. *Ant.* 16.5.2: "Herod [the Great] erected another city in the plain called Capharsaba ...: this he named Antipatris from his father Antipater."[15]

*Ant.* 16.5.2: "He also dedicated the finest monuments to his brother Phasaelus ... erecting a tower in the city itself, and a memorial for him that was deceased. He also built a city ... in the valley of Jericho ... and this he also called Phasaelus."[16]

4. *Ant.* 16.5.3 tells of even further benefits bestowed upon inhabitants of cities abroad such as the Rhodians, the Nicopolitans, and the Antiochians at Herod the Great's own expense.[17]

Imperial cults (generally confined to the period after their death and upon deification by the Roman senate) and subcults of distinguished members of imperial families were also multiplied in the dominated provinces and territories. It is possible that one such subcult was organized around the imperial wife, mother, patroness.

## THE PRACTICE OF HONORIFIC NAMING

Numerous negative charges have been (and continue to be) leveled at Josephus for being inconsistent, or inaccurate.[18] The major problem addressed here is that of inaccuracy. Moreover, there is the suggestion that according to one manuscript tradition, a homoioteleuton exists in *Antiquities* 18:2. That suggested solution/alternate would read:

> He also built a wall round Betharamptha, which was itself a city also and called it Julias, from the name of the emperor's wife.... He also advanced the village Bethsaida, located in front of the lake of Gennesaret, unto the dignity of a city, by the number of inhabitants it contained and its other grandeur, and called it Julias by the name of Julias [Caesar's wife, and Julias is], the same name with Caesar's daughter....[19]

The suggestion is based on there being only this one occurrence of a reference to Caesar's daughter, while the preponderance of allusions in *Antiquities* 18 are to Julia his wife, thus, a possible homoioteleuton. What is not clear from this suggestion is whether Josephus himself is unable to handle an account and maintain accuracy where multiple people bear the same name, or whether the hypothesized homoioteleuton is a product (and casualty) of manuscript transmission at a later time. To check the former, let us examine another reference in the same general text to the multiple appearances of the name Archelaus.

Archelaus is a name borne by (1) a son of Herod the Great, who had the title ethnarch/king and who ruled Judah and the Perea in the transjordan; (2) a king of Cappadocia and father-in-law of Herod Antipas' brother and later of Antipas himself. The latter situation gave rise to charges of incest (within Judaism) being leveled at Antipas by, among others, John the Baptizer; (3) a Herod Archelaus, a steward residing in Rome, and finally (4) the name of a great plantation of palm trees (*Ant.* 18:2:2). Here, in the same general text, Josephus is most reliable. Moreover, in *Antiquities* 17:13:1 Josephus reports that Archelaus built a village and "put his own name upon it, and called it Archelais," a further demonstration of his ability to keep the facts straight in reporting activities that concerned multiple people bearing the same name, but especially when honorific namings are concerned. This argues neither for nor against Josephus' total accuracy, however. Its purpose is merely to point out other places in the same text where there are no inaccuracies, thus to magnify the present problem, not trivialize it.

## THE HERODS AND THE IMPERIAL FAMILIES[20]

The alleged inaccuracy with which our present work is concerned occurs within the context of the Herodian family's official and unofficial relationships with the Roman imperial families in general and the honorific naming practices of certain members of this Herodian family in particular. The latter may or may not have occurred within the emperor (and empress) cults said to be existent in the Roman provinces in general and within its province of Syro-Palestine in particular. Imperial Rome vouchsafed to the Jews, and to the client-ruler Herods in particular, certain exceptions to normal ruling practices.[21] It is possible, and highly probable, therefore that the honorific namings reported by Josephus occurred more out of a personal relationship between certain Herodians and imperials than for cultic reasons or motivations. The personal aspect is reflected in an apparent giveback or return of the family favor gesture recounted in *Antiquities* 18 (supplied in a different context in the Problem section above): "... Marcus Ambivius came to be his [Coponius'] successor in that government under whom Salome, the sister of King Herod died, and left to Julia (Caesar's wife), Jamnia, all its toparchy ... upon whose death Tiberius Nero, his wife Julia's son, succeeded."[22]

Conversely, a personal giving on the imperial side is monitored in *Antiquities* 16:5:1, which depicts Josephus' recounting that: "... Julia, Caesar's wife, sent a great part of her most valuable furniture [from Rome] ..." to Herod the Great at Caesarea Sebaste (itself after an honorific naming). It is not obvious whether Salome's gifts were returns of specific properties which had been previously supplied by and named in honor of the empress.

Consolidating our categorizings thus far we note that (1) Josephus does maintain accuracy in relating information about the same person in multiple citings (Archelaus); (2) he reflects the practice of honorific namings of locales as something not only practiced in honor of imperial benefactors but in honor of fathers, brothers, and others deemed worthy of honor; and (3) honorific favors went both ways, client-rulers (or empowered family members such as Salome) donating, supplying, bequeathing specific Mediterranean-front real estate properties (Jamnia, modern-day Yavneh-Yam/Mesad Hashavyahu) to

Julia the wife of Augustus. Thus, granting that specific Julia cults (i.e., empress cults) existed, the solution to our problem of the honorific naming of Bethsaida-Julias points to a more personal practice of the Herodian family.[23] The negative, and confusing side of this equation has been severely reduced.

## A Second Ancient Literary Witness: Tacitus and the Julias

Anyone who delights in arguing that men historically have had all the political power concentrated in their hands will have to accept the opposite view when following the story of Julia the Augusta. The following mosaic, cobbled together from the *Annals* of Tacitus, demonstrates a power not from behind the throne but from above the throne and in plain sight for all to see. Only when she died and ceased to rule did things change. To be honest to the Augusta and to history, one may compare this with the earlier (ca. 176–167 BCE) relationship of the Jewish Hasmonean (king) Alexandra Salome and one of her sons, John Hyrcanus II (whom she elevated to the important position of high priest and thereby controlled the ecclesiastical aspect of her government also since no woman could serve in this capacity). But this Julia must be considered within a line of several other Julias of imperial families.

Women named Julia in the Roman, imperial, Claudian family are the core around which revolves a more positive identification of the city being excavated at et-Tell in Jordan Park of the Upper Galilee since 1987. Specifically, Josephan documents appear to intimate that honorific (re)namings of the same polis were made in honor of two women in the Roman imperial family, each named Julia. Putting together portraits of each woman may be helpful in determining whether both or only one of them would have been the object of honorific (re)namings by client-rulers of the Herodian family. But which Julia?

When one compares the records provided by Josephus (recorded above) and Tacitus it is evident that there are references to (1) Julia, wife of Julius Caesar (I); (2) Livia Julia (also called the Augusta), the wife of Augustus (II); (3) Julia, the daughter of Augustus (III); (4) Julia, the sister of Gaius and granddaughter of Augustus, who is also called Livia, the daughter of Drusus, and the wife of Nero Caesar (IV); and (5) Julia Livilla (the daughter of Germanicus and great granddaughter of Augustus (V). Tacitus refers to Julia, daughter of Augustus, as Julia III and to Livia Julia, wife of Augustus, as the Augusta. Moreover, three women other than Julia III bore this name after she had been discredited and banished for adultery and licentiousness. In fact, another of them, Julia III's own daughter, Julia IV, suffered the same fate, and for the same reasons as her mother. We must therefore keep in mind that to name a polis after even Julia (III) was in itself not impossible however improbable it may appear to modern researchers.The question of whether or not Josephus wrote about such an occurrence is our task.

## Julia (III): A Personal and Family Tragedy

Tacitus refers to Julia (III) only three times in his *Annals;* history is not kind to her. The first reference,[24] during the rule of Tiberias, holds:

> This was the year when Julia (III) died. Her father Augustus had imprisoned her—for immorality—first on the island of Pandateria and then in the town of Rhegium opposite Sicily on the strait. While Gaius Caesar and Lucius Caesar were still alive, she had been married to Tiberius, but had looked down on him as an inferior. That had been the fundamental reason for his retirement to Rhodes. When he became emperor, he eliminated her last hope by the removal of Agrippa Postumus. Then he let her waste away to death, exiled and disgraced, by slow starvation. He calculated that she had been banished for so long that her death would pass unnoticed. (p. 60)

One is thus tempted to make a strong case against anyone's naming anything honorifically after this Julia during the time of Augustus (after her being banished) and until the time of Tiberius' death. But we have more data to consult and observe. Tacitus further remarks that also one

> Iullus Antonius was executed for adultery with Augustus' daughter, that emperor (his great uncle) had dismissed him to Massilia, where study could be a cloak for exile. (p. 175)

And ending his account of Tiberius' reign of terror and his death through assassination, Tacitus writes:

> But Tiberius' position became most delicate of all after his marriage to Augustus' daughter Julia (III). For he had to choose between enduring her unfaithfulness or escaping it. (p. 221)

The picture painted of Julia (III) from the Tacitus accounts is not pretty even by empire-era standards, and certainly rubs rough even modern, ethical behavior standards. He intimates Julia might have been the victim and not the initiator of an illicit affair. In the case of another paramour, Iullus, however, it is left up to the reader to judge who initiated this deadly (for Iullus) liaison. Julia III's banishment occurred in 2 BCE. This date follows the death of Herod the Great by two years. Since neither of his three successor sons came to rule in Palestine until 4 BCE (having been present in Rome before Caesar at the reading and execution of their late father's will and thus knowing something about the imperial family "climate"), one is tempted to make prima facie a strong case against anyone's naming anything honorifically after this Julia from the time of Augustus until the death of Tiberius. At any rate, we now know why Julia (III) was banished, to where she was banished, the name of at least one reason why she was banished, and the results of her banishment. At this point we still don't know whether or not a polis could be (in good conscience and taste) still named in her honor or even memory. Let us see what our sources have to say about Livia Julia, the wife of Augustus.

## Julia/Livia/the Augusta: A Composite/Mosaic

In contrast to Julia (III), and because she was far more significant historically and the power behind one of the significant imperial thrones, one would expect far more references to have been made to Livia Julia, Augustus Caesar's wife, known as Augusta after his death and deification, and the ruling Tiberius' mother. In Tacitus' *Annals* one finds no less than twenty-five references to her.

This Julia—let us call her by all of her official names, Livia Julia (the) Augusta—like Julia (III) had no spotless, ethical plate off which she dined. She is referred to as a "feminine bully" (p. 31) and as "a catastrophe to the nation as a mother and to the house of the Caesars as a stepmother" (p. 36). Tacitus suspects her of having been involved in the deaths of her two stepsons, Lucius Caesar and Gaius Caesar. The Augusta (Livia) also had the aged Augustus exile his only surviving grandson, Agrippa Postumus, to the island of Planasia. This paved the way for Tiberius, another stepson of Caesar, to succeed him. Moreover, she is suspected of foul play with regard to the death of Augustus himself. He, it seems, had visited the exiled Postumus, became tearfully reconciled to him, and apparently somehow had given Livia the idea that he (the emperor) was about to change his mind and perhaps designate Postumus as his successor (p. 32). As soon as Tiberius was installed as Augustus' successor, the unfortunate Postumus was assassinated.

In the matter of one Quintus Haterius, whom Tiberius considered a threat to his position as emperor, according to Tacitus, Haterius

> went into the palace to apologize ... and groveled at his feet. Thereupon Tiberius crashed to the ground ... brought down by the grip of Haterius—who was then all but killed by the guards. However, the emperor's feeling's were not softened ... until Haterius appealed to the Augusta—as Livia was now called—and ... was saved. (p. 39)

Again, Tacitus has cause to allude to Livia's machinations following upon the death (and cremation) of Augustus. This time it is in reference to Germanicus, commander-in-chief of the armies of the Upper and Lower Rhine. He was the son of Tiberius' brother, Nero Drusus; the Augusta was therefore one of his grandparents. She also hated him—for reasons not particularly germane to our study—and saw him as a threat to Tiberius' security on the throne. Germanicus, however, worked tirelessly on behalf of Tiberius and remained loyal even though his armies were dissatisfied and in riot on the Rhine (pp. 49 ff.).

During the first set of treason trials, the Augusta, Livia Julia, in response to the honors (among them deification) that the senate had bestowed on the late Augustus, had instituted Games. Later this act was appealed to by Tiberius in order to save the life of one Falanius, who had been accused of admitting among the worshipers of the deified Augustus an actor/male prostitute and disposing of a statue of Augustus (during something like today's American yard/garage sale). Tiberius ruled that the gods—including the late Augustus—had to see to their own insults (p. 72).

Apparently the Augusta, his grandmother, was the stuff dreams were made of, for during the night before an important military engagement against the Germans, Germanicus dreamed that he was engaged in the ritual sacrificing of an animal and that when his garment had been spattered with too much blood from the victim, the Augusta handed him an unsoiled, finer robe (p. 81).

Also during these treason trials, and after the major wars with the Germans, one Lucius Calpurnius Piso (II) denounced numerous senate practices as corrupt; he threatened to leave Rome rather than continue to witness such obvious corruption. Because he was recognized by all as one of the few honorable and uncorrupted men left in the senate, Tiberius sought to mollify him, and entreating him to remain, extended to him certain legal powers. Using these new powers, and because she had openly displayed contempt for the law, Calpurnius had Urgulania, a friend of the Augusta's, summoned to court for offenses. Because of her high station and connections, Urgulania refused to appear; the Augusta, upon hearing of the summons, was outraged. Yet, Calpurnius was persistent: Urgulania was fined and an amount of the fine was fixed. Angrily, the Augusta agreed to direct that a sum be remitted by her. Tiberius, now to mollify both his mother and Calpurnius, played advocate before the senate on behalf of Urgulania, at no cost to his position of having been caught in the middle of this Calpurnius-led–mother-opposed matter (p. 91).

Due to an ever-growing popularity on the part of Germanicus, there developed at Tiberius' court such rivalries that a major split existed among the courtiers. Members, either openly or in secret, lined up behind either Drusus (Tiberius' son) or Germanicus (Tiberius' nephew). Not only was Germanicus more popular; so was his wife, Agrippina. The Augusta was bent on doing all she could to persecute this Claudian Ken-and-Barbie[25] pair; especially jealous was she of Agrippina.

Concerning the death of Germanicus, Piso, his arch rival, was advised by Domitius Celer, one of Piso's closest friends, how to conduct himself in order to win and maintain both imperial and popular support as governor of Syria. Domitius counseled:

> Why hasten to reach Rome at the same instant as Germanicus' ashes? If you do, the weeping Agrippina and the witless crowd will bring you down at once on hearsay, your defence unheard. You have the Augusta's complicity, the emperor's sympathy—secretly. No one is so delighted by Germanicus' death as its most ostentatious mourners. (p. 112)

When it was learned in Rome that Germanicus was ill, rumors began to spread concerning why he had been sent to such a faraway province; why his nemesis, Piso, had been given a governorship; and why the Augusta had had private talks with Plancina, Piso's wife (p. 114).

During the procession of Germanicus' ashes, Tiberius and the Augusta made no public appearance. According to Tacitus: "Either they considered open mourning beneath their dignity or they feared that the public gaze would detect insincerity on their faces" (p.118).

Eventually, and in turn, Piso, imperial tool and fool, became unpopular with the populace (and a potential liability to the crown). At issue were numerous unanswered questions concerning the mysterious death of Germanicus. At a hearing designed to determine his involvement in the death of Germanicus, Tiberius distanced himself. Plancina, equally hated but better connected, had promised her husband that she would share whatever vicissitudes he would have to undergo, including death if he were found guilty of all charges against him. However, the Augusta used her influence and secured a pardon for Plancina, herself suspected of having poisoned Germanicus at a banquet. Thereafter, she distanced herself from him and his eventual fate: a sabre-cut throat (p. 124).

Opinions (and rumors) continued to rage concerning how Germanicus died. Tacitus informs his readers that:

> Tiberius exonerated Marcus from the charge of civil war ... expressed pity for the terrible end of Piso himself. (p. 124)

And that:

> On behalf of Plancina he made a deplorable and embarrassed appeal, pleading his mother's entreaties. (p. 124)

Yet we learn that:

> All decent people were, in private, increasingly violent critics of the Augusta—a grandmother who was apparently entitled to see and talk to her grandson's murderess, and rescue her from the senate. (p. 124)

In essence, "the Augusta and the emperor were protecting Plancina" (p. 124).

Our composite/mosaic of the Augusta is by no means complete. Tacitus alludes to her yet twelve (or more) times in his *Annals*. During the fourth consulship of Tiberius, and the second of the now-elevated Drusus, Tiberius withdrew to Campania. He communicated often with the senate from there on various matters. However, later in his retirement there,

> the Augusta fell dangerously ill; and the emperor had to return urgently to Rome. Either mother and son were still good friends or if they were not, they concealed it. Indeed, shortly beforehand, when dedicating a statue to the divine Augustus, she had inscribed Tiberius' name after her own. This was believed to have given him grave, though unexpressed, offence as a slur on his imperial dignity. (p. 146)

During further wranglings with the senate, which attempted to rein in much of his power, Tiberius had to deal with numerous religious problems. The Augusta was ill and gentlemen outside the senate had vowed to place a gift to her, vowed by them, in a temple to Fortune-on-Horseback for her recovery. Since no such temples were located in Rome, one was finally found at Antium and their gift was deposited there (p. 149).

After the death of Drusus, Tiberius mourned him in the senate, while his body was awaiting disposal. Whether this mourning was accepted as genuine or not, Tacitus states that he attempted to be convincing and described the following scene:

> After referring sorrowfully to the Augusta's great age, his grandson's immaturity, and his own declining years, he said that the sons of Germanicus were his only consolation in his grief; and he requested that they should be brought in. (p. 157)

The reader of Tacitus' *Annals* follows numerous murders and conspiracies to murder. Attending the previously mentioned account of Tiberius' mourning, Sejanus, realizing that he could still be succeeded by one of Tiberius' grandsons (i.e., the sons of the late Germanicus), next decided to remove the latter's widow, Agrippina. Resolving not to kill the children, Sejanus "played on the Augusta's long-standing animosity against her" (p. 159). In addition to the naming of cities after the imperial mother (already noted in Josephus), ancillary honors were bestowed upon her when, named alongside Tiberius and the senate, a temple was decreed by the grateful cities of Asia Minor for (what was touted and doubted to be) an act of justice on their part: the punishment of one Gaius Junius Silanus. And related to this, after the death of an old priest of Jupiter, and Tiberius' replacing of him by

his son, a sum was donated to the upkeep of the sacred space. Moreover, "monies were donated to the upkeep of the theatre of the priest-
esses of Vesta, and it was also decided that the Augusta, whenever she
visited the theatre, should sit in the seats reserved for these priest-
esses" (pp. 161).

As the circle of crime, intrigue, and punishment shrank during
the reign of the elder Tiberius, those who had wielded legal power earlier in the senate now found themselves on trial before it. This certainly was the case with the earlier-mentioned Lucius Calpurnius Piso
(II), who had threatened to leave Rome because he found its legal
institutions corrupt. It was he who, "defying the Augusta's might, had
dared to haul her friend Urgulania into court from the palace itself"
(p. 163 ff.) He fell victim to a vicious prosecution and was saved total
humiliation and execution by dying suddenly.

This same Urgulania was involved in another prosecution case.
This one revolved around the praetor Plautius Silvanus' having been
found guilty of throwing his wife, Apronia, out of a window to her
death during a row. Tacitus writes, "Then Silvanus was sent a dagger
by his grandmother Urgulania. In view of her intimacy with the
Augusta, this was regarded as a hint from the emperor" (p. 164). Tiberius, upon hearing of the matter, had proceeded to Silvanus' house
and had inspected the bedroom himself and found signs of a struggle.

As Tiberius grew older and absented himself from Rome, rumors
raged as to why he had spent so much time away. According to Tacitus, one popular theory held that

> he was driven away by his mother's bullying: to share control
> with her seemed intolerable, to dislodge her impracticable—
> since that control had been given him by her. For Augustus
> had considered awarding the empire to his universally loved
> grandnephew Germanicus. But his wife had induced him to
> adopt Tiberius instead. The Augusta harped accusingly on this
> obligation—and exacted payment. (p. 182)

Tacitus notes once more during the time of Tiberius' long
absence from Rome that it was during this time that Julia (IV), granddaughter of Augustus and stepdaughter of the Augusta, died. Like Julia
(III), Augustus' daughter who had suffered a similar fate, Julia (IV) had
been condemned to banishment on an island—this one, Trimerum,
was located off the Apulian coast. The account states further that "the

Augusta had helped her" (p. 188). The references in Tacitus' *Annals* flesh out the thumbnail sketch he painstakingly provided of the Augusta; the remaining few describe circumstances in the aftermath of her death.

It was also during Tiberius' (and also Sejanus') time on the Campanian coast that the Augusta died. Describing the circumstances of her death, Tacitus provides a postage-stamp-sized biography, which is quite telling actually. Equally telling is the fact that Emperor Tiberius, elevated to and sustained in power by his mother, was conspicuously absent from the last public rites for the Augusta. What had been suppressed by Tiberius about his true feelings for her during her life was made known incrementally and obviously in a series of his rulings after her death. Among them was a curtailing of honors to her memory by the senate, which he deemed excessive. He also decreed that she not be deified, adding, however, that she had not wished it so (p. 190ff.).

Using her influence, the Augusta had elevated to consul a flatterer named Gaius Fufius Geminus; he had ridiculed Tiberius at an earlier time. His demise marked the beginning of a phase of payback, revenge, and tyranny inaugurated by both Tiberius and Sejanus, both of whom "had not ventured to outbid her parental authority" (p. 191).

To remove possible rivals within the imperial family "a letter was sent to Rome denouncing Agrippina and Nero Caesar" (p. 191). It was read so soon after the Augusta's death, that many held it had been received during her lifetime and suppressed until her death (p. 191). It resulted in Agrippina, Nero Caesar, and Drusus Caesar's being exiled. After Nero Caesar's death, Sejanus himself was accused and found guilty of conspiracy and executed. Livilla, his second wife and coconspirator, was either executed or she committed suicide after it was revealed by Apicate, Sejanus' first wife, that Tiberius' son Drusus had been poisoned to death by Sejanus and Livilla (p. 192).

Commenting on the reign of terror under Tiberius, Tacitus has cause to mention once again the influence of the Augusta. Plancina, wife of the previously mentioned Lucius Calpurnius Piso, had publicly shown her delight at hearing of the death of Germanicus. After Piso's own fall, her position became tenuous. According to Tacitus she was "rescued, after Piso's downfall, by the Augusta's intercessions and

Agrippina's hostility. Now that her patroness and her enemy were both gone, justice prevailed" (p. 207).

Tacitus' final reference in the *Annals* to the Augusta compares Agrippina's public deportment at the funeral of the late emperor Claudius (whom she poisoned) to "imitating the grandeur of her great-grandmother Livia, the first Augusta" (p. 273).[26]

### LIVIA JULIA THE AUGUSTA: A MINIBIOGRAPHY

The foregoing references allow us to produce the following outline in order of appearance of the Augusta's influence and activities leading to a minibiography of her. Honors to her are marked by asterisks.

1. Concerning Haterius, she saved his life.
2. She was opposed to anyone other than Tiberius' (her son's) becoming emperor after Augustus.
3. She instituted Games in honor of (the now dead and deified) Augustus.
4. She impressed Germanicus enough that he dreamed of her, and considered it a good omen before an important military engagement against the Germans.
5. She intervened in the treason trial of Urgulania—a friend—and had Tiberius function as defense counsel for her before the senate. When it was apparent that she would lose, the Augusta directed that a fine be paid by Urgulania.
6. She was drastically opposed to Germanicus' succeeding Augustus, and she took a personal disliking to his wife Agrippina.
7. She was an accomplice in Piso's machinations that led to the death of Germanicus. Domitius Celer advised him of the Augusta's conversance in the matter.
8. She also had private talks with Plancina, Piso's wife, concerning the matter.
9. She, along with Tiberius, failed to attend the funeral procession of Germanicus' ashes; they feared a knowing public gaze.
10. She and Plancina distanced themselves from Piso when he fell under suspicion of having had a hand in Germanicus' death. Actually, Plancina had administered the poison at a banquet.
11. As civil criticism mounted, Tiberius and the Augusta continued to protect the murderess Plancina.

12. Tiberius moved from Rome to Campania during his fourth consulship, but returned when the Augusta fell ill. Tacitus suspected that Tiberius was angry with her but concealed it for the time being.
13. *The ill Augusta was the recipient of a gift in her honor at a temple to Fortune-on-Horseback. She was highly admired by sections of the populace.
14. Now that the Augusta was ill, Drusus dead, and his own age advanced, Tiberius publicly showed favor to the sons of Germanicus.
15. The conspirator Sejanus could plot to remove Germanicus' wife Agrippina with full knowledge of the Augusta.
16. *The Augusta was awarded the status of priestess of Vesta, and alongside Tiberius and the senate, a temple was decreed by the cities of Asia Minor in her honor.
17. Piso, who had made an enemy of the Augusta in the Urgulania affair, fell victim to the senate but died suddenly before he could be humiliated publicly.
18. When the praetor Silvanus was found guilty of having killed his wife, Apronia, his grandmother sent him a dagger. He saw this as a hint from the emperor.
19. She was to Tiberius a bully, a controller, unable to be dislodged, for she had given him control and she never let him forget it.
20. Two other Julias, (III) and (IV), Augustus' daughter and granddaughter respectively, were banished for adultery; the Augusta helped the latter during her long exile from Rome.
21. Her son Tiberius hated her so much that when she died he did not attend her last public rites. He curtailed honors to her memory and decreed that she not be deified. It was his way of seeking revenge.
22. The flatterer Geminus, who had been elevated to consul by the Augusta's influence and had once insulted Tiberius, was victimized by the latter after the Augusta's death. It marked a period of payback.
23. Agrippina and Nero Caesar were denounced by Tiberius and exiled after the Augusta's death; Drusus Caesar was also exiled. Sejanus was found guilty of conspiracy and executed. His wife Livilla was also dispatched after Tiberius learned from Sejanus' first wife that the pair had poisoned his son Drusus.

24. Plancina, once protected by the Augusta, was dispatched by Tiberius after her death.
25. Her phony public deportment and sincerity at funeral processions was later imitated by Agrippina, the widow of the emperor Claudius (whom Agrippina had poisoned).

## CATEGORIES

The information supplied by Tacitus allows one to view the Augusta in seven ways (the reference numerals denominate mention by Tacitus of Livia-Julia):

1. Her role as protector and benefactor (1, 5, 20, 23, 26).
2. Her role as mother (2, 6, 9, 12, 19, 21).
3. Her role as wife (this information is supplied in full below).
4. Her role as power behind the imperial throne (3, 4, 5, 7, 8, 10, 11, 15, 17, 18).
5. Tiberius' activities shortly before and after her death (12, 14, 21, 23, 24, 26).
6. Those imitating her public insincerity (25).
7. Honors given her (13, 16).

Tacitus' twenty-second reference (in no. 3 above) thus allows him to provide the following minibiography, for he writes:

> By her own Claudian family, and her adoption into the Livii and Julii, she was of the highest nobility. Her first husband, and the father of her children, had been Tiberius Claudius Nero. The future Augustus, fascinated by her beauty, removed her from him—with or without his encouragement—and hastily conducted her to his own home even before the baby she was expecting (the future Nero Drusus) was born. That was her last child. But her connection with Augustus through the marriage of her grandson Germanicus to his granddaughter Agrippina gave them great grandchildren in common. Her private life was of traditional strictness. But her graciousness exceeded old-fashioned standards. She was a compliant wife, but an overbearing mother. Neither her husband's diplomacy nor her son's insincerity could outmaneuver her. (p. 190)

From this composite Tacitus mentions only three honors that the Augusta received abroad (no. 4): a gift at a temple to Fortune-on-Horseback, status as priestess of Vesta, and alongside Tiberius and the senate, a temple was decreed in her shared honor by the cities of Asia

Minor. From Tacitus, therefore, one is unable to glean any definitive information to explain how the Herodian family came to rename cities in honor of any of the Julias. We have alluded to personal relationships between certain members of the Herodian family from the information supplied by Josephus, and due to Tacitus' silence, one can only conclude that the honorific (re)namings were motivated out of personal admirations or relations. Tacitus does supply ample though sketchy information to suggest that because of the relationship between the Augusta and either Julia (III) or Julia (IV) it is extremely doubtful whether the Herodians, proven masters of survival and retention of power regardless of who was either on the imperial throne or the real power behind it, would have named locales in their territories of influence after either of the latter Julias. This was the most politically correct client family on Roman record!

## CONCLUSION

This then is the woman after whom Bethsaida was probably honorifically renamed. Seeing her presented here, alongside three other Julias, one gains tremendous insight into members of the Livii and Julii, and finds it possible to understand why so many honors could have been bestowed on these women by subject peoples in the provinces, if not in Rome: some to cull favor, others out of personal motives and, indeed, admiration. While Tacitus provides sufficient information about these women from the perspective of an observer of members of the imperial family as well as information about the foibles and peccadillos of some of its more notable members, the work of Josephus serves as a useful mirror from one of the dominated areas of how their power and influence were received.

While Tacitus provides no comprehensive biography of the Augusta, his twenty-seven brief insights provide the possibility that an honorific Julias could have been inspired in the territories by Julia (III). That is, we read that the Augusta showed kindness to the exiled Julia (IV). This might have been the case with Julia (III) as well, although we don't get this information from Tacitus. And this possibility might have been learned by those in the client-ruled territories, which were always prone to play their own form of sycophant politics.

While one could maintain that Bethsaida was most probably renamed in honor of the Augusta, Josephus never specifically states this; Tacitus is totally silent on the bestowal of such honors (especially of her having been worshippped as a goddess) in the Herodian-controlled territories. Moreover, the cobbled-together minibiography of the Augusta made possible by Tacitus does not exclude the possibility of a renaming of Bethsaida in honor of the Julia (III) to which Josephus appears to allude. As happens often with critical scholarship, we are thus certain why we must remain somewhat uncertain as to whose honor the fishing village/town Bethsaida was, definitely subsequently, honorifically renamed and upgraded to the status of the polis Julias.

## CHAPTER NOTES

1. Enslin (1938), 10.
2. Grant (1956), 147.
3. *Josephus* (1981), 377 (*Ant.*). One justifies "Julias, from the name of the emperor's wife" while the second justifies "Julias, the same name with Caesar's daughter."); 382 (*Ant.*) (concerning Philip) "He died at Julias; and when he was carried to that monument which he had erected for himself beforehand, he was buried with great pomp"; 478 (*Wars*) ("Philip ... built the city of Caesarea, at the fountains of the Jordan ...; as also the city Julias, in the lower Gaulanitis"); 504·(*Wars*) (Parts of the lands of King Agrippa began " ... at mount Libanus, and the fountains of the Jordan, and reaches ... in length ... from a village called Arpha, as far as Julias."); 520 (*Wars*) (The river Jordan, winding its way southward from its northern fountains, "... divides the marshes and fens of the lake Semechonitis: when it hath run another hundred and twenty furlongs, it first passes by the city Julias, ..."; 539 (*Wars*) At the northern end of the great plain and facing toward the south, the mountain range on the right (=West) was quite steep, barren, and uninhabited. Opposite this range, and east of the Jordan was another range which "... begins at Julias and the northern quarters, and extends itself southward as far as Somorrhon, which is the bounds of Petra, in Arabia"; 19 (*Life*) "Sylla (King Herod Agrippa II's commander) pitched his camp at five furlongs distance from Julias ..."; 20 (*Life*) "I (Josephus) sent two thousand armed men, ... who raised a bank a furlong off Julias, near the river Jordan"; 20 (*Life*) "Yet did they not go off with the victory ...; for when they heard that some armed men were sailed from Taricheae to Julias, they were afraid and retired."
4. Cf. McCown (1930), 35; Urman (1985).
5. Matt. 11:21, Mk. 6:45, 8:22; Lk. 9:10, 10:13; Jn. 1:44, 12:21.
6. Josephus (1981), *Ant.* 18.2.1:28, 18.4.6:108; *Wars* 2.9.1:168, 3.3.5:57, 3.10.7:515, 4.8.2:454; Life 398, 399, 406.
7. Kuhn and Arav (1991).
8. Niswonger (1988), 24, holds that: A true polis would adopt Greek styles of political and financial management and would provide fertile ground for social, intellectual, and business contact between Jew and Greek.
9. This account is imbedded within information provided by Josephus about the reorganization of the former client-kingdom of the late Herod the Great. Josephus refers to quite a bit of history all at the same time:
   (a) Herod the Great is dead;
   (b) his former kingdom has been divided among three of his sons as of ca. 4 BCE:
   1. Archelaus (king of Judea and Samaria)
   2. Herod Antipas (governor of Galilee and the Perea)
   3. Philip (governor of Bactria);
   (c) Archelaus has been removed from ruling and has been banished to Gaul;
   (d) the execution of Augustus' tax by Cyrenius had been completed (in the 37th year of Augustus' victory over Antony=4 BCE)
   (e) *Ant.* 17.13.2 holds that Archelaus ruled for ten years = until 6 BCE.
10. Strickert (1995).
11. Tacitus (1956).
12. Other examples are found in the presentation of speeches at which Josephus could not have possibly been present, such as the speech at Scythopolis (Beth Shean) by Simon son of Paul (*Wars*, 2.18.4); the speech by Titus before Taricheae (*Wars*, 3.10.2); and of course the speech by Eleazar son of Yair at Masada before its fall to the forces of Flavius Silva (*Wars*, 7.8.6).

13. The most obvious for the area under discussion are Caesarea Maritima (built by Herod the Great), Caesarea Philippi (built by Herod's son Philip), and Tiberias (built by Herod Antipas).
14. In Josephus (1960), *Ant.* 17.13.1, Archelaus built a village and "put his name upon it, and called it Archelaus."
15. This supplies the reason for the name similarity, but does not necessarily state that it was in honor of Antipater the Idumean.
16. Here there is no mistaking that these acts were in honor of his beloved brother.
17. Here the activity is primarily for self-gratification and self-aggrandizement through the bestowing of favors.
18. These are occasioned not least of all by his own actions as Joseph son of Mattathias the general and prisoner, and only later as writer. Palestinian Jews especially saw him as a renegade Jew and wanted nothing to do with him. While he, as Roman citizen and author, wrote to honor his fellow Jews, he wrote much in the service of his Roman patrons, the Flavian (imperial) family. Concerning specific writings, Whiston writes: "I believe, that in spite of his claim that he studied the Jewish sects at first hand, Josephus used other sources when he wrote about the Essenes. He does not exhibit the first-hand knowledge in this area as he does, for example, in describing the Jewish wars" (Josephus [1960], x).
19. This hypothesis is contained in a private correspondence dated 9 May 1994 between Professors Richard A. Freund of the University of Nebraska at Omaha and Professor Louis H. Feldman of Yeshiva University. The contents were shared with this writer by his colleague Professor Freund.
20. To understand this unique relationship and staying power of the Herods, one should read Sandmel (1967), Jones (1938), Perowne (1956), Grant (1977), and Hoehner (1980).
21. Since Rome was far more interested in Palestine's role as a buffer between its holdings in Egypt and threats from its enemies in Parthia, the Herodian client-rulers were given free hand to keep the buffer strong and self-serve at the same time. In turn, they showed their gratitude by erecting and honorifically naming cities after their emperor-patrons, their wives (and perhaps even their children).
22. Here, apparently, there was a strong personal friendship/relationship between the two women, both of whom had individual power and personal property holdings.
23. From Marc Antony's "standing up" for Herod at the Roman imperial court and supporting his right to be "King of the Jews" in the early 30s BCE, to the Rome-supported rulership of King Herod Agrippa the Second, during the latter half of the first century CE (the time of the first Jewish rebellion against Roman overlordship), this family enjoyed apparently unusual personal relationships with various members of the imperial families for a sustained period of time.
24. Parenthetical references are to the *Annals* of Tacitus (1956), edited by Michael Grant.
25. Barbie (a shapely teenage fashion doll invented in 1959) and Ken (Barbie's boyfriend doll) are popular children's and preteens' collector items manufactured by Mattel Toys, USA.
26. The 25th reference, concerning Marcus Aurelius Cotta Maximus Messallinus and describing a feast that he attended on the Augusta's birthday as a funeral feast, is essentially useless for our purposes herein; it is included for completeness (p. 197).

## LITERATURE CITED

Enslin, Morton Scott. 1938. *Christian Beginnings, Parts I and II.* New York: Harper & Brothers.

Grant, Michael. 1977. *Herod the Great.* New York: American Heritage

Hoehner, Harold. 1980. *Herod Antipas.* Grand Rapids: Zondervan.

Jones, Arnold. 1938. *The Herods of Judea.* London: Oxford University Press.

*Josephus: Complete Works.* [1960] 1981. Translated by William Whiston. Grand Rapids: Kregel Publications.

Kuhn, Heinz-Wolfgang, and Rami Arav. 1991. The Bethsaida Excavations: Historical and Archaeological Approaches. Pp. 91–106 in, *The Future of Early Christianity: Essays in Honor of Helmut Koester.* Edited by Birger A. Pearson. Minneapolis: Fortress Press.

McCown, C. 1930. The Problem of the Site of Bethsaida, *JPOS* 10:35.

Niswonger, Richard L. 1988. *New Testament History.* Grand Rapids: Academie/Zondervan.

Urman, Daniel. 1985. *The Golan: Profile of a Region during the Roman and Byzantine Periods.* BAR International Series. Oxford: Biblical Archaeological Review.

Perowne, S. 1956. *The Life and Times of Herod the Great.* London: Hodder and Stoughton.

Sandmel, Samuel. 1967. *Herod: Profile of a Tyrant.* Philadelphia: Lippincott.

Strickert, Frederick C. 1995. The Coins of Philip. P. 1 in *Bethsaida: A City on the North Shore of the Sea of Galilee.* Ed. Richard A. Freund and Rami Arav. Kirksville, MO.: Thomas Jefferson Press.

Tacitus. 1956. *Annals of Imperial Rome.* Translated by Michael Grant. Baltimore: Penguin.

*Mark D. Smith*

# A Tale of Two Julias: Julia, Julias, and Josephus

THE FIRST CENTURY CE WAS NOT THE BEST OF TIMES. Indeed, it often looked like the worst of times, at least from the perspective of the inhabitants of Roman Palestine. Not only Romans, but Jews and gentiles, pagans, and later, Christians all had a stake in the status and government of the eastern Mediterranean provinces and client kingdoms of Rome. Such ingredients made for a potent and volatile mix. In this turbulent era, Bethsaida-Julias seems to have played a significant role. It will come as no surprise that the most important early source for Bethsaida-Julias outside of the New Testament is Flavius Josephus, himself a significant player in these difficult times.

Josephus mentions the ancient city of Bethsaida more often than any other author in antiquity.[1] Although he only once calls the town Bethsaida,[2] he regularly refers to it by its herodian title, Julias—eight times in all, in three different works. Josephus claims that the son of Herod, Philip the Tetrarch, renamed the city Julias, in honor of a woman named Julia. The identity of this Julia, however, is the source of considerable difficulty. A close analysis of the evidence reveals that it is unlikely that Julias was named after Julia, the errant daughter of Augustus. Rather, it is more probable that the city was named in honor of Livia-Julia, the wife of Augustus.

The earliest extant reference to the renaming of the town appears in Josephus' *Wars of the Jews* (*JW*)[3]:

333

> Upon the death of Augustus ... the Roman Empire passed into
> the hands of Tiberias, the son of Julia. [On his accession],
> Herod [Antipas] and Philip continued to hold their tetrarchies.
> Philip built a city near the sources of the Jordan in Paneas,
> [which he named] Caesarea [Philippi], and, in lower Gaulani-
> tis, he built Julias; Herod, for his part, built Tiberias in Galilee
> and a city in Peraea, which also carried the name of Julias.[4]

In his later *Antiquities* (*Ant.*), Josephus revisits the same events, though
with considerable alterations:

> When Herod [Antipas] fortified Sepphoris, the ornament of all
> Galilee, he called it Autocratoris. He also erected a wall about
> another city, Betharamphtha, which he called Julias, after the
> name of the emperor's wife. Philip too made improvements at
> Paneas, the city near the sources of the Jordan, and called it
> Caesarea [Philippi]. He also raised the village of Bethsaida on
> Lake Gennesaret to the status of a polis by means of [adding]
> many residents and other power. He called it by the same
> name as Julia, the emperor's daughter.[5]

A cursory glance at these passages raises two sources of potential
confusion: There are two cities named Julias and two (or more)[6]
women named Julia. Which woman or which city may be referred to
in any particular passage is problematic.

We are fortunate with regard to the two cities renamed Julias by
herodian rulers (Betharamphtha and Bethsaida) that Josephus offers
hints that do not force us to depend on geographical context alone to
identify which is which. In addition, the relationship between the two
cities in Josephus' mind can help us disentangle the references to the
two women named Julia. Josephus mentions Betharamphtha, also
called Julias in Peraea, six times: four in his *JW* and two in *Ant.* (both
of which are merely parallels of passages in *JW*).[7] The parallel passages
of *JW* 2.252 and *Ant.* 20.159 discuss the redistribution of power under
the administration of Nero, who added Abila, Julias in Peraea, Taricheae, and Tiberias in Galilee to the domains ruled by Agrippa II. The
later version in *Ant.* adds little of substance: it neglects to mention
Abila, but it includes fourteen villages that were given to Agrippa,
along with Julias in Peraea.[8] *JW* 4.438 describes the Roman subjuga-
tion of Peraea, including the name of Julias among the conquered
cities. Finally, in *JW* 4.454, Josephus describes the mountains of Moab,
extending from Julias in the north, southward to Somora, near Petra.

The parallel passages *JW* 2.168 and *Ant.* 18.27 are quoted above. Both mention Bethsaida-Julias and Betharamphtha-Julias in the same context. There is little room for confusion between these two towns in these passages. An analysis of the two texts, however, raises the question of the women after whom these places are renamed. Of the five Julias identified by Greene, only three are named by Josephus (II, III, and IV) and only two are relevant to the issue at hand. Who was the Julia after whom Bethsaida was renamed? The problem stems from the respective reputations of Julia II and III. Julia (III)—the daughter of Augustus and Scribonia, the wife (consecutively) of Marcellus, Agrippa, and Tiberius—is renowned in Roman history as a woman of ill repute. At the very time when Augustus was busily tightening up the moral laws that governed the Empire, he learned that his daughter had been "indulging in every sort of vice,"[9] regularly engaging in "wanton drinking and revelling" with numerous men, "even in the forum, atop the very rostra."[10] The emperor therefore exiled Julia in 2 BCE, never to be reconciled with her. She died in 14 CE. On the other hand, Livia-Julia (II)—the wife of Augustus and mother of Tiberius (by her former husband)—was a paragon of Roman matronly virtue and represented all of the moral integrity that Augustan propaganda held dear, combining the highest noble lineage with fortitude, frugality, and faithfulness to her husband.[11] When Augustus died in 14 CE, Livia was, by his will, adopted into the *gens Iulia,* and given the name Julia Augusta.[12] Literary and epigraphic texts often refer to her by the latter name, particularly in the eastern provinces, where she was an integral part of the imperial cult and was worshiped as a goddess.[13] Her portrait appears on coins issued by Tiberius, in 22 or 23 CE.[14]

The problem for interpreting Josephus' references to Julia and Julias arises from his note in *Ant.* 18.27 that Philip renamed Bethsaida-Julias "after Julia, the emperor's daughter" according to Feldman's translation.[15] That Philip should have done such a thing is not impossible, but it would certainly be impolitic. Further, this is not a necessary interpretation of the evidence.

There are several ways one might attempt to alleviate this problem. One is chronological: Since Julia the daughter was not exiled until 2 BCE, there is a narrow time frame during which Philip could have named the city in her honor after he assumed his rule in 4 BCE but before she was exiled.[16] Recent analysis of Philip's coins, however, has shown that it is much more probable that Philip renamed Bethsaida in 30 CE. Two coins dated to the year 34 of Philip (30 CE) are of primary importance. The reverse of the first contains the inscription, ΕΠΙ ΦΙΛΙΠΠΟΥ ΤΕΤΡΑΡΧΟΥ ΚCΤΙC (by Philip the Tetrarch, founder), commemorating his founding of something significant, most probably, Julias.[17] The second coin features on the obverse a draped bust of Julia, surrounded by the inscription ΙΟΥΛΙΑ CΕΒΑCΤΗ (Julia Augusta).[18] Not only does the coincidence of these two coins, minted in the same year, make it probable that they are celebrating the renaming of Bethsaida, but the second coin is unambiguous in its reference to Livia-Julia. Julia the daughter of Augustus was never granted the title Augusta. In addition, that Livia-Julia should appear with such prominence in the year 30 CE is appropriate since she died the previous year. Now, even among the most sensitive of Romans, she could legitimately be celebrated as a goddess. Thus the proposed chronological solution is untenable.[19]

Another possible method of resolving this dilemma is textual: Perhaps Θυγατρὶ (daughter) is not the original reading of the text of *Ant.* 18.28.[20] That is possible, though not probable. There are no significant textual variants between manuscripts in this passage.[21] In addition, a scribe would be most unlikely to make such a change. It would make little historical or contextual sense, and this theory must ignore a fact with which a scribe would surely be familiar: of the many times Josephus uses the name Julia, the vast majority refer to the wife, not the daughter, of Augustus. A scribal emendation in the opposite direction would, therefore, be far more probable. There is, however, another, more supportable, textual explanation. This may be a case of homoioteleuton, in which an early scribe encountered two consecutive lines that ended with the same word—in this case, ᾽Ιουλίᾳ. The eye of the copyist then skipped to the second occurrence, unwittingly omitting the intervening line.[22] If this were the case, perhaps Josephus originally wrote a line noting that the city was named after Julia, Augustus' wife, followed by our extant line about Julia the daughter. This possibility, however, is not directly confirmed by any of the extant manuscripts. If some such error happened, the original scribal blunder must have taken place in one of the early generations of copying. All other copies must then have been lost, and only the errant copy must have served as the parent manuscript of all subsequent copies.

Another attempt to deal with this problem is to assume that Josephus is not using "daughter" in the literal sense. Rather, he is referring to Livia-Julia, not as the physical daughter of Augustus, but as the daughter of the Julian clan—a status officially conferred upon her when she was adopted into the *gens Iulia*. While this interpretation is tempting and would eliminate a jumble of exegetical gymnastics, it is difficult to reconcile with its context. Just two sentences earlier in the *Ant.* Josephus refers to Livia-Julia unambiguously as the wife of Augustus, after whom Antipas renamed Betharamphtha. If Josephus has just referred to her as wife, it is unlikely that he would, almost immediately afterward, refer to the same woman as daughter of Augustus without any explanation.

Another approach to the problem, which does not necessarily exclude some of those mentioned above, begins with the extant text and an analysis of Josephus' linguistic usage. Josephus uses Julia as a proper name sixteen times in two different works: the *JW* and *Ant*. Of those sixteen references, twelve refer to Livia-Julia.[23] Only three refer to Julia, the daughter of Augustus[24]; the only two other than the passage under consideration mention merely that she was the mother of the one-time heir to the empire, Gaius Caesar. Purely in terms of preference and the amount of attention he pays to each of these women there can be no question that Josephus considers Livia-Julia to be the more important of the Julias and, presumably, more worthy of having a city named after her. One might ask why he specifically mentions Julia the daughter in *Ant.* 18.28. Perhaps more importantly, why does he not mention her in the earlier account in *JW*?

One hint emerges from the parallel accounts. Where Josephus mentions the renaming of Bethsaida in his earlier *JW,* he does so in an important context. Archelaus has just been deposed and his ethnarchy reduced to a province (6 CE). Salome, at her death shortly thereafter, bequeathed her Toparchy to "Julia, wife of Augustus."[25] Upon the death of Augustus (14 CE), the helm of empire passed to Tiberias, "the son of Julia."[26] Philip and Antipas, meanwhile, continued to maintain their respective tetrarchies and built (κτίζει) cities, each of which was named for the imperial household: Caesarea, Tiberias, and the two towns renamed Julias. In this context, there is only one Julia, and she is mentioned repeatedly: the wife, Livia. In addition, Josephus makes no distinction here between the Julia after whom Betharamphtha is named and the Julia whose name Philip attached to Bethsaida.[27] The most reasonable interpretation of this passage is that both cities were named after the same woman. If we had only this description, there would be no controversy. This passage combined with Philip's coins featuring Julia Augusta clinches the matter, in my opinion, making it virtually certain that Philip renamed Bethsaida in honor of Livia-Julia, the wife of Augustus.

Why, then, did Josephus change his story when he covered the same ground in his *Ant.?* Here the context is somewhat different. By the time he reaches book 18, Josephus has already had occasion to mention Julia, the wife of Augustus, six times, most often to explain her close relationship with the house of Herod.[28] In addition, immediately after *Ant.* 18.28, the same Julia is mentioned two more times. Julia the daughter, on the other hand, has received only one mention, a passing reference that she was the mother of Gaius Caesar. The immediate context of *Ant.* 18.28 refers to the machinations of Quirinius after the deposition of Archelaus. Meanwhile, Herod Antipas fortified Sepphoris and Betharamphtha "which he called Julias after the emperor's wife."[29] Tiberias is not mentioned. Philip likewise made improvements in cities, including Paneas, which he called Caesarea, and Bethsaida, which he elevated to the status of a polis "by adding residents and strengthening the fortifications. He named it after Julia, the emperor's daughter," according to Feldman's translation.[30]

There are some significant translation problems with this sentence. First, what does Josephus mean by τῇ ἄλλῃ δυνάμει, which Feldman interprets as "strengthening the fortifications"? Since recent excavation has turned up no evidence of wall-building or strengthening of the fortifications in the Roman period, such a translation is suspect (though future excavation could, of course, overturn this verdict). In addition, Feldman's translation does not take into account Josephus' usage of δύναμις, a term that appears with considerable frequency, 538 times in four works: 328 in *Ant.*, 162 in *JW*, 30 in *Vita.*, and 18 in *Contra Apion*. Never in all of these occurrences does Josephus use the word δύναμις to refer to fortifications. Rather, four meanings of the word predominate. Thirty-one times Josephus uses it to refer to the power of God; 15 times it refers to the physical strength of a person; 47 times to political power. However, by far the most common way in which Josephus uses δύναμις is for military forces: 372 times it refers to bands of troops or armies, often appearing in the singular as a military force.[31] Only the last two usages are possible in the present context. It is possible that Josephus meant that Philip invested Julias with some political power it did not have before, but such an interpretation is hindered by the fact that Josephus commonly uses δύναμις to refer to the political power of a person, not of a city. In accordance with the preponderance of Josephus' usage, therefore, it is probably best to interpret this phrase as a reference to the stationing of an additional military contingent, perhaps a garrison, at Julias.[32]

Now that we have determined the meaning of δύναμις, we must analyze the use of the instrumental datives of which δυνάμει is a part. Do they denote means or cause? Should the sentence be rendered, Philip elevated Bethsaida to the status of a polis *by means of* [adding] many residents and another military garrison? or *because* [it already had] many residents and another military garrison? Both can claim some grammatical justification.[33] Here, the "another" seems to be the determining factor. Josephus uses ἄλλα δύναμις seven times; six of those seven appear with reference to two military contingents.[34] While one group handles a particular duty, the "other force" either does something else or reinforces the first group. The two closest parallels occur in *JW* 2.507 and 4.445. The first instance refers to one force sent to garrison Joppa, while "another force" would later come to reinforce them. In the second, Vespasian stationed a garrison at Ammaus, taking "the rest of his forces" to Bethleteptenpha.[35] Based upon such usage, as well as the context in which Josephus mentions the elevation of Bethsaida, the problematic phrase can only be meaningful if Josephus intended to convey the idea that Philip added another force (perhaps to bolster a minor contingent that was already stationed there), especially given the fact that the instrumental dative of means is by far the more common usage. Further, the idea of importing residents to bolster the prestige of a city is not without precedent: Antipas had done just that a few years earlier with Tiberias.[36] I therefore suggest that the problematic sentence be rendered "He also raised the village of Bethsaida on Lake Gennesaret to the status of a polis by means of adding many residents and reinforcing its military garrison."

Beyond the considerable problems of translating this passage, what is to be done with the reference to Julia, the daughter of Augustus? In context, Julia the wife appears with considerable frequency both before this passage, and immediately afterward.[37] Within such a context, Josephus' reference to the daughter of Augustus seems gratuitous and intrusive. Why is there this discrepancy between *JW* and *Ant.?* Did Josephus, in the intervening time between the writing of the two works, find out that he had been wrong to imply in his *JW* that Philip had named this city after Livia-Julia? Might he have been involved in some sort of imperial campaign to rehabilitate the reputation of the fallen daughter Julia? Such reconstructions are not only inherently improbable but lack any corroborating evidence.[38] In addition, it is difficult to imagine that Josephus was ignorant of Philip's coins struck in honor of Julia Augusta.

It seems to me that the simplest answer to this problem lies in the text itself. Josephus' reference in the *Ant.*, two sentences earlier, to the woman after whom Antipas named Betharamphtha is unambiguous—it is named after Julia the emperor's wife.[39] The later statement about the renaming of Bethsaida, however, is not nearly so clear. A literal translation is: "he called it the same name as Julia, the daughter of the emperor." Josephus does not write unequivocally, as he did above, that Bethsaida was *named after* this Julia. Rather, he says that the city and Julia the daughter share the same name. This may indeed mean that Philip named the city after her, but that is not a necessary interpretation. The crux of the problem is the translation of ὁμώνυμος, a term that Josephus employs twenty-four times in three different works.[40] In some instances it does indeed refer to something that is named after something or someone else. There are cases, however, where Josephus uses this word simply to express the idea that two things happen to share the same name. In *Ant.* 13.313 he notes that there are two places that share the name Straton's Tower.[41] Two men who are not related happen to share the name Pacorus, in *Ant.* 14.333.[42] Herod the Great had two sons who were named Antipater (with no implication that one was named after the other; *Ant.* 17.19). Similarly, two unrelated Egyptians bore the same name (*Contra Apion* 1.232–233). Although ὁμώνυμος can refer to something named after something else, such is not always the case, at least according to Josephus' usage, for it also may refer to a mere coincidence of names.

A knowledge of Josephus' linguistic habits is necessary to a sound interpretation of the final phrase of *Ant.* 18.28, but it is not sufficient of itself; one must ultimately take into account the literary and historical context in which it appears. Josephus may well have considered that he had already mentioned Livia-Julia so often, including what seemed to be an unequivocal connection between the Augusta and the city in Gaulanitis in his earlier *JW,* that it would be obvious to his readers that she is the only important Julia, the only Julia worthy of having a city named after her. He may well have assumed that his readers would know the importance of this Julia, her friendship with the house of Herod (which he discusses in depth earlier in the same work), her appearance on Philip's coins, and her association with the imperial cult. In short, precisely because it is so clear to Josephus that there is only one important Julia, he probably assumed that his readers would share his knowledge and assumptions. He could therefore think that he would add no confusion by tagging on an additional, if gratuitous, note mentioning that the daughter of Augustus also happened to share the same name as the newly elevated polis.[43]

In conclusion, Josephus' note in *JW* that Philip gave to Bethsaida the name of Julias clearly means that the city was named after the wife of the emperor. In the later *Ant.,* Josephus made some significant changes, including a reference that might be interpreted to mean that the newly designated polis of Julias was named after Julia the daughter of Augustus, and not Livia-Julia the wife. This interpretation, however, is not necessary and, given the precise wording of the relevant clause and the literary context in which it appears, it probably does not represent what Josephus was trying to communicate. Unfortunately, readers nearly two millennia removed do not have the luxury of sharing Josephus' literary and cultural context. From our point of view the prominence of Livia-Julia is anything but a given. Nevertheless, it is probable that Josephus assumed that his numerous references to Julia the wife and his earlier discussion of the naming of Julias, combined with the popularity of Livia-Julia and her association with the Herodian family and the imperial cult, made it unnecessary for him to make explicit what he considered obvious to his readers: There is only one Julia of sufficient dignity to receive such an honor, and it is not the profligate daughter.

If this interpretation is correct, if Philip did indeed elevate the status of Bethsaida, and renamed it Julias in 30 CE, the year after Livia-Julia died, the new polis may have served as a sort of memorial to the Augusta who had lavished her favor on the family of Philip. What then would be more appropriate than for Philip to equip his new polis with a new temple in her honor, complete with appropriate priests and rites, rites which may have required the use of an ornate bronze incense shovel and encouraged the manufacture of cultic figurines and the minting of coins featuring Julia's portrait? Whatever else the renaming of Bethsaida means, it surely represents a high point in the political fortunes of the new polis during the Roman period. It is, therefore, a fitting irony that Bethsaida's elevation in worldly status took place at perhaps the very time an itinerant rabbi from Nazareth made his way to Bethsaida, proclaiming that the Kingdom of God is not of this world.

APPENDIX OF JOSEPHUS' REFERENCES TO BETHSAIDA-JULIAS

The kingdom [of Agrippa II] beginning at Mt. Libanus and the sources of the Jordan, extends in breadth to the lake of Tiberias, and in length from a village called Arpha to Julias; it contains a mixed population of Jews and Syrians. (*JW* 3.57; trans. Thackeray)

The Jordan ... intersects the marshes and lagoons of Lake Semechonitis, then traverses another 120 stadia, and below the town of Julias, works its way through the middle of the Lake of Gennesar.... (*JW* 3.515; trans. adapted from Thackeray)

He [Philip] died in Julias. His body was carried to the tomb that he himself had erected before he died, and there was a costly funeral. (*Ant.* 18.108; trans. Feldman)

Sulla [commander of the troops of King Agrippa II] pitched his camp at a distance of five stadia from Julias, and put out pickets on the roads leading to Seleucia and to the fortress of Gamla, to prevent the inhabitants from obtaining supplies from Galilee. On receiving intelligence of this, I dispatched a force of two thousand men under the command of Jeremiah, who entrenched themselves a stadion away from Julias close to the river Jordan.... The next day, after laying an ambuscade in a ravine not far from their earthworks, I offered battle to the royal troops.... And my success on that day would have been complete, had I not been thwarted by some evil genius. The horse on which I went into action stumbled on a marshy spot and brought me with him to the ground. Having fractured some bones in the wrist, I was carried to a village called Cepharnocus [Capernaum].... [That night, Sulla launched a counter assault], killing six of our men. They did not, however, follow up their success; for, on hearing that reinforcements shipped at Taricheae had reached Julias, they retired in alarm. (*Vita* 398–406; trans. Thackeray)

## CHAPTER NOTES

1. Save rabbinic literature. For more on this, see Freund (1995).
2. *Ant.* 18.28.
3. *JW* 2.168; 3.57; 3.515; *Vita* 398; 399; 406; *Ant.* 18.28; 18.108.
4. μεταβάσης δὲ εἰς Τιβέριον τὸν Ἰουλίας υἱὸν τῆς Ῥωμαίων ἡγεμονίας μετὰ τὴν Αὐγούστου τελευτήν ... διαμείναντες ἐν ταῖς τετραρχίαις ὅ τε Ἡρώδης καὶ ὁ Φίλιππος, ὁ μὲν πρὸς ταῖς τοῦ Ἰορδάνου πηγαῖς ἐν Πανεάδι πόλιν κτίζει Καισάρειαν, κἀν τῇ κάτω Γαυλανιτικῇ Ἰουλιάδα, Ἡρώδης δ᾽ ἐν μὲν τῇ Γαλιλαίᾳ Τιβεριάδα, ἐν δὲ τῇ Περαίᾳ φερώνυμον Ἰουλιας; see Thackeray (1926–1927) *JW* 2.168. All translations are my own unless otherwise indicated.
5. καὶ Ἡρώδης Σέπφωριν τειχίσας πρόσχημα τοῦ Γαλιλαίου παντὸς ἠγόρευεν αὐτὴν Αὐτοκρατορίδα. Βηθαραμφθᾶ δέ, πόλις καὶ αὐτὴ τυγχάνει, τείχει περιλαβὼν Ἰουλιάδα ἀπὸ τοῦ αὐτοκράτορος προσαγορεύει τῆς γυναικός. Φίλιππος δὲ Πανεάδα τὴν πρὸς ταῖς πηγαῖς τοῦ Ἰορδάνου κατασκευάσας ὀνομάζει Καισάρειαν, κώμην δὲ Βηθσαϊδὰ πρὸς λίμνη τῇ Γεννησαρίτιδι πόλεως παρασχὼν ἀξίωμα πλήθει τε οἰκητόρων καὶ τῇ ἄλλῃ δυνάμει· Ἰουλίᾳ θυγατρὶ τῇ Καίσαρος ὁμώνυμον ἐκάλεσεν; (*Ant.* 18.27–8, ed. Feldman). Jones (1937), 283, suggests, despite Josephus' specific language, that Julias was not a polis: "It was merely the capital of the Toparchy of Gaulanitis."
6. It is possible to enumerate as many as five different women who are named Julia in the same period. According to Greene (1999), they are: Julia I, the wife of Julius Caesar; Julia II, Livia, the wife of Augustus; Julia III, the daughter of Augustus; Julia IV, the daughter of Julia III; Julia V, Julia Livilla, the daughter of Germanicus.
7. *JW* 2.168; 2.252; 4.438; 4.454; *Ant.* 18.27; 20.159. This last reference is curiously identified as Bethsaida-Julias in Rousseau and Arav (1995) 317.
8. Jones (1937), 79, considers this Julias also to be the capital of a Toparchy.
9. Suetonius, *Aug.*, 65.
10. Dio 55.10.12–16; cf. Syme, 425ff.
11. This is not to overlook her political manipulations or her tendency to lord it over her son, Tiberius, not to mention the numerous other faults, some of which may be nothing more than scurrilous gossip, collected in the pages of Tacitus. For further discussion, see Greene (1999); cf. Syme, 385; cf. Ferrero, 52.
12. Tacitus, *Annals* 1.8; Dio 56.46.
13. For further discussion, see Grether (1946).
14. Giacosa (1977) 24.
15. On the problematic relationship between the *JW* and the *Ant.*, see Cohen (1979) 48–66.
16. This is the solution suggested by Schürer (1973) 1:339; 2:171–172. Jones (1967) 174–175, seems also to have favored this solution.
17. Meshorer (no. 11), 42, 246; cf. Strickert (1995).
18. Meshorer, Supplement III (no. 1), 278; cf. Strickert (1995). Another coin issued by Philip features the jugate heads of Julia and Augustus on the obverse, together with the inscription, ΣΕΒΑΣΤΩΝ (of the Augusti). The genitive plural form of this inscription must include Julia as Augusta. Unfortunately, this is one of the few coins of Philip that do not bear a date, though it cannot have appeared earlier than 14 CE, when Julia was granted the title Augusta. Strickert (1995) argues that this issue should also be dated to 30 CE.
19. Cf. "Ktistes," in Rousseau and Arav (1995) 67.
20. So Rousseau and Arav (1995) 67; cf. Kuhn and Arav (1995) 87–90.
21. The only one is Ἰουλίαν for Ἰουλίᾳ, which offers no help with the problem at hand.
22. See Greene (1999), based upon a suggestion by R. Freund.

23. *JW* 2.167; 2.168 (twice); *Ant.* 16.139; 17.10, 11, 141, 146, 190; 18.27, 31, 33; 19.251. In addition, there are three places where Josephus refers to the wife of Augustus as Livia; see *JW* 1.566 and 1.641 (twice).
24. *JW* 2.25; *Ant.* 17.229; 18.28. The only other reference to a Julia is to the sister of Gaius (*Ant.* 19.251).
25. *JW* 2.167.
26. *JW* 2.168.
27. That Betharamphtha-Julias was named after Livia-Julia is confirmed by Eusebius, who refers to the town as Livias, seven times; Eusebius (1966) 12, 16, 44, 48 (thrice), 168. As late as the sixth century, Georgius Cyprius still referred to the town as Livias; ed. Gelzer, 1016, 1018, 1019. For further discussion, see Jones (1937) 273–77; cf. Kuhn and Arav (1991) 89.
28. For further discussion, see Grant (1971) 143, 191, 203.
29. ...'Ιουλιάδα ἀπό τοῦ αὐτοκράτορος προσαγορεύει τῆς γυναικός.
30. Καίσαρος ὁμώνυμον ἐκάλεσεν(*Ant.* 18.28).
31. One hundred ninety-six in *Ant.* alone, 29 in *Vita*, 12 in *C. Ap.*, 135 in *JW* .
32. Josephus does use δύναμις to refer to a garrison in a city, nine times (*Ant.* 8.303, 393, 13.16; *Vita* 411; *JW* 1.46, 210, 2.332, 448, 5.510). I owe this suggestion to Rev. Michael Turner, who was a volunteer at Bethsaida in 1996.
33. Smyth (1920) 346–49; cf. Kuhn and Arav (1991) 80.
34. *JW* 2.507; 4.445, 663; 6.243; 7.230; *C. Ap.* 1.277. The one completely different usage refers to political power: Agrippa did not seek "other privileges"; see *Ant.* 18.300.
35. Translation by Thackeray (1926–1927).
36. *Ant.* 18.36–38, only a couple of pages after the reference to Bethsaida.
37. *Ant.* 18.31, in which Salome wills her Toparchy to Julia, and *Ant.* 18.33, where Julia is noted as the mother of the newly ascendant Tiberius.
38. For further discussion, see Greene (1997).
39. See n. 29 above.
40. *JW* 1.80, 249, 418; 3.516, 521; 5.152; 7.180; *Ant.* 5.178, 9 p.5; 13.62, 313; 14.333; 16.145; 17.19, 28; 18.28, 140; 19.119, 125; 20.149; 236; *C. Ap.* 1.232, 233; 2.39.
41. Cf. *JW* 1.80.
42. Cf. *JW* 1.249.
43. This interpretation would, of course, be supported by the theory of a scribal error caused by a homoioteleuton. An additional line could certainly go a long way toward alleviating the awkwardness of Josephus' intrusive comment.
44. *JW* 3.57; trans. Thackeray (1926-1927).
45. *JW* 3.515; trans. adapted from Thackeray (1926-1927).
46. *Ant.* 18.108; trans. Feldman (1965).
47. *Vita* 398–406; trans. Thackeray (1926-1927). For a thorough discussion of the Battle of Bethsaida, see Greene (1995).

## LITERATURE CITED

Arav, Rami, and Richard A. Freund. 1995. *Bethsaida: A City on the North Shore of the Sea of Galilee.* Vol. 1. Kirksville, MO: Thomas Jefferson University Press.

Cohen, S. 1979. *Josephus in Galilee and Rome.* Leiden: E.J. Brill.

Dio, Cassius. 1914–1927. *Dio's Roman History.* Translated by Earnest Cary. Loeb Classical Library. 9 vols. London: W. Heinemann.

Eusebius of Caesarea. [1904] 1966. *Eusebius Werke.* Bd. 3.1, *Das Onomastikon der biblischen Ortsnamen.* Edited by E. Klostermann. Reprinted: Hildesheim: Olms

Feldman, L. 1965. *Jewish Antiquities,* books 18–20. Translated by L. H. Feldman. Vol. 9 of: Flavius Josephus (1958–1965; q.v.)

Ferrero, G. [1911] 1993. *The Women of the Caesars.* New York: Barnes and Noble.

Freund, R. 1995. The Search for Bethsaida in Rabbinic Literature. Pp. 267-311 in: Arav and Freund (*q.v.*).

Giacosa, G. 1977. *Women of the Caesars: Their Lives and Portraits on Coins.* Translated by R. Holloway. Milan: Edizioni Arte e Moneta.

Grant, M. 1971. *Herod the Great.* New York: McGraw-Hill.

Greene, J. 1995. Bethsaida-Julias in Roman and Jewish Military Strategies, 66–73 CE. Pp. 203–227 in: Arav and Freund (q.v).

———. 1999. The Honorific Naming of Bethsaida-Julias. Pp. 307–331 of this volume.

Grether, G. 1946. Livia and the Roman Imperial Cult. *AJP* 67: 222–252.

Jones, A. H. M. 1931. The Urbanization of Palestine. *JRS* 21, 78–85.

———. 1937. *The Cities of the Eastern Roman Provinces.* Oxford: Clarendon Press.

———. 1967. *The Herods of Judaea.* Oxford: Clarendon Press.

Josephus, Flavius. 1958–1965. *Works.* Loeb Classical Library. Cambridge, MA: Harvard University Press.[Reprint of 1926–1965 edition].

Klostermann, E. [1904] 1966. S.v. Eusebius of Caesarea.

Kuhn, H. W., and R. Arav. 1991. The Bethsaida Excavations: Historical and Archaeological Approaches. Pp. 77–106 of: *The Future of Early Christianity: Essays in Honor of Helmut Koester.* Ed. B. A. Pearson. Philadelphia: Fortress Press.

Meshorer, Ya'akov. 1982. *Ancient Jewish Coinage,* vol. 2, *Herod the Great through Bar Cochba.* Dix Hills, N.Y.: Amphora Books.

Rousseau J., and R. Arav. 1995. *Jesus and His World: An Archaeological and Cultural Dictionary.* Minneapolis: Fortress Press.

Schürer, E. 1973. *The History of the Jewish People in the Age of Jesus Christ.* 3 vols. Revised editon. Edited by Geza Vermes, Fergus Millar, and Matthew Black. Edinburgh: T&T Clark.

Suetonius. 1914. *Suetonius.* Translated by J. C. Rolfe. Loeb Classical Library. 2 vols. London: W. Heinemann.

Smyth, H. W. [1920] 1956. *Greek Grammar.* Cambridge, MA: Harvard University Press.

Strickert, F. 1995. The Coins of Philip. Pp. 165–189 in: Arav and Freund (q.v.).

Syme, R. 1939. *The Roman Revolution.* Oxford: Oxford University Press.

Tacitus, Cornelius. 1977. *The Annals of Imperial Rome.* Translated by M. Grant. Penguin Classics. Harmondsworth: Penguin Books.

Thackeray, H. 1926–1927. Volumes 1–3 of Flavius Josephus (1958–1965; q.v.).

*Fred Strickert*

# The Destruction of Bethsaida: The Evidence of 2 Esdras 1:11

A VERY CAREFUL READER of the New Revised Standard Version of the Bible may notice what may be critical evidence for dating the destruction of Bethsaida. The editors for the New Revised Standard Version of the Bible include a variant reading in a footnote for 2 Esdras 1:11: "Did I not destroy the city of Bethsaida because of you?'

At first glance, this note seems insignificant and one is tempted to discard it as a very late gloss derived from the imagination of a medieval reader of the Gospels. At second glance, one ponders numerous questions as seemingly insurmountable obstacles: How can something written in the Old Testament apocrypha shed light on the destruction of a town described as thriving in the time of the New Testament? Why does this detail show up in, of all places, such an obscure apocalyptic book? Why isn't the book even included in Catholic Bibles? Why isn't this detail even mentioned in any other modern English edition of the apocrypha?[1] Why is it only preserved in a footnote? With these questions before us, it would seem far-fetched to suggest that this detail could be valuable for our study of the history of Bethsaida. Yet in this chapter I argue that this statement was written in the mid-second century and that it is our most valuable piece of literary evidence concerning the destruction of Bethsaida during an early-second-century earthquake.

## The Development of 2 Esdras

One must begin with a brief discussion of the complex development of the apocryphal book called Second Esdras. This book is part of a body of literature that is often called pseudepigrapha because it is connected with a famous biblical figure—in this case the scribe Ezra who helped rally the returning exiles in the fifth century BCE around the law. Second Esdras is actually a composite work for which the core is a Jewish apocalyptic work that deals with the significance of the destruction of Jerusalem by the Romans in 70 CE.[2] For this reason it is sometimes included in the Old Testament apocrypha although it was in fact written at the close of the New Testament era, perhaps shortly before 100 CE.[3] This dating fits the author's own remarks, which set Ezra's speech to "the thirtieth year after the destruction of the city" (2 Esdras 3:1).[4] This work survives both independently in numerous manuscripts and in an expanded form of the Bible; at times it is treated independently under the title Fourth Ezra.

Fourth Ezra, however, was not included in the Septuagint—the Greek translation of the Old Testament—and its place in the apocrypha came about because of Christian additions to the work.[5] These Christian additions, known as Fifth Ezra and Sixth Ezra, were appended at beginning and end of the document so that the present 2 Esdras is structured as follows:

> 5th Ezra = 2 Esdras 1–2
> 4th Ezra = 2 Esdras 3–14
> 6th Ezra = 2 Esdras 15–16.[6]

Although this document was included in many manuscripts of the Vulgate of the Middle Ages, it was not accepted as either canonical or deuterocanonical[7] by the Council of Trent in 1563. The Clementine revision of the Vulgate in 1592 incorporated deuterocanonical works within the Old Testament, but placed 1 and 2 Esdras along with the Prayer of Manasseh as a supplement following the New Testament. Therefore, just as 2 Esdras is not usually included in Greek Orthodox Bibles because it was not in the Septuagint, so it is not usually included today in Roman Catholic Bibles because of sixteenth-century Tridentine decisions. Since Protestants often separated the Apocrypha into an appendix, 2 Esdras was often included in Protestant Bibles.[8]

## MANUSCRIPT HISTORY OF 2 ESDRAS 1–2

The section which concerns us—2 Esdras 1–2 = Fifth Ezra—survives in nine Latin manuscripts dating from the ninth through the thirteenth centuries. This may appear to be extremely late compared to New Testament textual studies. However, this is quite typical when compared to the preservation of many other ancient works. The reference to Bethsaida in 2 Esdras 2:11 first occurs in the tenth-century Manuscript Complutensis and then in six others.[9] The earlier Manuscript Sangermanensis (822 CE) and Manuscript Ambianensis (ninth century) do not include the reading of Bethsaida. On the basis of the principle of the earliest reading as most accurate, some reservation is merited. However, the issue is much more complicated.

Critical textual study demonstrates extensive variation among manuscripts so that two different recensions occur. MSS CKMNEVL all comprise the Spanish family of manuscripts while MSS SA comprise the French family. The problem is that no full critical edition has ever been published for the text. The Stuttgart Vulgate in Germany[10] and the Bensly edition in the United States[11] have followed the French text uncritically just as did the 1592 Clementine Revision of the Vulgate.[12] Thus English Bibles today are based on the French recension of 2 Esdras. At least the New Revised Standard Version has included Spanish readings in the footnotes.

All this is surprising, because there are a number of scholars who believe the Spanish recension to be authentic. Perhaps the greatest irony is that M. R. James wrote the introduction for the Bensly edition, published posthumously, and included a long list of readings from the Spanish recension—including 2 Esdras 1:11—which he considered authentic.[13] The commentary of W. O. E. Oesterley is very much dependent on the work of James and is in agreement with his assessment of the Spanish manuscripts,[14] while most other commentaries have continued to rely on the French family of manuscripts.[15] Interestingly, in the 1964 edition of the Hennecke-Schneemelcher *New Testament Apocrypha*, volume 2, *Writings Relating to the Apostles; Apocalypses and Related Subjects*, H. Duensing argues for the superiority of the French manuscripts, yet he does include several readings from the Spanish manuscripts including the mention of Bethsaida in 2 Esdras 1:11.[16]

More recently, Robert Kraft has demonstrated sympathy toward the readings in the Spanish text and has argued that scholarship on

2 Esdras cannot continue until the textual questions are dealt with and a critical edition is produced.[17] In fact, Kraft avoids the term "recension" suggesting that the major differences do not result from textual transmission, but from the process of translation from Greek to Latin. This is a point that needs to be stressed. In my opinion, the Spanish text reflects a Palestinian provenance and may represent a literal translation. The French text reflects a European provenance and appears to be a free revision. Kraft directed a dissertation by Theodore Bergren which carries out an extensive textual study that demonstrates the value of the Spanish manuscripts.[18] Bergren also includes a Latin edition that is highly dependent on these Spanish readings and opts for the Spanish reading—Bethsaida—in 2 Esdras 1:11. While the recent New Revised Standard Version has for the first time included in footnotes significant variants from the Spanish family, one can expect that many of them will be incorporated into future editions. What this means is that the Bethsaida reading in 2 Esdras 1:11—up until now mostly ignored—must be taken very seriously.

## 2 ESDRAS 1:11 IN CONTEXT: THE BAR KOKHBA REVOLT

While 4 Ezra (= 2 Esdras 3–14) is a Jewish reflection on the significance of the destruction of the Jerusalem temple in 70 CE, 5 Ezra (= 2 Esdras 1–2), in the words of Jacob Myers, "looks like a polemic against Jews on the part of a Christian leader who was himself involved in the conflict between mother and daughter."[19] It opens with Ezra commissioned as a prophet to contrast the misdeeds of the people with the mighty acts of God. These mighty acts begin with the Exodus and include deliverance through the sea, guidance by a pillar of fire, feeding with manna and quail, and providing water from a rock. In addition, God shows a strong arm destroying "many kings because of them" and culminating in the destruction of Tyre and Sidon, and, in the Spanish manuscripts, also of Bethsaida. According to this author, Israel's rejection of the Lord however leads to their own house becoming desolate: "I will hand over your houses to a people coming from far away, and those who have not known me will believe me" (1:35). Following this prophetic indictment of God's people, assurance of redemption is offered for the new people (2:10–48).

2 Esdras 1–2 has generally been dated to the middle of the second century with dates ranging from 130 CE to 200 CE.[20] Therefore, one must be open to any date up until the end of the second

century. However, there are a number of arguments which point per-
suasively to a date on the early end of this range. It accurately reflects
the situation shortly after the Bar Kochba Revolt in 132–135 CE.[21] Just
as 2 Esdras 3–15 reflects on the significance of the destruction of Jerusalem in 70 CE, so now this later section seeks answers and comfort in
the face of the further developments. The destruction in this region by
the Romans at this time was extensive as Dio Cassius reports:

> Fifty of their most important outposts and nine hundred and
> eighty-five of their most famous villages were razed to the
> ground. Five hundred and eighty thousand men were slain in
> the various raids and battles, and the number of those that
> perished by famine, disease and fire was past finding out. Thus
> nearly the whole of Judea was made desolate.[22]

This fits the description in 2 Esdras 2:6 of Jerusalem as destroyed and
her people scattered.[23] Because the Christians in the writer's community were also affected, the revolt has brought about the final split
with Judaism.

This revolt came about shortly after a visit to the area by the
emperor Hadrian around 129–131 CE. Two of his actions brought
about the revolt. First Dio Cassius reports that Hadrian attempted to
rebuild Jerusalem and establish a pagan shrine on the site of the
temple:

> At Jerusalem he founded a city in place of the one which had
> been razed to the ground, naming it Aelia Capitolina, and on
> the site of the temple of the god he raised a new temple to
> Jupiter. This brought on a war of no slight importance nor of
> brief duration, for the Jews deemed it intolerable that foreign
> races should be settled in their city and foreign religious rites
> planted there.[24]

While chapters 3–14 demonstrate a struggle over the fate of the
temple and chapter 10 especially speaks in detail of the fate of temple
furnishings, this later writer is no longer open to rebuilding the temple. Like the Old Testament prophets (Isaiah 1:10–17; Amos 5:21–24;
Jeremiah 7:1–15),[25] the writer speaks out in the strongest terms
against the temple:

> When you offer sacrifices to me, I will turn my eyes from you,
> for I did not command you to observe feast days, new moons,
> sabbaths and circumcisions. (2 Esdras 1:31)[26]

There is no doubt that the prophetic tradition is held in high esteem and most of the written prophets are mentioned by name. 2 Esdras 2:18 mentions the major prophets Isaiah and Jeremiah, while only Ezekiel is omitted perhaps because his message, following the destruction of the temple of Solomon, spoke in detail of its rebuilding. In the Spanish recension, the list of minor prophets in 2 Esdras 1:39 glaringly omits Haggai (and possibly Malachi[27] and the postexilic Zechariah), who would be out of place as a prophet who called for and witnessed the rebuilding of the second temple. While 2 Esdras 3–14 had mourned the destruction of the temple and struggled over its future, the later writer is resolved that it will not be rebuilt.

The one detail from 2 Esdras 1:31 that is not included in Isaiah 1:10–17—or in the prophets in general—is the comment about circumcision. This is significant, because the second cause of the Jewish revolt was a ban on circumcision. While Domitian and Nerva had previously banned castration, it was Hadrian who made circumcision illegal. Since this was the sign of the covenant with Abraham, the ban became the major issue of the revolt.[28] For Christians since the time of Paul, however, it was no longer a critical issue and thus cause for even further division between Jews and Christians. Since the ban was lifted for Jewish people after Antonius Pius became emperor in 138 CE, a date before this time is likely for the writing of 2 Esdras 1–2.

Finally, Justin Martyr notes that the Bar Kochba revolt was a time of persecution against Christians by those who recognized the messianic claims of the revolt's leader.[29] 2 Esdras 1–2 notes how they have experienced hardship and persecution (2:23–32), yet they have endured through their confession of the Son of God (2:42–48). This work shows evidence that the "separation of the church from Israel is felt so keenly in 5 Ezra that it may well have been a recent event."[30] Thus the metaphor of mother and sons occurs a number of times (2:10, 15, 17, 31) so that it is clear that Christians and Jews have shared the same mother (Jerusalem)[31] and now the coming people inherit the privileges of Israel.

## 2 ESDRAS 1–2 AND THE GOSPEL ACCORDING TO MATTHEW

This early date for 2 Esdras 1–2 is supported by a careful analysis of its literary relationship with other Christian documents. It is surprising that connections with the New Testament are extremely rare except for the Gospel of Matthew. It is true that commentaries often list phrases and parallels to other writings, but that does not establish dependence. In a very important article, "5 Ezra and Matthean Christianity," G. N. Stanton has taken the approach of demonstrating a close connection between 2 Esdras 1–2 and the themes of Matthew.[32]

Stanton notes that the themes of 2 Esdras 1–2 are a development of one particular section of Matthew, namely chapters 21 through 25. A key sentence is strategically placed among the parables of the Two Sons, The Wicked Tenants, and the Wedding Banquet: "Therefore, I tell you, the kingdom of God will be taken away from you and given to a people that produces the fruits of the kingdom" (Matthew 21:43).[33] This fits well the picture of the "people to come" (2 Esdras 1:35,38) taking the place of Jacob and Judah (1:24)[34] and inheriting the "kingdom of Jerusalem" (2:10).[35] He notes however, that 2 Esdras 1–2 is less polemical (against Jewish opponents) and more apologetic, trying to give comfort to Christians who are suffering in this separation[36] and emphasizing the continuity with the traditions of ancient Israel, especially the law and the prophets.[37]

While Stanton's approach focuses on a very close thematic relationship between 2 Esdras 1–2 and Matthew,[38] one can also establish a clear connection on the basis of redactional analysis. 2 Esdras 1:30–33 provides a close parallel to Matthew 23:34–38 (NRSV).

| 2 ESDRAS 1:30–33<br>(BERGREN [1989], 402) | MATTHEW 23:34–38<br>(NRSV) |
|---|---|
| [30] *"I gathered you as a hen gathers her chicks under her wings.* But now, what will I do to you? I will cast you forth from my presence! [31]When you offer sacrifices to me, I will turn my eyes from you, for I did not command you to observe feast days, new moons, sabbaths and circumcisions. [32] *I sent* my servants the *prophets to you,* but you took them and *killed them,* and tore to pieces the bodies of the apostles. I will require their souls and blood, says the Lord. [33]Thus says the Lord Almighty: *Your house is desolate!"* | [34] *"Therefore I send you prophets,* sages, and scribes, some of whom you will *kill* and crucify, and some you will flog in your synagogues and pursue from town to town, [35]so that upon you may come all the righteous blood shed on earth, from the blood of righteous Abel to the blood of Zechariah son of Barachiah, whom you murdered between the sanctuary and the altar. [36]Truly I tell you, all this will come upon this generation. [37]Jerusalem, Jerusalem, the city that kills the prophets and stones those who are sent to it! How often have *I* desired to *gather your* children together *as a hen gathers her brood under her wings,* and you were not willing! See, *your house* is left to you *desolate."* |

This Q material also is found in Luke, although it occurs in two different chapters (Luke 11:49–51 and 13:34–35). This is significant since Luke is generally thought to reflect the order of Q.[39] While it is possible that the writer of 2 Esdras 1–2 was drawing on Q or on the oral tradition, it is more likely that he was directly dependent on Matthew, who has joined this material together in one section.

One of the conclusions of Stanton is highly significant. Not only is 2 Esdras 1–2 dependent on Matthew, it was "not acquainted with any other part of the New Testament."[40] This would lead us to ask whether 2 Esdras comes from the same community, or at least a similar community, as that which produced Matthew's Gospel, yet perhaps a generation later. Bergren describes the situation:

> The author seems to be writing in a period where there is still lively debate between his own party [the Christians] and the opposition [Palestinian Judaism], and where the relationship between the two is still viewed in terms of continuity rather than diametric opposition.[41]

This fits well the situation shortly after the writing of Matthew's Gospel and would cause us to look in the vicinity of Syria as the location also of 2 Esdras 1–2.[42]

The connections between the Matthean community and 2 Esdras 1–2 are fitting since the reference to Bethsaida's destruction in 2 Esdras 1:11 is clearly related to the woe saying of Jesus in Matthew 11:20–24.[43] In that Q saying, Jesus' pronouncement of woe against Bethsaida, and also Chorazin, is linked to earlier destructions of Tyre and Sidon. Jesus had performed so many deeds of power in these two cities that even the ancient cities would have repented (Matthew 11:20–22 = Luke 10:13–14). The saying continues with a word of condemnation against a third city of Jesus' time, Capernaum, which will "be brought down to Hades" (Matthew 11:23 = Luke 10:15). Matthew 11:23b–24, but not Luke, goes on to compare Capernaum to another ancient city, Sodom. All three names listed in the Spanish recension of 2 Esdras 1:11 come from this saying. In addition, the description of Sodom and Gomorrah, "whose land descends to hell" in the Spanish recension of 2 Esdras 2:9, points to dependence on the Matthean version of the saying.

It is significant that 2 Esdras mentions all three Old Testament cities in 1:11 and 2:9—Tyre, Sidon, and Sodom. However, only one of the three New Testament cities, Bethsaida, is included while neglecting Chorazin and Capernaum. This points to the later writer's particular interest in Bethsaida, not merely a casual reference by a medieval scribe. It therefore requires a closer analysis of the two recensions of 2 Esdras 1:11.

## 2 Esdras 1:11—Two Recensions

The variation in 2 Esdras 1:11 between the two families of manuscripts is more than just a question of the inclusion or omission of the name Bethsaida. A more detailed comparison is in order. The two recensions read as follows:

> French MSS  I destroyed all nations before them, and scattered in the east the peoples of two provinces, Tyre and Sidon; I killed all their enemies.[44]

> Spanish MSS  Did I not destroy the city of Bethsaida because of you, and to the south burn two cities, Tyre and Sidon, with fire, and kill those who hated you?[45]

Our study of these variant readings will begin with a careful analysis of the traditionally accepted French recension.

### The French Recension of 2 Esdras 1:11

The French reading includes a number of difficulties.[46] First, the reference to the destruction of Tyre and Sidon is clearly anachronistic. It is generally assumed that the writer refers to the destruction of Sidon by Artaxerxes III in 351 BCE and of Tyre by Alexander the Great in 332 BCE. Yet the historical Ezra belongs to an earlier time period. The French manuscripts clearly identify the speaker with the Ezra of the return by listing his genealogy (2 Esdras 1:1–2) parallel to the list of names in Ezra 7:1–5 and setting him "in the land of the Medes in the reign of Artaxerxes, the king of the Persians" (2 Esdras 1:3). The Artaxerxes mentioned in Ezra 7:1, 7, is probably Artaxerxes I (465–425 BCE) or possibly Artaxerxes II (405–359 BCE), so the mention of the fall of these two cities is clearly out of place chronologically.

This may at first seem insignificant since the Spanish recension also mentions the destruction of the cities of Tyre and Sidon. However, the Spanish manuscripts include a totally different introduction so that neither "the land of the Medes" nor "the reign of Artaxerxes" is mentioned. Rather Ezra is placed in Babylon at the time of Neb-uchadnezzar.[47] The author of 2 Esdras has simply taken over the situation of Fourth Ezra in "the thirtieth year after the destruction of the city" (2 Esdras 3:1). This has a totally different effect on the reader since it does not give the aura of historical accuracy. The reader familiar with the apocalyptic genre immediately realizes that the setting is during the Roman era[48] in the shadow of the temple's destruction and with memory of the destruction of Tyre and Sidon as past events. The introduction is thus fitting. It is not difficult to see how it would have been changed by a later scribe to provide a historically accurate context for Ezra. As a result, we are left with an internal inconsistency with the reference to the destruction of Tyre and Sidon in the French manuscripts of 2 Esdras 1:11.

Second, the geography of 2 Esdras 1:11 is problematical in the French manuscripts. They refer to Tyre and Sidon "in the east" although the speaker, Ezra, is depicted as speaking from "the land of the Medes" (1:3), which is, of course, east of Tyre and Sidon. To refer to Tyre and Sidon in the east one would likely have a European perspective.[49] Is that the case with the author of 2 Esdras 1–2? This short document does include another reference to "the east" in 2 Esdras 1:38—a sentence for which both manuscript recensions are in agreement. It reads: "Now, Father, look with pride and see the people coming from the east." The situation is that a new people will be arriving now that the land has become desolate. A very close parallel occurs in Baruch 4:36–37: "Look toward the east, O Jerusalem, and see the joy that is coming to you from your God."[50] The expression "people coming from the east" is an apocalyptic designation of the returnees of the captives in Mesopotamia.[51] While the apocalyptic setting is the context of the aftermath of the sixth-century exile, a particular theme of Fourth Ezra is the return of exiles from both the Assyrian and Babylonian captivity so that there is an extensive elaboration concerning the return of the northern ten tribes (2 Esdras 13:39–50). The point is that the "land of the east" is Mesopotamia, not Tyre and Sidon.

The procession of returnees from the east is to be led by a group of "saints" from the past including the patriarchs and prophets. Here the two recensions give very different lists:

| SPANISH MANUSCRIPTS | FRENCH MANUSCRIPTS |
|---|---|
| Abraham | Abraham |
| Isaac | Isaac |
| and Jacob | and Jacob |
| Elijah | — |
| and Enoch | — |
| Zechariah | — |
| and Hosea | and Hosea |
| Amos | and Amos |
| — | and Micah |
| Joel | and Joel |
| Micah | — |
| Obadiah | and Obadiah |
| Zephaniah | and Jonah |
| Nahum | and Nahum |
| Jonah | and Habakkuk |
| Mattia | Zephaniah |
| Habakkuk | Haggai |
| — | Zechariah |
| — | and Malachi |
| and 12 angels with flowers | who is called messenger of the Lord |

In the Spanish recension the list culminates with "twelve angels bearing flowers" (1:40)—apparently symbolizing the totality of the return.[52] In the French recension, there is no mention of twelve angels, but rather Malachi is described as one "who is called messenger of the Lord." It is not difficult to see how the Latin: "et angelus duodecim cum floribus" became "et angelus domini vocatus est."[53] While the Spanish recension appears rough and spontaneous, the French recension shows signs of later development, presenting a perfect list of three patriarchs and the twelve minor prophets—in the exact order they occur in the Septuagint![54] What this demonstrates is that the French recension does not think of a procession from Mesopotamia to Palestine, but one from Jerusalem to Europe.[55] From this perspective one can understand the reference to Tyre and Sidon in the east (1:11), but not as original.

That perspective may also be reflected in a third difficulty in the French recension of 2 Esdras 1:11. Tyre and Sidon are referred to as "provinces." In reality they are cities and that is how they are mentioned in most prophetic words that recall their destruction. The French recension is the more difficult reading, but can be explained as the work of a distant scribe unfamiliar with the geography of the Middle East.

These three difficulties in the French recension of 2 Esdras 1:11 therefore cast doubt on their authenticity. However, there is one more serious question that needs to be addressed if the French manuscripts are original. How did "Bethsaida" enter the text?[56] Why would a later scribe add this detail in a book generally attached to the Old Testament? A lack of clarity suggests that the starting point must be the Spanish recension itself.

## THE SPANISH RECENSION OF 2 ESDRAS 1:11

In the Spanish recension Tyre and Sidon are not located "in the east." They are correctly listed as cities. While they are out of place in relation to the character of Ezra, they are appropriate as examples of the acts of God leading up to the destruction of Jerusalem by the Romans in the year 70 CE and the heavy-handed action in putting down the second revolt in 132–135 CE. How fitting then is the reference to a third city, Bethsaida?

THE DESTRUCTION OF BETHSAIDA. The Spanish recension of 2 Esdras 1:11 places the destruction in the context of the destruction of two other cities: Tyre and Sidon. It occurs at the end of a brief section (1:4–11) which has recounted the mighty deeds of God beginning with the defeat of the Egyptians at the Exodus and moving northward. The significance of Bethsaida is that it was located at the northern end of Palestine. It served as a boundary of separation between Eretz Israel and the diaspora. Positioned just east of the Jordan River and on the northern edge of the Sea of Galilee it was just outside the land. Its harbor provided access to cross the sea and a Roman road passed nearby for travelers on foot. The importance of Bethsaida must be linked to the return of people from the east, mentioned in 2 Esdras 1:39. A new people is coming to the land, now destroyed by the Romans, to take the place of those now scattered. Bethsaida is therefore the final stopping-off point to the land. The comments in 2 Esdras 1:11 must be understood in terms of that return.

It is important to pay close attention to the Latin texts of 2 Esdras 1:11. In the French recension the verbs are *perdidi … dissipavi … interfeci* (I destroyed … I scattered … I killed). In the Spanish recension the verbs are *everti … cremavi … interfeci*. These are translated in the New Revised Standard Version footnote as "I destroyed ... I burned ... I killed." The destruction of Bethsaida is thus contrasted with the burning of Tyre and Sidon—the burning of Sidon in 351 BCE is legendary. The verb *everto*—used with reference only to Bethsaida—literally means "overturn" or "throw down" (in contrast *perdo* means "destroy" or "ruin") and can refer to the destruction of cities by military force.[57] With regard to Bethsaida it is quite possible that the author was thinking of a destruction carried out by military activity. Josephus does mention such an important battle waged beneath the city of Bethsaida along the banks of the Jordan at the beginning of the Jewish revolt in 67 CE.[58] Yet he is completely silent regarding the status of the city. Did the battle move to the city itself? Was there a destruction? From Josephus' report it is impossible to tell. Archaeological evidence for such a battle is limited: a few arrowheads, perhaps some balustrades, but no evidence of a major conflagration.[59] More importantly, one must wonder how it is that Bethsaida would be so singled out among all the towns destroyed in the Jewish revolt and how this destruction could impact the writer more than a half-century later. What was it about this destruction that prevented them from rebuilding and continuing the history of this site. An understanding of the destruction of Bethsaida as a military defeat is possible, but not totally convincing.

The Latin term *everto*, however, more commonly refers to a natural, violent agitation of the sea or the uprooting of trees or even the ploughing up of land.[60] Thus the imagery is of structures overturned and upset. This terminology suggests that the writer was thinking not of destruction by warfare; rather it points to destruction by earthquake. The significance is that an earthquake would affect not only the city, but perhaps also the nearby Jordan River and Sea of Galilee. In other words, a shifting of the coastline outside Bethsaida and the course of the Jordan River—due to earthquake—could be interpreted as the fulfillment of this final sign, which leads to the return of the people coming from the east.

The possibility of an earthquake as cause of destruction for Bethsaida is quite high since the Jordan Rift is a major fault line. According to a recently published catalogue of earthquakes in Israel, major earthquakes are listed in 115 CE, 130 CE, 306 CE, and 363 CE.[61] The major earthquake in 363 CE destroyed twenty-one urban centers and the temple restoration project initiated by Julian in 361. Eusebius, in fact, noted the fourth-century destruction of Chorazin as the fulfillment of Jesus' words of woe in Matthew 11. Since Bethsaida was not mentioned, one can assume that it had already been destroyed.

The 115 CE earthquake is most significant for the 2 Esdras reading. This earthquake caused extensive damage in Antioch and was recorded in detail by Dio Cassius because Trajan was in the city at the time and barely escaped with his life.[62] The scene is described in vivid detail:

> While the emperor was tarrying in Antioch a terrible earthquake occurred; many cities suffered injury, but Antioch was the most unfortunate of all. Since Trajan was passing the winter there and many soldiers and many civilians had flocked thither from all sides ... there was no nation or people that went unscathed; and thus in Antioch the whole world under Roman sway suffered disaster. There had been many thunderstorms and portentous winds, but no one would ever have expected so many evils to result from them. First there came, on a sudden, a great bellowing roar, and this was followed by a tremendous quaking. The whole earth was upheaved, and buildings leaped into the air; some were carried aloft only to collapse and be broken in pieces, while others were tossed this way and that as if by the surge of the sea, and overturned, and the wreckage spread out over a great extent even of the open country. The crash of grinding and breaking timbers together with tiles and stones was most frightful.... As for the people, many even who were outside the houses were hurt, being snatched up and tossed violently about and then dashed to the earth as if falling from a cliff; some were maimed and others were killed. Even trees in some cases leaped into the air, roots and all.[63]

This earthquake appears to have been quite extensive, with evidence of even a tidal wave hitting Yavneh on the southern coast[64] and evidence of structural damage at this time for sites as scattered as Caesarea, Jerash, Masada, Petra, Heshbon, Avdat, Khirbet Tannur, and Mampsis.[65] Coins from the era of Trajan (97–117 CE) have been found in connection with the destruction material at Masada, Petra, and Avdat while coins of his successor Hadrian are absent. This supports a conclusion of a major earthquake's affecting all of Palestine and Syria in 115 CE.[66]

The archaeological excavations at Bethsaida between 1988 and 1997 have yielded evidence that fits this pattern of destruction in the early second century. In Area C, for example, a Roman house met a violent destruction. Courtyard walls on the west end have been twisted, with some stones moved out of place. Near the south entryway to the courtyard, a large number of stone slabs have collapsed from the roof. A lintel had fallen directly in the doorway at the north entry of the courtyard. On the south kitchen wall a large number of broken pottery vessels are stacked upon each other from what appears to be a collapsed shelf. Nearby on the floor was found a Roman key— perhaps evidence that the last inhabitants had to flee quickly. A similar picture occurs elsewhere on the site. Most significantly the pottery is predominantly Hellenistic/Early Roman. Coins from the entire site include a Domitian coin and four Trajan coins,[67] yet none from the era of Hadrian. A 115 CE date of destruction by earthquake fits the archaeological evidence.

Geological evidence from the area around Bethsaida confirms this picture. Two major landslides have been discovered in the Jordan Rift, about a mile north of Bethsaida. The presence of huge boulders 130 feet above the present level of the Jordan points in each case to such an extensive landslide which dammed up the river, creating a temporary lake which then broke through a week or so later with such intensive force as to carry debris upward to the top of the gorge and to deposit remains downriver at its mouth at the northern edge of the Sea of Galilee.[68] This corresponds to the report of Dio Cassius about the situation around Antioch:

> Even Mt. Casius itself was so shaken that its peaks seemed to lean over and break off and to be falling upon the very city. Other hills also settled, and much water not previously in existence came to light, while many streams disappeared.[69]

The activity in the Jordan gorge then altered the coastline so that Bethsaida—once on the shore of Galilee— is now situated a mile and a half from the sea. This is confirmed by probe holes in the Beteiha plain which show gravel deposited over silt and clay —signs of the earlier extent of the lake. Carbon 14 dating points to a major change about eighteen or nineteen hundred years ago.[70] With the port of Bethsaida now destroyed, one can understand that the fate of Bethsaida was permanent. While there is evidence that most sites affected by the 115 CE earthquake were rebuilt—including evidence from inscriptions at Jerash and Petra that Hadrian provided funding[71]— the city of Bethsaida came to an end after a long history of occupation.

How well does destruction by earthquake fit the literary evidence? 2 Esdras 3–14, as is common in apocalyptic literature (Mark 13:8; 2 Apocalypse of Baruch 27:7), does include earthquakes among the final signs that would precede the great return (2 Esdras 6:14; 9:3). 2 Esdras 13 also looks forward to a mighty act of God that will alter the courses of rivers and make possible a return for exiles from Assyria:

> The Most High will stop the channels of the river again, so that they may be able to cross over. (2 Esdras 13:47)

Previously the writer had described the exile at the time of Shalmaneser, king of Assyria, who took them "across the river" into another land (v. 40). These people who resolved to keep the laws of God while they were in exile therefore chose to journey even further to the north to an area where they would not be corrupted by their contact with others or where they might face assimilation. This writing describes another "sign" in which God stopped the channels of the Euphrates so they could cross over to safety (vv. 41–45). The descendants of these exiles remained faithful in that distant land until the last times when God would bring about a new Exodus from the north. Just as in the first Exodus, when God dried up the Red Sea (and later also the Jordan) for the people to pass through to the promised land, so God would bring about this latter-day return by diverting the waters that formed a barrier to Eretz Israel.

The writer of 2 Esdras 1:11 was surely thinking of the earlier-written 2 Esdras 13. In fact, in the Spanish recension these two chapters are located at the end of the earlier work. This would create an even greater dramatic effect since the mention of Bethsaida's destruction would follow closely after the prophetic words of 2 Esdras 13:47. This underscores his understanding of the destruction of Bethsaida as that final sign for the New Exodus. As was stated earlier, verse 11 comes at the end of a brief summary of the defeats brought about by the hand of God (vv. 4–11). Then the author continues by describing in detail the various mighty acts throughout the Exodus period (vv. 12–23). Most significantly, the reference to Bethsaida's destruction in v. 11 is followed directly (in the Spanish recension there is no verse 12) by a report of the passage through the sea:

Didn't I lead you across the sea, and make walls on the right and the left? I gave you Moses and Aaron as leaders. I gave you light in a pillar of fire. These are my great wonders that I have done for you, but you have forgotten me, says the Lord (v. 13–14).[72]

The expressions "on account of you" in verse 11 and "for you" in verse 14 link the Exodus and destruction together as great wonders of God. This is fitting because the writer is dependent upon the Matthew 11 woe saying against Bethsaida, which also spoke about the many unheeded signs in Jesus' lifetime.[73] It is no accident that the signs of Bethsaida portray Jesus as a new Moses (walking on water = crossing the sea; feeding five thousand = manna in the wilderness). His woe saying thus points ahead to this final sign.

There is no doubt that 2 Esdras 1:11 is dependent on the Q woe saying. However, only three of six cities are mentioned. The Q saying of Matthew 11:21–22 is based on the balance of two modern cities (Bethsaida and Chorazin) and two ancient cities (Tyre and Sidon). The balance continues in Matthew 11:23–24 so that the single city of Capernaum parallels the single city of Sodom, and Gomorrah is not even mentioned. The omission of reference to Chorazin and Capernaum may be due to their location within Eretz Israel, while Bethsaida is not. Recent archaeological research has yielded evidence in the case of Chorazin[74] and Capernaum[75] that both cities were thriving in the second century and continued uninterrupted for several centuries. Neither site offers any evidence of destruction in the early second century.

With regard to the ancient cities, 2 Esdras 1:11 does include both Tyre and Sidon. Along with diverted river channels, 2 Esdras 13:49 also refers to the destruction of a multitude of nations which might hinder the returning exiles. Sodom, by its location near the Dead Sea, would be out of place in this context. Yet in a later context, in 2 Esdras 2:8, Sodom is mentioned along with Gomorrah as cities "whose land sinks to hell."[76] This is striking because it is Capernaum in the Q saying that is brought down to Hades and only by way of association is Sodom connected with this description. What this demonstrates is that the author was clearly aware of the woes against Capernaum and Chorazin, yet chose to focus only on the destruction of Bethsaida. In 2 Esdras 1:11, the destruction of Bethsaida has already taken place, so the woe is transferred to "Assyria," which shall turn out like Sodom and Gomorrah (2 Esdras 2:8).

2 ESDRAS 1:11: "THE CITIES TO THE SOUTH". The Spanish recension of 2 Esdras 1:11 refers to the cities of Tyre and Sidon as "cities to the south" in contrast to "in the east" of the French recension. Because of the location of these in relation to cities to the north of Palestine, it is difficult to accept a reading of either south or east. A number of explanations for this geographical notation have been offered, including suggestions that originally the text referred to Sodom and Gomorrah; that it is a misunderstanding of Zephaniah 2:4, which speaks of cities taken at noonday;[77] or that it was merely confusion by a later author. However, because of the emphasis on the returning exiles both in chapters 3 through 14 and in chapters 1 and 2, it is more likely that these words are spoken from their vantage point north of the Euphrates River and are directed toward an entry into the land from the north at Bethsaida. The Woe saying against Assyria is thus appropriate in preparation for their return:

> Woe to you, Assyria, who hide sinners in your midst. Evil city!
> Remember what I did to Sodom and Gomorrah,
> whose land sinks to hell.
> I will do the same to those who have not obeyed me! (2:8–9)

In apocalyptic, "Babylon" often signifies Rome.[78] However, one might ask why the author chose to mention Assyria here instead of Babylon, as in 2 Esdras 1:3. Is it possible that this reference literally points to Syria?[79]

Is it possible that the author sees the community of 2 Esdras 1–2 as also part of the return? A parallel can be found within the history of the Qumran community in the Damascus Document.[80] Does this community see itself as similar to an earlier group who sojourned in "the land of the north"—that is, an area described as Damascus—and remained faithful while the "princes of Judah" awaited their destruction? It is clear that this group sees itself within the tradition of the prophets. Yet it is a tradition which is still alive. Malachi, the last of the prophets, is therefore omitted from the list of minor prophets in 2 Esdras 1:40; instead, one finds the name Matthia[81]—perhaps linking the first evangelist to this prophetic tradition. The present leader identifies himself with Ezra, but speaks with the voice of a prophet.[82]

A location in southern Syria fits the prophetic theme. Among the names of the prophets in 2 Esdras 1:39 are also Elijah and Enoch—often connected with apocalyptic.[83] The mention of Elijah recalls activity away from Jerusalem in northern Israel and also calls attention to his sojourn with the widow and son at Zarephtha.[84] Especially significant are connections with Mount Hermon and the transfiguration. Likewise, geographic references in 1 Enoch 12–16 mention the area around Dan and the headwaters of the Jordan.[85] Even though 1 Enoch has a positive view of the Jerusalem temple, this work has preserved notions of the validity of prophetic activity in the north.[86] This is especially significant since 2 Esdras 2:18–19 shows knowledge of 1 Enoch 24–25 and makes use of various symbols for paradise.[87] Interestingly, the tree of life (2 Esdras 2:12) will be transplanted *towards the north* in a holy place (1 Enoch 25:5). Like Peter near Caesarea Philippi (Matthew 16), the elect will offer their confession of "Son of God" (2 Esdras 2:47). Thus there is good reason to place 2 Esdras 1–2 in the far northern regions of Palestine or in southern Syria, in an area where familiarity with Bethsaida would be real. One may even speculate that some of the former inhabitants of Bethsaida had now joined the community of 2 Esdras 1–2 and were able to give firsthand accounts of the destruction.

Bethsaida had played an important role in the Gospel accounts as is attested by the reference to the many signs of Jesus mentioned in the famous Woe saying. One of those signs was the miracle of Jesus walking on the water near Bethsaida's shores. This miracle, described first by Mark, called attention to a recognition of Jesus as "Son of God" but because of its connection to the feeding miracle, it also portrayed him as a new Moses crossing the sea. The Gospel of Matthew added a new element to the story. Peter—a Bethsaida disciple—requests that he be allowed to come to Jesus on the water. Although he takes the first step, his lack of faith leads him to sink in the water. Now in response to its failure to believe, Bethsaida had been destroyed by a mighty act of God, with the mountain toppling into the sea and dry land emerging. For the writer of 2 Esdras 1–2, this was the beginning of the new Exodus for a new people of faith to cross over into the promised land.

## CHAPTER NOTES

1. The Revised Standard Version, New English Bible, and Good News Bible, while including 2 Esdras, do not mention the Bethsaida reading.
2. 2 Esdras 10 specifically describes the destruction of Jerusalem and the temple.
3. Beginning with Wellhausen, it has been clear that this work was composed in a Semitic language. However, the Semitic features of chapters 3–14 do not occur in chapters 1–2; Myers (1974) 116; Metzger (1983) 520.
4. With the common apocalyptic connection between Babylon and Rome, it is not difficult to place the actual author thirty years after the fall of Jerusalem to the Romans, or 100 CE. At the same time, there are some details of the fifth vision (chapters 11–12) that point to the reign of Domitian. So Stone (1990) 10, concludes: "This book was thus composed in the time of Domitian (81–96 CE) probably in the latter part of his reign." This view is the consensus of modern scholars such as Myers (1974) 129, Knibb (1979) 76, Oesterley (1933) xlv, Nickelsburg (1981b) 287, Metzger (1983) 520, Schürer (1924) 277.
5. Charlesworth (1981) 27–55.
6. In some manuscripts, 6 Ezra occurs first and 5 Ezra occurs last; Nickelsburg (1981b) 305.
7. The term Canon of Scripture (used also in a larger sense for a list or catalogue) gradually acquired a technical meaning for the books which were officially received as containing the rule of the Christian faith; in this sense the words "canon" and "canonical," which had already been employed by Origen, came into general use in the fourth century. The idea of a Canon of Scripture, however, goes back to OT times. The term Deuterocanonical is an alternative name for the books contained in the Greek (Septuagint) version of the OT, but not in the Hebrew; they are more commonly known as the Apocrypha.
8. 2 Esdras is also included in the Slavonic Bibles of the Russian Orthodox Church. In many editions of the Protestant apocrypha, 1 and 2 Esdras occur at the beginning. In the New Revised Standard Version, it occurs near the end of the apocrypha after those books accepted in Catholic and Orthodox Bibles. The names of books associated with Ezra are very confusing. The following chart may be helpful:

| NRSV (English 1989) | LXX Greek Orthodox | Latin Vulgate Catholic | Slavonic Russian Orthodox |
|---|---|---|---|
| Ezra | 2 Esdras | 1 Ezra | 1 Esdras |
| Nehemiah | 2 Esdras | 2 Ezra | Nehemiah |
| 1 Esdras | 1 Esdras | 3 Ezra | 2 Esdras |
| 2 Esdras | — | 4 Ezra | 3 Esdras |

9. MS C spells it *Bethsaydam*, MS K spells it *Bethsaiden*, MSS MNEVL spell it *Bethsaidam*; see Bergren (1990) 434.
10. Weber (1983).
11. Bensly (1895).
12. The Council of Trent directed a new edition of the Vulgate, which was completed in 1592 under Pope Clement VIII; see Bergren (1990) 7.
13. James (1895) xi–lxxxix, esp. lxiii, states, "My examination of the Spanish text of cc. i.ii. led me to the conclusion that it had preserved on the whole an older form of

the original version than the French." The text of MS C of the Spanish recension was printed as an appendix; Bensly (1895) p. 83–92.

14. Oesterley (1933) 3–4, accepts the Spanish reading for 2 Esdras 1:11.
15. Metzger (1983) 518, states, "In general the French family presents a superior text." Myers (1974) 140–147, mentions 119 significant variant readings from the Spanish text in his footnotes of the text of 2 Esdras 1–2. However, he treats only four of these variants in his section called "Notes" (pp. 148–153) and only five in his "comments" (pp. 152–158). He completely ignores the Bethsaida reading in notes and comments. In his introductory remarks (p. 114) he states, "According to textual critics the French group represents a superior text."
16. Duensing (1965) pp. 689–702.
17. Kraft (1986) 158–169.
18. Bergren (1990).
19. Myers (1974) 153.
20. Knibb (1979) 78, states: "we should probably think in terms of a date about the middle of the second century A.D." Oesterley (1933) p. xliv, concludes "it was written after the middle of the second century A.D." Myers (1974) 120, states that "chs 1 and 2 [derive] from the middle of the second century A.D."
21. Stanton (1977) 67–83. Knibb (1979) 78, sees this date as "an attractive, but somewhat uncertain, possibility."
22. Dio Cassius (1925) 69.14.1–2.
23. Knibb (1979), 87, notes that "your house is desolate" in 1:33 is "apparently a reference to the temple"; The reference, p. 90, to scattering could point to either the destruction in 70 CE or 132–135 CE. Oesterley (1933) 9, sees the reference to scattering as pointing to the destruction in 70 CE.
24. Dio Cassius (1925) 69.12.1–2.
25. Myers (1974) 155.
26. The French recension's "I repudiate" is weaker than "I did not command" in the Spanish.
27. Bergren and others suggest Matthia is a confusion of Malachi; cf. James (1895) p. liii, who says: "it is probable that 'Mathathia' must be regarded as a corruption of 'Malachias,' and not as the Maccabean hero."
28. "Moverunt ea tempestate et Iudaei bellum, quod vetabantur mutilare genitalia." *Vita Hadriani* 22.10; Fitzmyer (1974) 305–354; Nickelsburg (1981b) 311; Jagersma (1986) 155–160; Schürer (1924) 291–318.
29. Justin Martyr, *First Apology* 33:6.
30. Stanton (1977) 71. Myers (1974) 153, states "As it stands it looks like a polemic against Jews on the part of a Christian leader who was himself involved in the conflict between mother and daughter."
31. Isaiah 49:14–21 and 54:1–8; Baruch 4:5–29. Jerusalem during the exile is like a barren woman who mourns her loss and looks to the return of exiles as her new and larger family; Knibb (1979) 89; Oesterley (1933) 9; Myers (1974) 149. There is a contrast between the mother figure of 2:2–4 who has lost her children because of their own actions and the mother figure in verses 15, 17, 31 who is concerned about nurturing her children.
32. Stanton (1977) 67–83.
33. While the concept of turning to other nations occurs in the OT prophetic literature, it does not include an outright rejection of Israel. This is rather a Christian theme which is reflected in Acts 13:46 and Matthew 21:48; Myers (1974) 148. Charlesworth (1981) 47, notes that the Jewish view expressed in chapters 3–14 is pessimis-

tic about the number to be saved, while the Christian redactor is much more optimistic.

34. Stanton (1977) 73, notes the reading in the Spanish recension to be superior: *ad gentem alteram* in contrast to the French recension *ad alias gentes*. This points to the similar view of Christianity as a "third nation." Knibb (1979) 84, who relies heavily on the French recension, here accepts the Spanish reading. See also Oesterley (1933) 5.

35. This expression is never used in the OT or NT, but reflects the concept "kingdom of God"; Knibb (1979) 91; Oesterley (1933) 10.

36. Stanton (1977) 75.

37. Stanton (1977) 76–78.

38. Among other parallels, he notes the acts of mercy cited in 2 Esdras 2:20–22 to be very similar to those mentioned in the parable of Last Judgment in Matthew 25:32–36, the call for vigilance in 2 Esdras 2:34 and Matthew 24:36–25:13, the theme of the rejection of prophets in 2 Esdras 1:32 and Matthew 21:33 ff., and a special interest in the prophets Isaiah and Jeremiah in 2 Esdras 2:18 and in all of Matthew. See also James (1895) p. lvi; Bergren (1990) 189–193; Knibb (1979) 91.

39. Mack (1993) 93–98. Note that Matt. 23:37 and 2 Esdras 2:30 repeat the word 'gather' while Luke 13:34 has it only once.

40. Stanton (1977) 70, cautions against conclusions on the basis of a single word or phrase, especially in documents that have a long history of transmission; cf. James (1895), p. l–li, who sees Luke 11:49 as a source of 2 Esdras 1:32 because it includes *apostolorum*. See also Knibb (1979) 86; Oesterley (1933) 5.

41. Bergren (1990) 25.

42. Koester (1982) 172.

43. For arguments concerning the relationship of 2 Esdras 1:11 and the Matthean form of the Q saying see Strickert (1997), 113–117. See also Kloppenborg (1988), 74.

44. *Omnes gentes a facie eorum perdidi et in oriente provinciarum duarum populum, Tyri et Sidonis, dissipavi et omnes adversarios eorum interfeci;* Bensly (1895) 1.

45. *Nonne propter vos Bethsaidam civitatem everti, et ad meridianum duas civitates, Tyrum et Sydonem, igne cremavi, et eos qui adversum vos fuerunt male interfeci?* (Bergren (1990) 395; Bensly (1895) 83.

46. Knibb (1979) 80, refers to it as "an obscure passage, made more so by uncertainties about the text."

47. The description "Ezra, son of Cusi" in the Spanish recension draws a close parallel with Zephaniah 1:1 and places him in the prophetic tradition. Several manuscripts also include the designation "prophet." Later, verse 4 reads, "The Word of the Lord came to me," an expression that never occurs in the canonical Ezra but which clearly places this figure in the prophetic tradition. Most of the first chapter is a series of prophecies introduced by the words, "These are the words of the Lord Almighty." James (1895) xliv–xlvi; Oesterley (1933) 1–3; Knibb (1979) 79–82.

48. The use of Babylon as symbolic for the Roman power occurs in 1 Peter 5 and in Revelation.

49. According to Knibb (1979) 80–81, these words "suggest that 2 Esdras 1–2 was written in the west, but there are difficulties about the reading in the east." Oesterley (1933) 7, notes that on the basis of verse 11, "the writer would seem to have lived in the Western Dispersion and might therefore think of a people coming from Jerusalem, i.e. Jewish Christians coming from there to spread the faith in the west," but on the basis of verse 38 he suggests a Palestinian setting. See also Myers (1974) 156.

50. See Matthew 8:11.

51. Bergren (1989) 675–683. Oesterley (1933) 7, suggests that the author combines two thoughts: references to the returning exiles and the gentile wise men of Matthew 2.
52. James (1895) p. liii, sees a parallel with the Apocalypse of Baruch, where angels bearing flowers represent the ἀρεταί τῶν δικαίων; cf. Oesterley (1933) 8.
53. James(1895) p. liii.
54. James (1895) pp. lii–liii, states, "I cannot doubt that it [Spanish recension] is a more original one than the tame and obvious series of the French text." Oesterley (1933) 8, refers to the "haphazard order" of the Spanish reading as evidence of authenticity, but questions whether the names Elijah and Enoch belong since these are apocalyptic of the Jewish type in contrast to the Christian apocalyptic style of 2 Esdras 2.
55. Knibb (1979) 87, notes that the French recension possibly describes "Jewish Christians coming from Palestine to the West."
56. James (1895) p. xlvii, notes, "If we are to judge between the two texts provisionally on grounds of probability, it seems to me that we must here again decide in favor of the Spanish. Bethsaida might well have been cut out of the text, where it was felt to be absurd, and the far tamer and vaguer reference to 'all nations' substituted for it. But the temptation to insert Bethsaida merely because Tyre and Sidon were mentioned seems almost nil."
57. Livy, *Periochaè* 5.53.5; Cicero, *De Doma Sua* 101; Horace, *Epistulae* 2.2.34.
58. Josephus, *Life* 398–406.
59. Evidence to the contrary includes one Domitian coin and four Trajan coins from the end of the first century. One should also note that Pliny the Elder, *Natural History,* 5.15.15, in 77 CE refers to the city as if it were still standing.
60. Verg. A. 1.43; Ov. Ep. 7.42; Sen. Ep. 4.7; Pliny *Nat. His.* 16.130; see Glare (1982) 626.
61. Amiran, Arieh, and Turcotte (1994) 260–305.
62. Dio Cassius (1925) 68.24–25.
63. Dio Cassius (1925) 68.24.1–3.
64. Amiran, Arieh, and Turcotte (1994).
65. Russell (1985) 37–60, esp. 40–41.
66. Russell (1985) 40, notes that literary evidence for the 128–130 CE earthquake is questionable. It is based on Eusebius Pamphili's *Chronicon,* which reported in the 226th *Olympiad* that "Nicopolis and Caesarea collapsed from an earthquake." Yet this may show confusion in dating or also confusion of geography related to cities in Anatolia with similar names. Thus it may be more appropriate to speak of one major earthquake dating to the early second century CE.
67. Two coins of Trajan were minted in Tiberias and are dated to the 81st year of the city's founding, or 99/100 CE. A third coin dates to 108/109 CE. The other Trajan coin was minted in Rome and has no date.
68. Shroder and Bishop (1995).
69. Dio Cassius (1925) 68.25.6.
70. Shroder (1995).
71. Russell (1985) 41.
72. The French text differs slightly: "Surely it was I who brought you through the seas, and made safe highways for you where there was no road ... and did great wonders among you...."
73. "The Gospel of the Nazareans," Hennecke (1965) 151.
74. Yeivin (1987) 22–36. Yeivin's excavations from 1962 to 1986 uncovered evidence of a city from a second-century olive press, though the height of the city was marked by a third-century synagogue, destroyed by earthquake in the fourth century (Eusebius notes this earthquake as fulfillment of the woe saying of Jesus in Matthew 11).

The third-century Tosefta Makot 3:8 confirms Chorazin as a "medium-size town." Although the Talmud (Menahot 85a) supports the Gospel report of a city in the second temple period, no archaeological evidence has yet been produced. Later stages of a city exist from the fifth century through the ninth century. A three-century gap occurs before a small village was rebuilt in the twelfth to fourteenth centuries.

75. Loffreda (1984).
76. Osterly (1933) 10: "The simplicity of the Spanish text makes it perhaps more acceptable." The French manuscripts have "who lay in ashes." This may be an attempt to fit the reading in accordance with biblical history; James (1895) p. liv.
77. James (1895) p. xlviii: "The ambiguous κεσημβρία was taken to mean the quarter of the compass, not the time of day"; followed by Oesterley (1933) 3, and Myers (1974) 148.
78. Revelation 14:8; 16:19; 17:5; 18:2, 10, 21. Knibb (1979) 90, notes that "Assyria" is a "cryptic name for the Roman Empire," similar to usage in the Qumran War Scroll.
79. Zechariah 10:10; Isaiah 27:13. Oesterley (1933) 9. James (1895) p. liv, sees a parallel with Zephaniah 2:9,13: "Moab shall be as Sodom, and the children of Ammon as Gomorrah ... he will destroy Assyria." 1 QM 1:2, 6; 2:12; 11:11; 18:2 uses the expression "Kittim of Ashur" as the opponents of the sons of light. Ezekiel 32:22 and Zechariah 10:11 use "Assyria" to represent powers hostile to the Jews.
80. Damascus Document CD 7:12–15. See Strickert (1986) 333–335.
81. Bergren (1990) p. lii, and others suggest Matthia is confusion of Malachi; cf. James (1895) p. liii, who says that "it is probable that 'Mathathia' must be regarded as a corruption of 'Malachias,' and not as the Maccabean hero."
82. Nowhere in canonical literature is Ezra addressed as a prophet or are there prophetic formulas such as "The word of the Lord came to me..." (1:4) or "These are the words of the Lord Almighty"; see Knibb (1979) 80; Oesterley (1933) 3.
83. Elijah and Enoch are expected to usher in the last judgment in *Apocalypse of Elijah* 3:91.
84. 1 Kings 17:2–9.
85. "I went and sat by the waters of Dan in the land of Dan, which is southwest of Hermon"; 1 Enoch 13:7.
86. Nickelsburg (1981) 575–600.
87. Oesterley (1933) 12, states that "he was evidently familiar with the Book of Enoch."

## LITERATURE CITED

Amiran, D. H. K., E. Arieh, and T. Turcotte. 1994. Earthquakes in Israel and Adjacent Areas: Macroseismic Observations since 100 BCE, *Israel Exploration Journal* 44: 260–305.

Bensly, Robert L. 1895. *The Fourth Book of Ezra: The Latin Version Edited From the MSS.* Cambridge: Cambridge University Press.

Bergren, Theodore A. 1990. *Fifth Ezra: The Text, Origin, and Early History.* Septuagint and Cognate Studies 25. Atlanta: Scholars Press.

———. 1989. The "People Coming from the East" in 5 Ezra 1:38. *Journal of Biblical Literature* 108: 675–683.

Damascus Document. 1995. Pp. 95–113 in: *The Dead Sea Scrolls in English.* 4th edition. Ed. Geza Vermes. New York: Penguin Books.

Dio Cassius. 1925. *Roman History.* English and Greek. Trans. Earnest Cary, Loeb Classical Library, vol. 8. Cambridge, MA: Harvard University Press.

Duensing, H. 1965. The Fifth and Sixth Books of Ezra. Pp. 689–701 in Hennecke (1965) (q.v.).

Charlesworth, James H. 1981. Christian and Jewish Self-Definition in Light of the Christian Additions to the Apocryphal Writings. Pp. 27–55 in: *Jewish and Christian Self-Definition: Aspects of Judaism in the Graeco-Roman Period.* Ed. E.P. Sanders. Philadelphia: Fortress Press.

Fitzmyer, Joseph. 1974. The Bar Kochba Period. Pp. 305–354 in: *Essays on the Semitic Background of the New Testament.* Missoula, MT: Scholars Press.

Glare, P. G. W., editor. 1982. *Oxford Latin Dictionary.* Oxford: Clarendon Press.

Hennecke, Edgar. 1965. *New Testament Apocrypha,* vol. 2, *Writings Relating to the Apostles; Apocalypses and Related Subjects.* 3d ed. Ed. Wilhelm Schneemelcher, Robert McLachlan Wilson. English trans. R. McL. Wilson. Philadelphia, Westminster Press.

Jagersma, Henk. 1986. *A History of Israel from Alexander the Great to Bar Kochba.* Trans. John Bowden. Minneapolis: Fortress.

James, M.R. 1895. Introduction. In Robert L. Bensly, *The Fourth Book of Ezra: The Latin Version Edited from the MSS.* Cambridge: Cambridge University Press.

Josephus. 1958–1965. *Works. English and Greek.* Loeb Classical Library. 9 vols. Cambridge, MA: Harvard University Press.

Justin Martyr. 1981.The First Apology of Justin. Pp. 163–187 in: *Ante-Nicene Fathers,* vol. 1. *The Apostolic Fathers, Justin Martyr, Irenaeus.* Ed. Alexander Roberts and James Donaldson. Grand Rapids, MI: Wm. B. Eerdmans.

Kloppenborg, J. S. 1988. *Q Parallels: Synopsis, Critical Notes, and Concordance.* Sonoma, CA: Poleridge.

Knibb, M. A. 1979. The Second Book of Esdras. In R. J. Coggins and M. A. Knibb, *The First and Second Book of Esdras.* Cambridge: Cambridge University Press.

Koester, Helmut. 1982. *Introduction to the New Testament,* volume 2: *History and Literature of Early Christianity.* Minneapolis: Fortress Press.

Kraft, Robert A. 1986. Towards Assessing the Latin Text of "5 Ezra": The "Christian" Connection. *Harvard Theological Review* 79:158–169.

Loffreda, Stanislao. 1984. *Recovering Capharnaum.* Jerusalem: Terra Santa.

Mack, Burton. 1993. *The Lost Gospel: The Book of Q and Christian Origins.* San Francisco: HarperCollins.

Metzger, B. M. 1983. The Fourth Book of Ezra. In: *The Old Testament Pseudepigrapha: Apocalyptic Literature and Testaments,* vol.1, ed. James H. Charlesworth. Garden City, N.Y.: Doubleday.

Myers, Jacob M. 1974. *I and II Esdras: Anchor Bible.* Garden City, N.Y.: Doubleday.

Nickelsburg, George W. E. 1981a. Enoch, Levi, and Peter: Recipients of Revelation in Upper Galilee. *Journal of Biblical Literature* 100: 575–600.

———. 1981b. *Jewish Literature between the Bible and the Mishnah.* Minneapolis: Fortress Press.

Oesterley, W. O. E. 1933. *II Esdras: The Ezra Apocalypse.* London: Methuen.

Russell, Kenneth W. 1985. The Earthquake Chronology of Palestine and Northwest Arabia from the 2nd through the Mid–8th Century A.D. *Bulletin of the American Schools of Oriental Research* 260:37–60.

Schürer, Emil. 1924. *A History of the Jewish People in the Time of Jesus Christ,* vol. 1. Edinburgh: T & T Clark.

Shroder, John F., Jr. 1995. Geological and Physical Geographic Background to the Archaeology of Bethsaida Site. In: *Bethsaida: a City by the North Shore of the Sea of Galilee.* Ed. Rami Arav and Richard Freund. Kirksville, Mo.: Thomas Jefferson Press.

Shroder, John F., Jr., and Michael Bishop. 1995. The Geological Background for the City of Bethsaida. Paper presented at the 1995 International Meeting of the Society of Biblical Literature in Budapest, Hungary.

Stanton, G. N. 1977. 5 Ezra and Matthean Christianity in the Second Century. *Journal of Theological Studies* 28: 67–83.

Stone, Michael. 1990. *Fourth Ezra: A Commentary of the Book of Fourth Ezra.* Hermeneia Series. Minneapolis: Fortress Press.

Strickert, Fred. 1986. Damascus document VII, 10–20 and Qumran Messianic Expectation, *Revue de Qumran* 47:327–349.

———. 1997. 2 Esdras 1:11 and the Destruction of Bethsaida, *Journal for the Study of the Pseudepigrapha* 16:113–123.

Weber, R., editor. 1983. *Biblia Sacra Iuxta Vulgatam Versionem.* 2 volumes., 3d edition. Stuttgart: Deutsche Bibelgesellschaft.

Wellhausen, Julius. 1899. Zur apokalyptischer Literatur. *Skizzen und Vorarbeiter* 6: 215–249.

Yelvin, Ze'ev. 1987. Ancient Chorazin Comes Back to Life. *Biblical Archaeology Review* 13: 22–36.

*Mark Appold*

# Bethsaida and a First-Century House Church?

T HIS CHAPTER FOCUSES ON the potential relationships between an outstanding example of a first-century CE courtyard house on the summit of the Bethsaida mound and the development of the early Christian house church. Material finds at the Bethsaida excavation are weighed in the light of varying textual traditions connected with the places and structures of early Christian worship and the simultaneous emergence of synagogue and church. Special attention is given to the Johannine texts and their predecessor traditions, which provide suggestive clues to Bethsaida as a place of early Jewish-Christian beginnings where followers of Jesus gathered, told their stories, and gave definition to shared experiences. A confluence of textual, geographical, and archaeological factors conspires to make Bethsaida a city of pivotal significance before it began to fade from view after the turn of the first century CE.

## THE CONTEXT: FROM CHURCH TO BASILICA

A few general remarks are in order detailing the larger patterns of development from private domestic dwellings used for worship and gathering purposes, through successive stages of adaptation and renovation, and finally to the point at which edifices were either substantially reconfigured or built *de novo* as designated church structures during the period of basilical and memorial architecture.

Two landmarks stand out in the architectural tradition of the early church. On the one hand, there is the house church so richly attested to in the Pauline texts in the middle of the first century CE and alluded to as well in other New Testament texts through the end of the first century and beyond.[1] On the other hand, there is the basilica model of the Constantinian period which becomes the norm for church building in the fourth century. In between is a period of transition where domestic buildings were either partially or totally renovated for church purposes. The critical problem with the first stage of house church development is, simply put, the lack of any physical and archaeological evidence from the first and second centuries. While there is abundant reference in the literature, there are no clear and undisputed material finds to match the texts. To a large degree this is understandable when one remembers that the domiciles first used for church purposes had, apart from size, no distinguishing characteristics. There was as yet no architectural pattern for plan and style such as the Constantinian revolution would later provide. Christian congregations were limited to the realm of domestic architecture.[2]

By the end of the third and the beginning of the fourth centuries archaeological evidence supports a much clearer picture. Even before Constantine's introduction of the basilica, there is a clear record of Christians moving toward larger public structures and halls of assembly. Eusebius can speak of the "building boom" in the second half of the third century.[3] Porphyry in his deprecating view of the church can say that "the Christians erected great buildings" of their own, "imitating construction of the temples."[4] So dominating were the norms of architectural definition for the basilica that they often were mistakenly read back into and imposed on the period of the house church movement. Much of earlier scholarship was particularly prone to make these assumptions. Such anachronisms have not yet been completely put to rest.[5] The first century house church, on the other hand, is motivated by social and spiritual concerns unique to its time. It occupies a distinctive level in the evolution of the church building movement.

If the evidence for monumental and public buildings reflecting the largesse of the burgeoning Byzantine empire is clearly evidenced, the same cannot be maintained for the transitional period. Nonetheless, there are some well-attested examples. The best documented site is the Christian building in Dura Europos, that major Hellenistic and then Roman trade and military outpost in eastern Syria on the banks of the Euphrates. While these remains of the mid-third century cannot simply be projected back onto the house church development of an earlier period, they do provide an excellent model for the transition from a domestic edifice to a building used exclusively as a church, the oldest documented church on record, wonderfully preserved and never built on top of since its burial in the sands and rubble following its destruction in the Sassanian invasion of 256 CE. Although there is no direct evidence for the use of this building prior to its renovation in ca. 241 CE and whether it had any connection with Christian activity, the epigraphic, artistic, and architectural evidence is clear that the building subsequently was given over completely to the needs of the Christian community there. Other sites across the former Roman Empire, such as the "title churches" in Rome (*titulus Clementis* and *titulus Byzantis* [later the basilica SS. Giovanni e Paolo]) and the Lullingstone Villa in Roman Britannia, provide, through stratigraphic analysis, additional support for the adaptation and reconfiguration of existing buildings into structures designated either partly or wholly for church use.

## Cultic Movements and Their Meeting Places
What has been noted in this overview of the development and adaptation of buildings used for church purposes could also apply to other religious movements as well. Imperial Rome was thoroughly syncretistic. In contrast to the monumental public buildings and temples that dotted the landscape were the more private cultic forms that grew out of the household setting and adapted domestic structures for their activities. The Tyrian merchants association at Puteoli and the Serapis cult at Delos are cases in point. The mithrea of the romanized Mithras cult which had spread across the empire also offer many examples.[6] Of the more than sixty excavated Mithraic sanctuaries from across the Roman empire, only ten were constructed *de novo* for the cult. The remainder were found in renovated houses, apartments, shops, and warehouses.[7] In other cultic movements families themselves could establish cultic associations, as in the case of Pompeia Agrippinilla who founded a Dionysiac *thiasos* in Tusculum where household members constituted the hierarchy with Agrippinilla as priestess.[8] Both foreign and private cults typically used domestic quarters throughout the Hellenistic and Roman periods. A classic example

can again be found on the eastern edge of the empire in Dura-Europos, where on the same street one could see a Christian church, a synagogue, and a Mithreum, each of which had its origin in a house structure that was later modified to accommodate religious practices. Of the many temples scattered throughout the city, three Durene temples, one dedicated to Adonis, one to Zeus, and a third to a Palmyran deity, Gadde, were built on property previously occupied by private houses and shops.[9]

## EARLY SYNAGOGUES

A similar pattern may be observed in the development of the synagogue. The literature points not to the Homeland but to the Diaspora for the emergence of the synagogue and in particular to Ptolemaic Egypt, where inscriptions from the reign of Ptolemy III speak of the *proseuche* (place of prayer).[10] It should be noted, however, that this connection is not uncontested. Nonetheless, one looks in vain in Jewish literary sources for any mention of synagogues before or during the Maccabean revolt. Desecration of synagogue buildings or the disruption of synagogue worship would be expected as reprisals during the period of revolt, but no such mention is ever found. The New Testament texts are the earliest witnesses to synagogues as flourishing in pre–70 Palestine. But it is clear that the references are not to distinctive buildings normed by a set architectural code. Rather, they point to nondescript places of gathering *(bet ha-knesset)*, prayer *(bet ha-tefilah)*, study *(bet ha-midrash)*, court judgment *(bet ha-din)*, and worship within the context of homes instead of public buildings.[11] It could be said that the patterns of synagogal architecture paralleled rather than preceded the line of development noted with the church.

One should resist the temptation to read later Talmudic specifications into the earlier period. The rabbinic reference in the Palestinian Talmud (Megillah 3:1, 73d) that 480 synagogues were destroyed in Jerusalem by Titus is more than an exaggeration; it is basically worthless for historical reconstruction. The plethora of Galilean synagogues are all of Byzantine vintage and the claim that a first-century synagogue structure lies beneath the existing one at Capernaum is, while probable, still not fully documented.[12] Although archaeological data may point to the finds at Masada, Herodium (both built during the First Revolt), and Gamla (probably Herodian), the final assessments are also contested. The Theodotus inscription found on Mt. Ophel is strong epigraphic evidence for the existence of a synagogue in Jerusalem before its destruction under Titus, but further archaeological data has not been forthcoming.[13] In the Diaspora only six synagogues, ranging in date from the second century BCE through the sixth century, have been excavated extensively. They include the ones at Priene and Sardis in Asia Minor, Stobi in Macedonia, Delos in the Aegean, Ostia by Rome, and Dura-Europos in Roman Syria. Of these six, five were renovated from private homes. The Sardis synagogue stands out as a massive public building progressively reconfigured from earlier structures. The link between the synagogue and a domestic edifice in the first century CE is a strong one and should be remembered as we proceed to a further analysis of the house church. The difference between a synagogue and a house church in the first decades of the Christian movement, particularly in Palestine, would have been virtually nonexistent.

## WITNESS OF THE NEW TESTAMENT

It has already been noted that while archaeological evidence for the house church is virtually nonexistent, the textual traditions of the New Testament are notably strong. After the death of Jesus, we are told that the disciples continued gathering in traditional worship patterns "in the temple and at home" (Acts 2:46; 5:42) κατ' οἶκον has the sense of *in various private homes*. Conversions narrated in Acts depict "household" settings (Acts 16:15,34, Lydia/jailer at Philippi; 18:8, Crispus at Corinth). This picture is corroborated in the letters of Paul that date from the mid-first century, the earliest texts in the New Testament. Here Paul speaks of baptizing the household of Stephanas (1 Cor. 1:16) and he indicates that this household constituted the first converts in Achaia (1 Cor. 16:15). In 1 Cor. 16:18 he refers to Aquila and Prisca "and the church in their house." Likewise Philemon is addressed along with the church in his house (Philem. 2) as is Nympha in Colossae and the church in her house (Col. 4:15). The data gives prolific evidence of cellular groups that included extended family and household servants meeting in private homes hosted by a benefactor or *pater familias*.[14]

As many as a half dozen or more such groups or house churches would have existed in Corinth during Paul's ministry. And in Rome there would have been again as many, as indicated in the salutatory closing of his epistle to the church there. Significant also is the prominent role played by women. In the Roman period women could inherit personal estates and manage their own households. And so it is not surprising to hear of a Chloe in Corinth, a Lydia in Philippi, or a Phoebe, the well-known supporter of Paul and clearly identified as a benefactress (*prostatis*) of a house church in Cenchreae, a port town near Corinth. The house church phenomenon is not simply Pauline but can be noted in other circles as well. A case in point would be in the Johannine communities at the turn of the century where, as noted in third Letter of John, a certain Diotrephes exercised an unbounded control over those Christians who met under his patronage. He spread false charges and excommunicated members of his house church who welcomed itinerant missionaries from sister communities.

What significant information does all of this data about the development of the early Christian house church and its parallels with the synagogue or some of contemporaneous cultic movements yield for an analysis of a potential Bethsaida house church? Some of the following factors may be helpful. The actual structures of house churches followed the common norms for residential architecture of the area and failed to display any uniquely church characteristics in what was otherwise a strongly syncretistic environment. Ownership of the houses, however, may offer some clues. Owners typically were well-off economically and could afford dwellings that were more spacious. Such dwellings could provide room beyond immediate family needs for gatherings and meetings. Owners in these cases served as patrons capable of providing hospitality and support, such as Paul, for example, received when he arrived at Corinth and stayed and worked with Prisca and Aquila (Acts 18).

## A Model Courtyard House

When we turn our attention now to the two private houses thus far excavated on the top of the Bethsaida mound in Areas B and C, the following observations can be made. Both were built in a typical courtyard pattern with large open areas, kitchens, and residential quarters. Only the foundational stones have been left intact. There are no complete vertical walls. While the southernmost house (Area B), dubbed the fisherman's house, is noted for a variety of fishing implements found in the courtyard, the northernmost house (Area C), preserved in a better condition, contains also some fishing implements as well as a broader variety of other artifacts. It is on this structure, in particular on its basic ground plan and design that I would like to focus.

Fig. 1. Aerial view (1997) of House of the Vintner, looking east

Clearly, the architectural traditions here do not come from the West, from the Greek peristyle, the Italian villa and atrium houses, or the Roman insulae. The basic format and outline, on the other hand, are common to houses found throughout the Syro-Palestinian region.[15] They typically include an open courtyard, large kitchen area, and residential rooms which often have a second story. The house is unusually large when compared to the more modest dwellings that occupied an otherwise unpretentious fishing village. Perhaps larger structures were erected when Bethsaida was elevated to the status of a *polis* under Herod Philip, but none have been excavated.

Dimensions of the Bethsaida house in Area C are fairly impressive with a courtyard on the southwestern side that measures 10.9 x 11.5 m, almost half of the total area of the entire house. Partial pavement of a north-south street on the west side of the house may still be seen. An elongated kitchen, 9.9 x 4.49 m, is located on the east side and contains remnants of an oven and various kitchenware. On the north side are located three residential rooms: the westernmost, which measures 4.1 x 1.9 m; the center one, 4.5 x 5.4 m; and the eastern room, 3.5 x 2.1 m. In addition, off the kitchen and extending to the east is an amazingly well preserved cellar 4.5 x 3.5 m, which contained four Hellenistic jars and a cooking pot. Covering the cellar were ten basalt slabs, each about 4 feet long and more than a foot wide (approximately 1.3 x 1 m). The house has three doorways. The main entrance at the south wall led into the courtyard. Directly north across the courtyard is a door to the residential rooms, where a finely crafted lintel still rests in the place it had fallen just inside the doorway. A third doorway led from the courtyard to the kitchen. Iron nails found there may suggest the existence of a former wooden frame. The size of the house implies owners who were well off and whose home occupied a commanding position on top of the plateau.

For other material finds, the field diaries point to an enormous amount of Hellenistic and otherwise unidentifiable shards (11,604).[16] A whorl from a loom may indicate further domestic activity in the household. All of these finds point to an active household with substantial resources. As the reconstructed model shows, such homes often had a second story over the residential quarters.

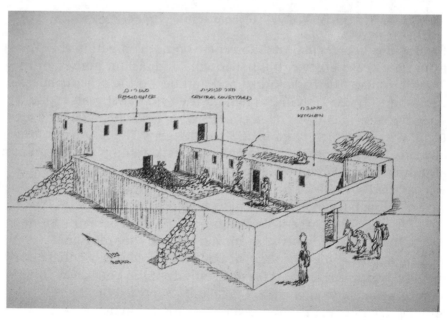

Fig. 2. Drawing of House of the Fisherman

The discovery of six partial or whole iron sickles and three iron grape hooks and the existence of what was presumably a wine cellar help shed light on the agricultural activities of the owners. Two lead weights, a fishing net weight stone, a stone anchor with a hole at the end (possibly a depth finder), and a fishhook would indicate fishing activity as well,[17] although the number of these artifacts would hardly support the idea of a commercial fishing operation. A bronze Hellenistic cosmetic spatula, one ring, a bead, and a very fine gold earring may say something about the economic status of the owners, while a *strigilis* found in the courtyard, definitely a non-Jewish instrument commonly used in the Greek gymnasium, underscores a syncretistic element. That element is strengthened by the many bone fragments unearthed, which include some pig and catfish bones, clearly ritualistically unclean foods. Other material finds include a spearhead and an iron key found in the kitchen as well as 6 iron nails in scattered locations. The overall picture suggests a household with substantial work and domestic activity.

The dating for all of this is problematic. That is corroborated by the discovery of 19 coins in the house,[18] 15 of which are Seleucid/Phoenician and date from the second century BCE, one from the late second century Hasmonean period, one from the fifth century BCE, and one from the Byzantine Justinian era of the sixth century CE. Considering that the overwhelming majority of shards, artifacts, and coins are from the Hellenistic period, one needs to ask whether there is evidence for occupation during the Roman period. These finds are few and include 27 shards from Herodian oil lamps, an additional 4 in the cellar, 5 late-first-century Roman oil lamp pieces, 1 decorated Roman oil lamp, 2 early Roman lid shards, 1 early Roman and 1 Herodian amphora shard, and 27 early Roman cooking pot shards. One should also add the 2 bronze coins minted by Herod Philip in 29–30 CE that were found in the house in Area B.[19] It is fairly apparent why there are not more artifacts. The level of destruction, marauding, plunder, and erosion was so complete that little on this top level remained. That alone precludes any viable stratigraphic analysis for the Roman level. There is no evidence for a conflagration such as was the case with the eighth-century BCE destruction by the Assyrians. Nor do material finds suggest anything like the military siege by the Romans during the First Revolt.

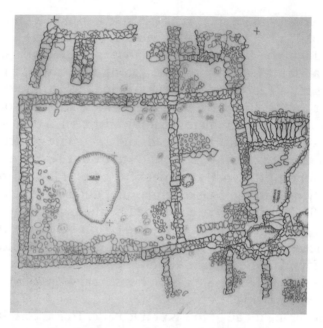

Fig. 3. Diagram of House of the Vintner

Other factors led to the demise of Bethsaida that would leave it uninhabited as a city for almost two millennia. No Byzantine church was built on the site and its memory faded fairly quickly. It is not difficult to identify a chain of causal events. Effects of the disruption in the Jerusalem community during the 40s with the execution of James, the son of Zebedee (Acts 12), and the severe famine that impoverished the land (Acts 11:27–29; Josephus, *Ant.* 19.343–352) would have been felt in the north. The advancing Roman legions and the battle that took place near Bethsaida in 67 CE must have led to a general abandonment of the city. Those who were against Rome would flee east to the fortified city of Gamla, while those who supported Rome would evacuate to the west. Final destructive blows were received by the devastating earthquakes in 115 CE and 130 CE, events that created major geological changes, the rerouting of the Jordan,[20] and the subsequent economic upheaval forcing emigration when the means of making a living were dramatically changed. The twisted appearance of some of the walls in the courtyard house, the collapsed roofing stones in the southwest corner of the courtyard house, and smashed cooking vessels on top of each other would corroborate an event of violent destruction.[21]

### THE JOHANNINE CONNECTION

Of enormous significance is the discovery of a pottery shard next to the entrance to the center residential room. On this shard of Galilean ware is a rather crudely incised cross, roughly 10.8 x 12 cm, and in its center is an imperfect circle with a 4.2 cm horizontal diameter and a 3.6 cm vertical diameter.[22] Although further analysis is needed, current assessment guardedly places this shard in the late-Hellenistic—early-Roman era.[23]

The use of crosses for religious, architectural, artistic and cultic purposes in the ancient world is widely documented. Also within Judaism the cross, drawn as a *taw* and used as a sign of the providence and protection of God (Ezek. 9:4)[24] and frequently used on ossuaria is widely attested.[25] But the Byzantinelike Bethsaida cross is strikingly different. Here we do not have simply two intersecting lines, a common symbol that occurs in a wide variety of pagan, Hellenistic, Jewish, and Christian contexts. Rather, what is notably different are

Fig. 4. Cross shard found in House of the Vintner (1.00 : 0.75)

the four equidistant arms with a circle in the middle. There is nothing exactly comparable in either the Jewish or Hellenistic world. At a time when the use of crosses in the Christian community lacks any hard evidence, this cross clearly intends to depict the symbol not as an instrument of execution or providence, but as a point of reflection on the meaning of the crucifixion. That kind of reflection is richly represented already in the middle of the first century with Paul, who depicts the cross dialectically as the sign of weakness and foolishness, strength and wisdom (I Cor. 1:23–25). But the Bethsaida cross with its circle in the middle points yet in a different direction, one that most closely parallels the thinking found in the Johannine tradition. With its high Christology the Johannine tradition presents the cross as a point of exaltation and glory. This is the home of the reflection behind the Bethsaida cross, embryonic in its development, yet aligned with the predecessor traditions that reach maturity in the Fourth Gospel.

It is in the Johannine tradition where we find the most provocative New Testament connections to Bethsaida. This is the tradition that preserves the memory of Bethsaida as the home for three of the disciples, Peter, Andrew, and Philip, and by implication perhaps also James and John, the sons of the fisherman Zebedee (John 1:43,44).[26] Why this unusual focus on the place of origin unless there was a subsequent history at this place involving these first followers of Jesus? In one of the dominant post-Easter traditions of the Gospels (Mark 16:7; Matt. 28:7) we find that the disciples are told to return to Galilee for it is there they will see Jesus. Indeed, where else would they initially have gone except to their home with its network of family and friends? Here is one of the primary places where post-Easter faith and the subsequent Jewish-Christian communities would develop. Experiences in the ministry of Jesus, such as the feeding of the multitudes in the area of Bethsaida, would be retold from a post-Easter perspective as is clearly suggested in the Johannine text. Bethsaida already had a tradition connecting it to the "mighty works" of Jesus, activities that also included memorable Jesus words of judgment and the call to repentance. It was a city also at the crossroads, located near the intersection between two major trunk routes, one north and south and one east and west. In the short three and a half decades after the crucifixion, itinerant groups of faithful Jews who had developed a Jesus connection and who may well have renounced any permanent abode would traverse the area with a message of radical discipleship.[27] They were the transmitters of the words and works of Jesus. In some cases, where support for this activity was provided, they would gather in the established patterns of synagogue worship. Could the Bethsaida house qualify for such an assembly? Could its patron have come from the family circle of the disciples? To be sure, such a house church would have been short lived. But the cumulative textual traditions and the archaeological data are both suggestive and supportive.

## BETHSAIDA AND THE DISCIPLES

We return to the two well-known Johannine statements in 1:45 ("Now Philip was from Bethsaida, the city of Andrew and Peter") and 12:21 ("They came to Philip, who was from Bethsaida in Galilee"). These two texts in the short history of Bethsaida studies have been among the most frequently cited since they document Bethsaida as the home of at least three apostles. Aside from the fact that the Fourth Gospel never refers to any of the followers of Jesus as "apostles," since all, including the community to follow, are designated "disciples," one could point out that these statements regarding three disciples constitute the *only* specific references to Bethsaida in the entire Johannine corpus. The name Bethsaida appears in no other place in John. Moreover, these references are unique to the Fourth Gospel and are found nowhere else in the canonical texts. Should such a paucity of direct references to Bethsaida in John be understood as restricting its significance or is the Bethsaida connection implicitly present in other situations where the broader traditions either presuppose or imply its involvement (e.g. multiplication of the loaves; epiphany on the water)? Of course, it is not called for to find Bethsaida behind every bush and tree in the pertinent texts. But it would be overly rigid simply to exclude possibilities just because the location is not specified or because the reference is viewed as redactional.

The great importance in these two citations is the clear identification of Bethsaida as the home of Philip, Andrew, and Peter. Normally in the Gospel tradition disciples' names commonly given are patronymics (James and John, sons of Zebedee, Simon bar Jona, James the son of Alphaeus, etc.). In John, on the other hand, the defining factors are not family relationships but places of origin. As a result new patterns emerge. In the Synoptic Gospels, Peter, James, and John constitute an inner circle of three persons. But in John they are never joined in that way. In the Synoptics, Philip and Andrew are linked

(Mark 3:18), but otherwise not as a pair with Peter. Added to this is yet another peculiarity. Nathanael, who is not given in the Synoptic lists but who is traditionally identified with the Synoptic Bartholomew, appears in the Fourth Gospel. Apart from his initial encounter with Jesus when he is presented as a serious student of the Scripture, seated under the fig tree and identified by Jesus as a true Israelite, he plays no other role except that care is taken to identify his home. He is Nathanael of Cana (20:2).

Why is this emphasis on place names so unique to John? When one reads of Bethsaida in 1:45 as the home of Philip, Andrew, and Peter, the question immediately surfaces: Why this information? By itself it is not necessary for the narrative and almost seems superfluous or intrusive—unless behind this geographical reference on a subsequent level of tradition there was lodged, additionally, the memory of Bethsaida as a place of worship or early Christian missionary activity associated with these three disciples (four, if you count Nathanael).[28] In his 1925 pioneering work on the *Topologische Überlieferungsstoffe im Johannes-Evangelium*,[29] Karl Kundsin was among the first to take the many unique geographical references of John[30] and connect them with early locations of worship, centers of Christian mission activity, or in some cases, organizational points for baptist movements associated with or derived from John. Kundsin laid great weight on the etiological dynamic at work whereby prominent centers for worshiping communities would subsequently identify their locations with biblical events. In other words, such congregations, which had grown in importance as places of pilgrimage and worship by the end of the century, would explain their importance by connecting with biblical references regardless of the actual historical worth of the references. The evidence, however, confirms just the opposite. Many of these unique place names, even when they add nothing to the narrative, appear nonetheless, not as literary devices and constructions, but precisely because of their association with the ministry of Jesus and his followers and the first generation of Christians.[31]

## BAPTISMAL MOVEMENTS: BETHSAIDA AT THE CROSSROADS

Another important aspect of the Bethsaida disciples is the relationship to John the Baptist and the places of his activity. At least one of the disciples, Andrew, is explicitly presented as belonging to the baptismal movement of John. Two, however, are mentioned. As already noted, there is good reason, along with the predominant witness of the subsequent tradition, for identifying this anonymous person with John the son of Zebedee. If John is in the picture here, what about his brother James? Did John lead James to Jesus just as Andrew led Peter? The larger Gospel tradition always links these pairs together. Although the Johannine text tells us nothing about the number of those who followed John the Baptist, it is clear that the size of his movement was considerable ("people kept coming and were being baptized," John 3:22). Since Andrew and John, initial followers of the Baptist, along with their brothers were fishermen, the connection with Bethsaida, a fishing village, is apparent. Was Bethsaida, then, one of the feeder towns for the baptismal movement of John? Were there other pious Jews from this area who responded to the message of John the Baptist?

In the final redaction of the Fourth Gospel the role assigned to John the Baptist is not only pivotal but a singular one as well. John has basically only one function and that is to give testimony to Jesus. In distinction to the Synoptics where he is pictured as the eschatological preacher preparing the way for the Messiah, in John he is viewed as the "primal disciple," the first real witness to Jesus. All that he had to say about Jesus is already Christian Gospel. Liturgical phrases combine with a high Christology indicating that in some sense he is already a disciple of Jesus. In the Fourth Gospel, which is so kerygmatically oriented and theologically structured, severe limitations in method and matter are placed on any attempt to retrieve historically precise information about earlier and successive levels of tradition and the events behind them. But the present text fairly bristles with inner tensions and suggestions that would allow us, with caution, to make some viable reconstructions. Behind the unified picture of John and his role must have been a mixed pattern of interaction and exchange. As John's following grew, Jesus' ministry also began to develop. The Fourth Gospel does not report a baptism of Jesus by John but does refer to a lively interaction between the two groups as disciples began to leave the fellowship of John and align with the Jesus movement. This interaction included elements of debate and conflict. In the successive decades there is evidence of open contention as the traditions diverged and separate communities such as the later Elchasaites, Hemerobaptists, and Mandaeans began to emerge.

All of this raises the next question. Where did the activity of John's movement take place? In the much discussed passage which occurs only in John we are told (1:28): "This took place in *Bethany across the Jordan*, where John was baptizing." This reference has plagued interpreters for centuries. There are eight πέραν τοῦ 'Ιορδάνου references in the Gospel tradition. This is the only one that is linked to Bethany. Already Origen was troubled by his inability to locate a Bethany on the other side of the Jordan. Even up to this day no such city has been located there. Origen resolved the problem by introducing into the text a substitute reading: Bethabara. Indeed, the Madaba mosaic depicts a Bethabara, but it is on the west side of the Jordan. Textual support for Origen's reading was never strong, and today textual criticism points to "Bethany" as the original reading.[32] It should be remembered that John baptized in many places, as Luke 3:3 points out: "he went into all the region around the Jordan." The traditional site for the baptismal activity of John is located in the south in the vicinity of Jericho in the Judean wilderness (Matt. 3:1) near the Wadi el-Charrar, where there is also a hill revered as the place where Elijah was taken into heaven. The Fourth Gospel mentions, in addition, Aenon by Salim where John baptized because there was abundant water there (3:23). Indeed, some eight miles south of Bet Shean we find a group of springs, on the west side of the Jordan, which would have provided more than adequate water resources and a suitable setting for baptizing. Also in the vicinity is Abel-Mehula where Elisha was called by Elijah (1 Kings 19:16–21). Neither the Jericho nor the Aenon site, however, fits the time and distance factors required, if one were to reconcile these places with the account of Jesus' journey to Bethany near Jerusalem to the home of Mary and Martha (ch. 11) or his journey to the wedding of Cana (ch. 2).[33]

Another solution therefore needs to be found. For well over a century various scholars independently and at different times have proposed identifying "Bethany on the other side of the Jordan" not with a city (indeed, such a city has never been located) but with an area; namely, the territory east of the Sea of Galilee, designated as Batanaea. The philological difficulty in equating the biblical Bethania with Batanaea (Josephus: Βατανέα, Βαταναία, Βατανεία) is eased when one considers the variants that occur in the Jerusalem Targum on Deut. 32:14 and the variants that occur in the Jerusalem Talmud.[35] Identifying John 1:28 with the region of Batanaea may also help to explain why John uses the word τόπος (a place or region) to describe Bethany and not πόλις or κώμη (a city or village). The territories to the east of the Sea of Galilee have a fairly unified history in terms of their designations. During the Ptolemaic and Seleucid period when the old Persian provinces were split up and Greek colonization was encouraged in these largely uninhabited regions, new hyparchies were established and distinguished by the Greek locative *itis*. Under the Seleucids an eparchy was created which included Gaulanitis, Batanaea (sometimes referred to as Basanitis or OT Bashan), and the cities beyond the Jordan: Trachonitis, Auranitis, and Moabitis.[34] During the Hasmonean period the area was populated with Jewish immigrants and under Herod (Jos. *Ant.* xvi.285) Batanaea was settled with Babylonian Jews, who succeeded in keeping down the highway robberies and provided the dynasty with a "house royal" of proven loyalty.

Given this background, it would be easy to understand how Batanaea convincingly fits into the Johannine geographical scheme. Batanaea, of mixed population, located in the north, east of the Golan and east-northeast of the Decapolis would develop into an area that was home to much of the baptismal activity of John. Indeed, as recent scholarship shows, it may well have been the home of some of Jesus' own forebears and extended family, a region where Jesus spent time in ministry, where there was lively exchange between his followers and those of John, where some of those followers aligned themselves with Jesus.[36] From here Jesus would have left after the encounter with Andrew and Peter. In following the road west and then north through Bethsaida, Jesus called Philip, and then went on to Cana on the western side of the Sea. Batanaea—not Peraea, which was still under the jurisdiction of hostile Antipas—would then also be the area to which Jesus retreated after the attempt to have him arrested and before his final journey to Jerusalem when we are told in John 10:40: "He went away again across the Jordan to the place where John had been baptizing earlier, and he remained there. Many came to him, and they were saying, John performed no sign but everything that John said about this man was true. And many believed in him there" (cf. Matt. 19:1).

Batanaea, where followers of John remained and later developed into separate communities, was a center of the sectarian baptist group which developed into the Mandaeans who remained in this area until the Bar Kochba Revolt in the first third of the second century.[37] Given this larger picture of an area of great activity on the east-northeast side of the sea complemented by Jesus' Galilean ministry on the west, one might imagine how Bethsaida, perched in between on the top of the Sea of Galilee could fulfill its role as a geographical junction that provided a point of crossing between both sides. This view is also supported by the existing roadways of the day with a major artery coming down from Damascus and extending in a north-south direction on the east side of Lake Hula connecting Caesarea Philippi with Bethsaida, the two major cities of Philip's tetrarchy. This north-south trunk road was intersected by an east-west artery just north of Bethsaida, leading in the west to Chorazin and beyond and in the east toward Gamala and beyond. Off of this east-west artery two roadways descend to the south, one on the west side of the Sea of Galilee and another on the east side. Off of this north-south road on the east side and in the northern part an additional two roads, initially separated by some 5 km, lead eastward. They converge some 11.5 km east of the Sea of Galilee and then separate again with the southern branch headed toward Batanea.[38] The overall picture confirms Bethsaida as a key intersection, the crossroads of the Galilee, with access to major roadways headed in all four directions.

## BETHSAIDA AND THE "MIGHTY WORKS" TRAJECTORY

Another vital aspect that may contribute to a fuller understanding of the significance of Bethsaida occurs in a pre-Johannine level of tradition that is associated with Bethsaida. The pericope in which the home of Philip, Andrew, Peter is identified with Bethsaida (1:35 ff.), contains a complex of verses which belong to a level of tradition predating the final redaction, decades later, by the Johannine school.[39] This body of material is uniformly referred to as the "signs source" (*SQ* or *Semeia Quelle*), unique because it comprises a collection of the "mighty works" of Jesus which, in distinction to the Synoptics, where the term δύναμις is used, are in John always and without exception interpreted as σημεῖον. Ever since the pioneering work of Faure[40] and the detailed study by Bultmann, extensive reconstructions by subsequent scholars have advanced the hypothesis that underlying the current text of the Fourth Gospel is a kind of protogospel, or at best a mission document, which presented the signs of Jesus as a demonstration of his messianic status.[41] Those who "came and saw" (1:39) recognized him as the one hoped for in Jewish expectation. Of course, it is difficult, if not impossible, to retrieve an exact profile and a precise description of this predecessor tradition which would be located in those shadowy years before and after the middle of the first century

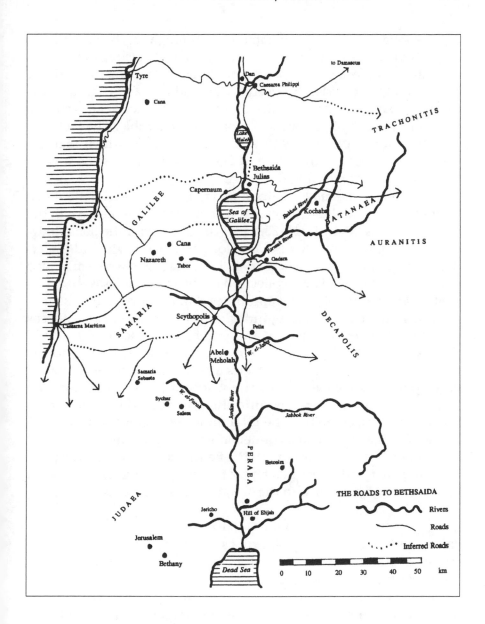

Fig. 5. Map of roads to Bethsaida

CE. The Johannine literary characteristics throughout the present text of the Fourth Gospel are so pervasive that any simple separation and delineation is precluded. And yet, the initial numbering, the striking aporias, and the collision between earlier tradition and later interpretation all make, at least in broad outline, the existence of an early collection of Jesus' "mighty works" more than plausible. The fact that this collection is prefaced with a "calling" pericope which makes a point of it to preserve the name of Bethsaida is highly suggestive of the area where this activity took place.

In a previous study,[42] I attempted to trace the development of a "mighty works" tradition associated with Bethsaida on the basis of the *Q-Logia* of Jesus (Matt. 11:21–23, Luke 10:13–15) with the harsh judgment pronounced over Bethsaida (along with Chorazin and Capernaum, the so-called evangelical triangle). Those *logia* were embedded in the Q document, a larger collection of the words of Jesus that shed light on the nature of the communities that collected them. Behind the woe statements are strong indications that the ministry of Jesus and the activity of early Jesus communities took place in the area of the evangelical triangle and in particular, Bethsaida. Parallel to the development of Q in the first decades after the death of Jesus was the development of a collection of the works of Jesus *(SQ)*. While the "word" tradition was absorbed into the Synoptics, the "work" tradition was later taken up into the Johannine texts. This "signs source," similar to Q, has a Bethsaida connection and its provenance may well be associated, at least in part, with the Bethsaida area. What is also significant is that both share in a larger trajectory of emerging tradition that is shaped by response to the "mighty works" of Jesus.

## Conclusion

Early house churches and synagogues share, to a point, a common history of development that runs along chronologically parallel lines. Their structures do not appear initially to have followed any distinctive architectural template. Instead, they are associated with normal domestic dwellings whose owners were essentially well off and who could afford larger quarters. Material finds at Bethsaida demonstrate that the courtyard house under discussion, or any at the project similar to it, falls within the parameters of the New Testament synagogue and house church traditions. The striking additional factor in the courtyard house was the discovery there of the Bethsaida cross shard, which provides an important link to the interior traditions of the Fourth Gospel. The Fourth Gospel was already important in Bethsaida research because of its statement that at least three of the disciples had their homes in Bethsaida. But now we have an ancient artifact which ties into the unique characteristics of the Johannine theology of the cross, centerpiece of the Fourth Gospel's story. Investigation of the baptismal movement of John so prominent in this Gospel, a movement to which at least two of the Bethsaida disciples originally belonged, brings an additional two factors into the picture. Highlighted here is the Johannine predecessor tradition focused on the "mighty works" of Jesus, understood as "signs." This tradition connects with those communities who in the same area and roughly at the same time gathered the words of Jesus in which are embedded the woe statements against Bethsaida because of its failure to heed the "mighty works" of Jesus. The tradition also underscores the geographically prominent position occupied by Bethsaida with easy access to the major areas of the ministries of Jesus and John and the subsequent communities that followed on both the western and eastern fronts. With Bethsaida at the crossroads and hometown connections in place what more likely locale would there be to find a center where faithful Jews intent on following Jesus would gather and share in worship?

## Chapter Notes

1. The existence of house churches stands in the background of the conflict so vividly portrayed in 3 John.
2. Krautheimer (1986) 23–25.
3. Eusebius. *HE* VIII.1.5.
4. Porphyry, Fragment 76.
5. Cf. the discussion in White (1996), 17–20.
6. Cf. MacMullen (1981) 118–119.
7. White (1997; in Meyers, 3:119).
8. Meeks (1983) 31.
9. White (1996) 40–44.
10. Hengel (1971) 57–184.
11. Urman and Flesher (1995) 1:xix; see also Horsley (1995) 224.
12. See also Rousseau and Arav (1995) 39–47.
13. Urman and Flesher (1995) 1:17–26.
14. White (1996) 102–110.
15. Cf. Hirschfeld (1995).
16. See Rami Aravi's chapter in this volume, esp. pp. 98–103.
17. See Sandra Fortner's chapter in this volume.
18. See A. Kindler's chapter in this volume.
19. Cf. Strickert (1995).
20. Cf. Shroder (1995) 65–98.
21. Memory of this devastation may be embedded in the otherwise anomalous reference in the Christian apocalyptic text of 5 Ezra (end of the second century CE). Cf. comments in Appold (1995) 234.
22. Bargil Pixner reports finding yet another cross sign incised on an oblong slab of stone found lying on the surface at the site of the Bethsaida excavation. The cross sign, which consists of two intersecting lines, has small v-like extensions at the end of each arm. The find was made before any excavations had begun on the mound, and since the stone slab was not in situ, no judgment can be made about age and significance.
23. No one would argue that isolated coins and pottery shards from the Byzantine, Islamic, and medieval periods could be used for this purpose. It is clear that such artifacts are the remains from transients, pilgrims, and travelers passing through the area.
24. The last letter in the Hebrew alphabet *(taw)* can be depicted either as a vertical + or as an X. Widespread usage of this sign in the tradition of Genesis 4:15; Ezekiel 9:4; 1 Kings 20:41; and Isaiah 44:5 can be documented within Judaism. The sign was used not simply as a decoration but as an indication of God's ownership and his protection.
25. Cf. Dinkler (1967) 1–54. See also the exhaustive collection of signs and symbols by Testa (1960) and particularly the chapter entitled "Il sigllo della Croce" 230 ff. Testa's understanding of "Jewish Christian" symbolism is, however, open to debate. He too readily assigns to Jewish/Christian groups that which can still be understood within the framework of Judaism.
26. One of the two disciples cited is specifically named Andrew, the brother of Simon Peter. The unnamed companion of Andrew is never identified. This, of course, fits well into the "beloved disciple" tradition (John 13:23; 19:20; 21:7,29) where John, the son of Zebedee, is never named. On the other hand, the unnamed disciple could also be James, the other son of Zebedee, who is almost always named before his

brother John in the Gospels; only in Luke 8:51 and 9:28 do the readings vary. The Gospel report that both the Zebedee family and the brothers Peter and Andrew shared in a common occupation is also another factor. But the simple fact that both sets of brothers were fishermen would by itself hardly justify placing the Zebedee family's home in Bethsaida.

27. Cf. Theissen (1992) 33–59.
28. Although the text demonstrates no interest in relating the narrative in terms of a historical reportage, the scene described in 1:43ff. ("the next day Jesus decided to go up to Galilee") could easily be connected with Bethsaida. In 12:21 the Fourth Evangelist speaks of "Bethsaida in Galilee." While Bethsaida was not identified as part of Galilee during Jesus' ministry, after the Jewish Revolt the extension of Galilee included Bethsaida. The final recension of the Fourth Gospel is written from this perspective.
29. Kundsin (1925) 14–34.
30. The list of place names unique to John is striking and includes the following: Bethany on the other side of the Jordan, Bethsaida, Cana, the Bethesda pools, the pool of Siloam, Aenon by Salim, Jacob's well by Sychar, Sea of Tiberias, and Ephraim by the wilderness.
31. P. Katz (1997) 130–134 convincingly argues against the Kundsin thesis in his analysis of the traditions behind John 11:54.
32. In the manuscript evidence Βηθανία represents the majority reading. It has the support not only of the codices Vaticanus (B) and Sinaiticus (א), but may be traced back to P[75] (third century) and P[66] (first half of the second century).
33. In a carefully argued study, R. Riesner (1987) 34–49 systematically investigates the options and concludes that "'Bethany beyond the Jordan' must be sought nearer to Galilee than to Judea" 34–48. See also Pixner (1994), 172–179.
34. See Jones (1984) 20.
35. For a fuller discussion of this philological issue, see Riesner (1987) 53–54.
36. Cf. Pixner (1994) 178–179.
37. Cf. Rudolph (1960) 248–252.
38. Cf. the maps, Tsafrir, Di Segni, and Green (1994).
39. For a detailed analysis of these verses see Fortna (1988) 40–47.
40. Faurè (1922) 99–121.
41. Other reconstructions add a version of the passion account (PQ).
42. Appold (1995) 229–242.

## LITERATURE CITED

Appold, Mark. 1995. The Mighty Works of Bethsaida: Witness of the New Testament and Related Traditions. Pp. 229–242 in: Arav and Freund (1995) (*q.v.*).

Arav, Rami, and Freund, Richard A. 1995. *Bethsaida: A City by the North Sea of Galilee.* Vol. 1. Kirksville, Mo.: Thomas Jefferson University Press.

Dinkler, Erich. 1967. *Signum Crucis.* Tübingen: J.C.B. Mohr.

Eusebius. 1980. *Ecclesiastical History* II. Loeb Classical Library. No. 265. Cambridge: Harvard University Press.

Faurè, A. 1922. Die alttestamentliche Zitate im vierten Evangelium, and die Quellenentscheidungshypothese," *ZNW* 21:99–121.

Fortna, Robert. 1988. *The Fourth Gospel and its Predecessor.* Philadelphia: Fortress Press.

Hengel, Martin. 1971. Proseuche und Synagoge: Jüdische Gemeinde, Gotteshaus und Gottesdienst in der Diaspora und in Palästina," pp. 157–84 in: Jeremias et al., eds., *Tradition und Glaube, Festgabe für K.G. Kuhn.* Göttingen: Vandenhoeck & Ruprecht..

Hirschfield, Yizhar. 1995. *The Palestinian Dwelling in the Roman-Byzantine Periods.* Jerusalem: Israel Exploration Society.

Horsley, Richard. 1995. *Galilee: History, Politics, People.* Valley Forge: Trinity Press International.

Jones, A. H. M. 1984. *The Greek City.* Oxford: Oxford University Press

Katz, Paul. 1997. Wieso gerade nach Efrajim? *ZNW* 88:130–34.

Krautheimer, Richard. 1967. *Early Christian and Byzantine Architecture.* Baltimore: Penquin.

Kundsin, Karl. 1925. *Topologische Überlieferungsstofffe im Johannes Evangelium.* Göttingen: Vandenhoeck & Ruprecht.

MacMullen, Ramsay. 1981. *Paganism in the Roman Empire.* New Haven: Yale University Press.

Meeks, Wayne. 1983. *The First Urban Christians.* New Haven: Yale University Press.

Porphyry. *Adversos Christianos.* Fragment 76 in: White, Michael. 1997. *The Social Origins of Christian Architecture.* Vol. 2. Valley Forge: Trinity Press International. No. 29, p. 104.

Pixner, Bargil. 1994. *Wege des Messias und Stätten der Urkirche.* Gießen: Brunnen Verlag.

Riesner, Rainer. 1986. Bethany Beyond the Jordan (John 1:28): Topography, Theology, and History in the Fourth Gospel. *Tyndale Bulletin* 38:29–63.

Rousseau, John J., and Rami Arav. 1995. *Jesus and His World.* Minneapolis: Fortress Press.

Rudolf, Kurt. 1960. *Die Mandäer.* Vol. I. FRLANT. Göttingen: Vandenhoeck & Ruprecht.

Schroder, John. 1995. Geologic and Geographic Background to the Bethsaida Excavations, in: Pp. 65–98 in: Arav and Freund (1995) (*q.v.*).

Strickert, Fred. 1995. Coins of Philip, Pp. 165–189 in: Arav and Freund (1995) (*q.v.*).

Testa, E. 1962. *Il Simbolismo dei Giudeo-Christiani.* Publicazioni dello Studium Biblicum Franciscanum 14: Gerusalemme.

Theissen, Gerd. 1992. *Social Reality and the Early Christians.* Minneapolis: Fortress Press.

Tsafrir, Yoram; L. Die Segni; and Judith Green. 1993. *Tabula Imperii Romani: Iudaea Palaestina.* Jerusalem: Israel Academy of Sciences and Humanities.

Urman, Dan, and Paul Flesher. 1995. *Ancient Synagogues.* Vols. 1 and 2. Leiden: E.J. Brill.

White, Michael. 1990, 1997. *The Social Origins of Christian Architecture.* Vols. 1 and 2. Valley Forge: Trinity Press International.

_____. 1997. House Churches, in: *The Oxford Encyclopedia of Archeology in the Near East.* New York: Oxford University Press. 118–21.

*Elizabeth McNamer*

# Medieval Pilgrim Accounts of Bethsaida and the Bethsaida Controversy

I N THE EARLY FIFTH CENTURY, writing from his cell in Bethlehem, Saint Jerome (c.347–419/20) tells of the importance of pilgrimage:

> Just as one can understand the Greek historians better when one has seen Athens or the third book of Virgil when one has sailed to Troas or Sicily, so also we understand Scripture better when we have seen Judea with our own eyes and discovered what still remains of the ancient towns. That is why I myself take care to travel through this land.[1]

About a thousand years later, Felix Fabri wrote:

> One returns wiser, able to argue about the Gospels and the prophets ... and one can sometimes overcome and set right learned divines in their interpretation of difficult passages of Holy Scripture.[2]

In the thousand years that spanned these two promoters of pilgrimage, many a holy person made the hazardous journey to the Terra Sancta in hopes of gaining a better understanding of Scripture and perhaps of challenging learned divines. We have some one hundred accounts of medieval pilgrims' journeys to the Holy Land. Twenty-seven of these (more than one in four) mention Bethsaida. The desti-

397

nation of most pilgrims was Jerusalem and places associated with the death and resurrection of Jesus. Travel into the remote countryside was dangerous—particularly between the time the Holy Land fell to the Arabs in 637 and the arrival of the Crusaders at the end of the eleventh century. Once the pilgrim was in the Holy Land he or she had the difficult task of identifying sacred sites. While the ingenuous pilgrim would have known from Scripture the names of the places associated with the ministry of Jesus, the ingenious guides might move the sacred sites around to accommodate the pilgrims' pious intentions. The fact that so many travelers mention Bethsaida is testimony to its importance.[3] That they give varying accounts of the location of Bethsaida is understandable.

### REASONS FOR CONFUSION OVER LOCATION

Difficulty in locating the site can be excused on at least two accounts. First, the Bethsaida of the Gospels was a fishing village located on the Sea of Galilee. Second, this village or city was known by two different names.

The references in the New Testament leave no doubt that Bethsaida was a fishing village. John 1:22 tells us that Philip, Andrew, and Peter, who were fishermen, came from this town. Mark 6:45 states, "As soon as it was over he made his disciples embark and cross to Bethsaida ahead of him." As a fishing town it would have been situated on the Sea of Galilee. Josephus tells us that Bethsaida was "situated on the lake of Gennesareth."[4]

So the logical place to look for Bethsaida would be on the shore of the Sea of Galilee. But the site is now two km from the sea; we do not know when it ceased to be a seaside town. Pliny the Elder, writing in the second century, notes that the Sea of Galilee was then fourteen miles in length;[5] it is now eleven miles long. Eusebius, writing in the fourth century, suggests that Bethsaida was no longer on the shore at that time: "Bethsaida, city of the apostles Andrew, Peter, and Philip, is in Galilee near the lake of Gennesaret."[6] Jerome, who wrote after Eusebius, muddies the waters somewhat by mentioning "the lake of Gennesareth on the shore of which Capernaum, Tiberius, Bethsaida, and Chorazin are situated."[7]

In any event it has now been established by geologists that in the past the sea actually came up to the present-day site.[8] Bargil Pixner has put forward the theory that at some point, possibly in the second century, excessive rain caused the Sea of Galilee to rise and its outlet at the lower Jordan river took a new course. When the rain subsided, the sea was smaller.[9] The changing topography, then, was one reason for confusion about the site of Bethsaida.

Another reason Bethsaida eluded identification was that its name was changed. Josephus tells us that Herod Philip renamed Bethsaida as Julius for the daughter of Augustus.[10] Recent scholarship has shown that it was probably renamed for the wife of Augustus, Livia-Julias, in about the year 30 CE.[11] However, none of the Gospels refers to this city as Julius even though they were written several decades after the renaming of the city; all four call it Bethsaida.

Bethsaida-Julius, as a viable city, ceased to exist at the time of the Roman war. For the next nineteen hundred years, it lay in its ashes and dust, its identity unknown.

### RUMORS OF A CHURCH

Interest in pilgrimages places associated with Jesus was heightened in the early fourth century by Helena (c. 248–c. 328), the mother of Emperor Constantine (who had afforded Christianity a legal status in the Roman Empire).[12] The saintly Helena made the journey to the Holy Land in 326 CE to seek out places associated with the founder of Christianity. She is known to have built the Church of the Holy Sepulchre in Jerusalem and the Church of the Nativity in Bethlehem (the Bethlehem church is still there).[13] Saint Willibald (700–786), who visited the Holy Land in the eighth century, wrote that Helena built a church at Bethsaida, that the church was still standing, and that he spent the night there:

> And then they proceeded from Capernaum to Bethsaida whence came Peter and Andrew. There is a church now there where their house formerly stood. They stayed there one night and in the morning went on to Corazin.[14]

The Bethsaida church is also mentioned seven centuries later by Franceso Suriano (1548/49–1621), who doubtless had access to the travel accounts of Willibald:

> The city of Bethsaida in which were born Peter and Andrew.... From the house of the apostles a church was made.[15]

Frater Bonifacius de Stephanis, who visited between 1551 and 1564, also wrote about the church:

> In that place Bethsaida, Helena built in the house of Peter a large church, of which vestiges until now still exist and the major capella served as a gift to God.[16]

And Johannes Cotovicus, writing in 1598, quotes a certain Nicephorus as having said that Helena built a church at Bethsaida on the foundations of the house of Peter:

> Helena built a church on the foundations of the house of Peter, according to the author Nicephorus; however there is nothing left today of this place. Here Christ cured the mother-in-law of Peter who had a fever, by only laying his hands on her, gave back vision to the blind man and cured many people afflicted with various illnesses.[17]

It is probable that Willibald, the first to mention a church at Bethsaida, spent the night at Capernaum (where indeed the remains of a church have been found) and not Bethsaida, and that others were led astray by his account. Nicephorus almost certainly meant Capernaum since he recalls the curing of Peter's mother-in-law, which Luke 4:39 says happened at Capernaum. Helena honored many places by building a church in them, but Bethsaida does not seen to have been one of those places; no remains of a church have been found at the site.

### Importance of Bethsaida in the New Testament

Pilgrims had three good reasons for wanting to find Bethsaida and to have it on their itinerary. First, it was, according to Saint Luke, the site of the multiplication of the loaves and fishes (one of the greatest miracles of Jesus). Second, John's Gospel claims that it was the home of three of the apostles (one of whom later was identified as the first pope). Third, it was, according to the Synoptic Gospels, associated with the miracles of Jesus. As such, it was important to medieval believers and earned itself a place on pilgrim agendas as worth seeking out.

### As the Site of the Multiplication of the Loaves and Fishes

Luke 9:10b–17 says Bethsaida was the site of the feeding of the five thousand:

[H]e took them with him and withdrew privately to a town called Bethsaida. But the crowds found out and followed him. He welcomed them and spoke to them about the kingdom of God, and cured those who were in need of healing. When evening was drawing on, the twelve came up to him and said "Send these people away; then they can go into the villages and farms round about to find food and lodging for we are in a lonely place here." "Give them something to eat yourselves," he replied. But they said to him "All we have is five loaves and two fishes, nothing more, unless perhaps we ourselves are to go and buy provisions for all this company." (There were about five thousand men.) He said to his disciples "make them sit down in groups of fifty or so." They did so and got them all seated. Then taking the five loaves and the two fish, Jesus raised his eyes to heaven, pronounced a blessing over them, broke them and gave them to his disciples for distribution to the crowd. They all ate until they had enough. What they had left, over and above, filled twelve baskets.

But Luke also mentions that this miracle happened at a lonely place (ἔρημος). Mark 6:32–445 gives the site of the multiplication of the loaves and fishes at "a lonely place" close to the sea, and immediately afterwards, Mark says that Jesus and his disciples embarked for Bethsaida. Matthew 14:13 says that Jesus, after hearing of the death of John the Baptist, withdrew "into a desert place" (εἰς ἔρημον τόπον) (14:13) where the five thousand were fed, and later went by boat to the other side and went into the mountains to pray. (Jesus may well have fled to the safer territory of Philip Herod, where Bethsaida lay.) The feeding of the four thousand (Matt. 15: 29-38) takes place near the Sea of Galilee in the mountains. Thus Jesus apparently sailed to a lonely place and went into the mountains after the miracle. (Mark 6:32, 35, 46; Matthew 14:13, 15, 23; John 6:15.)

Guides seem to have introduced the pilgrims to "the lonely place" instead of the town of Bethsaida.[18] The narrative of Arculf about the holy places, written in 650, mentions visiting the site of the feeding of the multitude on "a grassy and level place ... no buildings can be seen."[19] (He does not mention Bethsaida although he mentions Capernaum, Nazareth, and Mount Tabor.)

In the seventh century, the Venerable Bede (672/3–735), safe in his abbey in Northumbria, wrote a little book concerning the holy places by abbreviating the works of former writers. He places the site of the great miracle on the shore of the Sea of Galilee, on a grassy place, near a fountain, north of the city of Tiberius, and on the route from "Aelia to Capernaum."[20] (Aelia Capatolinia was the name given by Hadrian to Jerusalem in the first half of the second century CE and lasted to the seventh century CE.)

Between the time of the capture of the Holy Land by the Crusaders (1099) and the defeat of the Crusaders by Saladin (1187), a number of pilgrimages were recorded. Seawulf was the first to give an account during the time of the Crusaders. His visit took place between 1100 and 1105. He tells, somewhat tentatively, that Tiberius is on one end of the Sea of Galilee and Chorazin and Bethsaida on the other, and that the multiplication of the loaves and fishes took place about two miles to the east of the seashore, in the mountains.[21] A Russian pilgrim abbot named Daniel, who was escorted on his pilgrimage in 1106/7 by the Crusader Prince Baldwin, talks about the feeding of the five thousand as being a "verst" from the sea, a plain "covered with grass" (a later commentator describes the abbot's account as the "first example of thoroughly unintelligent topography"[22]). Belard of Ascoli, a monk who made his pilgrimage in 1155, is as vague as the abbot; he says that the place of the feeding of the five thousand "was on a mountain near Capernaum," where "there are many well cut stones lying about...."[23] Johannes Phocas, writing thirty years later in 1185, is no more reassuring; he positions the place "a little left of the Jordan" on a "slightly rising mound."[24] A tract by an anonymous pilgrim, dating from the time of Saladin's conquest of Jerusalem in 1187, mentions the place of the feeding of the five thousand as being near the marsh of Gennesaret, "a mountain covered with grass."[25]

Even a century and a half later, *A Guidebook for Palestine* described the feeding of the five thousand as taking place "two miles from Capernaum as you go down the mountain and then two miles from the descent."[26] Trying to follow these rather obscure directions might land one in the middle of the Sea of Galilee. Thus the argument as to the site of the miracle of the multiplication starts with the Gospel writers themselves and continues in medieval times.

As the Home of the Apostles
Bethsaida also appealed to pilgrims as the home of three of the closest friends of Jesus, Philip, Andrew, and Peter (John 1:44). Theodosius, a sixth-century pilgrim, added that it was also the home of John and

James, the sons of Zebedee: "From Capernaum, Bethsaida is six miles, where the apostles, Peter, Andrew, Philip and the sons of Zebedee were born."[27]

Nowhere in the canonical Gospels does it mention that James and John came from Bethsaida, although Mark 1:16–20 associates the "sons of Zebedee" with Andrew and Peter and the fishing business, and Luke 5:10 goes so far as to say that they were partners. Theodosius seems to have obtained his information from another tradition, as did several other writers. A twelfth-century pilgrim, the Count De Vogue, wrote, "A Bethsaida Petrus et Andreas, Joannes et Jacobus Alphei." He makes James "the son of Alphaeus" and ignores the fact that John and James were brothers and the sons of Zebedee.[28] Theodoric, a German bishop, in his *Description of the Holy Places* written in 1172, embellishes this account and makes both James and John sons of Alphaeus: "This is Bethsaida to which Peter and Andrew, John and James, son of Alphaeus, belonged."[29] The story is further colored by an anonymous pilgrim, referred to as Pseudo Bede, of the same century: "From Bethsaida came Peter and Andrew, James and John, and James the son of Alphaeus."[30] And a Magister Thetymarus, writing in 1217, mentions "From Bethsaida was Peter and John, Andrew and James springing from Alphaeus."[31] Philip has temporarily fallen by the wayside in these accounts, but James son of Alphaeus has been included among the Bethsaidans. This would make it the home of six of the twelve. Of course, if one assumes that Levi, son of Alphaeus (Mark 2:14), and Jude, the son of James (Acts 1:13), also came from the same town, the number is raised to eight.[32]

## As the Site of the Mighty Works of Jesus

Matt. 11:20-24 and Luke 10:13–15 mention Bethsaida in connection with the "mighty works" ($\delta\upsilon\nu\alpha\mu\epsilon\iota$) of Jesus, as does Josephus.[33] The city was condemned along with Chorazin and Capernaum for its lack of repentance. Mark 8:22–26 gives it as the place of the curing of the blind man. The medieval pilgrim would have sought out Bethsaida for this very reason, since miracles were of importance and the purpose of many pilgrimages was to obtain a miraculous cure for oneself or a loved one. It appears that guides were happy to place this town of miracles wherever it was convenient, leaving the innocent travelers to record various locations as being the same site.

## LOCATING BETHSAIDA

Theodosius, writing in 530, seems to have been in no doubt as to its location:

> From the seven fountains, Capernaum is two miles. From Capernaum it is six miles to Bethsaida.... From Bethsaida to Paneas is fifty miles. There the Jordan emerges from two sources, the Jor and the Dan.[34]

The Russian abbot Daniel is as vague about the location of Bethsaida as he was about the place of the multiplication of the loaves and fishes. He recounts: "a little farther distant from Magdala, in the mountain is Bethsaida...a little distance from there one finds Capernaum."[35] A guidebook associated with the name Fetellus, and composed by Count De Vogue in 1130, reads: "The Jor, not far from Paneas, becomes a lake, and afterwards forms the Sea of Galilee, beginning between Capernaum and Bethsaida.... Four miles from Bethsaida is Corozin."[36] Theodoric, in 1172, allows (correctly) that Bethsaida is four miles from Chorazin.[37] On the other hand, one Magister Thetmarus, writing in 1217, is not too helpful when he tells:

> Thence I crossed over above the banks of the sea of Galilee where the Jordan divides Galilee and Idumea. Thence from the sea of Galilee crossing to the cities of Bethsaida and Capernaum.[38]

Father Richoldus de Monte Crucis, writing in 1290, says that Bethsaida is "close to the Sea of Galilee."[39]

A fourteenth-century guidebook to Palestine (obviously an embroidered version of Fetellus' twelfth-century work) informs us that Bethsaida is "near the Sea of Galilee" and that "the Sea of Galilee begins between Bethsaida and Capernaum," and further, that "Bethsaida is four miles from Chorazin, where the world's seducer is to be nurtured."[40] Its location is given by Jacques De Vitry in his *History of Jerusalem*, written c. 1227:

> The Sea of Galilee is also called the Sea of Tiberius near which is Bethsaida the city of Peter and Andrew which the Lord glorified with his presence. It is also called the Lake of Gennesareth which is being interpreted "generating wind" because from the springs of the mountains that stand round about it a strong wind is often collected which causes a disturbance on

the lake and grows into a tempest whereby small ships are often overwhelmed by the high waves.[41]

Odoricus De Foro Iulii, writing in 1320, places Bethsaida near the lake and four miles from Chorazin; Jacobus De Verona, writing in 1335, places Bethsaida five miles from Magdala, above the Sea of Galilee; and Niccolo Da Poggibonse, in 1347, put the Sea of Galilee "below the city of Bethsaida and Capernaum."[42]

John Poloner made a very inaccurate map in 1422 but his description is colorful:

> Four leagues east of Nephtalim, beside the Sea of Galilee, is Bethsaida, the city of Andrew and Peter. Three leagues to the south of this is the castle of Magdalon, on the Sea of Galilee from which the Magdalen took her name. One league east of Bethsaida is the place where Christ stood on the seashore and said to the seven disciples "Children have ye any meat?" His footprint can be seen on a stone.... Galilee is nearly all flat and plain country. On one side it adjoins the Holy Land, wherein stands Bethsaida; on the other, Samaria is mountainous.[43]

At least one pilgrim disagrees with Poloner's statement that "Galilee is nearly all flat and plain country." Ludolph Von Suchem, in his *Description of the Holy Land*, written in 1350, calls Galilee

> a noble country rich in plains, hill, pastures, grass and other good things with exceeding fruitful and pleasant valleys. On its plains and the slopes of its hills stand the following cities to wit: Naim, Capernaum, Bethsaida, and Cana of Galilee. But all are now deserted and look as if they had never been of much account.[44]

The Italian Francesco Suriano, who made a pilgrimage in 1485, places Bethsaida on the coast of the Lake of Galilee but confuses it with Tiberius.[45]

Was Bethsaida on the main road from Syria to Egypt? Bouchard of Mount Sion, a German Dominican monk, writes in 1280:

> Two leagues from Nephtali, at the corner of the Sea of Galilee where it begins to curve from the north towards the south extends Bethsaida, the city of Andrew and Peter and Philip. At this day it has scarce seven houses which stand by the side of the road from Syria to Egypt. In ancient times it had a watercourse leading from the river which Josephus calls the little

Jordan which runs into the Sea of Galilee halfway between it and Capernaum. Traces of this may be seen to this day.[46]

While this account suggests that Bethsaida was on the road from Syria to Egypt, it may not be the case. Bouchard gives much inaccurate material: As the towns of the Decapolis he lists Tiberius, Sepher, Kadesh-Naphtali, Hazor, Caesarea-Phillipi, Capernaum, Iotapata, Bethsaida, Chorazin, and Beth Shan (Scythopolis). The only one of these towns that actually was in the Decapolis was Beth Shean. Bouchard thus is not trustworthy.

Marino Sanuto, who wrote *Secrets for the True Crusaders to Help Them Recover the Holy Land* in 1321, places Bethsaida near the highway "where the sea begins to trend to the southwards."[47]

## LATER CONFUSION

The double name Bethsaida-Julias led to confusion especially for later pilgrims. By 1562 an anonymous Franciscan wrote about coming out of Damascus to the Sea of Galilee, at the town called El Mini, to Bethsaida. By 1590 Christian Adrichom, a Dutch priest, wrote a book about the sites of the Holy Land and drew a map on which he indicates three places for Bethsaida—two on the east side of the Jordan, one of which he calls Julias and the other, farther south, "desertum Bethsaida," as well as one on the west side called Bethsaida. In 1600 Johannes Cotovicus wrote that it is a town where the Moors were making good use of the waters that flowed close by. In 1621 P. Franciscus Quaresmi spoke of two towns:

> Bethsaida and Julias were distinct, different places. Julias was a place at the other side of the sea which Philip the Tetrarch in the time of Christ encircled with walls and made into a city in honor of Caesar and his daughter Julia, and from that name, it is said, came Julias and Juliada. And Bethsaida was the town of Galilee at this side of the sea and this side of the coast. And now Bethsaida and the other penitent towns paid their fines. And the presence of ruins is at least some proof. From Tiberius it is a distance of twelve miles.[48]

In 1891 a Scot, George Smith, traveled the land on foot and corrected this:

> Bethsaida was a village on the east side of the Jordan, near the river's mouth that the Tetrarch Philip rebuilt and named Julias

in honor of the daughter of Augustus. This is the Bethsaida to which Jesus withdrew on hearing of the Baptist's death and near which was the desert place described by John on the other side of the Sea of Galilee. "Crossing over the Sea of Galilee" does not necessarily mean to cross to the opposite shore. Josephus speaks of sailing from Tiberius to Tarichea past towns that were on the same side of the lake.[49]

## Conclusion

There is little consistency in medieval pilgrims' accounts that mention Bethsaida. Later pilgrims seem to have reiterated what earlier pilgrims had stated. Willibald, for instance, mentioned that he spent the night in a church at Bethsaida. Others took up this idea. Chester McCowan deftly suggests that Saint Willibald "merely erred as to the name of the place where he spent the night,"[50] and this probably led to confusion on the part of others.

There is little agreement as to the place of the multiplication of the loaves and fishes. Theodosius puts it at what is known today as Tabgha. Bede corroborates this, at least to the extent of there being a fountain, and Belard of Ascoli also places the event near Capernaum, possibly in the same spot as Theodosius. Seawulf suggests it was some distance from the sea. None mention Bethsaida in connection with this miracle, but neither do they discount it.[51] It took place in a lonely place (ἔρημος), close to a mountain.

Some pilgrim accounts assert that Bethsaida was the home of three of the apostles (Peter, Andrew, and Philip), some say five (Peter, Andrew, Philip, James, and John), and others (by including James, son of Alphaeus) raise the number to six. If we add Jude (the son of this James), and Levi (James' brother), the number is raised to eight. This would make Bethsaida the home of two-thirds of the apostles, and thus of enormous importance.

There is no unanimity in medieval accounts as to the location of Bethsaida. It is listed variously as being twelve miles from Tiberius, eight miles from Tiberius, near Tiberius, three miles from Magdala, five miles from Magdala, "a little further distant" from Magdala, four miles from Chorazin (this is fairly consistent), right on the Sea of Galilee, where the Jordan divides Galilee from Idumea, by the side of the road leading from Syria to Egypt, a league from the seashore, close to El Mini, near Tabgha, four miles above Capernaum. As McCowan points out, one would have had to take very devious routes to find Bethsaida. Medieval pilgrims' accounts, charming and interesting, are at best unreliable for establishing the geographical location of the Bethsaida of the Scriptures or the Bethsaida-Julias of the Roman period.

## CHAPTER NOTES

1. Jerome. *Praef. In Lib. Paralip.*
2. Stewart (1971) 9:41.
3. However, there is only one recorded between 637 and 1099, that of an English pilgrim named Willibald; cf. Baldi (1982), 266.
4. Josephus (1958–1965) *Ant.* 18.2.
5. Pliny (1957), *Natural History* 5.15.15.
6. Eusibeus (1902) 58: βηθσαιδά πόλις Ανδρέου χαὶ Πέτροσ χὰι φιλίππου. χ̄ειτᾱι δέ ἐν τῇ Γαλιλάια πρὸσ τῇ Γεννησαρίτιδι Χμνη.
7. Jerome (1963) Comm. Isa. 9:1.
8. See Shroder and Inbar (1995) 65.
9. Personal interview with Bargil Pixner, June 1995. See discussion of rain in Galilee in Freyne (1980) 5.
10. Josephus (1958–1965) *Ant.* 18.28. Philip also raised the town to a polis (city).
11. Rousseau and Arav (1995) 21. This lady had pretensions of being a goddess. Neither her husband nor her son would confer this apotheosis, but Herod Philip renamed his town in her honor.
12. Several pilgrims visited the Holy Land prior to Helena. In his *History of the Church,* Eusebius tells us that the bishop of Mileto of Sardis made a pilgrimage in 160; Bishop Alexander of Cappadocia went there in 216; many pilgrims visited right after Helena's visit before the medieval period: Silvia of Aquatania journeyed to the Holy Land c. 385, Egeria visited in 380, Cassian in 385, Palladius in 388, and Posthominius in 401.
13. Murphy-O'Connor (1980) 148.
14. Baldi (1982) 266. "Et inde e Capernaum pergebant ad Bethsaidam: inde erant Petrus et Andreas. Ibi est nunc ecclesia, ubi prius erat domus ilorum. Et illic manentes unam noctem, mane pergebant ad Corozaim." Two accounts, both from c. 723, have come down to us of Willibald's pilgrimage. Roswida, a nun from Heidenheim abbey, wrote one and the other was written by a companion of Willibald's. He was the first English pilgrim of record to visit the Holy Land and his is the only account that mentions Bethsaida between the arrival of Arab Muslims and the Crusades.
15. Baldi (1982) 269: "la cita de Bethsaida, ne la quale nascete Pietro et Andrea…. De la casa de li Apostoli fo facta una chiesa.Æ
16. Baldi (1982) 271: In isto viculo Bethsaida Helena in domo Petri magnam construxit ecclesiam, cuius vestigia adhuc extant, et maior capella illaesa dono Dei servatur.
17. Baldi (1982) 270: "Helena hic supra fundamenta domus Petri Ecclesiam erexisse author est Nicephorus; eius tamen nulla hodie extant vestigia. Hic Christus Petri socrum febricitantem solo tactu sanavit, caeco visum restituit, multosque ante aedes Petri varijs afflictos morbis, daemonia cosque curavit." Egeria, who made a pilgrimage in 380, mentions that the walls of the church in which Jesus cured the paralytic were still standing at Capernaum. Egeria locates Bethsaida on the Jordan River just beyond the Hepta Pegai near what is today known as Tabgha.

18. Dalman (1935) argues that the feeding could not have taken place near Bethsaida since there are no mountains there to which Jesus could retire.
19. Stewart (1971) 3:43. Arculf has lived for nine months in Jerusalem and examined the holy places by daily visits.
20. Stewart (1971) 3:83. "The place where the Lord blessed the bread and the fish is on this side of the Sea of Galilee, to the north of the city of Tiberius; a grassy level plain which has never been ploughed, and which has no buildings on it showing only a fountain from which they drank. Those who come from Aelia to Capernaum pass through."
21. Stewart (1971) 4:25:"The city of Tiberius is on the seashore at one end. At the other end is Chorazin and Bethsaida, the city of Andrew and Peter. From the city of Tiberius, the plain of Gennesareth extends about four miles to the north.... From Gennesareth about two miles distance to the east is the mountain on which the lord Jesus fed five thousand men from five barley loaves and two fishes." Seawulf's manuscript was rescued from the destruction of monastic libraries in the sixteenth century by the then Archbishop of Canterbury, Matthew Parker.
22. Stewart (1971) 4:57; McCowan (1930) 37.
23. Stewart (1971) 5:29: "Moving your eyes to the left of the Jordan you will see the sea of Tiberias clearly and without any difficulty, on the opposite side of which appears a slight rising mound where the saviour blessed the words and fed five thousand."
24. Stewart (1971) 5:29 "Moving your eyes a little to the left of the Jordan, you will see the sea of Tiberius clearly and without any difficulty, on the opposite side of which appears a slight rising mound where the Savior blessed the waves and fed five thousand."
25. Stewart (1971) 6:54.This tract also tells of Jesus only eating the backs of the fishes and throwing them back in the water where they came to life again and swam round with bare backs! The writer also attests that Jesus was imprisoned until he paid the taxes for his passing, "and then Peter found a fish with a silver coin in its mouth and Jesus paid the taxes with that."
26. Stewart (1971) 6:36.
27. Baldi (1982) 266: De Capharnaum usque Bethsaida milia VI, ubi nati apostoli Petrus, Andreas, Philippus et filii Zebedae.
28. Stewart (1971) 5:244. The reader will recall that there were two among the twelve by the name of James, one a son of Zebedee and one a son of Alphaeus. They are often referred to, respectively, as James the Greater and James the Less.
29. Tolber (1851) 101: "Haec est Bethsaida, unde Petrus et Andreas, Johannes et Jacobus Alphaei fuerunt." Theodoric adds that while four apostles came from here, Philip came from Cana as did Nathaniel.
30. Stewart (1971) 6:53.
31. Tolber (1851) 5: "de Bethsaidam erant Petrus et Iohanes, Andreas et Iacobus Alphei oriu."
32. This is significant. Freyne (1980) 344, points out that while "Galilean Christianity" is frequently mentioned in contemporary New Testament studies, we have little direct evidence for its existence in the province.
33. See Appold (1995) 229. One must remember too that many pilgrims made the journey in search of a cure (a mighty work) for a loved one.
34. Baldi (1982) 266: "De septem fontibus usque in Capernaum milia 11. De Capharnaum usque Bethsaida milia VI.... De Bethsaida usque in Paniada milia L; inde exit Iordanis de duo loca Ior et Dan." Bethsaida is in fact 35 miles from Paneas.

35. Baldi (1982) 266: "Non loin de Magdalia, dans la Montagne, est située Bethsaide.... A peu de distance de là se trouve le village de Capernaum."
36. Baldi (1982) 266: "Ior Haut longe a Paneas lacum illius reddit ex se, postea mare Galilee, sumens initium inter Capharnaum et Bethsaida.... Quarto miliario a Bethsaida Corozain."
37. Stewart (1971) 5:432.
38. Baldi (1982) 266: "Inde transive super ripam maris galylee ubi iordanus exiens medio maris galylee dividit galyleam et ydumeam. Item inicit maris galylee transiens civitatem Bethsaidam et Capharnaum, Bethsaida."
39. Baldi (1982) 267.
40. Stewart (1971) 6:36.
41. Stewart (1971) 11:29.
42. Baldi (1982) 268, 269.
43. Stewart (1971) 6:24.
44. Stewart (1971) 12:123. Von Suchem was rector of the parish church of Suchem in the diocese of Paderborn and may have been identifying it with his own homeland.
45. Baldi (1982) 269.
46. Baldi (1982) 267: "De Neptalim per duas leucas in angulo maris Galilee, idem ab aquilone curvari incipit contra austrum, sita est Besayda, civitas Andree et Petri et Philippe. Nunc vix habet domos, iuxta viam, quede Syria ducit in Egyptum. Habuit ar quitus aqueductus de fluvio, quem Iosephus vocat parvum Ioronem, qui medio loco inter ipsam et Capharnaum ingreditur mare Galilee. Huius vestigia adhuc apparent.
47. Stewart (1971) 12:14. This writer seems to have had a copy of Bouchard before him since he reiterates the incorrect names of the ten cities of the Decapolis. He also states that he has located the well into which Joseph was cast by his brothers; he may be correct about this since there are not many wells in this area and the Genesis account indicates that Joseph was sold to a caravan group headed to Egypt from Syria.
48. Bethsaida et Juliam distinctas esse civitates.... Julia enim civitas est trans mare et Jordanem aedificata; erat enim vicus transmarinus ... quam Philippus tetarcha tempore Christi muris cinxit et in civitatem vertit ad honorem Caesaris et Juliae filiae eius, et es eius nomine Julias et Juliada dicta est. At Bethsaida fuit Galilaeae civitas cis mare Galilaeae, et in eiusdem littore sita.... Et nunc Bethsaida ut et aliae impoenitentes proxime civitates, solo aequatae debitas impoenitentiae poenas lunt; et illius in praesentia aliquae dumtaxat ruinae monstrantur. Distat a Tyberiade miliaria duodecim.
49. Smith (1966) 269.
50. McCowan (1930) 36.
51. Mccowan (1930) 42, points out that at least on pilgrim places the feast between Bethsaida and Jubb Yuseph.

## LITERATURE CITED

Appold, Mark. 1995. The Mighty Works of Bethsaida: Witness of the New Testament and Related Traditions. Pp. 229–242 in: Arav and Freund (1995) (q.v.).

Arav, R ami, and Richard A. Freund. 1995. *Bethsaida: A City by the North Sea of Galilee.* Vol 1. Kirksville, MO: Thomas Jefferson University Press.

Baldi, Donatus. 1982. *Enchiridion, Locorum Sanctorum.* Jerusalem: Franciscan Press.

Dalman, Gustaf. 1935. *Studies in the Topography of the Gospels.* New York: McMillan Co.

Eusebius, of Caesarea. 1965. *The History of the Church from Christ to Constantine.* Translated by G. S. Williamson. Penguin Classics. New York: Penguin.

———. 1902. *Eusebius Werke.* Vol. 3.1 *Das Onomastikon,* edited by Erich Klostermann. Leipzig: J. C. Hinrichs.

Fabri, Felix [1441] 1971. *The Wanderings of Felix Fabri.* The Library of the Palestine Pilgrims' Text Society. Vols. 7–10. Reprint of London 1887–1897 edition. New York, AMS Press.

Freyne, Sean. 1980. *Galilee from Alexander the Great to Hadrian.* Notre Dame, IN: University of Notre Dame.

Gingres, George. 1970. *Egeria: Diary of a Pilgrimage.* New York: Newman Press.

Hunt, J. 1982. *Holy Land Pilgrimage in the Later Roman Empire, A.D. 312- 460.* Oxford: Clarendon Press.

Jerome, Saint. 1963. *Commentariorum in Esaiam.* Corpus Christianorum. Series Latina; 73, 73A. Turnholti: Brepolis.

Josephus, Flavius. 1958-1965 (*Works,* English and Greek, 1958). Loeb Classical Library. 9 vols. Cambridge, Mass: Harvard University Press.; London: W. Heineman.

Klostermann, Erich. S.v. Eusebius (1902).

McCowan, Chester. 1930. The Problem of the Site of Bethsaida. JPOS 10:32–58.

Murphy–O'Connor, Jerome. 1980. *The Holy Land, an Archaeological Guide from Earliest Times to 1700.* Oxford: Oxford University Press.

Pliny, the Elder. 1957. *Natural History* 5.15:15. New York: Ungar Press.

Ptolemy. 1843–1845. *Geographia.* Edited by Carolus Fridericus Augustus Nobbe. Editio Stereotypa. Lipsiae: Sumptibus et typis Caroli Tauchnitii.

Rousseau, John J., and Rami Arav. 1995. *Jesus and His World.* Minneapolis: Fortress Press.

*Seawulf.* Canon Brounlow, trans. London: Palestine Pilgrims Text Society, 1892.

Shroder, John F., Jr., and Moshe Inbar. 1995. Geologic and Geographic Background to the Bethsaida Excavations. Pp. 65–98 in: Arav and Freund (1995) (q.v.).

Smith, G. A. 1966. *The Historical Geography of the Holy Land.* New York: Harper and Row.

Stewart, Aubrey, translator. [1895] 1971. Library of the Palestine Pilgrims' Text Society. Tracts and journals by unknown authors of the 11th and 12th centuries. The translation mainly from the text of Tober. Vols. 1–13. London: Palestine Pilgrims' Text Society, 1895. Reprinted edition, New York: AMS,1971.

*Textus Evangelici.* Bethsaida.

Theodericus, of Wurzburg. 1986. *Guide to the Holy Land .* Translated by Aubrey Stewart; with new introduction and bibliography by Ronald G. Musto. 2d ed. New York: Italica Press.

Tolber, J. 1851. *Thetmar Magistri Iter ad Terram Sanctam Anno 1217.* Bern: Saint Gallen.

Wilkinson, John. 1988. *Jerusalem Pilgrimage 1099–1185.* The Hakluyt society, 2d series, no. 167. London: Hakluyt Society.

*Richard A. Freund*

# The Incense Shovel of Bethsaida and Synagogue Iconography in Late Antiquity

A BRONZE INCENSE SHOVEL was found on May 7, 1996, at Bethsaida Excavations in an extremely disturbed Hellenistic–Early Roman layer of occupation in Area A, square G54, locus 152 (fig. 1).[1] The shovel was found under debris in close proximity to a large Iron Age Bit-Hilani-style palace structure and 9 m away from the southwest corner of a structure close to the city gate that measures 20 m by 6 m, which apparently was a Roman-style temple. The shovel was found in a first-century CE refuse pit, the contents of which seem to be related to the temple structure. If this Roman-style temple identification is confirmed through further investigations, then the hypothesis is that this is the site of the Julia cult established by Philip Herod, apparently when he raised the status of Bethsaida to a *polis* and renamed it Bethsaida Julias in the first century CE.

The last major site in Israel which produced an incense shovel in an archaeological context was the Bar Kokhba "Cave of Letters."[2] Yigael Yadin found three incense shovels together in a basket in one locus (and another shovel in a different locus) in the so-called Cave of Letters.[3] The incense shovels were found together with other bronze objects and Yadin quickly assigned the making of the shovels to the first century CE and their production to a non-Palestine locale.[4] According to Yadin, this was "the largest collection of Roman metal vessels found to date in Palestine and the neighbouring region."[5] The four incense shovels found in the caves were of four different sizes and

Fig. 1. Incense shovel found at Bethsaida Area A, square G54, locus 1521

suggested similar but distinct purposes.[6] It was Yadin's impression that the incense shovels were part of the booty taken by Bar Kokhba's troops: "... of the units of the Roman Legions or the Auxilia, which carried them about for ritual purposes."[7] He was not sure what the ritual purposes might have been, but he, like other investigators who had written about these bronze shovels, assigned them to some ambiguous pagan ritual. Apparently, Yadin did not consider why such a rich hoard of ritual objects would be located in a military camp. In addition, although Yadin himself pointed out that the incense shovels figure with a number of other well-known Jewish symbols such as the lulav (palm branch), ethrog (citron), and menorah (candelabrum) in synagogue iconography of the third to sixth centuries, he does not address the point of why synagogue iconography would adopt a pagan ritual object for presentation in a Jewish building.[8]

It is possible of course that all of these symbols—palm branches, citrons, candelabra, and incense shovels—were originally non-Jewish symbols which Jewish artisans adapted or adopted for use in synagogues, either with full knowledge that they were also pagan symbols or perhaps out of ignorance of pagan practices. There is evidence that all of these symbols, including the shovels, would have been meaningful in Jewish and non-Jewish circles of the period.[9] Moreover, depiction of the quintessential Jewish symbol—the seven branched menorah described in the Bible—was actually forbidden by rabbis for use after the destruction of the Temple in 70 CE and its appearance in synagogue iconography is itself problematic.[10] In order to accommodate this rabbinic injunction, small changes were sometimes made to the menorah so that it was slightly different from the one that had been in the Temple.[11] This point is important to our investigation of the incense shovel in synagogue iconography. The synagogue was not intended to be a replacement for the Temple, and the symbols of the synagogue were only intended to remind the worshipers of the Temple. This is especially true in regard to the investigation of the incense shovel in synagogue iconography.

The question is relevant since the incense shovels discovered in archaeological contexts such as Bethsaida and the Bar Kokhba Caves bear a striking resemblance to the incense shovels found in synagogue iconography. The locations of similar types of incense shovels at Pompeii and Herculaneum as well as Roman provinces of the East suggest that their original use was in the imperial cult[12] in the first centuries BCE and CE. According to Josephus, the city of Bethsaida-Julias was dedicated to the wife of Augustus Caesar by Philip Herod; since the imperial cult in the eastern provinces of the Roman empire was associated with the dedication of a temple and/or city to the imperial family (and especially Julia), it is reasonable to assume that a temple was built in her honor at Bethsaida upon the dedication of the city. The present assumption regarding the incense shovel found at Bethsaida is that it was used for the practice of the imperial cult in a temple dedicated to Julia at Bethsaida.The present chapter investigates another aspect of the incense shovel that remains unanswered: the continuing importance of the incense shovel of the type found at Bethsaida in Jewish life suggested by its prominent appearance in synagogue iconography from the third to sixth centuries. Two hypotheses will be explored:

1. The short-handled incense shovel was originally a pagan ritual object that became prominent in Jewish (i.e., rabbinic/synagogue) iconography and literature primarily because it was well known in the period.

2. The short-handled incense shovel was both a pagan and a Jewish ritual object which became prominent in Jewish (i.e., rabbinic/synagogue) iconography and literature because it was well known in the period, resembled (or was imagined to resemble) a ritual object used in the incense service in the Temple in Jerusalem, and because some sort of incense ritual continued to play a role in the synagogue after the destruction of the Temple in Jerusalem.[13]

### THE INCENSE SHOVEL OF BETHSAIDA

There are four parts to incense shovels in general: pan, cups or ear-brackets, handle, and feet. The pan of the Bar Kokhba Caves shovel (designated by Yadin as no. 3) measures 7.9 x 10.7 cm; the handle is 12.3 cm long; the overall length of this shovel is thus 23 cm.[14] The pan of the Bethsaida incense shovel is 9.1 cm long and 67.7 cm wide, and the handle is 11.2 cm long, for a total shovel length of 20.5 cm. This size is smaller than most of the incense shovels that are described below, but its precisely square size is important for comparative reasons—especially for comparison with the synagogue iconography (most are square and the pan is nearly equal in length to the shovel handle). The Bethsaida shovel is quite similar to those found in the Bar Kokhba Caves and especially to those designated by Yadin as incense shovels no. 5 and no. 6. The main reasons are: size, shape, design, decoration, and functionality suggested by other elements. Because these elements impact upon our understanding of the nature of the shovel, a detailed description of the Bethsaida shovel follows.

*Pan:* The rims of the sides are grooved. In the center of the pan and in each of its four corners there are stamped concentric circles. design. The flat bottom of the pan is somewhat shorter than the sides.

*Ear-Brackets:* The two closed corners of the pan terminate in ear-brackets which resemble leaf decorations. Some larger shovels, such as Yadin's incense shovel no. 3, have what can be described as cups[15] at the closed corners of the pan, which may have held other incense for mixture with the incense in the pan, but these smaller leaf decorations could not have been used for this purpose and may have had some other functional purpose.[16] The pan also has projecting sides that support rims. These are relevant to the investigation since according to Arav's assessment, these rims may date the pieces more conclusively.

*Handle:* The handle is a halved tube in the form of a Corinthian column; the shaft is plain except for a ring at the middle. The handle is joined to the pan by a Corinthian capital and the joint has been reinforced by a brace. The handle ends with a support that is square in shape with an arrowlike impression in the support. The importance of the short size of the handle should not be underestimated. It is approximately the same length as the pan, and the pan is nearly square. Yadin concluded that the "several parts may have been brazed together or more probably were molded in one piece by the *cire perdue* technique...."[17] Since the Bethsaida shovel broke at the handle during in situ removal, x-ray photographs were taken of the shovel to determine if this shovel had been molded in one piece from poor-quality bronze, which may indicate where it was produced and how it was to be used. In addition, although it was constructed from bronze, the metallurgical analysis[18] of the bronze reveals that it had a high percentage of lead (up to 15 percent) and a low percentage of tin up to 7 percent) in addition to copper.[19] The technique of casting in one piece may have been known in Palestine, but the raw materials (especially tin) for producing top-quality bronze was not. This clearly indicates a poor-quality bronze and may indicate that it was a local product of Palestine, produced from locally available raw materials for local use. Another possibility is that since only small amounts of tin were found, it could have been a reused bronze piece. Whatever its origins, the result is a shovel of low-quality bronze, which may not have been particularly useful, especially for frequent carrying of hot coals. In the case of Yadin's shovels, his own metallurgical analysis[20] reveals another poor-quality bronze shovel with a mixture of 15 to 20 percent lead and 65 percent copper. This composition, like that of the Bethsaida shovel, would not have held up as well as the traditional mixture of 60 percent copper and 40 percent tin used in Rome for high-quality bronze vessels. This analysis is important as we try to ascertain the exact use of short-handled incense shovels.

*Feet:* Four prongs form the feet, and the shovel remains free-standing when placed on a flat surface.

The shovel is made of bronze and has five concentric circular details in the four corners of the pan and in the center. The similarity between the Bethsaida shovel and the four bronze incense shovels from the Bar Kokhba Caves that date to the first or second century is striking. Yadin's descriptions of shovels no. 5 and no. 6 are very close to the description of the Bethsaida shovel, and the five concentric circles that appear in the pan of the Bethsaida shovel are the same as those on Yadin's shovels.[21] A shovel of similar dimensions and with similar concentric circle design appears at Hauran and seems to have been part of a set of three shovels.[22] Another similarly designed shovel, but without the concentric circle design, was found at Beitar in Israel.[23] This detail is noteworthy since Goodenough and Yadin suggest that the concentric circles were not merely aesthetic decoration, but served some specific purpose. The design is also seen another incense shovel found in Israel. These shovels, together with the Bar Kokhba Caves shovel no. 5, the Bethsaida shovel, and one of the Hauran shovels (no. 660), all have designs with the five concentric circles. The placement and number of the circles have not been explained sufficiently,[24] but in synagogue iconography in which a shovel of this sort appears, multiple round markings on the pans are clearly highlighted in some of the mosaics.[25] The suggestion that they may represent faux venting,[26] faux sifting,[27] or the possibility that they indicate the placement for coals (in contemporary usage or as representation of some ancient ritual) for a ceremony of incense burning, although the purpose of the symbols and the shovels themselves is still not known. The fact that the shovels found in the Bar Kokhba Caves were a set of different sizes found together and that the shovels from Hauran could also form a set of different sizes suggests a number of possibilities: (a) that different functions may have been assigned to each size shovel, (b) that the shovels were used by different individuals with different stature and hand size, or (c) that different ceremonies required varying amounts of incense. Only one shovel in each of these two "sets" has the concentric circle design and may indicate something about the use of that shovel in the ceremony. This type of symbol may be a cosmological design of the period, but it may also simply be an artistically grooved design. This design is found on metal bowls,[28] patera,[29] and the bases[30] of jugs and bowls among the other metal utensils found in the Cave of Letters.

Although Yadin mentions that burning is found on the shovel pans, this needs to be investigated further. He states that there were traces of burning in the center of the pans found in the Cave of Letters:

> The finds from the Cave of Letters further enable us to deliberate on the use of such shovels. The two cups preserved on our No. 3 indicate that the coals themselves were placed in the pan, while the cups served to hold various kinds of incense which was sprinkled from time to time over the coals. The two complete cups also explain the mysterious circles in the corners of censers depicted on several Jewish objects. Moreover, the concentric circles decorating our No. 5 and the shovel from the Hauran (No. 660) evidently represent the coals, like the dots decorating several other of the censers depicted on these objects.[31]

It is assumed by Yadin that incense would be placed in the pan of the shovel and the pan set upon some previously placed burning coals to produce plumes of incense smoke to be used in an incense rite. The Bethsaida incense shovel model could have been used in some freestanding capacity or in a ritual which did not require that the shovel be held throughout the service. The handle is too short to allow extended contact with an unprotected hand (unless some type of holder was involved) if hot coals were already in the pan. The four feet on the incense shovels of Bethsaida (and those from the Bar Kokhba Caves) would have allowed usage as a freestanding, portable, incense burner. More testing for evidence of burning would need to be performed to confirm whether the pans were used in this fashion. Portable censers are mentioned in some parts of the Bible, and Graeco-Roman Jewish interpretations for the most part suggest that the biblical shovel could have been used for (a) burning incense, (b) transporting hot coals, (c) transporting incense to the altar, or (d) carrying away the ashes after the ritual.

In sum, the short-handled, bronze incense shovels of Bethsaida and the Bar Kokhba Caves (and elsewhere) could have been used as a freestanding portable object in an incense ritual, as a freestanding incense carrier, or even as a cleaning shovel. The Bethsaida and Bar Kokhba Caves shovels do not appear to be fine bronze work (such as imports might be) but rather a local product of first-century Palestine. Finally, the shovels have characteristics that more likely suggest a freestanding incense carrier than a ritual incense burner. The implications of these conclusions for the interpretation of synagogue iconography are crucial since there appears in mosaics and other artifacts a representation of a square short-handled incense transporter (and not a censer) such as the one surveyed above. In this same synagogue iconography are found symbols that represent the ties between the Temple cult and the synagogue ritual. These symbols are at the heart of the major differences between the Temple and the synagogue. The lulav and ethrog symbols on synagogue iconography were central to the rabbinic celebration of Sukkot as was the Shofar to the holiday of Rosh Hashanah although they were peripheral to the cultic celebration of these holidays in the Temple. Instead of portraying a cult object from the Temple which was at the heart of a Temple incense ritual (for example, the censer), synagogue iconography had chosen a vessel for representation which although it might have been involved in a Temple ritual was not central to it. Instead of portraying a so-called holy vessel and suggesting (as it might be inferred) that the priestly incense ritual of the Temple could or should continue to be performed in the synagogue, a more profane and more peripheral object involved in the incense service had perhaps purposely been chosen for representation in the synagogue to imply that the synagogue ritual was to be similar but not equal to the Temple's.

### RITUAL OBJECTS: FROM TEMPLE TO SYNAGOGUE

Worship and prayer were defined in antiquity by many personal and public expressions. The Bible outlines the personal petitions of individuals that were made outside of the Tabernacle and Temple, and the need for public gatherings for expressions of national tragedy and success were common enough in antiquity that the existence of a gathering place for such activities may be inferred. Beyond the ritualistic prayers and services of the Temple, the existence of competing "temples" in Israel and Egypt suggests that the distance between Jerusalem and the communities of Israelites and later Diaspora Jews necessitated institutions to help mediate Jewish spirituality in an organized and ritualized manner. The Temple in Jerusalem has a unique place for Israelite and later Jewish public cultic worship, but its history was interrupted two or three times during the Iron Age and Hellenistic and Roman periods by destruction and exile. In the first Babylonian destruction of 586 BCE, the Jews were exiled to Babylonia, and during the generation which followed the origins of a new institution, the synagogue, supposedly were laid.[32] The relationship between the existence of the Temple in Jerusalem and the development of synagogues has been an issue of discussion for over one hundred years.[33] The present state of the question is that the synagogue as a separate and unique institution with a specific religious meaning and presence, in a building for liturgical activity originated in the Diaspora and largely remained a Diaspora institution until after the destruction of the Temple in Jerusalem in 70 CE. This is the definition of a synagogue for the prerabbinic period. The rabbinic definition of a synagogue—a unique structure described by and used in accordance with rabbinically defined norms for regular prayer services and Torah reading ceremonies, and which is oriented towards the east or Jerusalem—is a post-Temple innovation in Palestine.[34] Most standardized rabbinic synagogue construction took place during two major periods: the mid- or late third and early fourth centuries and the sixth century.[35] While construction and orientation seem to have been resolved by the third century, the ornamentation and iconography associated with the synagogue do not seem to have been resolved so early. With the rise of the rabbinic movement in the Galilee after the second century CE, questions about the synagogue and its furnishings were still up for debate. On the one hand, the rabbis seem to be the beneficiaries of not having a long and detailed history of prescribed iconography to deal with in Israel. On the other hand, the lingering emotional connection to the Temple of Jerusalem seems to have created a need to remember in symbols and prayer the rites and rituals of the Temple. The rabbinic calendar and liturgy were built around the holidays of the Temple and the sacrificial schedule. The synagogue service incorporated some literary references to rituals performed in the Temple together with active and passive participation by the congregant. The ceremonies of the waving of the lulav and the blowing of the shofar, for example, were incorporated into an active rite in the synagogue together with readings about the sacrifice rituals performed in the Temple. The main iconographic renderings in the synagogues seem to depict some of the objects used in the Temple, especially those that continued to play a role in synagogue ritual, but not those which were purely literary references and did not have some active synagogue role. For this reason, some of the most prominent Jewish symbols on the mosaics and synagogue iconography of Israel were the lulav, ethrog, menorah, shofar, and the Torah shrine. While these five are perhaps self-evident because they continued to find a role in the medieval and even modern synagogue, another symbol is found along with them in many synagogue mosaics: the short-handled incense shovel (see figs. 2–7 for examples).The presence of the incense shovel is a vexing one, because the incense shovel does not have a well-known ritual associated with it in the synagogue. The remainder of this chapter will argue that the short-handled incense shovel depicted on synagogue mosaics may not only have been the symbol of a long defunct incense ceremony of the Temple, but like the other symbols with which it is represented on these mosaics, it may not have had an ongoing synagogue ritual associated with it.

## THE INCENSE SHOVEL IN SYNAGOGUE ICONOGRAPHY: JEWISH OR PAGAN SYMBOL?

The fact that the incense shovel appears with some frequency in synagogue iconography of the third through the sixth centuries (in the Galilee in particular) is a point often missed in some studies.The following is an up-to-date listing of synagogue iconography found in Israel that features the incense shovel.[36]

The earliest use is attested only in the third century synagogues of Kohav HaYarden and Peqi'in. Its use continues in the fourth century synagogue of Hammath Tiberias (two instances), Ahmadiyye,[37] Yahudiyye,[38] the fifth century synagogues of Ein Nashot,[39] Danah,[40] Kafra,[41] Bet Samara at Sebaste, Beth Alpha (see figs. 2–3), Capernaum, Huldah (see fig. 6–7), Husifah (two instances), Sepphoris, the sixth century synagogues of Bet Alpha and Bet Shean (two instances) and Fiq,[42] for a total of sixteen sites and twenty instances in the Galilee and Golan over three centuries. While the number of instances is not extremely high, they are significant since the Torah shrine appears at eleven sites and thirteen instances, a Hercules knot appears in nine synagogues and eleven instances, and a depiction of a grapevine appears in nineteen sites and nineteen instances. What is most important is that the incense shovel always appears with the lulav, ethrog, shofar, torah shrines, and menorah. While the incense shovel does not always appear with the same frequency as the lulav, ethrog, menorah, and shofar, the incense shovel does appear regularly when these other symbols are present (see figs. 2–7).

The most frequently used symbols of the synagogue by far were the shofar (twenty-five sites and thirty instances), lulav (twenty sites and twenty-eight instances), menorah (over sixty sites and one

Fig. 2 (*above.*) Portion of a mosaic floor, Beth-Alpha synagogue (c. 5th century CE)

Fig. 3 (*left*). Detail of mosaic floor, Beth-Alpha synagogue (c. 5th century CE)

Fig. 4 (*above*). Portion of mosaic floor, synagogue at Tiberias Hamat (c. 5th century CE)

Fig. 5 (*left*). Portion of mosaic floor, synagogue at Tiberias Hamat (c. 5th century CE)

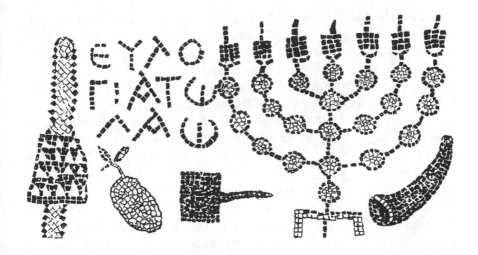

Fig. 6 (*above*). Portion of a mosaic floor, Huldah (c. 5th century CE)

Fig. 7 (*below*). Detail of a mosaic floor, Huldah (c. 5th century CE)

hundred instances), and ethrog (fifteen sites and twenty-two instances) from the third through the sixth centuries in the Galilee and Golan. These four items were the most frequently and routinely represented in all archaeological sites in Europe and the Middle East during the same period, presumably because they were powerful symbols with ritualistic importance in rabbinic Judaism of this period.

In volume four of *Jewish Symbols in the Greco-Roman World*, E. Goodenough attempts to interpret the nature of these symbols in the noncultic setting of the synagogue. He held that they were definitely Jewish symbols, as opposed to the wreath, Hercules knot, and others (which he saw as specifically pagan symbols) as well as the vines and pomegranates, for example (which were universal symbols). He held, however, that the menorah, lulav, ethrog, shofar, and incense shovel had been transformed into symbols "used in devotion, to have taken on personal, direct value,"[43] apparently linked to eschatological meanings. A. Nock, commenting on this, states:

> ... menorah, lulav, ethrog, Ark, and incense shovel were associated with the Temple and as such could remain emblems of religious and national devotion after its destruction; the details of the old observances were discussed with passionate zeal for centuries after their disuse. Goodenough has indeed made a strong case for the view that, as presented in art, they refer to the contemporary worship of the synagogue (as he has produced serious arguments for some use of incense in this). It may well be that they suggested both Temple and synagogue.[44]

What neither Goodenough nor Nock suspected was that the incense shovel may have figured in an ongoing synagogue incense ritual which may in fact have used a free-standing incense shovel like the one pictured in synagogue iconography and found at archaeological sites such as Bethsaida and Beitar.

## INCENSE: PRACTICES OF JEWS, GREEKS, AND ROMANS

Incense was a well-known part of rituals in the ancient Near East and the Mediterranean. In the myths of the Greeks, Romans, Egyptian Pyramid texts, Phoenicia, Ugarit, and Assyria as well as the Hebrew Bible, incense was a part of the spheres of medicine, religion, politics, economics, and the cultural and social milieu of the ancient world. Apparently it was used in private homes as well as in public religious ceremonies and although its purposes are well described in ancient literature, the delivery system and the vessels involved in its preparation and burning are not well known. This section will attempt to locate the incense shovel within the literature of the ancient world and the Bible. The problem of describing the incense shovel (i.e. as an artifact) and locating it in a specific literature such as the Bible (and its translations) is complicated by a number of interpretation layers. Archaeological excavations at Iron Age sites have identified what is thought to be three separate places (and artifacts) for incense burning, which are only partially confirmed by the literature: in pottery incense burners, on stone altars, and in specially created stone bowls. It seems that the incense was burned; then the ash and often the coals upon which the incense was burned were immediately carried away from the site of burning in a ritualistic act of transference during which the ash and coal were carried in a ritual object—the incense shovel.

In Leviticus 16:12–13, the Day of Atonement ritual indicates that the high priest was to take in one hand a shovel with charcoal and in the other hand incense. In the rabbinic interpretation of this section, the high priest would take a handful of incense from one location and put it in a shovel-like vessel called alternately a *kaf* (a biblical word meaning spoon or ladle) and *bazich* (a rabbinic term), although this vessel is not explicitly mentioned in the biblical text.[45] Although the ritual is mentioned in the Pentateuch as being part of the Tabernacle (and not the Temple), the interpretations of these sections take for granted that the Temple ritual is the same. In this ceremony, one of the most important of the ritual year, the high priest (using the shovellike vessel) put the incense on the charcoals in the other shovel and the resulting incense cloud gave the high priest a measure of protection while he proceeded to perform other Day of Atonement rites.

In Numbers 17:1–16 the material of the "censers" is bronze; these censers were portable and they were also used for ritual healing. The general English term "incense shovels" might be applied to ritual objects used by the priests for either the transporting or burning of incense. The vocabulary used in the Pentateuch to describe the ritual objects of the Tabernacle is not necessarily the same as the vocabulary used to describe the ritual objects in the Temple of Solomon or the later Temple reconstructions beginning under the Persians up through that of Herod the Great. One might reasonably extrapolate Temple practice from Tabernacle references because the lists of vessels used in both are similar, but they are not exactly the same. Also, biblical criticism of the past century demonstrates that this is to be expected since much of the Tabernacle material was produced during the periods of the Temples.[46] It is just not known with historical certainty whether the vessels of the Tabernacle are distinct from the vessels of the First (or Second) Temple, whether all the Tabernacle vessels were in use in the Temple(s), or whether any of the Tabernacle vessels were used in the Temple(s). The archaeological and literary information make varying contributions to our understanding of the question. The archaeological discoveries that relate to vessels from the period of the First and Second Temple are remarkably slim. One related piece of information regarding incense shovels can be drawn from the excavations at Tel Dan. In the Dan archaeological strata dating from the time of Jeroboam II (8th century BCE) there was discovered an altar with three iron shovels in close proximity.[47] The dimensions of these three iron shovels are important because A. Biran concluded that they are incense shovels and the altar was an incense altar.[48] Dimensions of two of the shovels that were found together are 54 cm long, with scoops 14 to 15 cm long, about 11 cm wide, and 2 to 5 mm thick. The handles are about 1 cm thick. The handles have hooks and rings at their ends, and according to Biran, the shovels were hung on a wall. The third shovel is 57 cm long and may have been longer but the end of the handle is missing. Biran admits that these Dan incense shovels are similar to the representations on synagogue iconography except that the shovel handles are so much longer. Furthermore, in excavations of Cyprus there were found similar long-handled shovels, which like the Bethsaida shovel, show extensive wear on the pan.[49] These Dan shovels may provide the missing link between the so-called incense shovels of the Roman period and those used in the Temples of the Iron Age. The wear and tear present on the Dan shovels and the length of their handles suggests that these shovels were probably used to carry burning substances. The handle of the Bethsaida shovel (11.1 cm) is only about one quarter the length of the Dan shovels (40 to 42 cm), which probably indicates that the incense shovel of Bethsaida was used only for the transporting of incense while a longer-handled shovel would have been used to transport hot coals or burning incense.

These problems will not be resolved in this chapter, but the investigation of the vessels for transporting and burning incense, known as censers, seems to be connected to another object referred to in the Bible as a ladle or spoon. Since our knowledge of all of these items is limited, the two words under investigation are *censer* and *ladle*. Three ambiguous Hebrew words are generally used in the MT for these vessels: כף, מחתה, and מקטרת.

The word כף is found throughout the Bible and is generally translated as ladle or spoon. In discussing the Tabernacle, one finds it is used for a ritual object in Exodus 37:16 (MT/LXX 38.12) and again when discussing the Showbread Table in Numbers 4:7: "And he made the furniture of the table, the plates (קערתיו) and כפתיו and the cups and the bowls...."

The כף in the Exodus passage and Numbers passage in LXX Greek is translated with the word θυισκη. In the rest of Numbers 7:14, 20,26, 32, 38, 44, 50, 56, 62, 68,74, and 80 in regard to the gifts of the tribal chiefs, the כף in the LXX Greek is translated with the word: θυισκη. This word is significant since it is also one of the Greek words used in the rest of the LXX for translating the MT word המחתה. The MT word המחתה is translated in a number of different ways in the LXX. It is translated in the LXX as the Greek word θυισκη in 1 Kings 7:50, 2 Chronicles 4:22, 2 Kings 25:15, and Jeremiah 52:17–19. It is difficult to determine how the LXX Greek rendered the words of the MT here (or whether it is rendering our MT or has a totally different underlying text![50]), but there is a discrepancy between the number of ritual vessels and the order of their presentation between the MT and LXX. The words המחתות and כפות both appear in Jeremiah 52:17–19, for example (כפות two times in the MT), and while only the Greek word θυισκη appears in this section as a recognizable parallel to these words, it is clear that the LXX vocabulary here is distinct from the LXX Exodus, Leviticus, Numbers, and even the Kings and Chronicles versions.

The MT word המחתה is also translated in the LXX Greek word το πυρειον in many cases; for instance, Leviticus 10:1, and 16:12, Numbers 4:14, 16:17–18, and in Numbers 16:37–46 (MT 17:1–11). The Numbers references are important since they refer to a portable incense burner or censer. The word also appears in Exodus 27:3:

> You shall make pots for it to receive its ashes, and shovels and basins and forks and firepans (המחתתיו); you shall make all its utensils of bronze.

One extremely interesting part of this is how different the description in the LXX version of this text is. The LXX has:

> You shall make a rim for the altar; and its covering and its cups and its flesh hooks and *its firepan* and all its vessels you shall make of brass [in the LXX Greek: το πύριον; singular].

One major difference is that while the MT has multiple firepans, only one is mentioned in the LXX, and this single firepan seems to be attached to the altar in some way in a later description.

Now we turn to MT Exodus 38:2–4 (=expanded LXX Exodus 38:22–23).

MT Exodus 38:2–4:

> [2] He made horns for it on its four corners; its horns were of one piece with it, and he overlaid it with bronze. [3] He made all the utensils of the altar, the pots, the shovels, the basins, the forks, and the firepans (המחתות; plural): all its utensils he made of bronze. [4] He made for the altar a grating, a network of bronze, under its ledge, extending halfway down.

Some additional information appears in this passage in the LXX Exodus 38:22-24 section, which is taken from the Numbers 16 Korah rebellion incident. In the Numbers 16 account, the bronze covering for the altar is made from the hammered out remains of the censers of the Korah supporters, while in this passage the actual censer seems to sit upon the altar and is attached to it. This does not exactly correspond to the earlier description of Exodus 27:3–5 of the bronze covering and grating where the LXX and MT basically agree. The LXX translator of Exodus does in many places expand and interpret apparently on the basis of the standards and terminology of the period during which it was translated[51] This is important, because it might imply that the LXX translator preserved an updated version of the way that the incense altar looked in the Hellenistic period.

LXX Exodus 38:22–24:

> [22] He made the brazen altar of the brazen firepans (πυρεια) which belonged to the men engaged in sedition with the gathering of Korah. [23] He made all the vessels of the altar and its firepan, and its base, and its bowls, and the brazen flesh hooks. [24] He made an appendage for the altar of network under the firepan (το πυρειον), beneath it as far as the middle of it and he

fastened to it four brazen rings on the four parts of the appendage of the altar wide enough for the bars so as to bear the altar with them.

Another Hebrew word also can be translated as incense shovel/firepan/censer/burner. The MT word מקטרה is translated in the LXX as the Greek θυμιατηριον. The use of the word *miqtoret* as a noun for the actual censer is limited to 2 Chronicles 26:19 and Ezekiel 8:11, but is still important since the word also appears in the so-called War Scroll of the Dead Sea Scrolls.[52]

A fourth word is apparently used to translate the MT word המחתה in the LXX Greek: επαρυστριδη. The word המחתה appears as a utensil for the menorah in Exodus 37:23:

And on the candlestick seven golden lamps, and its snuffers of gold and its מחתה of gold.

In the LXX, the מחתה are translated with the word τας επαρυστριδας. So too in Numbers 4:9, where the word appears as a utensil associated with the menorah and the conveyance of oil. Usually this Greek word is an indicator of a separate vessel for the transport of oil for the lamp or for transporting one substance to another, but here it is used as a translation for the word המחתה.

Finally, an additional word is used in the Greek to translate the concept of the censer of the Temple/Tabernacle. In the NT references of Revelation 8:3 and 8:5 "the censer" (το λιβανωτον) is named after the word which is used for frankincense and is the semitic loan word לבונה. In Revelation 8:3, the divine sees an angel with a golden λιβανοτος in his hands coming towards the divine altar. The Greek words το θυμιαματα πολλα ("much incense") is the description of the altar. It is clear that the translation of the MT word המחתה (censer) is not consistently translated in the LXX. It is difficult to know why, but among the possibilities might be that there were simply different types of *mahtot* which were used for a variety of distinct tasks and thus it seemed natural to designate them differently in the translation. Further, the translators lived in a time when they could only speculate on the ritual objects that were used during the time of the Tabernacle and Temple of Solomon. It is possible that the differences in translation may indicate different underlying Hebrew versions, confusion by later scribes, or even different hands translating different books and using a distinctive vocabulary. Four (or five) different Greek terms were used to describe Temple/Tabernacle utensils that might be described as incense shovels. They were:

1.  In the LXX Greek of 2 Chronicles 26:19 and Ezekiel 8:11: το θυμι-ατηριον. The word is also used in this sense in 4 Maccabees 7:11.
2.  In Exodus, Leviticus, and Numbers: το πυρειον.
3.  In Jeremiah 52:17–19 and 1 Kings 7:48–50 as well as other apparent references to the "ladle" but appear as the censers (τας θυισκη).
4.  In Exodus and Numbers the word τας επαρυστριδας.

What is obvious from this short survey of the Greek translations of the MT is that they employ a variety of distinct Greek terms for what might have been the incense shovel, censer, and ladle. It is not clear whether the Greek translators added new objects to the lists of vessels of the Tabernacle/Temple or whether the lists of objects remained the same from the time of the Tabernacle through the Second Temple since the lists of vessels are not standardized throughout the Hebrew Bible, Greek translations, or manuscript readings. What is clear is that there were a variety of words used to translate these specific objects, which may imply that Greek and Roman period translators and authors saw a number of different vessels being used for the Temple service and thus were forced to use a wider variety of Greek and Roman terms to describe the Temple incense service. The preferred translation for the object that was used to transport incense to the burning site (an incense transport shovel) is θυισκη. The word is apparently the translation for a spoonlike or ladlelike implement, the biblical כף. Hellenistic[53] and early Jewish Roman period writers such as Josephus and Philo[54] held that the מחתה and כף were different types of incense shovels in the sense that they were used to transport incense to the site of burning and/or they were portable incense bearers (an incense burner shovel). The כף is a vessel used specifically for carrying incense, while the מחתה is a portable incense burner. Since our knowledge of the objects used in the Temple service is so limited, the words used to describe the actual incense service is dependent upon interpretation and careful word analysis. Three ambiguous Hebrew words are generally used in the MT for the vessels involved in the incense burning services. They are *Machtah* and *Miqtoret,* translated as firepan or censer, and *Kaf,* translated as ladle or spoon. The original Hebrew words may have had a variety of meanings which are reflected in the Greek and Roman period translations. It is not surprising to discover that in the latter part of this same period, the rabbis' exegetical interpretations and their analyses of the Temple rite yielded a series of different Hebrew, Aramaic, Greek, and Latin loan words to describe the incense rites and vessels as well. Of particular interest is a short-handled shovel mentioned frequently in Rabbinic literature that was used for transporting incense from a storage facility in the Temple to the altar. This new term is *Bazich.*

## The Bazich [בזיך]: Was it the Incense Shovel of Synagogue Iconography?

As mentioned above, the burning of incense and the use of incense shovels or censers were an important part of the daily and holiday Temple service and would have been known to the Temple priests and the wider public. Many different types of utensils were used for a variety of purposes. For example, incense was burned twice each day, in the morning and evening, on the incense altar and different censers, incense holders, transporters, and ladles were used in this service. Two censers (actually incense holders) were used for frankincense for the Showbread Table and another special censer was used for the burning of incense on the Day of Atonement, among other utensils.[55] The burning and bringing of the incense to the altar and table required a number of steps, from its collection and processing until it was actually placed in its final resting place or was burnt. Unlike other rites which were mysteriously performed in the Temple without the public's awareness or appreciation, the fragrance and the cloud of smoke rising off the altar were well known in antiquity.[56]

While it is possible that the rabbis of the Talmudic era were aware of the items used in the Temple service, it is clear that the rabbis who codified the traditions were writing in a period significantly later than the Temple service—one to two hundred years later—when the services were no longer a reality. Their descriptions of the items and events, while important, cannot be considered to be firsthand information. The fact that the depictions of incense shovels on synagogue mosaics begin to appear two to three hundred years after the destruction of the Temple is significant.

The multiple examples in Israel and the Diaspora of a short-handled, flat, square-shaped item which is found in the floor mosaics of synagogues that date from the period of classical Rabbinic Judaism—the third through sixth centuries—and depicted on oil lamps from Israel and its environs[57] and on bone carvings, monuments, and tombs in Israel, North Africa, and Rome[58] demonstrates that this item was a powerful symbol in the rabbinic imagination. Although it may appear that the incense shovel was partially supplanted by the amphora in most tombs and inscriptions in Europe,[59] the symbol of the incense shovel still seems to have had a place in the synagogues and life of Middle Eastern Jewry. It is grouped together with the most famous Jewish iconography of the period (menorah, shofar, lulav, ethrog, and torah shrines). Even though the symbol is almost always found in synagogues in Galilee and not in the Diaspora, its importance cannot be underestimated. This short, flat, square-shaped item with a handle bears a striking resemblance to the incense shovels found in the archaeological contexts mentioned above. The logical conclusion might be that the incense shovel found in the archaeological contexts mentioned above and the symbol found on synagogue iconography in Israel are the same, that is, Jewish. The problem is obvious. If Yadin is correct and the proximity of the shovels located in a clearly archaeological context is an indicator of their use, the shovels can only be considered pagan. There is, however, another issue. Although one cannot be sure that the items mentioned in the Bible (for the Tabernacle) are the same items which were used in the First or Second Temple; it is nonetheless possible that the rather ambiguous "censer" of the books of Leviticus and Numbers may actually have been a distinct object and only later in the late Roman and early Byzantine periods did the rabbis need to "recover" the symbol as if it were actually the censer of the Temple in Jerusalem. If that is the case, then the bronze incense shovels found in the Hellenistic and Roman period may have little to do with the censer (מקטרת), firepan (המחתה), and ladle (כף) mentioned in the biblical text.

## CENSERS, FIREPANS, AND LADLES IN RABBINIC TEXTS

The firepan (המחתה) is a well-known rabbinic term in the midrashim and talmudim, appearing nearly fifty times. This is not unusual since these rabbinic texts are forms of biblical interpretation and must employ biblical terminology to ground their work. Other nonhomiletic Tannaitic works such as the Mishnah, Tosefta, and Halachic-Midrashim, however, employ the biblical terms only sparingly, together with new rabbinic terminology. It is important that the word המחתה appears only seven times in the Mishnah and three times in the

Tosefta: Mishnah Yoma 5.1, 7.4, Tamid 1.4, 6.2, Tosefta Yoma 1.9, 2.10, and 2.11.

The halachic midrashim, Sifra Tzav, 1.17, Acharei Mot, 3.1, 3.2, 6.2, and 6.5, all contain the word המחתה and it generally points to a difference between the ladle and the firepan. In addition, in Sifra Tzav, chapter 1, it is clear that the rabbis placed together their understanding of the fire for the menorah and the firepan together in their interpretation. In later aggadic midrashim the distinctions are similar.[60] The word firepan does appear in BT and PT discussions, but it is only because a citation from the MT is involved.[61]

The כף or ladle/spoon is a biblical word for one of the utensils used to transport elements for a variety of Tabernacle/Temple services.[62] This is important since the word כף is often rendered in Aramaic by Onkelos in his translation of the Pentateuch as בזיכא.[63] The בזך/בזיך/בזיכא (variant forms in varying manuscripts) is found extensively in rabbinic literature, but is seen as distinct from the כף. The כף was seen as a large ladle and the בזיך was a much smaller panlike object which had sides for the purpose of holding the incense heaped into it. The word בזיך does not appear in the Hebrew Bible and does not seem to be a Hebrew word at all.[64] בזיך appears in a number of sacrificial concepts in rabbinic texts and is not a word which appears in the Bible. The word appears in one rabbinic text clearly as an amulet with an incantation.[65] But in the Tosefta and Mishnah the word בזיך appears as a word for the shovel used to remove and carry items from one area to another.[66] The word בזיך appears almost one hundred times in rabbinic literature and is one of the main rabbinic terms used in the Mishnah, Tosefta, and BT to describe the vessel used to move and hold dry, unheated elements used in Temple services.[67] The largest number of appearances is in the Mishnah and Tosefta of Menahot.

In this section, which deals with the twelve loaves placed on the golden table each Shabbat, בזיכין is mentioned in Leviticus 24:5. According to the rabbinic account, there were two בזיכין, which were full of frankincense and placed on the same golden table with the loaves. The word is used also in Mishnah Menachot 2.2, 3.6, 13.3, but especially in 11.7–8:

> There were two tables within the antechamber at the entrance to the Temple building, one of marble and one of gold. They would place the loaves upon the one of marble when it was brought in and upon the one of gold when it was taken out....

There was one of gold upon which the loaves stood constantly. Four priests enter, two with the two arrangements in their hands, and two with the two בזיכין [of frankincense] in their hands. Four [others] precede them, two to take away the two arrangements and two to take away the two בזיכין.... They burned the בזיכין [of frankincense] and the loaves were divided among the priests.

The rabbis describe in detail this Bazich as a freestanding ritual object, which could be carried and which held a minimum amount of incense.[68]

In Mishnah Tamid 5.4:

The one [priest] who had been chosen to offer the incense took up the Kaf כף, which was in the shape like a big *tirkab* of gold. It held three *kabs*,[69] and the בזיך was in the middle of it heaped with incense. This had a covering over which was spread a kind of jacket.

The בזיך appears to be a much smaller object which would be in the middle of a much larger כף. The last part of this description is that apparently the smaller transporter, the *Bazich*, had a cover that fit over the top to keep the fine incense from blowing off the incense piled up in the middle. The word for the cover, מטוטלת, is a type of cloth or skin cover which was tied on in some way by cords.[70] This is important for our discussion of the incense shovel of Bethsaida, since this smaller shovel and others like it have at the closed corners of the pan smaller projections or decorations that could not have been used for tying on a covering. In addition, these shovels all have projected triple-ridge designs on the sides of the pans that also would allow for a covering to be placed on top. In Mishnah Tamid 6.2-3 it is clear that the בזיך was in fact the incense shovel for moving the incense from its place on the *kaf* onto the *machtah*.

[6.2] The one who had been chosen for the firepan (המחתה) made a heap of the cinders on the top of the altar and then spread them about with the end of the firepan and prostrated himself and went out. [6.3] The one [priest] who had been chosen for the incense took the *Bazich* בזיך from the middle of the *Kaf* כף and gave it to his friend or his relative.

According to the Mishnah, the firepan was used specifically for live coals and the actual burning of the incense. In Tamid 5.5:

> The one [priest] who had been assigned the shoveling took the silver firepan (המחתה) and ascended to the top of the altar and cleared away the live coals to this side, and then went down and emptied them into a gold [firepan].

Finally, however, there is a third object, a מגרפה. In Mishnah Tamid 5.6:

> When they came between the porch and the altar, one took the shovel (מגרפה) and threw it between the porch and the altar. People could not hear one another speak in Jerusalem from the noise [made] by the shovel.

The מגרפה is another larger vessel, which is not mentioned in the MT, and was used for cleaning, burning, and clearing larger objects associated with the incense service.

In total, the rabbis have four types of shovels in their conception of the daily incense service. Two, the מחתה and the כף are words found in the MT; two, the בזיך. and the מגרפה, are not. The מחתה was used to remove coals, the כף held a large quantity of incense, the בזיך. was used to move a smaller quantity of incense to the מחתה (or to the actual altar), and the מגרפה was apparently a larger shovel for use in cleaning, burning, or clearing away the incense.

The Mishnah of Yoma, chapter 5, contains details of the incense service on Yom HaKippurim in which the ladle (כף) and the firepan (המחתה) are used, and it adds some information about the use of the בזיך. It states:

> They brought the ladle (כף) and the firepan (המחתה) out to him. And he took handfuls [of incense from the firepan] and put [the incense] into the ladle (כף)—a large one in accord with the large size [of his hand] or a small one in accord with the small size [of his hand].

The rabbis debate how the incense was brought. This is extremely confusing in the BT, which states that there were actually two מחתה, one for hot coals and one in which the incense was to be initially carried to where it was burnt. Apparently a המחתה was used to transport the incense from the House of Avtinus, the official incense maker, and then another pan held the hot coals (BT 47a; SMALL CAPS indicates the Mishnah).

THE FIREPAN[?] (המחתה) But was it not taught: He took the fire-pan and went up to the top of the altar, took out the burning coals, and went down? — There the reference is to the pan of burning coals, here to the pan of the incense. For it was taught: One brought out for him the empty ladle from the Cell of Vessels, and the heaped pan of incense from the Cell of the House of Abtinas.

The ladle is simply a nonritual vehicle used to carry to the altar enough incense for one instance of burning and the firepan was used to carry burning coals. Depending on how large the individual priest's hands were, the ladle would need to be larger or smaller. The ladle was not the incense carrier in this case. As the amoraic explanation sets out (SMALL CAPS indicates the Mishnah's words):

HE TOOK HIS TWO HANDFULS AND PUT IT INTO THE LADLE, A TALL (HIGH PRIEST) ACCORDING TO HIS SIZE, AND A SHORT ONE ACCORD-ING TO HIS SIZE AND THUS WAS ITS MEASURE: For what purpose was the ladle on the Day of Atonement necessary? Surely the Divine Law said: [And he shall take] his hands full and bring it—Because [otherwise] it is impossible.

In BT Yoma 47a we learn an additional fact about the ladle (כף): While it is not a ritual object per se, it figures prominently in the actual ser-vice because it is used to carry the incense; additionally it was not used for the actual burning in the Temple and so it would be cold.

He took the firepan in his right hand and the ladle into his left hand.... This one [the ladle] is small, the other [coal pan] large, and even where both are alike, as with R. Ishmael b. Kimhith, the one is hot and the other cold.

Again, the BT Yoma 49b adds that the mysterious בזיך is used in the transference of incense as it was used in the daily sacrifice:

How does he do it? He takes hold of the בזיך. with his finger-tips—according to some with his teeth—and pulls it with his thumb until it reaches his elbows, then he turns it over in his hands and heaps up the incense in order that its smoke may come up slowly; some say he scatters it in order that its smoke may come up fast; and this is the most difficult ministration in the Sanctuary.

The PT amoraic discussion of the Mishnah of 5.1(42b), however, adds a new piece to our understanding of the objects used. The Mishnah reads:

> They brought the ladle (כף) and firepan (המחתה) out to him.

The PT amoraic discussion states:

> And has not the Mishnah already stated that he took the fire-pan and went to the top of the altar. [why state here that they brought the ladle and firepan out to him?]

> The mishnah should read (כיני מתניתא) "they brought the ladle and the בזיך to him" [instead of: "they brought the ladle and firepan out to him"]. What is a ladle? It is a מגיס.

The statement in the PT, "the mishnah should read (כיני מתניתא)" is an extremely important redactional statement which is much debated among scholars of the PT. It is thought that this is an interpretive device, which although it means to imply that this is actual meaning of the mishnah, does not imply that this is really a variant reading or that the written version of the Mishnah is incorrect.[71] It implies, however, that at the time of the PT's redaction, i.e. the fourth and early fifth centuries CE, the biblical word firepan (המחתה) had been replaced by the more current terminology for discussion of this object. The object was now being referred to by its function: a shovel for transporting incense to the altar. Its name was not מחתה but בזיך. The small and large sizes of the object mentioned in the Mishnah are now referring to the בזיך. This seems to be the view of the medieval interpreter Rashi, who writes concerning the Exodus 25:29: "the ladles are בזיכין in which were put the incense." In Exodus 25:37–38, Rashi describes the special vessels (called *mahtah* in the Bible but obviously not firepans) which were used for the menorah, and states: "מחתתיו are בזיכין קטנים which are used for collecting the ash from the menorah in the early morning ... in [Old French] *fourgeure*."

The word כף had also been changed from the "ladle" of the biblical period to מגיס (a Greek word written in Hebrew letters), meaning a plate. As mentioned above, the ladle is featured in Exodus 25:29: "And you shall make its plates and its ladles (קערתיו וכפתיו)." The Aramaic Targum Onkelos renders קערתיו as מגיס and וכפתיו as בזיך. Again, the word כף is rendered by Onkelos as בזיך. By the time of the Talmudim, the Greek [or Latin] terms בזיך and מגיס (both written in Hebrew letters) were being used to describe the terms for the firepan used for the transportation of the incense and the plate for holding the incense.

Terminologically, therefore, the small-handled incense shovel was called בזיך in the time of the fourth- and fifth-century-CE PT Rabbis, at approximately the same time that the iconography appears on the floors of Galilean synagogues. It is this short-handled shovel which is found in synagogue iconography, and it was probably a בזיך rather than the Temple's המחתה. It was probably used only for transporting the incense to the altar of incense for burning and was not a portable censer, but its importance seems to have gone beyond the time of the destruction of the Temple since it is found on synagogue iconography. The question is: Why depict this incense transporter on the synagogue? The answer is: Precisely because it was not the actual biblically ordained censer but was associated with the holiday incense service and was associated with the daily ritual of the Showbread. The case of the mysterious short-handled incense shovel in synagogue iconography seems to be similar to that of the symbolic renderings of the menorah and shofar. Instead of a copy of the biblically ordained objects (six- or seven-stemmed stylized menorahs and gold/silver trumpets), substitute (but similar) symbols were chosen to represent these items (various stemmed, unstylized menorahs and simple rams' horns), which continued to be used in synagogues and rabbinic rituals. The short-handled incense shovel was a replacement symbol for the biblically ordained censer and incense altar which simultaneously symbolized the daily incense offering, the Day of Atonement, and the offering of frankincense associated with the Showbread and perhaps was a part of an ongoing synagogue ritual, like the other symbols. The proximity of the incense shovel to the menorah in almost all of the synagogues surveyed raises the question of whether it was somehow linked to it in a textual and symbolic context.

The offering of frankincense associated with the Showbread appears in Leviticus 24:7. The free-standing frankincense offering stood with the Showbread ("... and you shall put the frankincense with each row, that it may go with the bread as a memorial portion). The section concerning the incense offering follows that of the commandment for the menorah (Leviticus 24:1-4). In this case, both Leviticus 24:4 and 24:8 close with the same pronouncement: that this injunction shall be done "continually" (תמיד), "a statute forever throughout your generations" (Lev. 24.4; in the case of Lev. 24:8: עולם

בריח). This is important because one of the questions concerning the synagogue iconography is the juxtaposition of the incense shovel with the menorah. Only here do they appear together with the pronouncement that they are to be done "continually" and "forever" (תמיד and חקת עולם). The words "continually" and "forever" were important for the rabbis since they were key derivation words for continuation of a Temple ritual in the synagogue.[72] The symbol of the בזיך in synagogue iconography in direct juxtaposition with the menorah is probably because of this textual connection. In many cases the shofar is found in synagogue iconography in direct juxtaposition with the incense shovel. A dual connection is therefore suggested. The incense shovel and shofar may both be linked to the High Holidays. The Shofar was used in the synagogue during the holidays of Rosh HaShanah and Yom Kippur, and the use of incense is found (at least textually) in connection with the Day of Atonement. The use of the terminology of the בזיך as the incense shovel for the transporting of incense during the Day of Atonement ritual is aided by a late medieval reference. In the tenth century, Rabbi Meshullam ben Kalonimos' piyyut on the worship service of the High Priest (Avodah) for the Day of Atonement, called "Amitz Koah," the incense service as it was known to the rabbis of the Talmudim is summarized and elaborated. This piyyut consistently substitutes the word בזיך for the word כף in the Rabbinic texts.[73]

*Conclusion:* The בזיך is a non-Hebrew word used by the rabbis to represent a vessel used during the incense service. The Mishnah continues to use the Hebrew terminology of the Bible (firepan and ladle), but introduces the Bazich as the implement used to transport the incense. The PT makes the word the equivalent of the firepan used for removing the incense from its storage area to the incense altar. The BT makes the word the equivalent of the ladle used for the handfuls of incense picked up by the high priest. The shovel apparently comes in a number of sizes (according to the different-sized handfuls of the priests) and is a freestanding holder for incense in the case of the showbread ritual. In many ways, therefore, it is the equivalent of the biblical "ladle" and "firepan," and yet is distinct from them. It is not the long-handled firepan used for hot coals. It is therefore the equivalent of a ritual Temple object, but not an actual ritual object mentioned in the Bible—in short, a perfect compromise symbol for the rabbis and for use as synagogue iconography. The rabbis allowed the depiction of symbols from the Temple on synagogue mosaics in the Galilee and Golan if the symbols were not exactly like the vessels and ceremonies used in rituals performed by the priests. The development of synagogue rituals surrounding these symbols may have developed in tandem with the iconography. These non-Temple synagogue rituals may have included menorah lighting and incense burning ceremonies, developments that may be assumed by the depiction of these symbols on the synagogue mosaics. All of these rabbinic rituals continue in synagogues to this day. The least well known of these rituals is the rabbinic incense ritual, which seems to have continued in synagogues until the Middle Ages and then disappeared.

## Literary Evidence for Jewish Incense Ceremonies and Incense Use

Although the use of incense in the Temple in Jerusalem is well documented, other Jewish uses (outside the Temple) are not. Scant references to certain times of incense burning in one's home could be documented from Tobit 6.17–18 and 8.1–2, although in these passages it seems to be linked with a marriage ceremony of some kind. One well-known non-Temple rabbinic use of incense is in the Havdalah (literally "Separation" from the Sabbath) service. Spices used in the service, while not burned, have a ritualized purpose and a special ritualistic holder, which by the Middle Ages resembled some of the incense burners found in Jewish burials. In addition, rabbinically ordained blessings were said over a variety of naturally occurring events, including the pleasant aromas of trees and incense.[74] Blessing *'al hamugmar,* is apparently placing incense on top of live coals.[75] Even into the Middle Ages, a type of ritual holder for this burning incense was called *mahtah* shovel.[76] While it is possible that a short-handled bronze shovel may have continued to be used as a ritual transporter of the incense, evidence both literary and archaeological points to the use of a conical incense burner in the medieval synagogue.

It is also difficult to assess the possibility of synagogue incense use, since hundreds of Talmudic discussions involving incense usually focus on biblical and Temple practices. One citation, however, which relates to a ruling of Rabban Gamliel (who lived at the time of the Temple) and a post-Temple continuation of the practice suggests that an incense burner was used. BT Beitzah 22b related the three controversial rulings of Rabban Gamliel, one of which concerns the burning of spices on a festival:

> He (Rabban Gamliel) furthermore gave three lenient rulings: One may sweep a dining room and put the spices (on the fire) on a festival, and one may prepare a 'helmeted kid' on Passover. But the Sages forbid these.

The Babylonian Gemara relates that this refers to the perfuming of clothes, not a ritual burning of spices. But the actual incense burning in the synagogue on holidays is alluded to in the discussion:

> And one may not put the spices [on the fire] on a Festival, but in the house of Rabban Gamaliel they did put. Said R. Eleazar b. Zadok: Frequently I accompanied my father to the house of Rabban Gamaliel and [observed that] they did not put the spices [on the fire] on a Festival but *they used to bring in iron censers*[77] and fill them with the perfume of the incense on the eve of the Festival and stop up the vent-holes on the eve of the Festival. On the morrow when guests came they opened the vent-holes with the result that the room was automatically perfumed. They said to him: If so, it is permitted to do the same even on a Sabbath.[78] [Emphasis added]

This same discussion is found elsewhere in the BT and seems not to have been resolved in this period.[79] Most medieval legal commentators did not allow "incense burning" at the close of the Sabbath festivals, although Rabbenu Gershom and Tam are in favor of using incense on these occasions.[80] The large number of conical incense burners found in Syrian locations may have led to the designation of this incense burner as a *Damasca*.[81]

When one finds that the rabbis include any narrative insight from daily life such as in BT Berachot 53a, where the observation is made that Jewish women use incense for witchcraft, it is difficult to determine for sure whether this is a historical insight or a contemporaneous one from the late Roman–early Byzantine period,[82] for example, in Midrash Shir HaShirim Rabbah 5.1:

> Formerly God used to receive sacrifices from on high, as it is written, "And the Lord smelled the sweet savour" [Gen. viii, 21]. Now he receives them below, and so it is written, "I am come into my garden, my sister, my bride. I have gathered

myrrh with my spice": this refers to the incense of spices and
the handful of frankincense.

The Babylonian and Palestinian Talmudim contain second-century
narratives about the Abtinas family, who were the incense makers for
the Temple, and to note that the recipe for the ritual incense was not
lost after the destruction of the Temple in 70 CE.[83] However, the
incense which was a part of the synagogue service probably had no
direct connection to the incense ritual of the Temple, but was used to
provide a fragrant environment to the building, to link the people
indirectly to Temple rituals of old, and to provide a defense against
lurking demons and evil spirits.[84] Clearly the rabbis saw the incense
symbol as one that was associated with both the healing of sins and
atonement as well as possessing the power to overcome a variety of
other problems.[85] The use of spices for personal hygiene and stimula-
tion was not forbidden, but on the contrary, in the context of so-called
Oriental or Middle Eastern cultures incense burning was a recom-
mended and highly meritorious part of daily life.[86]

Given the importance of incense burning, why didn't the
Jewish artisans and rabbis of Israel choose to put conical incense burners in the synagogue iconography? First, it appears that some did.
Although E. Goodenough, who surveyed the Dura-Europos synagogue
extensively in his *Jewish Symbols* volumes, did not find any in the synagogue iconography there, closer observation does reveal the appearance of conical incense burners in a number of contexts in the Dura-
Europos synagogue and on incense shovels. In four of the panel paint-
ings found on the walls of the synagogue, C. H. Kraeling found depictions of conical incense burners and an incense shovel. In the depiction of the "Ark in the Land of the Philistines" (WB 4),[87] for example,
although the right side of the mural is supposed to represent the rav-
aged Temple of Dagon, the implements in the right lower corner of
the mural resemble the elements of the Roman imperial cult more
than they do ancient Near Eastern/Philistine wares.[88] There are a
number of elements that closely resemble objects found at the Dura-
Europos Hellenistic and Roman excavations, including an incense
shovel (no. 17) and four conical incense burners (nos. 11–14).[89]

C. H. Kraeling noted several different freestanding incense
burners in the murals: In "Consecration of the Tabernacle and its
Priests" (WB2), there are freestanding incense burners on the two sides

of the menorah,[90] and in the "Wilderness Encampment and the Miraculous Well of Be'er" (WBI), two items to the right and the left of the menorah can be distinguished as freestanding incense burners.[91] The bronze incense burners in the "Consecration of the Tabernacle and its Priests" show incense smoke coming from the top of the conical object. In the "Destruction and Restoration of National Life" panel (NCI),[92] a freestanding conical incense burner is found.[93]

The incense shovel was apparently known in Dura-Europos in antiquity. In a *dipinto* from another part of Dura-Europos excavations from the Roman period, one finds within a niche a drawing of an eagle mounted on a horned altar with an individual off to the left side of the altar who is holding a shovel with a square pan.[94] In the same excavations from the Hellenistic and Roman periods, two glazed clay incense burners (one conical) adorned with a sacred animal (a deer) were discovered in the temple of Atargatis as well as a bronze incense shovel from a private building near the temples.[95]

Second, although it might have been possible to preserve in mosaic form a conical incense burner, this was probably seen as a post-Temple innovation and not representative of the Temple ritual. Third, the incense shovel seems to have been seen as having some role in the Temple ritual while not a biblically ordained part of the service. Finally, during the latest periods of synagogue iconography (sixth century) the conical incense burner may have already been proscribed as a symbol because of its use in Church ritual.

### Evidence for an Incense Ritual in the Synagogue?

As mentioned above, an incense shovel was found at Dura-Europos in excavations from the Hellenistic and Roman period.[96] It was assigned as a pagan incense shovel and assumed to be a "brazier." In the same excavations, two glazed clay incense burners (one conical) in the temple of Atargatis adorned with the sacred deer were discovered as well as the bronze "brazier."[97] The Dura-Europos incense shovel is freestanding and decorated ornately. The presence of the two clay incense burners suggests that perhaps the brazier was only a shovel for transporting the incense and not for the burning of incense. Despite Yadin's perception of slight traces of burning on his shovels (which still needs scientific confirmation), it does not appear that the primary purpose of the shovel was the burning of incense but rather the transporting of incense to the place where it was burned. While it is possible that the shovel could have been used to burn incense, that does not appear to be its primary purpose.

The synagogue iconography suggests a freestanding shovel that could be placed on a flat surface (over hot coals if used for burning) and then sprinkled with incense or could be used for moving incense from place to place, as the rabbinic texts suggest. There is archaeological evidence for a freestanding bronze incense burner in the early Hellenistic period in the ancient Near East. These Hellenistic incense burners or censers generally are mounted on top of a splayed foot with a pan or receptacle "in the form of a cup with a splaying foot, one side of the cup being raised up and surmounted with knobs. It seems to act as a sort of shield from heat, while the handle is in the form of an ibex standing facing outwards on a plinth."[98]

There are also examples of bronze incense burners found both in synagogue excavations and in iconography in Israel. In the fourth-century synagogue of Beth Shean, which features a mosaic of an incense shovel, a two-part conical bronze incense burner was found,[99] which had four feet and could be freestanding (although it had a bronze chain connected to the upper part for hanging). The decorated sides of the pan or receptacle are ornate, with bronze latticework, and resemble the side panels of the Dura-Europos Hellenistic pan. N. Zori, who excavated the synagogue, says that the side panels of the burner are designed to look like animals. Zori also states that this incense burner is similar to some found in Syria.[100] He assigns the incense burner to the sixth or perhaps seventh century. This is the same synagogue where a mosaic with an incense shovel was found, in what is known as Beth Shean A.[101] It is interesting that two elements related to an incense service were found in this one location. In the synagogue mosaic an incense shovel is featured, while in another part of the excavations, an entirely different type of incense burner is found. It is clear that the incense burner and the mosaic are from different periods. The earliest stratum of the Beth Shean mosaic is assigned to the fourth century, while the incense burner found in the sixth- to early-seventh-century remains of the Beth Shean synagogue resembles those that were a part of the Byzantine church service. One explanation of the discrepancy is that the two may represent different developments of the same incense ritual. Another is that the two elements were parts of an ongoing incense ritual in the synagogue. The shovel may have continued to be used only for transporting incense to a conical incense burner.

What all of this suggests is that incense burning was not in fact a Christian practice, but rather a Roman and Jewish practice through the fourth century CE. The Byzantine Church did not at first accept the use of incense in services, apparently because of the imperial cult use of incense in the pre-Christian period. Trypho and Irenaeus in the second century CE see the incense as totally a spiritual metaphor. Irenaeus states: "The incense is the prayers of the saints."[102] This trend continued into the third century as witnessed in the writings of Tertullian, perhaps because of the attacks of Marcion against the practices of the Hebrew Bible.[103] In addition, during this period, trade in incense by Christians was forbidden.[104] Arnobius in his assaults against heathen practices denigrates the use of incense in the late third and early fourth centuries.[105] Although early Christians did use incense at graves, it was not a Church ritual until the fifth and early sixth centuries.[106] A Byzantine incense shovel from Sardis, decorated with a large cross[107] very similar to the ones surveyed above, demonstrates that the shovel was used by the fourth century CE in Christian contexts. The shovel was replaced by the bronze conical censer in eastern and western churches. In the late fifth and early sixth centuries, it was introduced with blessings taking place; by the ninth century it had become a regular part of eastern and western Church ritual.[108]

Synagogue iconography of the late Roman and Byzantine period, therefore, implies that an incense burning ritual may have survived into the synagogue service as well. Whether it was performed with a conical burner or on an incense shovel is not clear, but the iconography suggests that the shovel was a part of an active synagogue ritual.

The next question is whether there is any evidence of an incense ritual in the literature of the rabbis. Very little is known about rituals of the synagogue in the Amoraic-Geonic (late Roman and Byzantine) period for a number of reasons. One reason is that the standardization of rabbinic practice took place at the end of this period (tenth and eleventh centuries) and any practices that were not continued in the medieval synagogue were not written about after this period. Remnants of variant practices can be found in polemical responsa literature written by the Geonim to criticize variant practices of certain communities in Palestine and among the Diaspora and the Karaites. Rabbinic literature is the main source of our information on the synagogue and it is Babylonian Judaism (and its practices) that became the predominant standard for Rabbinic Judaism. One of the main targets for this polemical responsa literature is the Karaites, who criticized the "Rabbanites" for introducing practices into the synagogues that were not in the Bible. Some of these practices continued into medieval rabbinic Judaism, while others did not. An example of the former is the introduction of the ritual lighting (and blessing) of Sabbath candles in the period of the Geonim; Rabbi Saadiah Gaon took the final action of obligating Jews to kindle the Shabbat light and say a blessing over its light apparently in reaction to the Karaite Sabbath practice of not lighting candles or any other fire during the Sabbath.[109] While the Rabbis and the Karaites were at odds over theological and religious authority issues, the most prominent areas of divergence that separated them were both the rabbinic development of ritual that is not mentioned specifically in the text of the Bible and the practice in the synagogue of a ritual that was to be conducted only within the confines of the Temple—practices that enhanced the position of the synagogue and the rabbis. To the Karaites, both practices seemed to be improper. In the rabbinic prayer book developed by the rabbis in the period of the Tannaim and Amoraim, the incense service of the Temple figures prominently both in the opening and closing of the morning services. The ritual of incense is clearly suggested again in a polemic against the Karaite Daniel al-Qumisi by Rabbi Saadiah Gaon. Al-Qumisi's writings (like many of the controversies and the rabbinic responses) are preserved in only manuscript form but express the major differences between the rabbis and the Karaites. The Gaon Natronai ben Nahshon, for example, composed a treatise refuting the Karaite views on the Jewish calendar, which was discovered only in manuscript form.[110] Apparently, once the controversy was finished and the Karaites were no longer a force to be reckoned with, the rabbis felt no need to preserve the original content of the arguments. This is the case regarding the incense ritual. Al-Qumisi, in a Cambridge Geniza manuscript about his dispute with Saadiah Gaon, writes:

> If they say that we should burn incense and light candles because they (synagogues) are a "Temple in miniature," we will say to them: It is not as you argue, even more so, God forbade the incense and the lighting of candles in synagogues because there is in this pagan worship, because they are placing the synagogues in the same level as the Temple of God (in

Jerusalem) in the holiness and the doing of these things ... this is forbidden to put the synagogues in the same level with the Holy Temple in regards to the bringing in of impurities, because synagogues are not holy. And every one who lights candles in them or burns incense in them because they are holy is transgressing the commandments of God and is making holy that which is not holy and is not preparing his heart for the God of his fathers ... but those who obligate the lighting of candles and the burning of incense in synagogues are the Rabbis, and they bring evidence (to support this view) of the holiness of the synagogue from the writing that it shall be "a Temple in miniature....[111]

In his assessment of the incense shovel, Goodenough presents a number of sources which also seem to imply that the burning of incense continued in the period following the destruction of the Temple.[112] Evidence of open-top square boxlike incense burners associated with Jewish burials may reflect refinements of the incense shovel burner. Goodenough's more anthropological approach to the use of the incense burner among Jews found that it continued in the East but not in the West. Evidence for incense burning in synagogues and in homes can be found among Ethiopian Jews, Syrian Jews, and especially among Yemenites up until the modern period.[113] Most used incense burners similar to those now used in the Eastern Orthodox tradition of Christianity. Although incense burning may have survived in eastern/oriental Jewish rites, the Western and Eastern European Jewish rites removed it entirely, perhaps because it was too similar to the ritual of medieval Church ritual. Jewish liturgy continued to have a disproportionately large number of readings on incense for the daily, Sabbath, and holiday services. The mystical Medieval Jewish tradition also incorporated elements of the incense service (and perhaps even the conical incense burner) into a new/old ritual called Havdalah, performed with an ornate spice box at the end of the Sabbath. It would seem that just as with other parts of the synagogue service, the rabbis in Eastern and Western Europe moved to a new level of symbolic understanding of the mysteries of the Temple—from the incense altar to the incense burner and shovel to the incense liturgy—from one physical symbol of the Temple service to another physical symbol of the remembrance of the Temple in liturgy and ritual.

## CHAPTER NOTES

1.  In the preceding days (May 2–6, 1996), the following items were found in the same locus above, below, and around the find: Hellenistic cooking pots, casserole bowls, juglets, jars, decorated ware, so–called Galilean bowls, Roman glass, a bow-spouted Herodian lamp, and Eastern Terra Sigillata pottery shards among hundreds of other small finds.

2.  Yadin (1975), 55–57, lists nine incense shovels in Palestine, one in Gaul, three from Pompeii and Herculaneum, four from Lebanon and Syria (indicating that others are in the National Museum in Damascus); but this is not a complete list. Most of the shovels that have been discovered come from the eastern parts of the Roman empire and the Bethsaida shovel is one of the few that come from a documented archaeological context and not from a hoard, a random discovery, or a private collection. In Yadin's section marked "Varia," for example, he lists only one shovel in the Rockefeller Museum and a significant number from other collections. The one from the Rockefeller that Yadin lists bears the inscription "Good luck to the purchaser," which may indicate private use. Two others are presently found in the collection of the Rockefeller Museum. One apparently comes from the vicinity of Hebron, and it is said to have been found together with a coin struck by a procurator in the first half of the first century CE. Other shovels listed in Yadin's work are no longer in their original locations. This list of shovels is, therefore, far from exhaustive. A fourth shovel was found in another locus.

3.  Yadin (1975), 18–22. On Friday, April 1, 1960, while working in Niche 4, Hall A, locus 57, after removing a medium-sized stone and an additional half-meter of dirt, a basked containing a cache of metal utensils was discovered. The basket contained nineteen metal objects, including bowls, patera, three incense shovels, and jugs. On Sunday, 3 April 1960, at a distance of several meters north of locus 57 and near the metal utensils, a scroll fragment of Psalms was found. Then later that day in an adjoining crevice was found the waterskin containing the Letters. In March 1961, in the second season of excavations, in a locus designated 61.3, Hall C, another incense shovel was discovered in the same area as the cache of Babata, textile fragments, a bag of deeds, and other personal items.

4.  Yadin (1975) 45.

5.  Yadin (1975) 44.

6.  The largest's overall length is 35.8 cm, the next largest is 28.7 cm. The two smaller shovels had an overall length of 24.7 cm and 23 cm.

7.  Yadin (1975) 45. Other views of where the "booty" came from are more plausible given the richness and diversity of the hoard, especially in light of the other discoveries in the Bar Kokhba caves. They are: (1) an imperial cult site close to the Dead Sea such as Livias (formerly Betharamphtha in Transjordan); (2) an imperial cult site close to the Dead Sea such as Jerusalem; at the time of the Bar Kokhba Rebellion (132–135 CE) there was a temple dedicated to Jupiter built by the emperor Hadrian on the Temple Mount; (3) the Second Temple of the Jews in Jerusalem before its destruction in 70 CE. Since Yadin held that the vessels were made a century before their deposit in the Bar Kokhba caves, the vessels could be those donated by the emperor for use in the temple mentioned in Josephus, *Wars*, 5.562–564. The retaking of the Temple Mount and the reinitiation of the Temple cult was a major objective of the Bar Kokhba rebellion and perhaps for this reason the vessels were taken and buried in the caves along with other important "Judaica." The claim that Bar Kokhba even started to reinitiate Temple worship can be found in a number of sources. See, for example, M. Avi-Yonah in his book, *The Jews under Roman and Byz-*

*antine Rule (Jerusalem*: Magnes Press, 1984) P. 13 states: "Bar Kokhba established his government in Jerusalem and probably resumed the Temple ritual as far as possible."

8. Yadin (1975) 58.
9. Rubenstein (1995) 94ff., demonstrates that the symbol of palm branches and citrons were both non–Jewish and Jewish symbols.
10. BT Avodah Zarah 43a: "A person may not make ... a menorah after the design of the [Temple's] menorah. One may, however, make one with five, six, or eight branches, but with seven he may not make it even though it be made of other metals [than those used in the Temple's menorah]."
11. For a detailed study of the question see, Cohen (1984) 151–174.
12. Taylor (1931) 215ff. It should be remembered that the Roman imperial cult had a priest of Augustus at Pompeii soon after 2 BCE. The fact that the Roman imperial cult is found in Herculaneum is important. The Shrine of the Augustales excavated at Herculaneum is a testament to the elite group who saw to the cult functions before the destruction of the city in 79 CE. Yadin (1975) 58, contends that the shovels were used: "I think there is little doubt that none of the shovels are described above are Jewish in origin and that they belong to the Greek and Roman—and later, Christian—rituals. This supposition is strengthened by their having been found together with the pagan patera in centers of pagan worship and in stations of the Roman Legions and Auxilia." Some of the other shovels found in an identifiable archaeological setting might also fit this description.
13. Other authors have assigned different meanings to this type of shovel for many of the reasons cited above; see Narkiss (1935), Avi-Yonah (1940), Braslavi (1967).
14. Yadin (1975) 53–56, no. 5–57.23 (Pl. 16; fig. 14) and no. 6–57.24 (pl. 16, fig. 15).
15. Yadin (1975) p. 50, no. 3.
16. They may have been used as posts for tying off a covering, for example. See the full discussion from Mishnah Tamid 5.4 below (p. 436ff.)
17. Yadin (1975) 48. The technique generally called for a shovel pattern to be created in wax first; then a clay enclosure was created around the wax pattern. In the second stage of developing the shovel, the clay model was baked, at which time the wax disappeared, or melted, hence the term "disappearing wax." Next, molten metal was poured into the baked clay mold to form a one-piece shovel.
18. The shovel was examined by Mrs. Hana Ziv at the metallurgical laboratories of Raphael Institute in Israel on November 20, 1996. Two spots were selected for the analysis, at the rear side of the handle and at one of the legs of the pan. The samples were polished and analyzed with a scanning electronic microscope (SEM) for chemical elements. The results did not show conformity of materials and therefore element mapping was carried out. The analysis was made on a small enlargement in order to obtain maximal surface analysis. Three analyses were performed on the leg, four were performed on the handle, and one was performed on an 800x enlargement of a lead grain. Element mapping was produced and demonstrates clear grains of lead within the copper surface.
19. The analysis shows clearly that there is no uniformity of elements throughout the shovel, which indicated that the raw material used to produce the shovel was not homogenized. This low-quality bronze was produced in low melting temperature or by a poor stirring of the different elements. The main element in the shovel is copper. It comprises between 77.18 percent and 82.46 percent of the material. In the point analysis of the lead grain there was only 16.16 percent copper. Tin was found in a relatively low percentage of 6.39 percent to 7.28 percent. Lead, an element that

normally is not mixed with bronze, was found in relatively large concentration of 81.69 percent.

20. Yadin (1975) 48, n. 21: "In Dr. Minkoff's opinion, the lead was accidentally introduced into the alloy instead of tin."

21. Yadin (1975) no. 5–57.23 (pl. 16; fig. 14)

22. Yadin (1975) p. 56, "*c*. No. 660. The overall length is 25.4 cm. The rims of the sides of the pan are grooved. Concentric circles are stamped on the upper side of the blade [pan], in each corner and in the center; there are four prong feet and two ear brackets." Richter (1915) 236.

23. Yadin (1975) p. 56, "*d*. A shovel; the rim of the sides on the pan are grooved. There are two ear–brackets. Found at Bettar (?). Traces of the soldering are visible. The columnar handle is partly fluted; near the joint with the pan, the handle terminates in a stylized Corinthian capital. At the other end of the handle, there are a knob and a support, as on our No. 5. The overall length is 29.5 cm."

24. The circles may have been functional for an incense burning ceremony; i.e., usage of the five circles for strategic placement of coals to produce a dramatic plume of incense may actually be documented in a short narrative about the Abtinas family, who prepared the incense for the incense ceremony in the Temple of Jerusalem; see BT Yoma 38a.

25. Holes of this type, in varying numbers, are found on the mosaics of incense shovels in the synagogue iconography in such places as Hamat Tiberias (see figs. 4–5), Huldah (see figs. 4–5), Husifah, and Beit Shean A, for example; see figs. 2 and 3 for details of the Huldah and Hamat Tiberias shovels, which show these holes.

26. Goodenough (1953–68) 4:197: "... might be draught holes, but such perforations would have made them more useful, and Jews may have been clever enough to construct them in this way."

27. Faux venting or sifting might indicate that originally the ceremony involved an incense shovel with holes for accumulated ash to pass through or for air to circulate among the coals. The incense shovels under discussion, therefore, may no longer have been used for the actual burning of incense, but were only symbolic of the original, more ancient ceremony. Most of the synagogue mosaics that have incense shovels show decorations on the pan of the shovel. This may indicate that at least the artists of the rabbinic period tried to incorporate the decorations of the real incense shovels into their mosaics. The decorations on the pan in the mosaics may also be an attempt to portray coals and/or incense piles.

28. Yadin (1975) 47, fig. 10.

29. Yadin (1975) 59, fig. 16.

30. Yadin (1975) 71, fig. 21

31. Yadin (1975) 51, 54.

32. *The Iggeret Rav Sherira Gaon* states that the foundations of the first synagogue were made from earth and stones from the ruins of the First Temple that the refugees brought with them from Jerusalem; see Neubauer (1959) 25–26.

33. For the latest literature on this question see Urman and Flesher (1995).

34. PT Berachot 8b–c: "Towards the Land of Israel for those outside of the Land, for those in the Land of Israel towards Jerusalem, those in Jerusalem towards the Temple Mount, and those on the Temple Mount towards the Holy of Holies." However, there was disagreement on this point.

35. Hachlili (1988) 399. At Dabbura in the Golan the famous lintel inscription with R. Eliezar HaQappar's name on it may date it to the end of the second century or early third century sage or to his memory in a later period.

36. Based upon (and updated here) Neusner (1991) 145–59.
37. Nine-branched menorah, shofar, and incense shovel; Urman and Flesher (1995) 1:455.
38. Nine-branched menorah and a tripod base with reliefs of a shofar on one side and an incense shovel on the other; Urman and Flesher (1995) 1:498.
39. On an Ionic capital made of basalt a large, ten-branched menorah with a two-legged base and a shofar and incense shovel on the sides; Urman and Flesher (1995) 2:440
40. A lintel from Danah has two incense shovels with a menorah in between them; Urman and Flesher (1995) 1:168.
41. Lintel from Kafra with incense shovel, shofar, menorah and lulav; Urman and Flesher (1995) 1:169.
42. Lintel with a medallion containing a menorah, a shofar, and an incense shovel; Urman and Flesher (1995) 2:584.
43. Goodenough (1953–68) 4:67 ff.
44. As cited from Neusner (1991) 230.
45. The Mishnah, Tosefta, and BT of Yoma, chap. 5.
46. Friedman (1987) 174 ff., regarding the opinions that place the Tabernacle description into the Second Temple period as well. The consensus of scholarly opinion holds that the Temple ritual was retrojected into the ancient Tabernacle ritual by the Bible's redactors.
47. Biran (1994) 192.
48. Biran (1994) 193–94.
49. Richter (1915) no. 657, p. 235; 49.1 cm long. More importantly, the long-handled ritual shovels continued throughout the Roman period; see Ulansey (1991).
50. This question is still not been resolved totally; see Würthwein (1987).
51. See, e.g., Freund (1990) 1:87 ff. where I demonstrate that the LXX translator(s) did more than simply translate; they added Greek terminology and ideas to make the biblical text fit the reality of their own time.
52. (מקטרת) 1QM 2.5.
53. The word *thuiskei* has the added meaning of sacrifice and fragrant incense as well and is additionally found in 1 Maccabees 1:22 and Josephus, *Antiquities;* see Goldstein (1978) 209. The 1 Maccabees passage is important since Goldstein notes that this word "... is best translated as ladle and not censer." Goldstein is assuming that the word being translated is כף, although it appears that *thuiskei* also is applied to מחתה in this period. The 1 Maccabees section is also an abridged version of a number of passages in the MT.
54. It is not clear if Philo's information on the Temple service was firsthand. His description from the Tabernacle period is quite confusing and metaphoric regarding the altars and vessels; Philo, *Moses* 2.21.94–105. In relating the story of the rebellion of Korah in *Antiquities* 4.33, Josephus uses the word το θυμιατηριον for the portable censer; this reference is significant since it adds information not found in the MT: "... let all claimants for the priesthood bring each a censer from his home, with incense and fire...." The reference to each bringing "a censer from his home" indicates Josephus' knowledge of information not found in the LXX or MT, i.e., a home incense ritual using the *thumiaterion*—a portable censer. The word *thumiaterion* appears again, in *Antiquities* 4.54, where Josephus relates how Aaron and the company of Korah had portable censers. In 4.57, when relating the reason for the brazen altar, he states that it was made from the melted bronze censers of Korah. In *Antiquities* 3.150, Josephus uses *thuiskei* to describe one of three vessels he mentions there. He is apparently writing about the vessels found in Exodus 27:3 (although his

list seems to differ from the LXX and MT lists of the vessels in the Tabernacle/Temple so it is difficult to determine which vessel is meant by *thuiskei*), and the word מחתה is found in the list of MT Exodus 27.3. Josephus, in *Antiquities* 3.220, uses *thuiskei* for incense to describe the gifts brought by the leaders of the tribes (where the MT Numbers 7 texts use כף), which leads one to assume that while the two words מחתה and כף are not interchangeable, Josephus believed there was some similarity between the two objects. None of these sources suggests the shape or style of the object, but the composition in some of these cases is bronze. It is possible, therefore, that two objects or one object with two names is meant by the incense shovel in the writings of Josephus. Thus, Josephus, an eyewitness to Temple worship, describes a portable bronze object, used for home ritual (as well as for public worship) as an incense shovel. The possibility exists that the same object (when listed among the utensils of the Temple/Tabernacle) was known by the either *thumiaterion* or *thuiskei,* or that they were two separate utensils.

55. Although partially an imagined version of the first century, Maimonides' assessments provide a good insight into the way the entire service was understood based on rabbinic texts. His *Mishneh Torah*, The Book of Temple Service, The Temple (chap. 4), Daily Offerings (chap. 3) among others deal with the incense of the daily service and Table of Showbread as do some short references in The Day of Atonement (chap 5); see Maimonides (1957 trans.).

56. Maimonides (1957 trans.) chap. 3.

57. Six lamps:
a. Goodenough (1953–68) vol. 3, fig. 293: Torah shrine, menorah, paterae (?), and an ascia with a shovel (at right) that has six holes or concentric circle designs on the pan.
b–e. Ibid., figs 334–37: Four lamps. Central menorah with a shofar on one side and a shovel on the other. Three shovels have a small mound in/on them; one is empty (see fig. 334).
f. Ibid., fig. 340: One lamp with vase, with a vine growing from one side of a central menorah; lulav, ethrog, shofar, and shovel on the other side.

58. Goodenough (1953–68) vol. 4, p. 196.

59. A review of the relevant symbols in Frey's collection reveals that the incense shovel does appear in some places during the Diaspora, but for the most part the shofar, menorah (variously labeled candelabra), lulav, ethrog, and amphora predominated in the European Diaspora. This may be because the shovel was so identified in Europe with the imperial cult or simply because the shovel was only a relevant symbol in the eastern parts of the empire as was shown above.

60. Midrash Rabbah Numbers 4:16, 5:7, 18:19, Tanhuma Tetzveh, 16, 96.9; Korah, 9, Tzav, 96.12, Korah 23, Midrash Proverbs 30:2, Pesiqta Rabbati, 20.3.

61. Shabbat 47a, BT Pesahim 65b, Yoma 25b, 32a, 43b, 45b,46b, 47a, 48b, 52b, 60a, 60b, Zebachim 50b, 64a, Tamid 28a, 33a. PT Shabbat 27b, Yoma 22a, 24a and 24b, 26a and 26b, 37a, and Shavuot 11a. In almost every one of these cases, the Bazich appears to be a flat, shallow, freestanding palm-of-the-handlike object (to fulfill the biblical injunction of "handfuls" of incense) and not a deep cuplike object as suggested by some. Although it is possible that a clay incense shovel (such as one found at Sepphoris, for example) might be fashioned rather than a bronze vessel, the preponderance of evidence suggests that a bronze, not clay, vessel was in use during the Roman period.

62. Of the more than one hundred times this item is mentioned in the MT, it applies most of the time in the MT to the hand, palm of the hand, or a measurement of the hand; only a small number of times does it refer to an actual ritual object.

63. Exodus 25:29, 37:16; Numbers 7:14, 20, 26, 32, 38, 44, 50, 56, 62, 68, 74, 80, 84, 86.

64. Although it is possible to indirectly link it to a Hebrew/Aramaic word, its usage is unusual. Jastrow attempts to connect the word to a Hebrew and Aramaic root בזז, but it is not clear what formative ending ך would fit this model; see Jastrow (1926), s.v. בזיך. The word is perhaps linked to the Greek root βασκανος—which forms the word for a bronze amulet or charm (see Liddel–Scott, p. 310). Another possibility is that the word is derived from the general Latin term for a small vessel (*vasculum*); see Oxford Latin Dictionary (1968–1982) 8:2014, *s.v.* Fascicle. The dropping of Greek or Latin endings (or the adding of a new ending) when a word is borrowed by Rabbinic literature is common. The Greek word βυρσευς (tanner) appears in Rabbinic literature as בורסי (and sometimes בורסקי); the Greek word παρθικος (scarlet colored) appears in Rabbinic literature as בורדיקא; the Greek word and Latin word *vivarium* appears in Rabbinic literature as ביבר.

65. BT Shabbat 67a.

66. Tosefta Menahot 11.15; BT 14b; Midrash Rabbah 4.14; PT Yoma 9a. Maimonides, *Mishneh Torah*, Daily and Additional Sacrifices, 5.2, explains what the *Bazich* was. It appears directly next to the instructions for the ordering of the *Lehem HaPanim* or Showbread; therefore is assumed to have been flat.

67. In Mishnah Menahot 2.2, 3.6, 11.7, 11.8, 13.3, Mishnah Tamid 4.3, Mishnah Meilah 2.7, Tosefta Shekalim 1.8, Tosefta Nedarim 1.7, and Tosefta Menahot 3.1, 3.6, 4.7, 11.7, 11.9, 11.10. In the BT Shabbat 133b, Pesachim 58a, 64b, 68a, Yoma 24b, 29b, 34a, Megillah 21a, Zebachim 14a, 63a, Menahot 7a, 7b, 8a, 9b, 11b, 13b, 15a, 16b, 19a, 27a, 90a, 94b, 96a, 97a, 99b, 100a, 106b, and Meilah 9a. PT Yoma 12b.

68. Mishnah Menahot 13.3 states: "....the two בזיכין [of frankincense] require two *kematzim*." This amount fits into the cavity formed by the three middle fingers of the priest's right hand when he folds them over the palm of his hand according to Menahot 1.2. But as noted later in the discussions from tractate Tamid, this amount differs depending on how large the priest is and therefore there were different sizes of בזיכין.

69. Weights and measures are extremely unpredictable in rabbinic texts and are only relative measures at best. Approximations to relative measures, however, would put three *kabs* as a large measure, approximately six liters according to the standard which puts a *kab* in the two-liter range see *Anchor Bible Dictionary*, s.v. "Weights and Measures." Since the Bazich fits inside this large-measure Kaf it was quite a bit smaller than the Kaf. For the purposes of this chapter, it is important to note that the Kaf is not seen as a small spoon/ladle but as a large measure vessel into which could be set a smaller vessel.

70. The pad or cushion was made to be tied on a number of different items in the Mishnah and post–mishnaic language; Jastrow (1926), s.v. מטוטלת. This tying off is important for our investigations since the incense shovels have two closed corners of the pan that terminate in small ear brackets that jut out and have no functional purpose. The ear brackets are also found on the synagogue mosaic iconography (see figs. 2 and 3).

71. On this statement see Epstein (1995), s.v. at כיני מתני.

72. Although not all rituals were to be performed in exactly the same way as they had been in Temple times (witness the fact that the sacrifices were not made in the syn-

agogue), but a version of the ceremony was performed. Examples abound of how the rabbis derived the ongoing ceremonies and legally binding prohibitions of the synagogue from the biblical injunctions. The continuation of Sabbath observance is derived from the pronouncement of "a statute forever" in Exodus 31 and Leviticus 16, and the rabbinic regulation of and prohibitions about the major holidays derive from pronouncements that use the words "a statute forever" in Leviticus 16 and 23; see, e.g., BT Yevamot 6a–b.

73. *Artscroll Mahzor* (1987) 564–65. Translation: "He would gather glowing coals by scraping with a shovel (*machtah*) of reddish gold / Which was light, thin-walled, and long-handled. / Into it he shoveled three kabs of coals. / They brought him a ladle (*bazich*) filled with fine incense. / He scooped up [incense] with both hands and emptied it into a ladle. / He quickly grasped the shovel in his right hand and the ladle in his left."

74. Mishnah Berachot 6.6 and BT Berachot 43a–b: "R. Zera said in the name of Raba b. Jeremiah: When do they say the blessing over the perfume? As soon as the smoke column ascends. Said R. Zera to Raba b. Jeremiah: But he has not yet smelt it! He replied: According to your reasoning, when one says 'Who brings forth bread from the earth,' he has not yet eaten! But [he says it because] it is his intention to eat. So here, it is his intention to smell."

75. Rashi on BT Beitzah 22b. "Mugmar is incense on top of a live coal."

76. Rashi on BT Berachot 42b.

77. ערדסקאות. There is apparently some dispute about the way this word is to be written: דסקאות, indicating its origins in Damascus; see *Diqduqei–Sofrim*, (1976). These were apparently closed incense burners similar to those found by N. Zori at Beth Shean.

78. Despite attempts by later (thirteenth and fourteenth centuries, esp. European) commentators and scribes to the contrary, the prescribed practice of burning in a closed incense burner seems to be allowed by the major eleventh- and twelfth-century commentators; see *Diqduqei–Sofrim* (1976).

79. Ketubot 7a.

80. Or Zarua II.92. Orah Hayim no. 624.

81. If this word is to be written דסקאות, indicating its origins in Damascus. Zori (1967) 163, notes that there were many conical incense burners that resemble the one at Beth Shean in Syria. Ross (1962) pp. 42–45, pls. XXXII:47, XXXIII: 48–49.

82. Our Rabbis taught: If one was walking outside the town and smelt an odour [of spices], if the majority of the inhabitants are idolaters he does not say a blessing, but if the majority are Israelites he does say a blessing. R. Jose says: Even if the majority are Israelites he does not say a blessing, because the daughters of Israel use incense for witchcraft. Do all of them use incense for witchcraft? — The fact is that a small part is used for witchcraft and a small part for scenting garments, with the result that the greater part of it is not used for smell, and wherever the greater part is not used for smell a blessing is not said over it" (BT Berachot 53a).

83. BT Yoma 38a, PT Yoma 40a.

84. Zohar, Vayaqahel, 208b. Lauterbach (1927) 196.

85. BT Yoma 44a–b.

86. BT Sanhedrin 70a, Horayot 13b, Yoma 76b. "That is why Raba said: Wine and odorous spices made me wise."

87. Kraeling (1956) 101–102.

88. The reason is obvious: First, the artisans of Dura probably had no idea what the implements/ritual objects of the ancient Philistine cult of Dagon looked like, but they were familiar with the Roman imperial cult. Second, this art form was social

and religious polemic retrojected into the Philistine cult. This was a common way for Jews to deal with current social and religious issues which would be polemical; see Moore, ed. (1985) 29 ff.

89. Kraeling (1956) 101 (fig. 30), 102.

90. Kraeling (1956) 119.

91. Kraeling (1956) 119.

92. Kraeling (1956) 195.

93. One might expect to find an incense shovel in the Torah shrine panel since it has the major symbols found elsewhere with an incense shovel. The main Torah shrine niche of the Dura-Europos synagogue features a painted panel with a seven–branched menorah, a round shaped object (ethrog?), and a lulav next to a portal of a structure with a columned facade, but neither the shofar nor the incense shovel is found; Kraeling (1956) 59.

94. Goldman (1966) p 123.

95. Rostovtzeff (1939) 46, and pl. VIII.

96. Yadin (1975) 57. Goodenough (1953–68) 1:174, 3:439.

97. Rostovtzeff (1939) 46 and pl. VIII.

98. See Barnett (1964) 5.

99. Zori (1967) 163. The bronze incense burner was found in room 10, with pieces from the sixth to early seventh century.

100.Zori (1967) 163. Ross (1962) 42–45, pls. XXXII:47, XXXIII: 48–49.

101.Hachlili (1988) fig. 103.

102.*Ante–Nicean Fathers* (1976 reprint) 1:574.

103.*Ante–Nicean Fathers* (1976 reprint) 3:346.

104.*Ante–Nicean Fathers* (1976 reprint) 3:67.

105.*Ante–Nicean Fathers* (1976 reprint) Arnobius, "Against the Heathen," 428–29.

106.Cited in Goodenough (1953–68) 4:200.

107.Yadin (1975) 57, n. 36 as: G. M. A. Hanfmann, Excavations at Sardis, 1958, *BASOR*, 154 (1959) pp. 5ff., fig. 11.

108.*Ante–Nicean Fathers* (1976 reprint) 7:537, 552–56, 563–64.

109.Hoffmann (1979) 86–89.

110.Zucker (1959) 5.

111.Zucker (1959) 170–71, n. 666. There is other evidence suggested there of this incense ritual as well.

112.Goodenough (1953–68) 4:199 ff.

113.Goodenough (1953–68) 4:204–5.

## Literature Cited

*Ante-Nicean Fathers: The Writings of the Fathers Down to A.D. 325.* Vol. 1, The Apostolic Fathers. 1976. Grand Rapids, MI: Eerdmans (reprint of 1885 edition).

*Artscroll Mahzo.* 1987. New York: Mesorah Publications.

Avi-Yonah, M. 1940. The Meaning and Use of Incense Shovels. *Journal of the Palestine Oriental Society,* 18:87-97.

Avi-Yonah, M. 1984. *The Jews Under Roman and Byzantine Rule, Jerusalem*: Magnes Press.

Barnett, R. D. 1964. A South Arabian Ivory Vessel. *Eretz-Israel 7.* Jerusalem: Israel Exploration Society.

Biran, A. 1994. *Biblical Dan.* Jerusalem: Israel Exploration Society.

Braslavi, J. 1967. *Symbols and Mythological Figures in the Early Synagogues in Galilee in All the Land of Naphtali.* Jerusalem: Hebrew University.

Cohen, S. J. D. 1984. The Temple and the Synagogue, in *The Temple in Antiquity.* Ed. T. Madsen (Provo: UT: Brigham Young University Press.

*Diqduqei-Sofrim.* 1976 reprint. Edited by R. Rabbinovicz. Vol. 1, on Betzah 22b-23a. New York.

Epstein, Y. N. 1955. *Mavo LeNusah HaMishnah* [Hebrew]. Jerusalem: Magnes.

Freund, Richard A. 1990, 1993. *Understanding Jewish Ethics.* 2 vols. San Francisco: EM Texts.

Frey, J. B. 1936. *Corpus Inscriptionum Judaiacarum.* New York: Ktav, reprinted 1975.

Friedman, R. E. 1987. The Sacred Tent, in *Who Wrote the Bible?* (New York: Harper and Row.

Goldman, B. 1966. *The Sacred Portal.* Detroit: Wayne State University Press.

Goldstein, J. 1978. *I Maccabees,* The Anchor Bible, vol. 41. Garden City: Doubleday.

Goodenough, E. R. 1953–68. *Jewish Symbols in the Greco-Roman World.* New York: Pantheon.

Hachlili, R. 1988. *Ancient Jewish Art and Archeology in the Land of Israel.* Leiden: Brill.

Hanfmann, G.M. A. 1959. Excavations at Sardis, 1958. *BASOR,* 154: 5ff.

Jastrow, Marcus. 1926. *A dictionary of the Targumim, the Talmud Babli and Yerushalim, and the Midrashic literature: with an index of Scriptural Quotations.* New York.

Hoffmann, L. 1979. *The Canonization of the Synagogue Service.* Notre Dame: University of Notre Dame Press.

Josephus, *Antiquities.Medieval Jewish Chronicles.* Ed. A. Neubauer. 1887–1895. New York: Menorah, 1959, reprint.

Kraeling, C. H. 1956. *The Synagogue.* New Haven: Yale University Press.

Lauterbach, J. Z. 1927. A Significant Controversy between the Sadducees and Pharisees. *Hebrew Union College Annual 4.*

Lewittes, M., trans. 1957. Chap. 4 of *Mishneh Torah.* Vol. 12. New Haven: Yale University Press.

Maimonides, Moses. 1957 trans. *Mishneh Torah,* The Book of Temple Service. Vol. 12, trans. M. Lewittes. New Haven: Yale University Press.

Moore, Carey A., ed. 1985. Introduction, in *Judith.* Anchor Bible Series, no. 40. Garden City: Doubleday.

Narkiss, M. 1935. The Snuff Shovel as a Jewish Symbol. *Journal of the Palestine Oriental Society,* 14–28.

Neubauer, A., ed. 1959. *Medieval Jewish Chronicles.* New York: Menorah (reprint of the Oxford 1887–1895 edition).

Neusner, J. 1991. *Symbol and Theology in Early Judaism.* Minneapolis: Fortress Press.

Philo. *Moses.*

Richter, G. M. A. 1915. *Greek, Etruscan and Roman Bronzes.* New York: Metropolitan Museum of Art.

Ross, M. C. 1962. *Catalogue of the Byzantine and Medieval Antiquities in the Dumbarton Oaks Collection.* Washington, D.C.

Rostovtzeff, M. 1939. *Dura-Europos and its Art.* Oxford: University Press.

Rubenstein, J. 1995. *The History of Sukkot in the Second Temple and Rabbinic Periods,* Brown Judaic Studies, 32. Atlanta: Scholars Press.

Taylor, L. R. 1931. *The Divinity of the Roman Emperor.* Chico, CA: Scholars Press (reprint).

Ulansey, D. 1991. *The Origins of the Mithraic Mysteries.* New York and Oxford: Oxford University Press.

Urman, D., and P. V. M. Flesher. 1995. *Ancient Synagogues.* 2 vols. Leiden: Brill.

Würthwein E. 1987. *The Text of the Old Testament.* Trans. E. R. Rhodes. Grand Rapids, MI: Eerdmans (reprint of 1973 edition).

Yadin, Yigael. 1975. *The Finds from the Bar Kokhba Period in the Caves of Letters.* Jerusalem: Israel Exploration Society.

Zori, N. 1967. The Ancient Synagogue at Beth-Shean. *Eretz Israel.* Jerusalem: Israel Exploration Society.

Zucker, M., ed. 1959. *Rabbi Saadya Gaon's Translation of the Torah.* New York: Feldheim.

# Index

*Bethsaida*

*Notes*

*Bethsaida*

*Notes*

*Bethsaida*